i

Uncle John's
SLIGHTLY
IRREGULAR
BATHROOM
READER

By the
Bathroom Readers'
Institute

Bathroom Readers' Press
Ashland, Oregon

OUR "REGULAR" READERS RAVE!

"This is one of the best books I've ever read. What are the other best books I've read? Why, the other *Uncle John's Bathroom Readers*, of course! Thanks—you make doing #2 my #1 priority!"
—*Robert D.*

"I found nirvana when I found your books. Thank you, thank you, thank you."
—*Donna K.*

"This is just a note to thank you for the valuable knowledge that you have dumped on me. You have given me great pleasure and kept me quite regular. My wife also thanks you, for since our introduction to the world of the *Bathroom Reader*, I had to build her a second bathroom. Humble thanks and keep up the good work."
—*James M.*

"I started reading your books after a colleague, ordinarily not much of a conversationalist, started to get smarter and smarter by the day. We couldn't figure out what was going on until we caught him reading one of your books. I bought my first one that night."
—*Ernie P.*

"You guys are the best. My girlfriend thinks I spend too much time in the can, but I just tell her that I am improving my cognitive thinking and am full of information, not what I'm usually full of."
—*Marty M.*

"I'm a huge fan of *Bathroom Readers*, but they are *too* good. Everytime someone sees me with one of your books, they ask to see it, read it, then borrow it. The bad part is I never get them back. Keep on flushin'!"
—*Ted C.*

"I just purchased my 16th *Bathroom Reader* and will not stop until I own every one. You have given me many days and nights of enjoyable reading. I look forward to future editions. Keep up the good work!"
—*Karyn L.*

UNCLE JOHN'S SLIGHTLY IRREGULAR BATHROOM READER®

For information, write
The Bathroom Readers' Institute,
P.O. Box 1117, Ashland, OR 97520
www.bathroomreader.com
888-488-4642

Cover design by Michael Brunsfeld,
San Rafael, CA (*Brunsfeldo@comcast.net*)
BRI "technician" on back cover: Larry Kelp

Uncle John's Slightly Irregular Bathroom Reader®
by The Bathroom Readers' Institute

ISBN: 1-59223-270-1

Library of Congress Catalog Card Number:
2004110248

Printed in the United States of America

First Printing
10 9 8 7 6 5 4 3 2

*   *   *

"Seattle Windsheild Pitting Epidemic" by Alan J. Stein for History Link.
Copyright © 2003. Reprinted by permission of History Link.

THANK YOU!

The Bathroom Readers' Institute sincerely thanks the people whose advice and assistance made this book possible.

Gordon Javna
John Dollison
Thom Little
Jay Newman
Julia Papps
Brian Boone
John Gaffey
Laura BlackFeather
Jeff Altemus
Sharilyn Hovind
Michael Brunsfeld
Bryan Henry
Angela Kern
Lori Larson
Sam Javna
Sydney Stanley
Gideon Javna
Jim McCluskey
Janet Spencer
Paul Stanley
Jenny Baldwin
Nancy Toeppler
Raingirl Thering
Joe Diehl

JoAnn Padgett
Amy Briggs
Allen Orso
Lyne Brennanski
Jolly Jeff Cheek
Scarab Media
Stephanie Spadaccini
Jef Fretwell
Maggie Javna
Andy Peterson
John Staedler
Larry Bograd
(Mr.) Mustard Press
Steven Style Group
Mana Manzavi
Matt Rosenberg
Jim Koweek
Barb Porshe
Paula Leith
Chris Olsen
Rich Skrenta
Porter the Wonder Dog
John Javna
Thomas Crapper

*   *   *

...AND BEST FLUSHES

to the millions of bathroom readers out there.

"Doing nothing is very hard to do... you never know when you're finished." —Leslie Nielsen

CONTENTS

Because the BRI understands your reading needs, we've
divided the contents by length as well as subject.
Short—a quick read
Medium—2 to 3 pages
Long—for those extended visits, when something
a little more involved is required
* Extended—for those leg-numbing experiences

*   *   *

Oops! A popular British hiking magazine had to apologize to its readers. Its February 2004 issue contained faulty directions for how to get down safely from Ben Nevis, the country's highest peak. As printed, the route led hikers over the edge of a cliff.

HERE WE GO AGAIN!

Another year...another amazing *Bathroom Reader*. Why do we keep doing this? Two reasons: 1) We love learning new things; and 2) We love sharing what we've learned. We just can't help it. For instance, did you know that the world's safest mode of transportation is...the elevator? See? The urge is still uncontrollable—even after 16 years!

On our quest for perfect bathroom reading, we tried to shake things up a bit this year: Instead of writing about dumb crooks, we decided to find some smart crooks. We couldn't find any. So we settled for nice crooks, like the guy who handed a bank teller a robbery note that ended with "Sorry for your inconvenience."

We also came up with a few new wordplay pages. We have a crazy word game based on Fed chairman Alan Greenspan, and our regular page of palindromes turned into a three-page sci-fi epic of absurd proportions. (Speaking of palindromes, we discovered a town called Adaven, Nevada.)

And why settle for the best when the worst is a lot funnier? We have a bunch of worsts, including the world's worst novelist and two terrible poets (one of whom only writes about cheese).

This book truly is...slightly irregular.

But wait, there's more. (Okay, you can stop waiting.) Even with the few new touches, this is still a bona fide classic *Bathroom Reader*. It runs the gamut from the useless (Michael Jackson has a pet llama named Louie) to the useful (how to get out of a speeding ticket) to the sublime (our "Creative Teaching" award to the guy who punishes his students by making them listen to Frank Sinatra) to the very core of what makes us who we are ("The History of Civilization" begins on page 110). We also answer some of life's nagging questions, such as, "How come so much stuff is made in China?" and "How do you kill a zombie?"

As always, these books would never make it to press were it not for the committed (they should be) staff at BRI headquarters in Ashland, Oregon.

- Thanks to our writers, John D. (check out his harrowing tale of "The Gimli Glider," perhaps the most nail-biting story we've ever told) and Little Thom (he gave us "The History of Civilization" and "Forgotten Founding Father").

- Then there's Brian, who knows far too much about pop culture and proves it with his great article about the lost *Star Wars* movie. And we can't forget Ol' Jay, who left the BRI, but somehow still shows up every day...and one day he showed up with a terrific piece on Woodstock.

- Laura does a bit of everything, from answering the mail, to revamping our store, to writing about Jackie Chan's most brutal injuries. Thanks to John G. for his typesetting prowess and creative eye (and to Jeff for helping during crunch time!). And thanks to Rain for filling all of our customer orders with a smile.

- Sam came to Ashland, said "Whassup?" wrote some articles ("Upstanding Citizens," for instance), then said "Later," and flew back to New York City. Who was that masked man?

- Special props: to Michael B., the world's best (and most patient) cover designer; to Angie, who provided hundreds of great running feet (including Uncle John's new favorite: "This page is about 500,000 atoms thick"); to the Godfather, Allen Orso; to Jenny Baldwin and Paul Stanley, our cohorts at Banta; and to our copyeditor, Sharilyn (Weer verry sad two sea you goe., but dont wurrry—weel bee just find).

- Holding it all together is our production manager, Julia, whose grace and perseverance make our lives a whole lot easier.

- Thank you to Mrs. Uncle John from the BRI for sparing your wonderful husband for most of the summer and fall so we could get this book done. You can have him back now. (He may need a nap.)

- And last, but most, thank you to our dedicated readers. You're a part of our family, too. See you next year.

And in the meantime,

Go with the Flow!

—Uncle John, the BRI staff, and Porter the Wonder Dog

YOU'RE MY INSPIRATION

It's always interesting to find out where the architects of pop culture get their ideas. These may surprise you.

SUPER MARIO BROTHERS. Mario, the Italian-American plumber in dozens of Nintendo video games, was modeled after the landlord at Nintendo's New York offices in the 1970s.

GOLLUM. Actor Andy Serkis provided the voice and movements for the character in the *Lord of the Rings* films. He based the voice on the sound of his cat coughing up a hairball. Special effects artists modeled Gollum's wiry, bony frame on punk rocker Iggy Pop.

"SMOKE ON THE WATER." In 1971 the band Deep Purple was about to perform at a casino in Montreux, Switzerland. Just before they went on, a fan fired a flare gun into the crowd (the opening act, Frank Zappa, was performing). The casino burned to the ground, spreading huge plumes of smoke across Lake Geneva. The image stuck with the band and inspired the classic rock song.

NBA LOGO. The National Basketball Association's logo is red and blue with the white silhouette of a player dribbling a ball. The model: 1960s Los Angeles Lakers star Jerry West.

TAXI DRIVER (1976). Paul Schrader created Robert De Niro's creepy Travis Bickle character after reading the published diaries of Arthur Bremer, the man convicted of trying to assassinate presidential candidate George Wallace in 1972. In turn, John Hinckley, Jr. claims *Taxi Driver* inspired his attempt to murder President Reagan.

COLUMBIA PICTURES LOGO. The woman in a toga holding a torch aloft is not based on the Statue of Liberty. The model for the logo—used since 1925—was Evelyn Venable, a bit player at Columbia.

AMERICAN FLAG BUMPER STICKERS. Peter Fonda got the idea to use American flags to decorate the motorcycle he rode in his 1969 film, *Easy Rider*, from John Wayne's flag-emblazoned jacket in *Flying Tigers* (1942). But when Fonda rode the motorcycle through Los Angeles, police stopped him for *desecrating* the flag. "By 1970," says Fonda, "every cop car had a flag on its fender."

Princess Diana's favorite band was Duran Duran.

COURT TRANSQUIPS

*The verdict is in! These real-life courtroom exchanges make
some of the best bathroom reading there is. These were
actually said in court, and recorded word for word.*

Q: Do you recall telling the police that you passed out at that time?
A: I passed out, yes. I passed out. I think I blacked out. I passed out, but I don't know if I was really out. I just remember blacking out, and I assume I passed out. If I didn't pass out, maybe just my mind blacked out.

Judge: Had you been drinking that day? Alcohol, I mean?
Defendant: Uh-huh.
Judge: Had you?
Lawyer: Answer it audibly.
Judge: Had you been drinking alcohol that day?
Defendant: Audibly.

Lawyer: Do you now wear corrective glasses?
Witness: There are three of you?

Judge: How do you plead, guilty or not guilty?
Defendant: I'm guilty as hell.
Judge: Let the record reflect the defendant is guilty as hell.

Lawyer: Officer, at this point in your mind, did you consider him to be a suspect in the homicide?
Officer: No. I really did not have enough intelligence to make that decision.

Q: I take it you helped milk the cows?
A: I milked them.
Q: Did you help with breeding at all?
A: The bulls did the breeding. I couldn't do that.

Lawyer: When you said that, there was some hesitation. Have you heard of others that you haven't heard about yet?

Q: So you don't recall the exact distance?
A: That he was from me? Or I was from him?

Lawyer: What about the research?
Witness: I don't think there is any research on that. There's a logical hunch that may be true, but I know of no research study that would support that.
Lawyer: What about just common sense?
Witness: Well, I am not here using common sense. I'm here as an expert.

Lawyer: Now, Doctor, which way would someone fall after receiving a twelve-gauge shotgun blast directly in the chest?
Witness: Down.

Eight percent of pet owners dress up their dogs and cats for Halloween.

NOT EXACTLY SEABISCUIT

Here's the story of a pokey little horse who has won the hearts of Japanese racing fans...by losing every race she enters.

STEED WITHOUT SPEED

In the summer of 2003, the owners of a struggling track in Kochi, Japan, were looking for a way to keep from going under. Someone noticed that one of the horses competing in an upcoming race, an eight-year-old named *Haru-urara* ("Glorious spring"), was just a few races away from losing her 100th race in a row—why not try to get some publicity out of it?

They got a local newspaper to do a story on Haru-urara, and the national press picked it up. Until then she'd been just another unknown loser, but Haru-urara turned out to be just the right horse at just the right time: Japan had been on a losing streak of its own—the economy had been in bad shape for more than a decade and unemployment was high—and the losing horse that kept on trying was an inspiration to Japanese workers worried about their own economic futures. Attendance at the race track soared from an average of 1,600 fans per day to 5,000 on Haru-urara's 100th race. (She lost.) Thirteen thousand showed up on her 106th. Japan's top jockey rode her...and she lost again.

NEVER GIVE UP

Haru-urara has become the most famous horse in Japan. Fans expect her to lose but bet on her anyway, just to get a ticket with her name on it—it's considered good luck. So many people place bets on her, in fact, that she's usually favored to win, even though everyone knows she will lose. Like a pro athlete, she endorses products (she races with a pink Hello Kitty riding mask), appears in beer commercials, has her own line of merchandise, and has been the subject of both a pop song and a major motion picture.

Best of all, she has been saved from the fate of many losing horses—the slaughterhouse. Her trainer, Dai Muneishi, has arranged for her to retire to a farm on the northern island of Hokkaido. "I don't really know why she's so popular," Muneishi says, "but I guess the biggest reason is that the sight of her running with all her heart gives comfort to people's hearts."

YOUNGEST & OLDEST

Some people seem to be able to overcome any obstacle—including age.

HIT RECORD
Youngest: In 1992 a 4-year-old named Jordy had a hit in France with "Dur Dur d'Être Bébé!" ("It's Not Easy Being a Baby!")
Oldest: Louis Armstrong was 62 in 1964 when "Hello, Dolly!" hit #1.

PRO HOCKEY PLAYER
Youngest: Bep Guidolin joined the Boston Bruins in 1942 when he was 16.
Oldest: Gordie Howe played professionally from 1946 to 1980, when he was 52 years old.

MAYOR
Youngest: Jeffrey Dunkel won the mayorship of Mount Carbon, Pennsylvania, in 2001 at the age of 18.
Oldest: Dorothy Geeben was still leading Ocean Breeze Park, Florida, at age 96.

CONVICTED MURDERER
Youngest: Thirteen-year-old Nathaniel Abraham was convicted in 2000.
Oldest: Leonard Nathan Sherman of Daly City, California, was 85 in 1999 when he got life in prison for shooting his sister.

OSCAR WINNER
Youngest: Tatum O'Neal won for *Paper Moon* at the age of 10.
Oldest: Jessica Tandy won for *Driving Miss Daisy* at age 80.

POPE
Youngest: Benedict IX, elected pope at age 11 in 1032.
Oldest: Adrian I, elected at age 80 in 772.

PERSON TO SWIM THE ENGLISH CHANNEL
Youngest: Thomas Gregory did it in 1988 when he was 11.
Oldest: Clifford Batt did it in 1987 at 67.

AUTHOR
Youngest: Dorothy Straight was 4 years old in 1964 when her book, *How the World Began*, came out.
Oldest: Sarah Louise Delany's book, *On My Own at 107*, was published in 1997. She was 107.

SATURDAY NIGHT LIVE HOST
Youngest: Drew Barrymore hosted in 1982 at age 7.
Oldest: Miskel Spillman was 80 when she won an "Anyone Can Host" contest in 1977.

Average life expectancy worldwide: 66 years old.

OOPS!

Everyone's amused by tales of outrageous blunders—probably because it's comforting to know that someone's screwing up even worse than we are. So go ahead and feel superior for a few minutes.

AVANT GARBAGE

"Damien Hirst, an avant-garde artist, saw his brand-new installation at London's Eyestorm Gallery go missing briefly. The work is a collection of found objects recovered from an artist's launch party (cigarette butts, beer bottles, soda cans, candy wrappers, etc.). A cleaning man mistook the 'exhibit' for the nightly garbage and tossed it out. Gallery officials recreated it later by referring to a photograph of the trash to get the exact placement of the items."

—News of the Weird

LEAST WANTED

"Two Mexican criminals, Alfredo Ramirez and Alvaro Valdes, were recently withdrawn from a highly publicized 'Most Wanted' list distributed to police stations all over Mexico. The reason: officials discovered that the two men were already in prison. The state prosecutor's office released a congratulatory statement saying that it 'recognizes the unmatched cooperation of the citizens and authorities of the country...which allowed us to locate these two dangerous evil-doers, who are already in jail.'"

—Reuters

DUMMY

"When Claudia Sassi, 57, heard a voice from inside her husband's casket, she collapsed and died. Jacques de Putron, a ventriloquist friend of the husband, told police he thought mourners would find it uplifting to hear 'Let me out!' coming from his coffin."

—Stuff magazine

YOU LIGHT UP MY LIFE

"A lovestruck German man burned down his house after candles he lit for his girlfriend sparked a fire. The unnamed man had laid out hundreds of candles in the shape of a heart carrying the words

In ancient Greece, sick people slept in medicine temples to dream about how to get better.

'You set my heart on fire.' The 18-year-old had hoped the gesture would impress his girlfriend. Instead the heat was so intense it melted the candle wax onto the floor, where it ignited. Ten fire-fighters fought the blaze for an hour before getting it under control. No one was hurt but emergency services said damage to the property came to about £33,000 ($60,000). The young man told police: 'My girlfriend didn't even see the message, all I have left of it is a photograph…and she was not in the mood to look.'"

—Ananova

MP3, M16—WHAT'S THE DIFFERENCE?

"A Canadian student who ordered an MP3 player over the Internet from the U.S. was shocked to receive a licensed handgun instead. Brandon Buchan, 21, an English student at the University of Saskatchewan in Saskatoon, bid for the MP3 player on eBay, the *Star Phoenix* newspaper said. The pawnshop that auctioned the device sent him an unloaded .22-caliber Smith & Wesson gun and a license by mistake. 'I was mostly confused about it all. I'm not a hit man,' Buchan insisted. 'I figured it must just be a mistake.' The student called the police, who removed the weapon. He also e-mailed the shop, who are arranging for his MP3 player to be sent to him. Mr. Buchan says he is keeping a photocopy of the gun license as a souvenir."

—BBC News

SORRY, WRONG CAR

"A German woman became so furious after a telephone quarrel with her husband that she stormed out of the house armed with a hammer and smashed up his car—before realizing that the car didn't belong to her husband. The 43-year-old from Essen told police she shattered the windshield, broke the headlights, and wrenched off the wing mirrors, causing more than $1,200 in damage. After going back indoors she realized she had attacked her neighbor's blue Opel Corsa and not the blue Ford Fiesta belonging to her spouse."

—Reuters

* * *

Huh? "If crime went down 100%, it would still be fifty times higher than it should be."

—Washington, D.C., Councilman John Bowman

What crime led to Billy the Kid's first run-in with the law? Stealing butter.

WOULD YOU RATHER LIVE IN...

Check out these real town names.

Sun, Mississippi, or Moon, Mississippi?

Black, Alabama, or White, Arkansas?

Paradise, California, or Hell, Michigan?

Rock, Kansas, or Roll, Oklahoma?

Devil Town, Ohio, or Angel, Ohio?

Papa, Hawaii, or Mummie, Kentucky?

Cat Creek, Montana, or Dog Creek, Oklahoma?

Smart, Virginia, or Dumbell, Wyoming?

Hungry Horse, Montana, or Fuller, Montana?

Sound Beach, New York, or Silent Grove, Arkansas?

Democrat, Arkansas, or Republican, North Carolina?

Start, Louisiana, or Stop, Georgia?

War, West Virginia, or Peace, Alabama?

Straight, Oklahoma, or Gay, Oklahoma?

Duet, Virginia, or Solo, Tennessee?

Liberty, Kentucky, or Justice, Kentucky?

Can Do, North Dakota, or Defeated, Tennessee?

Chance, Montana, or Fate, Texas?

Boring, Oregon, or Rapture, Indiana?

Rich, Tennessee, or Poor, Tennessee?

Hate Cove, Massachusetts, or Love Cove, Maine?

Darkesville, West Virginia, or Lightville, Ohio?

Push, Arkansas, or Pull Tight, Alabama?

Life, Tennessee, or Death Valley, California?

What does the word "pizza" mean in Italian? Pie.

FAMILIAR PHRASES

Where do these familiar terms and phrases come from? The BRI has researched them and come up with some interesting answers.

GIVE A DAMN
Meaning: To assign little or no significance to something
Origin: "Originally 'I don't give a *dam*,' probably brought back to England from India by military men in the mid-18th century. A *dam* was an Indian coin of little value." (From *Encyclopedia of Word and Phrase Origins*, by Robert Hendrickson)

LICK INTO SHAPE
Meaning: Make ready or presentable
Origin: "Bears are central figures in numerous superstitions. According to one belief, a cub is absolutely shapeless at birth. The mother and father bear were thought to lick their newborn into shape with their tongues. Persistence of the legend is due in part to the fact that few persons saw newborn cubs and lived to describe them." (From *Why You Say It*, by Webb Garrison)

AT FIRST BLUSH
Meaning: Without prior knowledge; at first glance
Origin: "The earliest use of this expression dates from the 16th century, when 'blush' meant not a reddening of the cheeks with embarrassment, but 'glimpse'." (From *Have a Nice Day: No Problem: A Dictionary of Clichés*, by Christine Ammer)

CAKEWALK
Meaning: Effortless; something easily accomplished
Origin: "From a contest popular in the African-American community in the 19th century. Couples competed strolling arm in arm, with the prize—a cake—being awarded to the most graceful and stylish team. Cakewalking demanded both skill and grace, so victory was rarely a 'cakewalk' in our modern sense. That use came from the boxing ring, where an easy victory over an outclassed opponent was a 'cakewalk' compared to the ordinarily brutal and prolonged nature of the matches." (From *The Word Detective*, by Evan Morris)

Dumb joke: What does an educated owl say? Answer: "Whom."

I HATE CLEANING!

Even professional house cleaners draw the line at doing windows, and nobody enjoys cleaning the toilet. Now you don't have to.

PRODUCT: "Cleartect" self-cleaning glass
BACKGROUND: Japan's Nippon Sheet Glass Company began test-marketing the glass for large office buildings and airports, but they were soon overrun with requests from individual customers, so now it's made for homes, too.
HOW IT WORKS: The glass is coated with titanium dioxide, which is *photocatalytic*, meaning that it has a chemical reaction to light. When sunlight hits the glass, that reaction breaks down organic material on the window into smaller and smaller particles. The coating is also *hydrophilic*, meaning that rainwater won't form droplets on the glass—it forms an even sheet that flows down the window, taking dirt away with it. (If it doesn't rain often enough, you have to hose down the window.)

PRODUCT: The "CWS Best CleanSeat" self-cleaning toilet seat
BACKGROUND: Designed for high-traffic public restrooms, these seats have been clinically tested to kill such microorganisms as staph, E. coli, hepatitis A, and strep.
HOW IT WORKS: After every use, the seat automatically spins in a circle. The sensor-activated rotation takes it through a washing device—located on the back of the seat—that cleans and disinfects the seat in 15 seconds. Not satisfied with the first cleaning? Simply signal the sensor (wave your hand in front of it) for another sanitizing round and you're good to...er...go.

PRODUCT: Self-cleaning clothes
BACKGROUND: Scientists at Hong Kong's Polytechnic University discovered that titanium dioxide—the same stuff that's used for self-cleaning windows—can be used for clothes, too.
HOW IT WORKS: The titanium dioxide, when applied to cotton (no other fabric will work) breaks down dirt and other pollutants into smaller and smaller particles, the same way it does on glass. Sunlight and movement, they hope, will eliminate the dirt.

The Chinese have been painting their fingernails for 5,000 years.

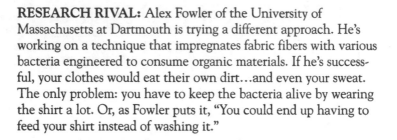

RESEARCH RIVAL: Alex Fowler of the University of Massachusetts at Dartmouth is trying a different approach. He's working on a technique that impregnates fabric fibers with various bacteria engineered to consume organic materials. If he's successful, your clothes would eat their own dirt…and even your sweat. The only problem: you have to keep the bacteria alive by wearing the shirt a lot. Or, as Fowler puts it, "You could end up having to feed your shirt instead of washing it."

PRODUCT: Self-cleaning house

BACKGROUND: By 1952 a 37-year-old designer and professional builder named Frances Gabe of Newberg, Oregon, had had enough of the "thankless, unending, and nerve-twangling bore" of housework. So she designed and built a self-cleaning house.

HOW IT WORKS: The house is built of cinder block to avoid termites and other wood-burrowing insects, and each room is fitted with a ceiling-mounted cleaning, drying, heating, and cooling device. The inside of the house is covered with resin to make it waterproof. The furniture is made entirely from waterproof composites. There are no carpets. The beds are covered automatically with waterproof material that rolls out from the foot of the bed. Easily damaged objects are protected under glass.

At the push of a few buttons, soapy water jets out from the ceiling to power-wash the rooms like an automatic car wash. The same jets then rinse off the water, and a huge built-in blower dries everything. The floors are sloped slightly at the corners so that any excess water can run into a drain. The sink, shower, toilet, and tub clean themselves, too. So do the bookshelves and fireplace. The clothes closet serves as a washer and dryer, and the kitchen cabinets are also dishwashers. The house can be cleaned all at once or one room at a time, as often as needed.

Gabe's been living in her prototype for the past 50 years (she's 89) and only cleans the entire house two or three times a year (unless her grandchildren are coming to visit).

*   *   *

"Cleanliness is next to godliness." **—English proverb**

"Cleanliness is next to impossible." **—Pigpen**

Eeww! Eyes change color after death, usually to a greenish-brown.

STALLED CARS

The old saying that there's nothing new under the sun is especially true in the auto industry. Ideas that seem new today may have been floating around for years, but for some reason didn't succeed the first time around. Here are a few examples.

B & S HYBRID (1980)

B **Ignition:** Milwaukee-based engine maker Briggs & Stratton is best known for its lawn mower engines. But in 1980 B & S introduced a unique vehicle: a "hybrid" car—one that improves fuel economy and reduces air pollution by having both an electric and a standard gasoline-powered engine. Today hybrids made by Toyota, Honda, and Ford are common, but at the time this was a strange and exotic concept. The company did not plan on selling the cars itself. Instead, it hoped that by building and demonstrating a prototype, it could interest major automakers in using Briggs & Stratton engines to power their own hybrid cars.

Car Trouble: The idea looked good on paper, but it was more than 20 years ahead of its time—the battery technology that was necessary to make hybrid cars practical didn't exist. The 12 rechargeable batteries the B & S hybrid carried in its trunk added so much weight to the car (about half a ton) that it needed a second set of rear wheels just to hold them up. The car had only a 60-mile range, after which the batteries needed a full eight hours to recharge. Even when both the gasoline and the electric engine were firing at the same time, it took 22 seconds for the car to accelerate to 40 mph. Top speed: a paltry 68 mph.

Out of Gas: GM, Ford, and Chrysler weren't interested. Briggs & Stratton went back to making engines for lawn mowers. The first practical hybrid sold in the United States, the Honda Insight, didn't arrive in American showrooms until 1999.

FORD CAROUSEL (1970s)

Ignition: In the early 1970s, a group of Ford Motor Company executives had an innovative idea: create a van large enough to hold seven passengers, yet small enough to handle like a car and park in an ordinary garage. They were convinced that it would be

---

Bad car-ma? 40% of car theft victims admit they left their keys in the ignition.

a big seller and might even replace the station wagon as *the* suburban family car. In 1972 the company created a full-size clay model of the concept, which it called the Carousel, and the following year commissioned a consumer survey to gauge public interest. Their findings: Demand was so high that Ford commissioned a second survey out of fear that the results of the first study were too good to be true. The results of the second survey were identical—so Ford set to work designing a prototype and made plans to introduce the car during the 1975 model year.

Out of Gas: Ford president Lee Iacocca liked the Carousel, but his boss, Henry Ford II, hated it and didn't care how well the car tested. "I'm not a big survey man," he explained years later. "I think that if you're in the business you ought to know what the hell you want to do and you can't rely on a survey to pull your bacon out of the frying pan." On his orders, the Carousel was shelved.

Aftermath: Henry II fired Iacocca in 1978, and when Iacocca went to work for Chrysler, a lot of Ford execs went with him, including several who had worked on the Carousel. Chrysler commissioned its own consumer survey to see if a Carousel-type van would still be popular. It was, and in 1983 the first Dodge Caravan—which looked virtually identical to the clay model Ford created in 1972—rolled off the assembly line. By 1988 Chrysler was selling more than 450,000 minivans a year, making it one of the most successful automobile launches in history.

LINCOLN FUTURA (1955)

Ignition: If ever there was a concept car that was appropriately named, it was the Lincoln Futura. The car looked like something out of *The Jetsons*: it was a two-seater like the classic Ford Thunderbird, except that it had sharklike headlights, long tail fins and a "double-bubble" windshield—the driver and the passenger each sat inside their own glass bubble, just like a spaceship from a 1950s science fiction movie.

Out of Gas: As with most concept cars, Lincoln never planned to put the Futura into production; they just built it to test some design ideas and then put it on tour in the car show circuit. The Futura also made a prominent appearance in the 1959 movie *It Started with a Kiss*, starring Debbie Reynolds and Glenn Ford. Then, when Lincoln was done with it, they sold it to a custom car designer in Los Angeles named George Barris.

Q: What do California, Delaware, Florida, Oregon, Idaho, Kansas, Nevada, New Hampshire...

Aftermath: The Futura might never again have seen the light of day, had 20th Century Fox not hired Barris to design a car for their new *Batman* TV series—and given him only three weeks to do it. It wasn't enough time to build a Batmobile from scratch, so Barris gave the Futura a Bat-makeover instead, putting a bat-like snout in the front, installing a rocket "afterburner" in the back, and adding lots of other bat features in between. Reborn as the Batmobile, the Futura has gone on to become one of the most recognizable cars in the world.

THE CHRYSLER D'ELEGANCE (1952)

Ignition: In 1952 Virgil Exner, the head of Chrysler's styling department, came up with a design for a two-seater fastback coupe with beautiful, curvy lines. To save costs Exner sent his sketches and a plaster scale-model to Carrozzeria Ghia, an auto design firm headquartered in Turin, Italy. They built a full-sized prototype and sent it back to Chrysler.

Out of Gas: At the time Chrysler was in a financial crunch. Exner thought a two-seater sports car like the D'Elegance would be a popular seller...but Chrysler didn't want to spend the money to put the car into production. Big mistake—in 1953 Chevrolet introduced the Corvette, and the following year Ford rolled out the Thunderbird. Both cars were huge sellers; Chrysler had nothing like them.

Aftermath: What happened to the D'Elegance? Although it never made it into production, if you saw a picture of it, the lines might look familiar. While Carrozzeria Ghia was building the full-scale model of the D'Elegance, they were also working on a sports car for Volkswagen. Ghia claims the new design was totally original, but the car's resemblance to the Chrysler D'Elegance is remarkable. Did they "borrow" the design? Car buffs still argue over exactly what happened—all anybody knows for sure is that Ghia raced out the design for VW's prototype sports car in a record five months and VW arranged for Karmann Coachwerks, a specialty German body maker, to assemble the car. Introduced in 1955, the VW *Karmann-Ghia* sold more than 485,000 units before it was discontinued in 1974...and Chrysler didn't make another two-seater sports car until it introduced the Dodge Viper in 1992.

LOVE...AND MARRIAGE

Someone once called marriage a "souvenir of love." Here are some other observations about this blissful institution.

"I love being married. I was single for a long time, and I just got so sick of finishing my own sentences."
—**Brian Kiley**

"They say marriage is a contract. No, it's not. Contracts come with warranties."
—**Wanda Sykes**

"My husband and I celebrated our 38th wedding anniversary. You know, I finally realized that if I had killed that man the first time I thought about it, I'd have been out of jail by now."
—**Anita Milner**

"The only thing that keeps me from being happily married ...is my husband."
—**Andra Douglas**

"Getting married is a lot like getting into a tub of hot water. After you get used to it, it ain't so hot."
—**Minnie Pearl**

"We were happily married for eight months. Unfortunately, we were married for four and a half years."
—**Nick Faldo**

"Marriage is like putting your hand into a bag of snakes in the hope of pulling out an eel."
—**Leonardo da Vinci**

"Before we got engaged, he never farted. Now it's like a second language."
—**Caroline Rhea**

"There is so little difference between husbands, you might as well keep the first."
—**Adela Rogers St. Johns**

"Marriage is like a phone call in the night: first the ring, and then you wake up."
—**Evelyn Hendrickson**

"Why can't someone invent something for us to marry besides women?"
—**Fred Flintstone**

"The Wedding March always reminds me of the music played when soldiers go into battle."
—**Heinrich Heine**

"Never get married in the morning—you never know who you might meet that night."
—**Paul Hornung**

INSTANT JUSTICE

*Sometimes crooks get a dose of instant karma—
and sometimes that's just funny.*

CRIME: In September 2003, two men attempted to break into a bank in Kansas City.

INSTANT JUSTICE: Cops in a police cruiser saw the two thieves running down a street with crowbars in their hands and chased them into a grassy field. When they lost sight of the fleeing suspects, the officers stopped and got out of the car—and then heard moans. It turned out that one of the robbers was hiding in the tall grass and the cops drove over him. The lucky thief suffered only a scrape on his forehead.

CRIME: Wanton Beckwith, 27, stole a car in Monrovia, California, in May 2003. After a high-speed chase by police, he exited the car and ran into a house to hide.

INSTANT JUSTICE: Somebody was home—and that somebody had a samurai sword. He pointed it at the intruder's face, led him back outside and held him—at swords length—until police arrived.

CRIME: In September 2003, 18-year-old Michael Watt walked into a health food store in Uttoxeter, England, pulled out a knife, and demanded money.

INSTANT JUSTICE: The sole employee, 48-year-old Lorraine Avery, refused. "I thought, 'He's not having our money, I've worked hard for it.'" She looked for something to hit the thief with but couldn't find anything. So she grabbed an industrial-sized bottle of salad dressing, pointed it at him, and told him to get out of the store. Watt wouldn't go—so she started squirting him with the dressing. "He kept coming at me with the knife," Avery told reporters, "and I kept squirting him." It worked! The would-be robber left the store, and police were able to track him down...by following the trail of salad dressing.

CRIME: In January 2004, an unknown man grabbed a bag out of a car stopped at a stoplight in Sydney, Australia.

INSTANT JUSTICE: The car belonged to Bradley McDonald, a local snake catcher. In the bag was the snake he had just caught— a four-foot-long, venomous, red-bellied black snake. "It might teach him a lesson," McDonald said.

CRIME: Roy A. Gendron, 45, broke into a home in rural Alabama.

INSTANT JUSTICE: The homeowner's son, Richard Bussey, caught Gendron loading furniture and other items onto his truck. Bussey had a gun in his car, so he pulled it on Gendron. But he didn't have a telephone and didn't know what to do next, so he made the burglar mow the lawn—with a push mower—while he thought about it. He eventually took Gendron's driver's license, which the police used to track down and arrest the thief a short time later. Assistant D.A. Brian McVeigh told reporters that if he ever found himself in a similar situation, "I'll try to get some yard work out of the guy."

CRIME: An inmate at the county jail in St. Charles, Missouri, attempted to escape.

INSTANT JUSTICE: The escapee ran into the prison's darkened parking garage and headed for an open door marked "Fire Exit." Sensing that freedom was about to be his, he turned around, gave the approaching deputies a salute, and dashed through the door…running smack into the brick wall behind it. Deputies took the unconscious man to a nearby hospital.

CRIME: In July 1996, 37-year-old Willie King snatched a wallet from the coat of an old woman on a street in Greenwich Village, New York City.

INSTANT JUSTICE: The woman was 94-year-old Yolanda Gigante. Who's that? The mother of Vincent "The Chin" Gigante, reputed head of the Genovese crime family, one of the country's most powerful criminal organizations. King was caught a short time later, and as soon as he realized who he'd mugged he agreed to plead guilty to grand larceny. Sentence: 1-1/2 to 3 years in prison. "My client admitted his guilt at the earliest opportunity, because he wants to put this incident behind him," King's lawyer told the judge. "He hopes the Gigante family will, too."

Elvis Presley shared a bed with his mom until he reached puberty.

UPSTANDING CITIZENS

Before this page became a Bathroom Reader *page, it was a tree.
While we can't bring back the poor tree that sacrificed its life for
your reading pleasure, we can honor these other special trees.*

FREDERICK DOUGLASS' WHITE OAK

In 1877 Frederick Douglass, former slave, author, public speaker, presidential advisor, minister, and antislavery activist, purchased one of the most beautiful and desirable homes in the Washington D.C. area. He called it Cedar Hill. In front of the house stood a towering white oak tree. On February 20, 1895, Douglass left a women's rights conference and walked home, feeling ill. Once home, Douglass sat beneath his white oak, suffered a heart attack, and passed away. Cedar Hill is now a National Historic Site and on a clear day, the immense oak can still be seen from downtown Washington.

THE "SMOKEY" ROOSA SYCAMORE

In 1969 NASA announced its third trip to the moon for January 1971. One of the Apollo 14 astronauts, Stuart Roosa, had been a smoke jumper for the U.S. Forest

Service before joining the space program (he was nick-named "Smokey"). When Ed Cliff, Management Research Director for the Forest Service, heard about the lunar mission he asked his friend Smokey Roosa to take a variety of seeds (pine, sweet gum, fir, sycamore, and redwood) to the moon so that they could be planted on Earth as "moon trees." Roosa liked the idea and took the seeds into space. But they were subjected to a post-return decontamination process that appeared to have killed them. Undaunted, Cliff planted them anyway...and a few actually grew. One of them, a sycamore, still stands in front of the Forestry Science Building at Mississippi State University.

THE BUDDHA BODHI TREE

The Bodhi, or peepul, is a species of fig tree that is native to India. The most famous one grows in the town of Bodh Gaya. It is there, Buddhists believe, that while the monk

---

Now *that's* a buzz: Orchids release a chemical that makes bees drunk.

Siddhartha Gautama sat beneath a Bodhi tree in 528 B.C., he gained enlightenment and became the Buddha. A descendant of that same tree still stands at the site. Another famous Bodhi: In the third century B.C., a cutting from the "Buddha" tree was planted in Sri Lanka, where it has been protected ever since and still flourishes today— 2,300 years later.

TREATY OAK
Once the largest in a circle of 14 oaks that Tonkawa Indians called the Council Oaks. Treaty Oak was the spot where, according to legend, Stephen Austin signed a treaty with the Tonkawas for the land that is now Austin, Texas. With a 127-foot canopy spread, the 500-year-old tree was one of the finest examples of oaks in the world. But in 1989 someone tried to poison Treaty Oak. Arborists were able to save the tree, but it lost more than half of its canopy, making it a shadow of its former self. Good news, though: In 1997 Treaty Oak, the last of the Council Oaks still standing, produced its first acorns since the attack, and will hopefully make a full recovery.

WASHINGTON'S TULIP POPLARS
George Washington: President, general, landscaper. Landscaper? At Mount Vernon, his estate in northern Virginia, Washington found solace in creating gardens. One of his favorite American trees was the tulip poplar. A pair of 100-foot specimens, planted by Washington himself, still thrive on the grounds of Mount Vernon. The Marquis de Lafayette, a close friend of Washington's, was also fond of the tulip poplar and brought a few saplings back to France. He presented them to Marie Antoinette, who had them planted at Versailles. The last of the Lafayette poplars died during the winter of 1999, but, as a reminder of the two men's friendship, the trees were replaced with offspring from Washington's original tulip poplars at Mt. Vernon.

* * *

"Except during the nine months before he draws his first breath, no man manages his affairs as well as a tree does."
—George Bernard Shaw

FOUL BALLS

Lots of people go to baseball games hoping they'll
catch the next ball that gets hit into the stands.
These fans got lucky...or did they?

T he Fan: Robert Cotter, an 11-year-old boy who went to a
Philadelphia Phillies game in 1922.
The Catch: One of the players hit a foul ball into the
stands, and Cotter managed to catch it. He wanted to keep it, but
in those days baseballs were too expensive for teams to give away,
so fans who caught fouls were expected to give them back. Cotter
refused—even when security guards ordered him to hand the ball
over. That evening he became the first and probably the only kid in
professional baseball history to spend the night in jail for refusing to
give back a ball.

What Happened: The next day, Cotter was hauled before a judge,
who ordered that he be set free. "Such an act on the part of a boy is
merely proof that he is following his most natural impulses," the
disgusted judge told the court. "It is a thing I would do myself."

Cotter never did get his ball back, but that summer he got
something better: A woman in New York who read his story invited
him to New York to watch the Yankees play the Philadelphia
Athletics. At the game, he got an autographed baseball and even
got to meet Babe Ruth.

Aftermath: As home runs became increasingly common in the
1920s, teams realized they'd have problems if they kept jailing fans
who kept the balls hit into the stands. So they gave in and decided
to allow the practice. Do we have Cotter to thank for it? It's hard to
say—even Cotter doesn't remember. "I'm not sure if I caused that,"
he told *USA Today* in 1998. "I was only eleven."

The Fans: Alex Popov, a health food restaurant owner from Berkeley,
California, and Patrick Hayashi, a college student from San Diego.
The Catch: In October 2001, both men were at Pac Bell Park in
San Francisco when Giants slugger Barry Bonds hit his record-
setting, single-season 73rd home run into the stands. A camera crew
recorded the scene: the ball landed in Popov's glove and he man-

aged to hang on to it for only six-tenths of a second before he was enveloped by a mob of glove-wielding fans who were also trying to catch it. Popov lost the ball. It was at this point that Hayashi says he saw the ball on the ground, grabbed it, and held it up for everyone to see. Security guards escorted him to a room where officials authenticated the ball as genuine and certified him as the owner.

It's not uncommon for home run balls to bounce from one fan to another. But Popov was adamant that the ball landed in his glove first, making him the rightful owner. When Hayashi would not give it back, Popov sued him.

What Happened: The case wasn't tried until 13 months later; then, following a two-week trial, the judge deliberated for an entire month before finally arriving at his decision: *both* claims of ownership were legitimate, so the ball would have to be sold at auction and the proceeds split evenly between them.

Aftermath: Initially the ball was expected to fetch $1 to 2 million, but by the time the lawsuit was resolved, the economy had worsened and public interest in the ball had dropped significantly. In the end it sold for only $450,000, or $225,000 each for Popov and Hayashi. How much money did Popov get for his troubles? Less than zero—in July 2003, his attorney sued him to recover $473,500 in unpaid legal bills relating to the case.

The Fan: Jay Arsenault, a construction worker from Vacaville, California.

The Catch: In August 2002, three of Arsenault's buddies gave him a ticket to a Giants game at Pac Bell Park. At the time Barry Bonds was approaching another record: he was about to become only the fourth player in pro baseball history to hit 600 home runs in his career. The friends all agreed that in exchange for giving Arsenault the ticket, if he caught the 600th ball, he would sell it and they'd all split the proceeds. Amazingly, Arsenault *did* catch the ball—but rather than honor the agreement as promised, he hid from his friends. They filed a lawsuit, claiming breach of an oral contract.

What Happened: In October, Arsenault, claiming he'd been "totally overwhelmed by the situation," backed down and agreed to sell the ball and split the money just like he'd promised. "This is better for both sides," Eric Bergen, one of the friends, told reporters. "This is what we wanted from the beginning."

Big picture: The first VCR, made in 1956, was about the size of a piano.

The Fan: Nick O'Brien, a four-year-old boy whose parents took him to a Texas Rangers-St. Louis Cardinals game in June 2004.

The Catch: Right fielder Gary Matthews, Jr. hit a foul ball into the stands. It landed at Nick's feet, but as he was reaching down to pick it up, a grown man pushed him away and grabbed the ball.

What Happened: Nick's mother, Edie O'Brien, confronted the man. "You trampled a four-year-old boy to get this ball!" she yelled at him, but he refused to give the ball back. The incident, caught on camera, was replayed on the park's giant video screens. Outraged fans started chanting "Give him the ball!" and the mood turned ugly, but still the man that the Rangers announcer called "the biggest jerk in this park" refused to give the ball back. He was literally booed out of the stands. Nick fared a little better: the Rangers invited him and his parents down to the dugout and gave him two autographed bats and four autographed balls, including one signed by Hall of Famer Nolan Ryan.

That might have been the end of it, had the *Dallas Morning News* not identified the Biggest Jerk in the Park as 28-year-old Matt Starr, a married landscaper and former youth minister living in a Dallas suburb. By Wednesday, when Nick and his mom and dad were in New York telling their story on *Good Morning America*, reporters were camped out in front of Starr's house. He was nowhere to be found.

Aftermath: Three days was all it took: on Wednesday night Starr caved in, called the Rangers, and told them he would give the ball to Nick, along with a letter of apology and tickets to an upcoming game. "He doesn't want any more publicity about this," a Rangers spokesperson told reporters. "He's hoping this will bring some sort of closure."

*   *   *

CAUGHT WITH THEIR PANTS DOWN

In January 2004, three men in Spokane, Washington, decided to have a little fun by running through the local Denny's at dawn, wearing just their shoes and hats. Their only mistake: leaving the car engine running. While they were streaking through the restaurant, someone stole their car and their clothes. The three naked pranksters had to hide behind parked cars until police arrived to take them to jail.

FLUBBED HEADLINES

These are 100% real, honest-to-goodness headlines.
Can you figure out what they were trying to say?

Doctor Testifies in Horse Suit

DIET OF PREMATURE BABIES
AFFECTS IQ

Oprah, Madonna Talk
Marriage

COMPLAINTS ABOUT NBA
REFEREES GROWING UGLY

Groom Sues Bride of 4
Mouths

GENERAL EISENHOWER FLIES
BACK TO FRONT

God Gets a Parking Caution:
"No Exceptions" Say Police

Dumped Fish Remains Upset

AIRLINE TRAVEL SAFER DESPITE
MORE ACCIDENTS

American Ships Head To
Libya

WOMAN NOT INJURED
BY COOKIE

LACK OF WATER HURTS
ICE FISHING

L.A. Voters Approve Urban
Renewal by Landslide

LAWYER CALLS SOUL AS
WITNESS

Thanks to President Clinton,
Staff Sgt. Fruer Now Has a Son

TORTOISES HELD
HOSTAGE AS LOBSTER
WAR TURNS NASTY

SNOW STORMS MAY BE
PRECURSOR OF WINTER

Blind Bishop Appointed to See

Diaper Market Bottoms Out

Ancient Blonde Corpses
Raise Questions

LAWYERS GIVE POOR
FREE LEGAL ADVICE

California Governor Makes
Stand on Dirty Toilets

REASON FOR MORE BEAR
SIGHTINGS: MORE BEARS

Ban on Soliciting Dead in
Trotwood

CUTS COULD HURT ANIMALS

NUDE SCENE DONE
TASTEFULLY IN RADIO PLAY

BOX OFFICE BLOOPERS

Everyone loves bleepers, er, bloppers, er, we mean bloopers.
Here are a few great ones from the silver screen.

Movie: *Lethal Weapon 2* (1989)
Scene: Martin Riggs (Mel Gibson) is placed in a strait-jacket and thrown into a river.
Blooper: Struggling to escape from the straitjacket, Riggs purposely dislocates his left shoulder. Back on dry land, he slams his *right* shoulder against a car to put it back in place.

Movie: *Fear.com* (2002)
Scene: The entire movie is about a woman who is a hemophiliac.
Blooper: This is one of our favorites—the whole movie is a blooper. How so? It's physically impossible for women to be hemophiliacs. They are carriers of the disease, but only males can contract it.

Movie: *Terminator 2* (1991)
Scene: The Terminator (Arnold Schwarzenegger), Sarah Connor (Linda Hamilton), and John Connor (Edward Furlong) escape from a mental hospital in a car, driving in reverse.
Blooper: The stunt driver is driving from the trunk of the car, and you can see his head pop up just inside the rear window.

Movie: *Panic Room* (2002)
Scene: When the group of robbers first enters the house, Meg (Jodie Foster) runs into her daughter's room and dumps a bottle of water on the girl to wake her up.
Blooper: They quickly make their way to the panic room, but once they're inside, the girl is completely dry.
Bonus Blooper: The survival pack inside the panic room is well-stocked with almost everything they need—except food. (It does have another "essential," though: sugar-free breath mints.)

Movie: *Gladiator* (2000)
Scene: After the battle with the Germans, Maximus (Russell Crowe) feeds his horse an apple.

First actor to refuse an Oscar: Marlon Brando (for *The Godfather* in 1973).

Blooper: You can see a crewman standing in the background (wearing blue jeans).

Movie: *One Hour Photo* (2002)
Scene: Nina (Connie Nielsen) drops off three rolls of film.
Blooper: Although the film she drops off is clearly labeled "Fuji Superior," when Sy (Robin Williams) runs the film through the machine all the negatives say "Kodak."

Movie: *The Last of the Mohicans* (1992)
Scene: The British troops leave Fort Henry.
Blooper: As the Huron warriors begin to attack the British, the camera moves behind the procession, and in the middle of the commotion a man in a blue hat can be seen raising a megaphone.

Movie: *Star Wars* (1977)
Scene: Stormtroopers break into the control room.
Blooper: One unfortunate trooper rushes in and slams his head against the door frame.

Movie: *The Lord of the Rings: The Two Towers* (2002)
Scene: Just before the final battle at Helm's Deep, the villagers run into caves for safety.
Blooper: As the camera pans the rocky interior, one of the villagers leans against a stalactite…which wobbles back and forth.

Movie: *The Scorpion King* (2002)
Scene: Opening narration.
Blooper: The film is said to have taken place long before the time of the pyramids, yet all the swords seem to be made of steel, which would not be invented for thousands of years to come.

Movie: *Signs* (2002)
Scene: Merrill (Joaquin Phoenix) is in an Army recruiting office.
Blooper: The "Army" poster in the background shows a soldier in a Marine Corps uniform.

(B)AD CAMPAIGNS

*Advertisers are always trying to come up with
new ways to sell their products. Sometimes
they end up achieving the opposite result.*

BRILLIANT MARKETING IDEA: In April 2000, IBM launched its "Peace, Love and Linux" ad campaign to promote their Linux operating system. The plan: hire graffiti artists in Chicago, Boston, New York, and San Francisco to stencil hundreds of peace symbols (for "peace"), hearts (for "love"), and smiling penguins (the Linux logo) on sidewalks in biodegradable chalk. Rain and normal foot traffic would cause the ads to disappear after about a week.

ON SECOND THOUGHT: They were *supposed* to use biodegradable chalk, but somehow the artists in San Francisco either didn't get the message or decided to improvise, because they didn't use chalk—they used spray paint, which isn't biodegradable and doesn't disappear in a week. Some of the artists were caught in the act, but IBM wouldn't fess up. "At first they feigned ignorance," a San Francisco city supervisor told the *Los Angeles Times*. "Then they refused to give the name of the local ad agency. That's when we parted ways about being amicable." IBM eventually admitted guilt and paid San Francisco more than $100,000 in compensation. "I guess we got a little carried away," an IBM spokesperson told reporters.

BRILLIANT MARKETING IDEA: In the early 1980s, Pan Am Airways decided to run a promotion for its New York to San Juan, Puerto Rico, route by serving a special meal on the flight: salami, cheese, and an apple in a basket, along with a small bottle of Mateus wine and a tiny tablecloth. The airline made plans to publicize the promotion by running newspaper ads.

ON SECOND THOUGHT: The idea seemed simple enough… until the 2,000 pounds of sliced salami arrived. Pan Am's agreement with its in-house food preparers stipulated that only *they* could slice meats served on the airline. So Pan Am rescheduled the newspaper ads and ordered 2,000 pounds of fresh, unsliced salami…only to learn that the little bottles of wine were delivered to New York, and

---

Cosmic question: Did Adam and Eve have belly buttons?

the baskets were sent to San Juan. It rescheduled the newspaper ads again...only to learn that while New York was shipping the wine to San Juan, San Juan was shipping the baskets to New York. The ads were rescheduled again. Finally, when everything was in order, the ads ran, the special meals were served on the flight...and the flight attendants realized that the bottles had cork tops instead of screw-off caps. (The planes didn't carry corkscrews.) Pan Am replaced the corked bottles with screw top bottles and a short time later switched the small jumbo jets on the New York to San Juan route over to much larger 747s. When the flight attendants complained that preparing baskets for all 300 passengers was too time consuming, the airline scrapped the promotion altogether.

BRILLIANT MARKETING IDEA: In 1998 Toyota launched an ad campaign aimed at young African Americans.

ON SECOND THOUGHT: An ad for a Toyota Corolla that ran in *Jet* magazine had the slogan, "Unlike your last boyfriend, it goes to work in the morning." And then in 2001 they ran an ad that showed a young smiling black man with a gold outline of the RAV4 on his front tooth. Jesse Jackson and other civil rights leaders were incensed. When they threatened a boycott of Toyota and Lexus, Toyota diffused the crisis by negotiating a 10-year, $7.8 billion campaign to improve corporate diversity.

BRILLIANT MARKETING IDEA: In 1989 Kraft General Foods launched its "Ready to Roll" game promotion: customers who bought Kraft Singles cheese slices could match a "left half" game piece inside the cheese package with a "right half" coupon inserted into Sunday newspapers in Chicago and Houston. Prizes included bicycles, skateboards, cheese, and a 1990 Dodge Caravan. Odds of winning the $17,000 van: 15 million to 1.

ON SECOND THOUGHT: Kraft only planned to issue one grand prize-winning game piece...but the printer made a mistake and printed 10,000 of them, plus another 10,000 winning pieces for the bikes, skateboards and free cheese. "Essentially all of the game pieces appear to be winning ones," a Kraft spokesperson told reporters. When the company tried to cancel the promotion, the "winning" contestants sued; Kraft ended up paying $700 to everyone who won a van—and giving smaller prizes to other winners. Total payout: $10 million.

FIGHTING WORDS

Wartime leaders with an ear for a memorable phrase.

"War is cruelty. There's no use trying to reform it, the crueler it is the sooner it will be over."
—**William Tecumseh Sherman**

"I prefer fifty thousand rifles to fifty thousand votes."
—**Benito Mussolini**

"Next to a battle lost, the greatest misery is a battle gained."
—**The Duke of Wellington**

"It is easier to find men who will volunteer to die than to find those who are willing to endure pain with patience."
—**Julius Caesar**

"I want you to remember that no son of a bitch ever won a war by dying for his country. He won it by making the other poor dumb bastard die for his country."
—**Gen. George S. Patton**

"Political power grows out of the barrel of a gun."
—**Mao Zedong**

"In war, you win or lose, live or die—and the difference is an eyelash."
—**Gen. Douglas MacArthur**

"Do not forget your big guns, the most respected arguments of the rights of kings."
—**Frederick the Great**

"If men can develop weapons that are so terrifying as to make the thought of global war include almost a sentence for suicide, you would think that man's intelligence and his comprehension would include also his ability to find a peaceful solution."
—**Dwight D. Eisenhower**

"Voice or no voice, the people can always be brought to the bidding of the leaders. That is easy. All you have to do is to tell them they are being attacked, and denounce the pacifists for lack of patriotism and exposing the country to danger. It works the same in any country."
—**Herman Goering**

"They are in front of us, behind us, and we are flanked on both sides by an enemy that outnumbers us 29 to 1. They can't get away from us now!"
—**Gen. Chesty Puller**

Snobs? Rabbits and hares never mate with each other.

THE WORLD'S (UN)LUCKIEST MAN

Is he lucky…or unlucky? You decide.

T HE SELAK ZONE
On a cold January day in 1962, a Croatian music teacher named Frane Selak was traveling from Sarajevo to Dubrovnik by train. Well, that's where he *thought* he was going. Little did he know that he was actually about to embark upon a strange 40-year odyssey marked by freak accidents and near-death experiences.

• The train carrying Selak in 1962 inexplicably jumped the tracks and plunged into an icy river, killing 17 passengers. Selak managed to swim back to shore, suffering hypothermia, shock, bruises, and a broken arm, but very happy to be alive.

• One year later, Selak was on a plane traveling from Zagreb to Rijeka when a door blew off the plane and he was sucked out of the aircraft. A few minutes later the plane crashed; 19 people were killed. But Selak woke up in a hospital—he'd been found in a haystack and had only minor injuries.

• In 1966 he was riding on a bus that went off the road and into a river. Four people were killed—but not Selak. He suffered only cuts and bruises.

• In 1970 he was driving along when his car suddenly caught fire. He managed to stop and get out just before the fuel tank exploded and engulfed the car in flames.

• In 1973 a faulty fuel pump sprayed gas all over the engine of another of Selak's cars while he was driving it, blowing flames through the air vents. His only injury: he lost most of his hair. His friends started calling him "Lucky."

• In 1995 he was hit by a city bus in Zagreb but received only minor injuries.

• In 1996 he was driving on a mountain road when he turned a corner and saw a truck coming straight at him. He drove the car through a guardrail, jumped out, landed in a tree—and watched his car explode 300 feet below.

BAD NEWS (AND GOOD NEWS) TRAVELS FAST

By this time he was starting to get an international reputation for his amazing knack for survival. "You could look at it two ways," Selak said. "I am either the world's unluckiest man or the luckiest. I prefer to believe the latter."

How does the story of Frane Selak end? Luckily, of course. In June 2003, at the age of 74, Selak bought his first lottery ticket in 40 years...and won more than $1 million. "I am going to enjoy my life now," he said. "I feel like I have been reborn. I know God was watching over me all these years." He told reporters that he planned to buy a house, a car, and a speedboat, and to marry his girlfriend. (He'd been married four times before and reflected, "My marriages were disasters, too.")

Update: In 2004 Selak was hired to star in an Australian TV commercial for Doritos. At first he accepted the job, but then changed his mind and refused to fly to Sydney for the filming. Reason: He said he didn't want to test his luck.

*　　*　　*

BACKWARD TOWN NAMES

The names of dozens of U.S. cities come from other words spelled backward. Most were forced to do it after realizing that the town name they wanted was already taken. Others have quirkier origins.

• **Enola, South Carolina.** Originally named "Alone," but residents began to feel too isolated.

• **Nikep, Maryland.** Changed because it kept getting Pekin, Indiana's, mail by mistake.

• **Adaven, Nevada.** America's only city with its state's name spelled backward. It's a palindrome!

• **Tensed, Idaho.** Named for a missionary named DeSmet, the name was reversed when it was discovered there was already a DeSmet, Idaho. The town submitted their new name, Temsed, to Washington, D.C., but a clerical error resulted in the misspelling.

THE ETERNAL TWINKIE

*We at the BRI have an insatiable appetite for finding
misinformation, including these food myths.*

Myth: French fries aren't really French—they're Belgian.
Truth: Fried, salted potato strips *did* originally come
from Belgium (they were introduced to America by soldiers returning home from World War I). But French fries are also
French. How so? The term refers to the way they're cut—long,
thin strips are called julienne, or French style.

Myth: Belgian waffles are Belgian.
Truth: They're American. Some enterprising food vendor in the
Belgian Village pavilion at the 1964 New York World's Fair added
yeast to normal waffle batter so they'd be fluffier. To make his new
creation sound more exotic, he called them "Belgian" waffles.

Myth: The Chinese invented pasta.
Truth: Legend has it that Marco Polo discovered noodles during his
travels to China and brought his discovery back to Italy. But actually, the Italians already had noodles. They'd been making them for
centuries. The difference: Chinese noodles are made from rice or
buckwheat. Italian pasta uses semolina flour, a type of wheat.

Myth: Twinkies will stay fresh forever.
Truth: True, Twinkies have a longer shelf life than most other
baked goods. But that's because they contain no dairy products,
not because they're full of preservatives. How long do they really
stay fresh? According to Hostess, a mere 25 days.

Myth: Sugar makes kids hyper.
Truth: For years scientists have conducted studies, trying to link
sweets with hyperactivity...without success. A 1995 double-blind
American Medical Association test concluded that there is
absolutely no chemical link between sugar and behavior problems.
There may be a psychological link, however: parents who expect
sugar to affect their child tend to imagine the kid is misbehaving.

FAMOUS PEOPLE'S PETS

*Do you think an animal cares that its owner
is a celebrity? Probably not...but we do.*

MADONNA has a Chihuahua named Chiquita.

ERNEST HEMINGWAY had Springer Spaniels named Black Dog and Negrita (and 30 cats).

LEONARDO DICAPRIO has a Poodle named Rufus and a lizard named Blizzard.

MARTHA STEWART has cats named Beethoven, Mozart, Vivaldi, Verdi, Teeny, and Weeny.

PINK has a Jack Russell terrier named F**ker.

VIRGINIA WOOLF had a marmoset named Mitz.

ADOLF HITLER had a German Shepherd named Blondi.

JESSICA SIMPSON has a pot-bellied pig named Brutus.

MICHAEL JACKSON has a llama named Louie.

CALVIN COOLIDGE had raccoons named Rebecca and Horace.

MUHAMMAD ALI has a tabby cat named Icarus.

CAMERON DIAZ has a cat named Little Man.

GEORGE CLOONEY has a pot-bellied pig named Max.

SIGMUND FREUD had a Chow named Jo-fi.

DREW BARRYMORE has a Lab/Chow mix named Flossie.

TRUMAN CAPOTE had a Bulldog named Bunky.

SYLVESTER STALLONE has a Boxer named Gangster.

BRITNEY SPEARS has a Yorkshire Terrier named Baby.

SLASH has a Golden Retriever named Belle.

GEORGE ORWELL had a dog named Marx and a goat named Muriel.

CHRISTINA AGUILERA has a dog named Jackson (for her idol, Michael Jackson).

CHARLES DARWIN had a dog named Bob.

Pet tip: If your dog has bad breath, he may need to have his teeth cleaned. (Or maybe he's just a dog.)

THE CHAUCER OF CHEESE

Have you heard of one James McIntyre?
His unusual verses set the world afire.
Think of this while eating your Cheerios:
In the 1800s he was the bard of southwestern Ontario.
His work is published this day still,
If you read his poems, they'll make you ill.

A BARD IS BORN

James McIntyre (1827–1906), known to his admirers as the "Chaucer of Cheese," was born in the Scottish village of Forres. He moved to Canada when he was 14 and lived most of his life in Ingersoll, a small town in Ontario, where he worked as a furniture and coffin maker. But what earned him his reputation was his hobby—writing poetry. McIntyre wrote poems on a variety of topics: He described Ontario towns, saluted his favorite authors, and sang the praises of farming and country life. He even composed tributes to his furniture.

WHAT RHYMES WITH GOUDA?

Most famously, he wrote poems to promote the local economy. And in the mid-1800s, the economy of southwestern Ontario was cheese. In 1866, for example, Ontario dairy farmers produced what was then the world's largest block of cheese—it measured more than 21 feet across and weighed 7,300 pounds. The giant inspired two of McIntyre's best-known poems: "Ode on the Mammoth Cheese" and "Prophesy of a Ten Ton Cheese."

When the *Toronto Globe* printed some of his work, including such poems as "Oxford Cheese Ode," "Hints to Cheesemakers," "Dairy Ode," and "Father Ranney, the Cheese Pioneer," his fame spread across Canada and then around the world. What makes McIntyre's poetry fun to read isn't just his choice of subject matter (cheese) or his weird rhymes (pairing "fodder" with "Cheddar," or "shoes Norwegian" with "narrow toboggan").

"If you read his poetry, what comes out is his enthusiasm," says

Michael Hennessy, mayor of Ingersoll. "People might say they are terrible poems, but McIntyre was a trier, and that is a great quality in a writer."

WHO IS THE WORST?

Giving new meaning to the term *cheesy*, many of McIntyre's admirers argue that he, not Scotland's William McGonagall (see page 145), deserves the title of World's Worst Poet. But McGonagall's fans steadfastly disagree. "McGonagall is by far the worst poet in the English language," says Scottish poet Don Paterson. "He could write a bad poem about anything. This cheese guy may be a bad poet, but it seems he could write bad poetry about only one subject."

A MCINTYRE SAMPLER

A few excerpts from our favorite McIntyre poems:

"Hints to Cheesemakers"

All those who quality do prize
Must study color,
taste and size,
And keep their dishes
clean and sweet,
And all things round
their factories neat,
For dairymen insist that these
Are all important points
in cheese.

Grant has here a
famous work
Devoted to the cure of pork,
For dairymen find it doth pay
To fatten pigs
upon the whey,
For there is money
raising grease
As well as in the
making cheese.

"Dairy Ode"

Our muse it doth
refuse to sing
Of cheese made early
in the spring.
When cows give milk
from spring fodder
You cannot make
a good cheddar.

The quality is often vile
Of cheese that is
made in April,
Therefore we
think for that reason
You should make cheese
later in the season.

Cheese making
you should delay
Until about the first of May.
Then cows do feed
on grassy field
And rich milk they
abundant yield.

Utensils must be
clean and sweet
So cheese with first class
can compete,
And daily polish up
milk pans,
Take pains with vats
and with milk cans.

And it is important matter
To allow no stagnant water,
But water from
pure well or stream
The cow must drink
to give pure cream.

Though 'gainst spring cheese
some do mutter,
Yet spring milk also makes
bad butter,
Then there doth
arise the query
How to utilize it in the dairy.

🔹

"Oxford Cheese Ode"

The ancient poets
ne'er did dream
That Canada was
land of cream
They ne'er imagined
it could flow
In this cold land
of ice and snow,
Where everything
did solid freeze,
They ne'er hoped or
looked for cheese.

🔹

"Ode on the Mammoth Cheese"

We have seen thee,
queen of cheese,
Lying quietly at your ease,
Gently fanned by
evening breeze,
Thy fair form no flies dare seize.

All gaily dressed soon you'll go
To the great Provincial show,
To be admired by many a beau
In the city of Toronto.

Cows as numerous
as a swarm of bees
Or as the leaves upon the trees,
It did require to
make thee please,
And stand unrivalled,
queen of cheese.

May you not receive a scar as
We have heard that Mr. Harris
Intends to send you off as far as
The great world's show at Paris.

Of the youth beware of these,
For some of them might
rudely squeeze
And bite your cheek,
then songs or glees
We could not sing, oh!
queen of cheese.

We'rt thou suspended
from balloon,
You'd cast a shade
even at noon,
Folks would think
it was the moon,
About to fall
and crush them soon.

At its thickest point, the ice in Antarctica is 15,700 feet thick.

BILLION-DOLLAR BABIES

How does a fad start? What makes millions of people all jump on the same bandwagon at the same time? Is it coincidence...or careful planning? Here's a look at an interesting craze of the late 1990s.

TOYCOON

In 1980 Ty Warner left his sales job at a San Francisco stuffed animal company to start one of his own. He named it after himself—Ty Inc. The business did well from the start, but it wasn't until 1993 that Warner hit on the idea that would put it on the map. Why not make a stuffed animal so affordable that kids could buy it with one week's worth of allowance?

So he came up with tiny stuffed animals made of polyester plush fabric that could sell for about $5. The critters came with a heart-shaped paper tag that gave the animal's name, its "birth date," and a four-line poem describing it. He called them "Beanie Babies."

The Beanie Babies' most novel feature was their filling—as the name suggests, they were loosely filled with plastic "beans" that gave them the feel of a beanbag instead of a stuffed animal. They looked slightly deflated, not stuffed, and when Warner showed his tiny slumping cats, dogs, bears, and other animals to people in the toy industry, they thought he was nuts. "Everyone called them roadkill," Warner told a reporter in 1996. "They didn't get it. The whole idea was that they looked real because they moved."

GET 'EM WHILE THEY'RE HOT

To help boost sales, Warner adopted a clever "strategy of scarcity":

• He avoided giant retailers and toy store chains in favor of small gift shops and specialty toy stores, and he limited sales to these stores, too. No store was able to buy all the Beanie Baby characters that were available, and those they did get were limited to 36 of each character per month. Collectors came to perceive them as scarce—they had to buy them quickly before they were gone.

• Instead of manufacturing as many as he could sell, Warner regularly "retired" Beanie Baby characters by posting a notice on the company Web site. Some were retired only after a long run; others

---

Japan produces more solar power than any country on Earth.

were retired quickly. There was no logic to it, so when a new character appeared in stores people had to act fast if they wanted one.

• Warner made small changes in each character. If the first production run of Shasta the Bear had an orange ribbon around its neck, Warner would then change the ribbon to yellow, and then green on the next runs. Or he might change the color of the bear from white to red, and then to blue. Hardcore collectors felt compelled to buy several versions of each character.

• But Warner's most brilliant stroke of all: a near-total information blackout on his company, so that nobody had a complete picture of what was going on. How many Seaweed the Otters was the company going to produce? In how many versions? Which stores would get them? How soon would they be retired? He wouldn't divulge his plans, which further fueled the frenzy to buy.

FROM BEANS TO NUTS

Warner's clever marketing paid off. Kids spending their allowance money on Beanie Babies were quickly overtaken by crazed adult collectors racing from store to store looking for newly retired Beanie Babies before they disappeared forever. Since no information was coming, Ty collectors organized phone and e-mail networks to compare notes and keep up to date.

New Beanie Baby characters came out all the time priced at $5 to $7, but as the fad grew, the value of the oldest and rarest of the retired Beanie Babies began to soar on the collectors' market. Skyrocketing prices drew more people into the craze, which in turn pushed prices even higher. People bought every character they could get their hands on, in the hope that, like the royal blue Peanut the Elephant, one or more of them might one day be worth $5,000.

NOTHING LIKE IT IN THE WORLD

So how crazy did it get? Collectors made daily calls to their local toy stores to see when new shipments were expected, then on delivery day lined up hours before the store opened to be the first to buy whatever new Beanie Babies might be in the shipment. But why wait? Some people drove around looking for UPS trucks that might be carrying Beanie Babies. People fought over stuffed frogs and crabs in the parking lots of strip malls, and in West Virginia a security guard named Harry Simmons was shot and killed by his "business partner" during an argument over their Beanie Babies.

In 1997 McDonald's announced that it would include a "Teenie Beanie Baby" prize with each Happy Meal. The giveaway turned into the company's most successful sales promotion ever: Crazed collectors stampeded the restaurants, buying dozens of Happy Meals at a time, tossing out the food and getting back in line to buy more. The promotion was supposed to last a month, but the company ended up giving away all 100 million Teenie Beanie Babies—one for every child in America—in ten days.

And over the course of the Beanie Baby craze, Ty Warner, a man who basically sells little *bean bags* for a living, pocketed about $6 billion. In 2003 *Forbes* magazine listed him as the world's 44th richest person—in a league with software giants, media moguls, and Arab sheiks.

WHAT GOES UP...

Nothing could postpone the inevitable: With factories in Asia churning out new Beanie Babies by the hundreds of millions, sooner or later people were bound to get bored and even the most diehard collectors would despair of ever collecting them all. By mid-1999 Beanie Babies were beginning to pile up on store shelves, so Warner announced that the company was retiring *all* of its remaining Beanie Babies on December 31. The "last" Beanie Baby ever? A black bear named "The End." Sales shot up again.

Then on Christmas Eve he announced he would put it to a vote: Beanie Baby fans could phone in (at 50¢ a call) and vote on whether Beanie Babies should be saved. Guess what happened!

The fake retirement boosted sales in the short run, but in the long run it probably killed the craze. The Ty company still manufactures Beanie Babies, but today they're what they should have been all along: toys for kids. New ones sell for about $6 in toy stores, but on eBay shell-shocked collectors who hoped to pay for their kids' educations by hoarding Beanie Babies are now dumping them in bulk. Even when offered for a penny apiece, they don't always attract bidders.

Moral of the story: Beanbags are great toys. They're just not good investments.

Trinidad's paradoxical frog starts as a foot-long tadpole and "grows" into an inch-long frog.

WHAT'S UP, DOC?

Some doctor shows on TV may seem far-fetched, but these stories prove that truth is stranger than fiction.

YIP/TUCK

In Rio de Janeiro, Dr. Edgard Brito is now offering a wide variety of the latest surgical procedures, such as Botox injections and wrinkle-reductions. Brito's patients, however, happen to be dogs. For a reasonable price, the vet performs full face-lifts including ear straightening and eyebrow corrections. When asked by reporters about his surgical packages, Brito said, "We all like to talk to someone who looks good. It is the same for dogs."

WORKS EVERY TIME

In April 2002, doctors told Trizka Litton that she was going to need a hernia operation, but that her condition didn't require immediate surgery. Finally, after seven months on the hospital waiting list, Litton had had enough. She concocted a cocktail of crumbled biscuits and cranberry juice, microwaved it, and called the paramedics, claiming that she had just vomited blood. An ambulance immediately took her to the hospital (where she promptly disposed of the evidence before docs could test it). Doctors performed emergency surgery and discovered that her stomach was pressing dangerously on her heart. Litton later said, "I carried a heavy burden of guilt and shame at being forced to cheat and lie. But it vanished when doctors told me just how near death I had been."

HAIRY HEARING

In 2002, 24-year-old Yu Zhenhuan was listed in the *Guinness Book of World Records* as the "World's Hairiest Man" (thick hair covers 96% of his body). But due to the growth of hair inside his ears, Zhenhuan, star of the film *China's Number One Hairy Child* when he was six, was losing his hearing and suffering from pounding headaches. In order to restore the "hairy child's" hearing, doctors performed a unique operation: a four-hour "hairectomy," removing hair follicles two to three centimeters long from his inner ear. Yet despite the apparent dangers of a hairy physique, Zhenhuan refuses to shave any part of his body but his beard.

Q & A:
BODY OF KNOWLEDGE

*Everyone's got a question they'd like answered—basic stuff,
like "Why is the sky blue?" Here are a few questions,
with answers from the nation's top trivia experts.*

O
PEN WIDE

Q: *Why are yawns contagious?*

A: "The action of a mouth opening is not what compels others to yawn, according to Dr. William Broughton, director of the Sleep Disorders Center at the University of South Alabama. Studies have demonstrated that showing someone a photo of a wide-open mouth does not induce a yawn. Conversely, holding a hand over the mouth while yawning doesn't prevent it from being contagious. Contagious yawns appear 'basically to be a visual response.' Between 40 and 60% of people who watch videos or hear talk about yawning also end up doing it, too. Researchers from the State University of New York tested people to find out what kind of person is most susceptible to contagious yawning. Their conclusion: people who are self-aware or empathetic are more likely to catch yawns." (From *The Mobile* (Alabama) *Register*)

X MARKS THE SPOT
Q: *What causes liver spots?*

A: "Liver spots, also called age spots or *lentigenes*, are the result of hyperpigmentation—the buildup of excess pigment in patches of the skin. Liver spots have nothing to do with the liver; they most often result from a lifetime of exposure to sunlight. Other possible causes include surgery, pregnancy, and some medications." (From *The New York Times Second Book of Science Questions and Answers,* by C. Claiborne Ray)

BAD TASTE
Q: *Why does orange juice taste so bad after you brush your teeth?*

A: "The detergent used in most toothpastes—sodium lauryl sulfate—temporarily modifies the taste system, according to Dr. John

DeSimone of Virginia Commonwealth University. It reduces your ability to taste sweetness and saltiness, and makes sour foods intensely bitter. Right after brushing, anything will taste less sweet. Don't worry, though: the reaction won't harm you." (From *Newsweek*)

DRY YOUR EYE

Q: *Why do we have eyebrows?*

A: "We have eyebrows for two reasons. The first is to keep water from running into your eyes. Your forehead can perspire more than other parts of the body. Perspiration is salty, and if you didn't have eyebrows it would run into your eyes and cause them to smart. If it is raining hard, water running off your head and down your forehead is stopped by the eyebrows so the water doesn't get into your eyes and hamper your vision. You'll also notice that the bone under your eyebrows sticks out slightly. If you bump that bone, the eyebrows soften the blow to prevent damage to the bone. It is believed that early humans had much thicker eyebrows to provide more padding." (From *What Makes Flamingos Pink?*, by Bill McLain)

GESUNDHEIT!

Q: *Why do you close your eyes when you sneeze?*

A: "It's a reflex thing. Your eyes snap shut as soon as you sneeze, and it's pretty much impossible to keep them open. The nerves serving the eyes and the nose are very closely connected. The stimuli to one often trigger some response in the other. There's an urban myth that if you keep your eyes open when you sneeze, your eyes will pop out. Well, you can't do it, and even if you could, it wouldn't happen." (From *Return of the Answer Lady*, by Marg Meikle.)

LEAKY PIPES

Q: *Why does running water make you have to go to the bathroom?*

A: "Scientists say it's the power of suggestion. It's totally psychological. The sound of going to the bathroom is very similar to the sound of water filling a sink. The brain hears water running and connects it with the need to urinate, so it sends a message to the bladder telling it that it's full, even if it isn't. The phenomenon even occurs in dogs." (From *Why Knuckles Crack and Other Body Facts*, by Jeremy M. Barker)

The cold truth: Scientists say you have more nightmares when your bedroom is cold.

KIND OF KINKY

What do Bill Clinton and George W. Bush have in common? They're both fans of Texas novelist/songwriter/satirist Kinky Friedman.

"A happy childhood is the worst possible preparation for life."

"In six days the Lord created the heavens and the Earth and all the wonders therein. There are some of us who feel that He might have taken just a little more time."

"If you have the choice between humble and cocky, go with cocky. There's always time to be humble later, once you've been proven horrendously, irrevocably wrong."

"I came from an upper-middle-class home, which is always a hard cross for a country singer to bear."

"If you're paranoid long enough, sooner or later you're gonna be right."

"The distance between the limousine and the gutter is a short one."

"We're all worm bait waiting to happen. It's what you do while you wait that matters."

"Seventeen publishers rejected the manuscript, at which time I knew I had something pretty hot."

"No matter where you go, you always see yourself in the rearview mirror."

"I don't believe in carrying a weapon. If somebody wants to shoot me, he'll have to bring his own gun."

"If you're patient and you wait long enough, something will usually happen. And it'll usually be something you don't like."

"On the whole, I prefer cats to women because cats seldom if ever use the word 'relationship.'"

"I'm not afraid to die. I'm not afraid to live. I'm not afraid to fail. I'm not afraid to succeed. I'm not afraid to fall in love. I'm not afraid to be alone. I'm just afraid I might have to stop talking about myself for 5 minutes."

"I knew I wasn't as stupid as I looked. No one was."

Actor Mark Wahlberg has three nipples.

McLIBEL

You might have heard about it on the news: In 1991 McDonald's sued two unemployed vegetarians for distributing leaflets disparaging the mega-chain's practices. McDonald's won the case—or did they? Here's the story.

THE McMURDER PAMPHLETS

In 1990 environmental activists David Morris and Helen Steel distributed copies of a controversial pamphlet outside a McDonald's restaurant in London, England. It had been written by a small environmental group called London Greenpeace (not linked to Greenpeace International) and was entitled "What's Wrong With McDonald's? Everything They Don't Want You To Know." The cover showed the famous "golden arches," along with the words "McDollars," "McGreedy," "McCancer," and "McMurder." The six-page pamphlet made some strong accusations: that McDonald's knowingly promoted unhealthy diets; that cattle raised for their burgers caused destruction of rainforests; that they caused starvation in developing countries, were hostile to trade unions, exploited children, and abused animals. McDonald's was not amused.

The Illinois-based corporation sued Morris and Steel for libel (they sued in England, because English law makes it easier to win a libel case than U.S. law) and Morris and Steel, surprisingly, decided to fight. They counter-sued, accusing McDonald's of libeling them by calling their accusations "lies." Because Morris was unemployed and Steel was a part-time bartender, the two had to act as their own lawyers against the McDonald's legal army.

OUTCOME: McDonald's won. The award: the penniless defendants had to pay McDonald's $94,000 in damages. Justice Rodger Bell also ruled against the activists in their countersuit, saying that the restaurant chain had a right to defend itself against the accusations.

THE OTHER OUTCOME: McDonald's lost—big time. The trial dragged on for years. Amazingly, when it ended, "McLibel" was the longest trial in English history. It didn't get officially started until 1994 and wasn't decided until 1997. Justice Bell's opinion was more than 800 pages long and took two hours just to summarize orally. For the duration of the trial McDonald's was regularly grilled in the international press as the big bully beating up on the little guy at best, and as the above-the-law mega-corporation suppressing the right of free speech at worst. The $94,000 turned out to be hardly an award since they never received it anyway, and since McDonald's spent an estimated $16 million on the case!

Another blow to the company: It was revealed during the trial that they had hired people to infiltrate London Greenpeace. These spies actually became members of the group—they even handed out some of the leaflets.

McCULPABILITY

While the judge found in favor of the chain, he also made it clear that some of the accusations were accurate. The *McSpotlight* Web site, created by the defendants so supporters could follow the trial (it's still active today) happily reported the rulings:

• Justice Bell found that Morris and Steel had not sufficiently proven the allegations against McDonald's on rainforest destruction, heart disease and cancer, food poisoning, starvation in the Third World, and bad working conditions.

• But they had proven, he said, that McDonald's "exploits children" with their advertising, falsely advertises their food as nutritious, risks the health of their most regular, long-term customers, are "culpably responsible" for cruelty to animals, are "strongly antipathetic" to unions, and pay their workers low wages.

• In March 1999, the English Court of Appeal made two further rulings, saying that a regular McDonald's diet is indeed linked to heart disease and that the defendants had the right to say that McDonald's employees suffered "bad working conditions" because it was an opinion.

And the offending pamphlets? Thanks to all the press the case received, at least three million more "McMurder" pamphlets were distributed around the world.

* * *

"Do not spit into the well—you may have to drink out of it."

—Russian proverb

In her witchcraft trial, Joan of Arc was also charged with disobeying her parents.

BE A POCHEMUCHKA!

In 2004 a British company called Today Translations commissioned a worldwide poll of 1,000 professional interpreters and translators to find the world's most difficult-to-translate words. Here's their top 10.

ND THE WINNERS ARE:
10. *Klloshar.* The closest meaning for this Albanian term: "loser."

9. Pochemuchka. Russian for "a person who asks a lot of questions." *Pochemu* means "why" in Russian, so a *pochemuchka* is kind of like a "why-man" or "why-woman."

8. Selathirupavar. A word in the Tamil language (spoken in India and Sri Lanka) that refers to a particular form of truancy.

7. Saudade. It refers to "a certain type of longing" in Portuguese.

6. Gezellig. Dutch for "cozy."

5. Altahmam. An Arabic word that refers to a particular kind of "deep sadness."

4. Naa. Spoken only in the Kansai region of Japan, it's a modifier that's used to "emphasize statements or agree with someone."

3. Radioukacz. The Polish word for "a person who worked as a telegraphist for the resistance movements on the Soviet side of the Iron Curtain."

2. Shlimazl. A "chronically unlucky person" in Yiddish, a language spoken by central and eastern European Jews and their descendants around the world.

...and the most difficult-to-translate word in the world is:

1. Ilunga. A word in Tshiluba, a Bantu dialect spoken in the Congo region of Africa. Meaning: "A person who will forgive any abuse for the first time, tolerate it a second time, but never a third time."

ODD MUSEUMS

The next time you're traveling across America, take
some time to visit these unusual attractions.

MUSEUM OF BAD ART
Location: Dedham, Massachusetts
Background: MOBA is the only museum in the United States that *admits* it shows bad art. When it opened in 1993, the museum was housed in someone's basement, but it's now located in the Dedham Community Theater, just outside the men's room. Most pieces in the collection were found in thrift stores or in the garbage.
Be Sure to See: "Sunday on the Pot with George," a painting in pointillist (made up of dots) style depicting a heavy man wearing only his underpants, sitting on a toilet. One reviewer called the work "the single most memorable artistic experience in my life—a bit like my recent bout with the shingles."

BARBED WIRE MUSEUM
Location: La Crosse, Kansas
Background: Sure, barbed wire is an important part of American history. (It provided an inexpensive way for "sodbusters" to keep cattle off their land, effectively ending the open range.) But wire's wire, right? Apparently not. This museum holds 18-inch segments of more than 1,000 different types of barbed wire, lining its walls from floor to ceiling.
Be Sure to See: A real bird's nest made almost completely from bits of barbed wire (it weighs 72 pounds) and a piece of barbed wire taken from the top of the Berlin Wall when it fell.

SPAM MUSEUM
Location: Austin, Minnesota
Background: Next door to the top-secret facility where the Hormel Corporation makes Spam, fans of the canned meat can see a giant Spamburger sandwich (with its own 17-foot spatula), visit the 3,390-can "Wall of Spam," don hardhats and work on a simulated Spam production line, and marvel at the 4,700 cans

that document 70 years of Spam's worldwide popularity.

Be Sure to See: The talking wax figure of company founder George Hormel.

TRAGEDY IN U.S. HISTORY MUSEUM

Location: St. Augustine, Florida

Background: In the same town as the supposed location of the Fountain of Youth and Ripley's Believe It or Not! Museum is this attraction that celebrates the grislier parts of history. Curator Buddy Hough said, "Tragedy is what makes America great." He began collecting in 1963, making several trips to Dallas to get whatever artifacts he could from the Kennedy assassination.

Be Sure to See: The ambulance that took Lee Harvey Oswald to the hospital after he was shot, the furniture from the Dallas room Oswald stayed in before the assassination, the car Jayne Mansfield died in, and the bullet-riddled 1933 Ford in which Bonnie and Clyde were supposedly killed. There's also a copy of Elvis Presley's will, antique torture equipment, and a Spanish jail cell from 1718 with real skeletons inside.

Update: Want to visit the museum? You can't. Tragedy struck in 1996, when Buddy Hough died. His wife auctioned off the museum's contents two years later. (The ambulance sold for $17,500, Bonnie and Clyde's car went for $1,900, and Ripley's Believe It Or Not! Museum bought Lee Harvey Oswald's furniture for $6,000.)

FUTURE BIRTHPLACE OF CAPTAIN KIRK

Location: Riverside, Iowa

Background: Boldly going beyond a single building, the entire town is a *Star Trek* museum. According to the TV series, Captain Kirk will be born here on March 22, 2233. The town wanted to erect a statue of William Shatner as Kirk, but Paramount Pictures, which owns *Star Trek*, wanted a $40,000 licensing fee. So instead, docked in the town square is the *U.S.S. Riverside*, which bears a striking (but not copyright infringing) resemblance to the *U.S.S. Enterprise*.

Be Sure to See: The annual Kirk Birthday celebration in March. Souvenirs are available. The bestseller: Kirk Dirt, a $3 vial of soil dug from the fictional space captain's future birth site.

STRANGE LAWSUITS

These days, it seems that people will sue each other over practically anything. Here are some real-life examples of unusual legal battles.

THE PLAINTIFFS: Sixteen violinists
THE DEFENDANT: The city of Bonn, Germany
THE LAWSUIT: In March 2004, violinists from the Beethoven Orchestra sued for a pay raise on the grounds that they play more notes than musicians in the woodwind or brass sections. They demanded an extra $123 per rehearsal (or performance) for the "extra notes" they have to play, adding that they were actually being generous by not asking for more. "We could have calculated the surcharge per eighth note, but we chose to take an easier course," one violinist said. Orchestra director Laurentius Bonitz said, "The suit is absurd."

THE VERDICT: The violinists changed their tune and took an even easier course: they dropped the suit.

THE PLAINTIFF: Isabel Barros of Santiago, Chile
THE DEFENDANT: A bank
THE LAWSUIT: Barros was making a withdrawal when one of the cashiers loudly asked, "Who is the lady for the £9,000?" When Barros left the bank with the money ($16,000), she was robbed, so she filed a lawsuit to get the money back, saying it was the clerk's fault. "Why I was so stupid to answer him when he asked who was the £9,000 lady I don't know, but it was his unsubtlety that drew attention to me. Plus he counted the money out loud so everyone could hear." The bank denied that the clerk shouted, and said they have video footage to prove it.
THE VERDICT: Pending.

THE PLAINTIFF: Donald Johnson of West Palm Beach, Florida
THE DEFENDANT: Shoney's Restaurant
THE LAWSUIT: Johnson ordered potato soup from the restaurant and they gave him clam chowder by mistake. He's allergic to clams, but he ate the whole bowl. He had an allergic reaction that

required a visit to the emergency room and sued the restaurant for giving him "psychological sleep disorders" when they served the wrong soup.

THE VERDICT: He won, but didn't get the $4,070 he wanted to cover his medical bills. The jury said that Shoney's was 10% responsible for serving the wrong soup—but that Johnson was 90% responsible for eating it, and awarded him $407.

THE PLAINTIFF: Will Wright
THE DEFENDANTS: Producers of *Wheel of Fortune*
THE LAWSUIT: In 2003 Wright won a $48,000 jackpot on the game show. It was a big moment for everybody, but Wright claims host Pat Sajak got too carried away. "I stick out my hand thinking he's going to shake it," Wright said. "Instead he jumps onto me." Wright sued the show for $2 million, claiming that Sajak's assault resulted in his needing back surgery. "They say I signed a release," he said, "but that was for things like if you hurt yourself spinning the wheel. It doesn't cover the host jumping on a contestant."
VERDICT: Pending.

THE PLAINTIFFS: Lance and Misty Westmoreland
THE DEFENDANT: Scenic Igloo Village, Cordova, Alaska
THE LAWSUIT: The Westmorelands visited the tourist site in 1997 with their six-year-old son Cody, who "wanted to see Eskimos." There were no Eskimos, but they did see John "Chico" Williams, 47, an actor at the village, dressed as a woman. "I don't know what you call it up there," Lance Westmoreland later said from his Texas home, "but down here it's just plain sick." Igloo Village manager Dave Moka said, "I tried my best to placate them. I told them they were lucky—Chico once came to work dressed as the Madonna. Another time he showed up wearing only a bagel. I refunded their money, and thought that would be the end of it." It wasn't: the couple sued for $600,000 in damages, claiming the "cross-dressing Eskimo" traumatized their son. "Eskimos are supposed to be normal Eskimos," Misty Westmoreland said. "You go to a tourist igloo village, you want to see whale blubber and mukluks and stuff like that." Williams kept a sense of humor about the incident. "I am an Aleut, not an Eskimo," he said.
THE VERDICT: None. The trial ended in a hung jury.

HAIRY HOUDINIS

Are humans really the smartest primates?

THE BALLAD OF KEN ALLEN

As a baby at the San Diego Zoo, an orangutan named Ken Allen taught himself to take his crib apart and to unscrew lightbulbs. By adulthood, he was breaking other orangutans out of their cages and leading them on covert trips around the zoo. During the 1980s, Ken broke out nine times, delighting zoo visitors and frustrating zoo workers. How'd he do it? Keepers discovered dozens of makeshift finger and foot holds in the artificial rock walls of Ken's pen. The holes were smoothed over, ending Ken's escapes, but he'd already become a media hero, with magazine profiles, a fan club, T-shirts, and even a country song: "The Ballad of Ken Allen."

MMMM...PASTRIES

In 2001 a gorilla in the Pittsburgh Zoo leapt eight feet over a moat and grabbed onto an inch-wide bamboo stem leaning against the enclosure wall. Then she climbed the bamboo like a rope, all the way up the 16-foot wall. Easily hopping over a short retaining wall, the gorilla began foraging...for junk food. She raided a concession stand, consuming muffins, pastries, and orange soda. Some resourceful zookeepers finally figured out how to lure her back into captivity: they used Hershey's Kisses as bait. The gorilla was tranquilized and returned to her habitat, and the bamboo was immediately trimmed.

TARZAN THE APE APE

The Los Angeles Zoo assumed an area designed to hold bears would be sufficient to house gorillas. Wrong. In October 2000, a gorilla named Evelyn took a running jump, grabbed a hanging vine, and vaulted over a 15-foot-wide moat. For the next hour, Evelyn leisurely wandered around the zoo, visiting the orangutan, giraffe, and elephant houses. She also played in flower gardens, rummaged through garbage cans, and played hide-and-seek with the frantic zookeepers trying to catch her. Evelyn broke out several more times, even after the walls of her enclosure were raised. The Los Angeles Zoo finally gave up and sent her to a new home in the Denver Zoo, from which she continues to escape.

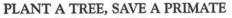

PLANT A TREE, SAVE A PRIMATE

After Jonathan the orangutan escaped from his enclosure numerous times, the Los Angeles Zoo designed a state-of-the-art, escape-proof outdoor habitat. They were so sure it would hold Jonathan, they arranged for local officials and reporters to witness him enter his new home for the first time. Bad idea: as zookeepers, dignitaries, visitors, and the media watched in disbelief, the ape went straight to a tree, uprooted it, leaned it against a wall, and climbed out.

BRIDGE OVER TROUBLED WIRES

After the headaches Jonathan caused in Los Angeles, the Kansas City Zoo didn't take any chances with Jonathan's son, Joseph. Keepers lined the ground around Joseph's enclosure with electrified wires, which would give Joseph a potent jolt should he ever try to break out. It didn't work. He took an old rubber tire he'd been given as a toy, laid it across the wires, and simply walked to freedom. Nobody even noticed that he was gone until visitors found him in the petting zoo playing with the sheep.

GREEN THUMBS

An orangutan in a Texas zoo figured out how to overcome the electric fence around his cage. He ripped out big chunks of grass from the ground and held them in his hands and feet. Using them as insulating mittens, he climbed over the electrified wires without getting zapped.

GIMME A "C," GIMME AN "H," GIMME AN "I"...

Resembling a cheerleading squad, chimpanzees at the Arnhem Zoo in the Netherlands formed a pyramid to collectively escape from their pen. They stacked on top of each other until they were high enough to scale the walls. The first one to the top then reached down and helped the others get out.

*   *   *

Zoologist Ben Beck once said that if you give a screwdriver to a chimpanzee, it will use the tool for everything except its intended purpose. A gorilla will first be scared of it, then try to eat it, and finally forget about it. An orangutan, however, will hide it and then, when the coast is clear, use it to dismantle the cage.

There are no rhymes in the English language for orange, silver, or purple.

CELEBRITY TWO-TIMERS

*One of the nice things about living in anonymity is that if you make a
mess of your private life, the whole world doesn't have to find out about
it. Here's what can happen when your private life is made public.*

JACQUES COUSTEAU

Claim to Fame: Oceanographer, inventor of the aqualung, and
host of TV's *The Undersea World of Jacques Cousteau* from
1968 to 1976.

Secret Life: Not long after Cousteau's wife of 50 years, Simone,
passed away in 1990, the famous oceanographer revealed to his
son, Jean-Michel, that he'd been carrying on a 13-year affair with
a former flight attendant named Francine Triplet, and had
fathered two children by her. Cousteau married Triplet in 1991,
and his relationship with Jean-Michel, already tense, soon got
worse.

A year later, Cousteau transferred control of his nonprofit
Cousteau Society to his new wife, prompting Jean-Michel to
resign in protest. When Cousteau passed away in 1997, Francine
Cousteau seized full control of the Cousteau Society, appointing
herself president and chairwoman and reserving for herself "the
exclusive use of the Cousteau name." Cousteau's children and
grandchildren from his marriage to Simone were forbidden from
using their last names to promote their own oceanographic ventures. Soon the entire family was in court, battling it out to see
which Cousteaus had the right to use the family name.

Update: Francine won. In a 2003 settlement, Cousteau's grandchildren won the limited right to use the family name on a Web
site, but amazingly, Francine was awarded sole ownership of
"Cousteau" as a trademark.

THE REVEREND HENRY LYONS

Claim to Fame: From 1994 to 1999, leader of the National
Baptist Convention, USA, Inc., the largest organization of black
churches in the United States, with 8.5 million members.

Secret Life: The first sign that something was amiss in Lyons's life
came in 1997 when his wife was arrested and charged with setting

---

What do Cary Grant and Billy Joel have in common? Neither graduated from high school.

fire to a waterfront mansion in St. Petersburg, Florida. The mansion turned out to be owned by the reverend and a church employee, Bernice Edwards, whom Lyons described as his "business partner." Mrs. Lyons hadn't known about the house until she found the deed in her husband's briefcase. So she drove to the house to look around and discovered some of her husband's clothing hanging in the "business partner's" bedroom closet. Drawing her own conclusions, she set fire to the house.

Update: The fire touched off an investigation into National Baptist Convention's finances, which culminated in Lyons being charged with grand theft, racketeering, tax evasion, money laundering, and bank fraud. In 1999 he was convicted of swindling companies that did business with his organization out of more than $4 million and was sentenced to five years in prison.

CHARLES LINDBERGH

Claim to Fame: "Lucky Lindy" became an international hero in 1927 when he made the first nonstop solo flight across the Atlantic Ocean.

Secret Life: Lindbergh fathered six children by his wife, Anne, but apparently six was not enough. In August 2003, three grown children of a Munich hatmaker named Brigitte Hesshaimer came forward to claim that Lindbergh was *their* father as well.

For Dyrk Hesshaimer, 45, Astrid Bouteuil, 43, and David Hesshaimer, 36, piecing the story together had taken most of their lives. When they were growing up, a tall, mysterious American they knew as "Careau Kent" visited them a few times a year, cooking them huge breakfasts of sausages and banana pancakes, and telling them tales of his adventures around the world...before disappearing again a week or two later. Their mother, Brigitte, confirmed that he was their father, but she refused to tell them his real name. Furthermore, she warned, if they ever talked about him outside of the immediate family, he might disappear forever.

Their father's true identity remained a mystery until the late 1990s, when Astrid Bouteuil was cleaning out a storeroom and accidentally discovered a bag containing more than 100 love letters written to her mother. The letters were signed only with the initial "C," but the bag also contained a magazine article about Lindbergh. When Astrid confronted her mother with the evidence, Brigitte confessed—Careau Kent was Charles Lindbergh, and he was their father.

Brigitte begged her children not to reveal the secret while she was alive, and they respected her wishes. Two years after Brigitte died, they went public.

Update: In October 2003, Dyrk, Astrid, and David agreed to let the University of Munich test their DNA to confirm their story. Result: The test came back positive—Lindbergh is their father.

So is that the end of the story? Maybe not—the German magazine *Focus* reports that Lindbergh also had an affair with Brigitte Hesshaimer's sister, Marietta. So far Marietta's two sons are refusing to take DNA tests.

CHARLES KURALT

Claim to Fame: CBS newsman from 1960 to 1994 and host of the popular news segment *On the Road with Charles Kuralt.*

Secret Life: Kuralt passed away suddenly and unexpectedly from an autoimmune disease called lupus in 1997. Had he lived long enough to put his financial affairs in order, the biggest secret of his life might never have become known: for nearly 30 years, he'd carried on a relationship with a woman named Patricia Shannon and had supported her financially to the tune of $80,000 a year.

Shannon lived in a cabin that she and Kuralt had built at his 110-acre fishing retreat in Montana. Kuralt had promised to leave it to her upon his death and had even given her a notarized letter to that effect. In fact, he was in the process of transferring ownership to her when he died, but he passed away before the transaction was complete...so his wife and daughters inherited it.

Kuralt's wife of 35 years apparently had no inkling of his secret life until Shannon showed up at his funeral with the notarized letter and tried to stake her claim on the fishing retreat. When that failed, Shannon filed suit against the estate, and her relationship with Kuralt became public.

Update: Shannon won. Not only did she inherit the cabin and the 110 acres, but Kuralt's daughters (his widow had since passed away) were ordered to pay $350,000 in property taxes out of *their* share of the estate.

UNCLE JOHN'S
STALL OF FAME

*Uncle John is amazed—and pleased—by the unusual way
people get involved with bathrooms, toilets, toilet paper,
and so on. That's why he created the "Stall of Fame."*

Honoree: Heraclio "Rocky" Nazarano, deputy press secretary
for Philippine president Gloria Macapagal Arroyo
Notable Achievement: Getting lost on the way to the airplane lavatory
True Story: In September 2003, Nazarano was on a chartered
flight from Paris to Manila with President Arroyo when he had to
pee. So he got up from his seat and made his way to the restroom.
At least that's what Nazarano *thought* he was doing. It turns out
he'd had a little too much to drink, mistook the emergency exit
door for the toilet, and peed on it.

Nazarano was mortified when he sobered up. "How I wish I
could deny it," he said in a cell phone text message to reporters.
"But it was a moment of weakness. I deeply apologize about all the
shattered expectations."

Honoree: Cody Yaeger, 10, a fourth grader at Jamestown
Elementary School in Hudsonville, Michigan
Notable Achievement: Striking it rich in the bathroom...and
being honest enough to report it
True Story: In May 2004, Cody was making a pit stop at school
when he found something unusual inside a roll of toilet paper—a
neatly folded $100 bill. The bill was so perfectly tucked into the
roll that it seemed like it must have been put there by someone at
the toilet paper factory. Cody knew the money didn't belong to
him, so he took it to a teacher.

The school's lost-and-found policy states that if, after two
weeks, nobody claims the item, the person who found it gets to
keep it. Two weeks later, no one had claimed the money so Cody
became $100 richer. His mom, Terri, says she isn't surprised that he
acted so honestly. "When it comes to school or church, when he

---

finds something, he turns it in," she says. "But if it has anything to do with his sister, he'll keep it."

Honoree: Monica Bonvicini, an Italian artist
Notable Achievement: Turning a toilet into "performance art"
True Story: In December 2003, Bonvicini had a stainless-steel toilet installed on the sidewalk across the street from the Tate Britain, a national museum in London. Then she had it enclosed in a cubicle made entirely of one-way glass, and opened it to the public. Result: People using the toilet can see out, but people outside can't see in—it looks like a big mirrored cube stuck in the middle of the sidewalk. Of course anyone inside has the feeling of doing their business right out in the open.

"It will arouse curiosity," says a spokesperson for the art project. "People can just come and use it, although there is a question of whether they will feel comfortable doing so."

Honoree: Chien (Taiwan's TVBS cable network isn't releasing his full name.)
Notable Achievement: Getting fired for poor marksmanship
True Story: In October 2003, Chien received a letter of dismissal from his company. Reason: When answering the call of nature, Chien routinely missed the urinal. According to the letter, cleaning ladies complained repeatedly about his poor aim, so he was let go. (No word on how the cleaning ladies knew that *he* was the one responsible.) Chien doesn't buy a word of it. "The company had planned to lay off a number of employees," he told TVBS. "This was just an excuse to dismiss me."

* * *

FIVE REAL PLACES TO SPEND YOUR NEXT HOLIDAY

1. Christmas Valley, Oregon
2. Easter, Texas
3. Passover, Missouri
4. New Years Lake, Idaho
5. Valentine, Texas

Survey says: 95% of us put our left sock on first.

THE RISE AND DEMISE OF ULYSSES S. GRANT

You've seen Grant on the $50 bill; you know that he was a president and also the general who won the Civil War. Here are some things you probably didn't know about him.

SCHOOL OF HARD KNOCKS

In 1839 an Ohio tanner named Jesse Grant managed to obtain an appointment to the U.S. Military Academy for his son, Ulysses. Ulysses wasn't the slightest bit interested in a military career, but Jesse didn't think his son had much of a head for business. West Point was free, and it offered Ulysses his best chance for a good education. So off he went.

Ulysses graduated from West Point in 1843, fought in the Mexican War, and remained in the military until 1854, when he resigned and became a civilian again.

Ulysses promptly proved his father's suspicions correct: he had no head for business. He took up farming and failed at it; then got a job in real estate and failed at that, too. By 1860 Grant, a graduate of West Point, was back working as a clerk in his father's store. He was 37, and a failure. But the Civil War was about to save him.

The first shots were fired at Fort Sumter, South Carolina, on April 12, 1861. The fort fell to the Confederacy the following day, prompting President Abraham Lincoln to call for troops. Grant returned to the army and was quickly promoted to brigadier general. "Be careful, Ulyss, you are a general now," Jesse Grant wrote him after learning of the promotion. "It's a good job, don't lose it!"

ITCHING FOR A FIGHT

In the early months of the war Grant was assigned mostly defensive tasks, but he wanted to go on the offensive. In February 1862 he won approval for a plan to attack two key Confederate strongholds: Fort Henry, on the Tennessee River, and Fort Donelson on the Cumberland. Grant, with 17,000 troops and the assistance of gunboats commanded by Commodore Andrew Foote, planned to attack the forts.

This page is about 500,000 atoms thick.

Fort Henry fell after just a few hours of fighting; the attack on Fort Donelson began a week later and raged for two days. By February 15, defeat was imminent.

As was the custom in 19th-century warfare, the fort's commander, General Simon Bolivar Buckner, sent a message to Grant proposing a truce so that the two men could negotiate terms of surrender. Buckner had served with Grant in the Mexican War and had even lent him money, but if he was expecting generous terms from his old friend, he was soon rebuked. Grant's reply was swift and blunt: "No terms except an unconditional and immediate surrender can be accepted." Buckner, complaining that he had no choice but "to accept the ungenerous and unchivalrous terms," gave in.

Capturing the two forts marked the first major Union victories in the war, and turned "Unconditional Surrender" Grant, as his admirers nicknamed him, into a national figure. He was promoted to major general. And "purely by accidental circumstance," as Grant himself later put it, the campaign caused him to pick up the habit that would eventually claim his life—cigars.

THE SPOILS OF WAR

Up to this point, Grant had smoked a pipe, but only occasionally. When Commodore Andrew Foote was wounded in the assault on Fort Donelson, he asked Grant to confer with him aboard his ship, and offered him a cigar. Grant was still smoking it on his way back to his headquarters when a staff officer informed him that Confederate soldiers were attacking. Grant recalled in 1865:

> I galloped forward at once, and while riding among the troops giving the directions for repulsing the assault I carried the cigar in my hand. It had gone out, but it seems that I continued to hold the stump between my fingers throughout the battle. In the accounts published in the papers I was represented as smoking a cigar in the midst of the conflict; and many persons, thinking, no doubt, that tobacco was my chief solace, sent me boxes of the choicest brands from everywhere in the North. As many as 10,000 were soon received. I gave away all I could get rid of, but having such a quantity in hand, I naturally smoked more than I would have done under ordinary circumstances, and I have continued the habit ever since.

STILL SMOKIN'

Inundated with free cigars, Grant was soon addicted. In March 1864, he was promoted to lieutenant general and given command of all the Union armies. By then he was smoking his first cigar of the day right after breakfast as he stuffed the pockets of his uniform with another two dozen. When he accepted General Robert E. Lee's surrender in 1865, Grant was still puffing away. And after the war the gifts of free cigars and related paraphernalia—ashtrays, cigar holders, cigar stands, and so on—only increased.

Even in those days people had an idea that smoking was unhealthy, and in 1866 Grant tried to cut back on the stogies. "I am breaking off from smoking," he told a newspaper reporter. "When I was in the field I smoked eighteen or twenty cigars a day, but now I smoke only nine or ten." (One large cigar can contain as much tobacco as an entire pack of cigarettes.) Grant was elected president in 1868 and reelected in 1872. He smoked his way through both terms; though he still tried to quit on occasion, he never managed to cut back much.

WHAT GOES AROUND...

Grant was still smoking heavily in the summer of 1884 when he experienced throat pain while eating a peach. Doctors found a small cancerous growth in the soft palate of his mouth; at the time of discovery it may still have been small enough to be surgically removed, but by the time Grant got around to having it treated in the fall, the mass had grown to the point that it was inoperable.

Grant struggled with the disease for about a year before dying on July 23, 1885. The man who never wanted a military career and never smoked more than an occasional pipe before the Civil War, died a war hero...from smoking.

*   *   *

WHERE THERE'S A WILL

• The world's longest will was 95,000 words and took more than 20 years to complete.

• The world's smallest will was written on the back of a postage stamp. It included the required signatures of two witnesses.

JACKIE CHAN'S GREATEST HITS

He's one of the greatest action stars of all time. And what's most
amazing is that he does his own stunts. So how does he do all that
fighting and perform all those daredevil feats without getting
injured? He doesn't—he's been injured dozens of times.
Here's a sample of what you (almost) never see.

Body Part: Head
The Movie: *Armour of God* (1987)
The Stunt: Jumping from a castle wall to a tree, Chan
missed the branch and fell headfirst onto the rocky ground below.
Result: a broken skull and a brain hemorrhage. With blood pour-
ing from his ears, Chan was rushed to the nearest hospital for
emergency brain surgery. He now has a permanent hole in his
skull, filled with a plastic plug. The same fall shattered his jaw,
knocked out some teeth, and broke his nose.

Body Part: Arm
The Movie: *Snake in Eagle's Shadow* (1978)
The Stunt: In a sword fight scene, his opponent's sword was supposed to be blunt—but it wasn't. Chan's arm was slashed and blood
went everywhere. He screamed in pain, looked up at his opponent in
surprise...and kept right on fighting. The camera kept rolling, and
the scene—and the real blood—appeared in the final cut of the film.

Body Part: Neck
The Movie: *Mr. Nice Guy* (1997)
The Stunt: A stunt called for Chan to be pushed backward into a
wheelbarrow on the second floor of a construction site, then fall out
of the wheelbarrow to the ground two stories below, where he would
land on mats that were out of camera range. Chan missed the mats:
He jumped up to let everybody know that he was okay, then immediately passed out. X-rays revealed torn ligaments and dislocated
vertebrae in his neck. (He broke his nose filming another scene.)

The combined area of the entire United Kingdom is smaller than the state of Oregon.

Body Part: Nose
The Movie: *First Strike* (1996)
The Stunt: You'd think this would have happened during one of the film's snowboarding stunts—considering Chan did them with only four days of snowboard training. But it was actually in a scene where he jumped through an extension ladder. He got tangled in the rungs and couldn't escape before it crashed to the ground, breaking his nose and knocking him unconscious.

Body Part: Shoulder
The Movie: *Supercop* (1992)
The Stunt: One of his most dangerous stunts ever. Chan had to jump from a building and catch a rope ladder that was hanging from a passing helicopter—with no air bags or cushions below him to break the possible 100-foot fall. Did he fall? No—but the rope ladder crashed through several billboards, breaking Chan's shoulder.

Body Part: Ankle
The Movie: *Rumble in the Bronx* (1994)
The Stunt: Chan jumped from a bridge onto the deck of a hover-craft, turning his body as he landed to avoid hitting a wall. But his ankle didn't turn with him. It stayed planted on the craft's non-slip deck, breaking in two places. Chan's doctor set the bone and told him to stay off it, but Chan put a sock over the cast, painted it to look like a sneaker, and finished the movie.

Body Parts: Hands, pelvis, back
The Movie: *Police Story* (1985)
The Stunt: Chan leaped 10 feet from a narrow handrail (70 feet above the ground) to a nearby pole, slid down the pole, then crashed through a glass ceiling and fell to the ground on his back. The slide peeled the skin off his hands (he was treated for second-degree burns), and the fall dislocated his pelvis and pushed several of his lower vertebrae into the surrounding organs, causing internal bleeding. When he managed to stand up, blood gushed from his mouth. Chan later told reporters that this was the only time in his career when he actually thought he might not survive a stunt. A few hours later he was back on the set.

THE DIGITAL AGE

Uncle John's brother Stumpy's advice: Be
careful where you stick your fingers!

NO RETURN

When 46-year-old Emanuel Fleming of East St. Louis, Illinois, lost 50 cents in a pay phone, he stuck his middle finger in the coin return slot and tried to get it back. Not only did he not get his change back, he almost didn't get his finger back. He tried calling his wife, but the line was busy. Two passersby tried to help him, to no avail. He finally called 911, but fire department and ambulance crews couldn't free him either—so they cut off the entire pay phone and drove Fleming (together with the phone) to the hospital. ER doctors gave him a painkiller, put on some lubricant, and finally freed his finger. Another painful part of the four-hour ordeal: the phone was near a busy bus stop. The embarrassed Fleming recalled, "People on the bus who know me were laughing at me."

GAS ATTACK

In July 2000, a Danish woman traveling in Germany stopped at a gas station near Hannover. For some reason, after she filled up she put her finger in the fuel tank flap...and got it stuck. The station attendant couldn't free her, so he called the police. The police couldn't help, so they called the fire department...who called in paramedics...who couldn't free the finger either. Finally a mechanic stopped to help. He spent an hour removing the gas tank and filler pipe, then took them, the woman still attached, to a doctor. Luckily, the doctor was in and managed to get the finger out.

THE MACHINE FIGHTS BACK

Two 15-year-old boys were trying to steal candy bars from a vending machine in Melbourne, Australia, when one of them got his thumb stuck. Unable to free the digit, the boys finally gave up and called the police. It took 10 cops and rescue workers an hour to get the thumb loose...after which the lad was immediately arrested.

ANOTHER GAS ATTACK

In 1994 Sergeant Arnie Ziegler of the Royal Canadian Mounted Police answered a call from a TV station in Oliver, British Columbia, saying there was a thief in the parking lot. Sergeant Ziegler arrested 24-year-old Hugo Murdock—but couldn't take him directly to jail. Murdock had been busy stealing gas from a van when his siphoning hose got stuck. He used his pinky finger to free it—and the finger got stuck, too. "The fire department had to push the van out of the parking lot with the guy attached so they could work on him," Ziegler reported. They removed the gas tank pipe and took it (and Murdock) to a hospital, where doctors freed his pinky and handed him back to the police. "The guy was pretty embarrassed," said Ziegler. "He said, 'I think this is gonna be the end of my criminal career.'"

RING OF POWER

A seven-year-old Welsh boy named Joel Withey found a small copper ring in his dad's toolbox in January 2003. It was a compression device commonly used by plumbers to seal pipes, but Joel thought it looked like the ring from *The Lord of the Rings*. He and his younger brothers had been acting out scenes from the film *The Two Towers*, and the ring seemed perfect. Once he put it on, though, he couldn't get it off. His finger swelled up and his parents eventually took him to a local fire station, where they cut it off (the ring, not the finger). Joel's father decided to keep the ring to teach the boy a lesson. "We've kept Joel's ring in a jar," he said, "to show to his girlfriends and embarrass him when he grows up."

MUNCHING MANCHAS

In 2004 employees of the Rio Grande Zoo in Albuquerque, New Mexico, found a finger on the ground next to the jaguar cage. One of the staff remembered seeing a man the day before running into the bathroom with his hand in his pocket and a dark stain on his pants. The man was a member of the zoo and a daily visitor, so they called him and asked if perhaps he was missing a finger. He said he wasn't. But police weren't convinced. They got a print from the finger, and it was a match. Apparently the man had been trying to pet the jaguar, whose name is Manchas. Officials didn't press charges, saying that losing a finger was punishment enough, but the zoo barred him from ever coming back.

Hey, technophiles! What was the first domain name ever registered? Symbolics.com

HAPPY EOSTRE!

*Ever wonder why a sacred Christian holiday is celebrated
with candy, baskets, and a bunny? Wonder no more.*

T HE HOLIDAY: Easter comes from *Eostre*, a pagan festival. Before Christianity, early Germans held an annual celebration in honor of Eostre, goddess of spring and fertility. As Christianity spread across Europe in the first and second centuries, the Church often modified or adopted pagan holidays. Because Eostre was the goddess of spring and her festival celebrated renewal and rebirth, the Church's belief in Christ's resurrection made for a good match.

THE EASTER BUNNY: Rabbits breed notoriously quickly. Eostre's association with fertility led to her frequent depiction with a rabbit's head. But the concept of an Easter Bunny originated with the Germans, who settled in Pennsylvania when they emigrated to the United States in the 1700s. Their "Pennsylvania Dutch" children believed that if they were well-behaved, the *Oschter Haws* (literally, "Easter rabbit") would leave a nest of brightly colored eggs on Easter morning. The idea began to catch on nationwide after the Civil War.

Some countries don't have the Easter Bunny. Switzerland has the "Easter cuckoo," while Australia has the "Easter bilby," a marsupial with rabbitlike ears. (Rabbits aren't native to Australia— they were imported in the mid-1800s and destroyed thousands of acres of crops, so they're not considered a symbol of growth.)

EASTER EGGS: In a folktale, Eostre turns her pet bird into a rabbit to entertain some children. The rabbit performs a trick: it lays colorful eggs. Eggs are also a common symbol of rebirth in many ancient cultures, including those of Egypt, Persia, China, Gaul, and Rome.

The first concrete historical association of colored eggs with Easter is in the 1200s, when English servants were given painted eggs by their masters as Easter gifts. Today, different countries have different egg-coloring traditions:

• **Greece:** They're painted red to symbolize Christ's shed blood.

What would Jesus wear? According to some scholars, he wore a size 10-3/4 sandal.

- **Germany:** They're dyed green and distributed on Holy Thursday, the day of the Last Supper.
- **Poland:** They're decorated with colored dots, which represent the tears that Mary wept over Christ's crucifixion.
- **Armenia:** They're hollowed out and decorated with religious scenes.
- **Ukraine:** Melted beeswax is applied to the shell, and the egg is dipped repeatedly into a series of dyes. The wax peels off to reveal intricate, colorful patterns. The ornate eggs are called *pysanki*.

EASTER SUNDAY: In the early years of Christianity, Easter was an informal holiday, celebrated sometime in the spring. Early Christians were widely persecuted and could not worship openly, but conditions eased when Constantine became the first Roman emperor to convert to Christianity. In 325 A.D., he issued an edict: Easter was to be celebrated on the first Sunday after the first full moon after the vernal equinox (the first day of spring).

According to that schedule, Easter will always fall on the same weekend as Passover, the time when Christ was condemned. Linking Passover, Easter, and the vernal equinox ensures that Easter will be on a Sunday between March 22 and April 25 every year.

EASTER BASKETS: This is also from the "Pennsylvania Dutch" Germans. Children would build a little "nest" and leave it overnight somewhere in the yard or home for the Oschter Haws to lay it's colored eggs in. This eventually evolved into the bright-ly-colored baskets of eggs and candy we have today.

* * *

TOO MUCH EGGS-CITEMENT

The annual Easter Egg Hunt is the White House's largest public gathering. The first one was held in 1872 on the grounds of the U.S. Capitol. Children were so rambunctious and tore up so much of the lawn that Congress passed a bill banning recreation on Capitol grounds. The event returned in 1878, this time to the White House lawn, and was attended by President Rutherford B. Hayes.

Bunny-noculars: Rabbits can see forward and backward at the same time.

THE WORLD'S FIRST MUSCLE CAR

*Ever seen—or heard—a muscle car? They were big sellers in the
mid-1960s, but by the early 1970s they were gone. Here's
a look at the car that started it all: the Pontiac GTO.*

BREAKDOWN
In the summer of 1956 General Motors appointed an engineer named Semon "Bunkie" Knudsen general manager of
the company's Pontiac division. Knudsen's marching orders were
simple: he had five years to improve the division's sales and if he
couldn't do it, GM might shut Pontiac down for good.

In those days Pontiac was America's sixth largest automaker.
The cars were affordable and reliable, but they were slow and their
styling was outdated; they were the kind of cars that grandparents
drove. That was the biggest problem, Knudsen figured. "You can
sell a young man's car to an old man," he liked to say, "but you'll
never sell an old man's car to a young man."

Knudsen hired E.M. "Pete" Estes, formerly the chief engineer at
Oldsmobile, to head the engineering department, and he hired a
31-year-old Packard engineer named John Z. DeLorean to be Estes'
assistant. Changes came quickly: They immediately began manufacturing high-performance versions of their existing models. The
following year they created the Pontiac Bonneville, a racy full-
sized convertible with a big V-8 engine and fancy bucket seats.

WIDE-TRACKING

For 1959, Knudsen had the designers come up with a new wide-
bodied car with extra-wide tires to boot. These "Wide-Track"
Pontiacs had an athletic, broad-shouldered look that caught on
quick with younger drivers. By 1960 they were the bestselling mid-
priced car in the country.

By 1961 Pontiac had done so well that Knudsen was promoted to
general manager of Chevrolet. Pete Estes replaced him as the head of
Pontiac, and John DeLorean became the chief engineer. Together,
they were about to come up with the most famous Pontiac ever.

True or false: Mythomaniacs are people who lie constantly. (True)

OUT OF THE RACE

From 1959 to 1963, Pontiac had dominated the NASCAR circuit with their custom-built race cars, but then GM decided to stop producing them so they could focus on selling higher-profit consumer vehicles. All auto divisions were banned from any participation in motorsports. The divisions weren't even allowed to assist professional race car drivers. Estes was miffed about the restriction—he didn't want to lose the association with sports. So he decided that if he couldn't put a race car on a race track, he'd start putting them on the street.

He and DeLorean used the same trick that hot-rodders had used for years: They took the giant engine out of the full-sized Pontiac Bonneville and dropped it into the mid-sized Pontiac Tempest/LeMans. They added lots of other goodies, too: high performance carburetors, a heavy duty clutch and suspension, dual chrome exhausts, an air scoop on the front hood, and an optional 4-speed manual transmission with a stick shift on the floor.

SECRET WEAPON

It's not uncommon for auto companies to hide new models from the public, but Estes and DeLorean hid it from their bosses at GM. Putting such a huge engine into a car that small was against company rules, so rather than introduce the car as a new model, they called it an "option package" for the Pontiac LeMans instead, hoping that nobody would realize what they were up to.

DeLorean named the souped up LeMans the GTO, which was short for Gran Turisimo Omologato. *Omologato* is the Italian word for homologous, which means "all coming from the same thing." Whereas most custom-built hot rods of the time were pieced together from different cars and "aftermarket" parts, the GTO was truly homologous—all of its parts came from Pontiac. This made it America's first "factory hot rod," or "muscle car."

Calling the GTO an option package for the LeMans paid off: by the time the bosses at GM realized what was happening, car dealers had already placed orders for 5,000 of the cars, so GM grudgingly agreed to let the car be built. Whatever anger the company had toward Estes and DeLorean disappeared when more than 32,000 GTOs sold that first model year alone, and 75,000 in 1965. The car was a smash hit, and GM not only allowed the GTO to

That's all? An elephant can hold up to a gallon and a half of water in its trunk.

become a model in its own right for 1966 (it sold nearly 97,000 cars that year), it also made plans for its other divisions to produce their own muscle cars, including the Chevy Chevelle SS, the Buick Regal Gran Sport, and the Oldsmobile Cutlass 442.

MUSCLE CARS EVERYWHERE

Over the next few years the Big Three automakers got into the act, too: Ford introduced the Fairlane GT, the Mercury Cyclone GT, and the Ford Torino Cobra. Chrysler came out with the Dodge Charger and the Plymouth Road Runner, to name just a few. Each year the engines got bigger and more powerful. The 1964 Pontiac GTO had a 325 horsepower engine; by 1971 the Plymouth Road Runner had a 425 horsepower engine.

END OF THE ROAD

Muscle cars were popular because they were cheap and fast—a brand-new 1964 GTO convertible cost only $3,081—and though many got less than 10 miles to the gallon, gas only cost about 25¢ a gallon so it wasn't a problem. Muscle cars took to the road by the tens of thousands in the late 1960s and early 1970s.

And then by 1973 they were gone.

What happened? For one thing, when the auto insurance industry realized that muscle cars were little more than street-legal race cars, they raised their rates so high that many people paid more for insurance than they did for their monthly car payment. Then in 1973 the Arab oil embargo caused the price of gasoline to soar. Suddenly cheap muscle cars weren't so cheap anymore. To make things worse, they were also coming under increased criticism from environmentalists and car safety advocates.

The automakers were also being pressured by the federal government to build more fuel-efficient cars that could run on regular or unleaded gas. In 1974 Pontiac came out with a muscle car without any muscle, a GTO with only 200 horsepower. In 1975 they didn't even bother. The GTO bit the dust, just like nearly every other muscle car it inspired.

If you missed your chance to own a GTO, cheer up. Pontiac brought a new one to market in 2004. Price: $32,495, quite a lot more than a new GTO cost forty years ago, but about as much as you can expect a classic GTO in excellent condition to cost you today.

You can estimate the age of a star by its color...typically, the redder, the older.

BANNED BOOKS

Sometimes even the most popular, critically acclaimed, and even kid-friendly books can be removed from libraries and schools.

Book: *Are You There God? It's Me, Margaret*, by Judy Blume
Banned in: Fond du Lac, Wisconsin
Reason: In 1982 concerned parents challenged this novel about a young girl dealing with puberty because it was "sexually offensive" (Margaret experiences her first menstrual cycle) and "amoral" (Margaret wonders if God is real).

Book: *American Heritage Dictionary*
Banned in: Eldon, Missouri, and Anchorage, Alaska
Reason: This dictionary used to be one of the only dictionaries that included curse words. (Who hasn't looked up dirty words in the dictionary for a cheap laugh?) Then in 1978, the Eldon public library banned it for containing 39 objectionable words. Hoping to avoid further controversy, the editors of the dictionary elected not to include the naughty words in future printings. However, in 1987 the Anchorage School Board banned the censored version because it still contained slang definitions of words, such as *knocker* and *balls*.

Book: *Little Red Riding Hood*, by the Brothers Grimm
Banned in: Two California school districts
Reason: Big Bad Wolf eating people too violent? Nope. In 1989 school officials thought the story might encourage children to drink because it shows a bottle of wine among the food Red brings to her grandmother.

Book: *Where's Waldo*, by Martin Handford
Banned in: Saginaw, Michigan
Reason: The public libraries of Saginaw tried to ban *Waldo* in 1989 because some of the pages supposedly contained "dirty things," including the bare back of a topless sunbather in a beach scene. (As if Waldo himself wasn't hard enough to find.)

Book: Mickey Mouse comics
Banned in: Italy
Reason: In 1938 Italy's National Conference of Juvenile Literature banned all materials featuring the Disney icon. The organization thought he encouraged children to be individuals, a concept that clashed with the fascist politics of dictator Benito Mussolini.

Book: *Complete Works of William Shakespeare*
Banned in: England (almost)
Reason: Though many think Shakespeare was the greatest writer who ever lived, poet Samuel Taylor Coleridge ("The Rime of the Ancient Mariner") didn't. In 1815 Coleridge attempted to ban all of Shakespeare's plays and poems throughout England because he found them crude and vulgar. Coleridge's efforts actually had the opposite effect: He didn't get the Bard banned, but the attention led to England's first real academic interest in Shakespeare.

Book: *To Kill a Mockingbird*, by Harper Lee
Banned in: Eden Valley, Minnesota
Reason: Required reading for schools across the nation, *To Kill a Mockingbird* delivers a strong message of racial tolerance. Nevertheless, Eden Valley removed it from schools in 1977, and was soon followed by schools in New York, Illinois, and Missouri. Protestors said the book's violent depiction of a hate crime actually encouraged racism.

Book: *Fahrenheit 451*, by Ray Bradbury
Banned in: Foxworth, Mississippi
Reason: In 1998 this novel about the dangers of book banning... was banned. West Marion High School in Foxworth took it off the required reading list when parents protested the book's use of the phrase "g*dd*m." (We added the asterisks because Uncle John banned the letters "o" and "a." Hppy reding and g with the flw!)

*　　　*　　　*

"There are worse crimes than burning books. One of them is not reading them."
　　　　　　　　　　　　　　　—Joseph Brodsky

In the 1800s, people segregated their books by the sex of the author.

THE NAKED TRUTH

Let it all hang out.

"Take off all your clothes and walk down the street waving a machete and firing an Uzi, and terrified citizens will phone the police and report: 'There's a naked person outside!'"
—**Mike Nichols**

"On the fourth day of telecommuting, I realized that clothes are totally unnecessary."
—**Dilbert**

"I often think that a slightly exposed shoulder emerging from a long satin nightgown is far more sexy than two naked bodies in bed."
—**Bette Davis**

"I've posed nude for a photographer in the manner of Rodin's 'Thinker,' but I merely looked constipated."
—**George Bernard Shaw**

"I can't bear being seen naked. I'm not exactly a tiny woman. When Sophia Loren is naked, this is a lot of nakedness."
—**Sophia Loren**

"And they were both naked, the man and his wife, and were not ashamed."
—**Genesis (2:25)**

"I used to sleep nude—until the earthquake."
—**Alyssa Milano**

"What spirit is so empty and blind, that it cannot recognize the fact that the foot is more noble than the shoe, and skin more beautiful than the garment with which it is clothed?"
—**Michelangelo**

"My school colors were clear. We used to say, 'I'm not naked, I'm in the band.'"
—**Steven Wright**

"When you've seen a nude infant doing a backward somersault, you know why clothing exists."
—**Stephen Fry**

"I think onstage nudity is disgusting, shameful and damaging to all things American. But if I were 22 with a great body, it would be artistic, tasteful, patriotic, and a progressive religious experience."
—**Shelley Winters**

"There are few nudities so objectionable as the naked truth."
—**Agnes Repplie**

Fred Rogers took a morning swim every day in the nude.

JUST PLANE WEIRD

*The fact that hundreds of thousands of pounds of aluminum
and pretzels can fly is weird enough, but it gets weirder.*

COMPLAINT DEPARTMENT

Artyom Chernopup, a passenger on a Russian Aeroflot flight, was upset because some of the flight attendants were obviously intoxicated. When he complained about it, three of the drunken crew members beat him up. Chernopup planned to press charges; Aeroflot announced that the entire crew would be "temporarily dismissed."

WALK THIS WAY

A 35-year-old man was asked to remove his belt while he was going through airport security in Cologne, Germany. He refused. When told that he *had* to do it to get on the plane, he angrily took off his belt—and his pants—and walked through the detector in his underwear. (No alarms sounded.)

HAPPY BIRTHDAY

Louis Paul Kadlecek of Angelston, Texas, started celebrating his 21st birthday on February 25, 2004. He was still drunk four days later when he decided to break into the Brazoria County Airport and steal an airplane (he had never flown one before). He got into a single-engine Cessna (with a case of beer) and took off. A mile later he flew the plane into a 100,000-volt power line, cutting off electricity to a large portion of the county, and plunged 100 feet to the ground. The drunken man then got up and walked the three miles back to his home. Police arrested him the next morning. When asked where he had planned to take the plane, he answered, "I don't know—Mexico, maybe." He faces up to 20 years in prison.

IT'S NOT FUNNY

A week after two America West pilots were fired for showing up drunk, a passenger was thrown off an America West plane in San Francisco when she jokingly asked flight attendants if they had "checked the crew for sobriety." The airline said the woman's remarks "constituted a potential security problem." David Stempler, president of the Air Travelers Association, called it an abuse of authority. "They ought to put up a big sign with an 'H' and a slash through it for 'No Humor Zone' because there's no joking allowed."

DID THEY SEE ANYTHING?

Several security screeners at Denver International Airport were reprimanded in 2004 after they sent themselves through the X-ray machine "to see what their brains looked like."

HOW MANY WERE DETAINED? NUN.

An American Airlines plane was evacuated in Dallas because someone thought they detected a strange smell onboard. No problem was found, so they let all the passengers back on, except for four nuns. The four Indian-born nuns, who were returning home to California from their Christmas vacation, were questioned for six hours before they were allowed to get on another flight. The explanation: "The crew members didn't feel comfortable taking you inside." "We didn't know we looked suspicious," said Sister Tessy Pius. (American Airlines later sent them a formal apology.)

JAILBIRD

Perhaps they saw a telltale bump in his pants. Or heard chirping noises. Or maybe it was just because he was arriving from Cuba. Whatever the reason, airport inspectors were suspicious of Carlos Avila when he landed in Miami in October 2001. They asked him to raise his pant legs...and discovered he had 44 birds strapped to his legs. Smuggling charges were made worse by the fact that Avila had signed papers specifically stating that he was not bringing birds into the United States. He was sentenced to six months in prison.

BETTER THAN A SEAT BELT

In 2002 the BBC reported that a woman on a Scandinavian Airlines flight got stuck to the airplane toilet when she pushed the button for the vacuum-powered flush. Sealed to the seat, she was unable to get up until technicians pried her loose hours later, after the plane had landed in the United States. (Great story, huh? Unfortunately it never really happened. At first Scandinavian Airlines confirmed the story, then later claimed it was all a big mistake—probably a fictional emergency from a training manual.)

THAT'S DEATH!

We often write about weird things that happen in everyday life. Turns out they happen in death, too.

DON'T WORRY, BE HAPPY

"A Thai ice-cream truck driver died laughing in his sleep, the newspaper *The Nation* reported. Damnoen Saen-um, 52, laughed for about two minutes and then stopped breathing. The newspaper said Damnoen's wife tried to wake him but he kept laughing. 'It is possible that a person could have a heart attack while laughing or crying too hard in their sleep,' said Dr. Somchai Chakrabhand, deputy director of the Mental Health Department. 'But I have never seen a case like this before.'"

—*Herald Sun,* **Australia**

BRITON OF THE SEA

"An Englishman has applied for permission to be fed to Great White sharks off South Africa after he dies. Robert Blackwood, a property developer, wants his dead body thrown into waters off Gans Bay, Cape Town. He admits he has never seen a live shark or been to South Africa—he made his decision after watching a television documentary by the author of *Jaws*. Gans Bay resident George Smit, who has been diving with sharks for 23 years, says the idea wouldn't work because white sharks aren't interested in human blood. 'The sharks wouldn't give it a second glance,' he said. 'It would rot and be eaten by crayfish.'"

—*Sunday Times,* **South Africa**

DEATH INSURANCE

"A cemetery in Santiago, Chile, is offering its clients coffins with sensors that detect any movement inside after they have been buried. According to a spokesperson for the cemetery, 'We want to be pioneers and avoid catalepsy cases, in which a person gets completely paralysed for a few hours and ends up buried as if they were dead. We want families to rest assured that if a case like this ever happens their loved ones will be immediately rescued.'"

—**BBC News**

A single tiger can eat six tons of meat a year...the equivalent of 60,000 hamburgers.

TO MAKE IT UP TO YOU...

"An Italian family recently learned they had been praying at the wrong grave for 15 years. The Belforte cemetery, near Varese, exhumed the body in an unrelated legal matter and discovered that the tombstone on the grave had been mixed up with that on the grave next to it when the person was buried, Italian newspaper *Corriere della Sera* reported. The family have said they plan legal action over the mix-up but local authorities have apologised and offered a 'free grave plot' as compensation."

—*Ananova*

SHOTGUN FUNERAL

"The widow of an expert on shotguns had her husband's ashes loaded into cartridges and used by 20 close friends for the last shoot of the season. A total of 275 12-bore cartridges were produced from the mix and were blessed by a minister before they were used. The widow, Joanna Booth, of London, said it was a marvelous day out and her husband would have loved it. 'It was not James' dying wish,' she said, 'but he had read somewhere that someone had done it and he thought it was very funny.' The special cartridges accounted for 70 partridges, 23 pheasants, seven ducks, and a fox."

—*The London Telegraph*

DEATH OF THE FUTURE?

"Concerns about the environmental impact of cremation and burial has led Swedish firm Promessa Organic AB to a chilling alternative—freezing bodies in liquid nitrogen, then using sound waves to smash the brittle remains into a powder. Bodies would be dipped in liquid nitrogen with a temperature of $-196°C$. Extracted from the super-cold solution, the bodies would be brittle as glass and could be broken down with bursts of sound. 'The method is based upon preserving the body after death, while avoiding harmful embalming fluid,' said Susanne Wiigh-Maesak, a spokesperson for Promessa. The remains, buried in a coffin crafted from cornstarch, would take about a year to break down and return to the soil. 'On top of the grave you can set a plant that would take advantage of the nutrients in the 'compost',' Wiigh-Maesak said, adding that she herself would very much like to become a white rhododendron."

—**Associated Press**

On average, men spend 45 seconds in a public restroom stall. Women typically spend 80.

WORD ORIGINS

Ever wonder where words come from? Here are the interesting stories behind some everyday words.

MARMALADE

Meaning: A jellylike preserve made from the pulp and rind of fruits, especially citrus fruits

Origin: "It was said that when Mary Queen of Scots was out of sorts, she would refuse to eat. The only food that could tempt her was a conserve of oranges. Hence the name of this jam after the Queen's indisposition: *Marie malade* ('sick Mary'). The word's *true* ancestor, however, is the Latin *melimelum*, meaning 'sweet apple.'" (From *The Story Behind the Word*, by Morton Freeman)

OSTRACIZE

Meaning: To banish or exclude from a group

Origin: "In ancient Greece, the Athenians voted against a statesman by placing his name on an *ostrakon*, an earthenware tablet. Six thousand adverse votes constituted a decree of banishment." (From *Classical Word Origins*, by Harry E. Wedeck)

DUMBBELL

Meaning: A short bar with weights at each end, used for exercise

Origin: "Some 250 years ago someone noticed that bell ringers attained a remarkable muscular development of the chest, shoulders, and arms. Whoever he was, he invented a device which simulated the bell ringer's gallery, but without the bells. Because there was no bell attached, it became known as a *dumb bell*. Someone else discovered that one could get the same exercise without most of the cumbersome contrivance, using only a wooden or metal bar." (From *Thereby Hangs a Tale*, by Charles Earle Funk)

DISMAL

Meaning: Causing gloom or depression; dreary

Origin: "First mentioned in 1256 as the Anglo-French name for French *les mals jours*, the evil days, from the Latin *dies mali*, or unlucky days. First computed by Egyptian astrologers, the *dies*

Q: What are *ephelides*? A: Freckles.

mali were the days of the medieval calendar when it was unwise to begin any undertaking: January 1 and 25, February 4 and 26, March 1 and 28, April 10 and 20—and so on, two per month, through the year." (From *More About Words*, by Margaret S. Ernst)

CAPITAL

Meaning: Wealth in the form of money or property

Origin: "From Latin *caput*, a 'head' of cattle. Cattle are one of the oldest forms of wealth: they are movable; grow; bear interest (milk); and provide capital gains (calves)." (From *Remarkable Words*, by John Train)

GIBBERISH

Meaning: Unintelligible or nonsensical talk or writing

Origin: "This word was influenced by the 11th century Arabian alchemist, *Geber*, who, to avoid death on a charge of dealing with the devil, wrote his treatises in apparent nonsense." (From *Dictionary of Word Origins*, by Joseph T. Shipley)

CHAUFFEUR

Meaning: One employed to drive a private automobile

Origin: "The French word *chauffeur* comes from the verb *chauffer*, 'to heat.' A *chauffeur* was originally the 'fireman' on a steam train, whose job it was to shovel fuel into the boiler and maintain a head of steam. Steam-powered cars worked on the same principle (it took as long as 15 minutes to produce steam from a cold boiler) but this time the *chauffeur* was often also the driver." (From *The Chronology of Words and Phrases*, by Linda and Roger Flavell)

JINX

Meaning: An omen of bad luck

Origin: "At the turn of the 20th century, some people used animals and birds for fortune-telling. One of the most popular was the wryneck woodpecker—commonly known in the Southeast as the *jinx*. Many who paid for information from a jinx regretted it: Too often the good predictions didn't come true, while the bad ones did. Disaster followed a reading so often that the bird's name came to stand for bad luck." (From *Why You Say It*, by Webb Garrison)

In Switzerland, it is illegal to flush a toilet or pee standing up after 10 p.m.

SPIDER? MAN?

Can he really do anything a spider can?

COMIC BOOK SCIENCE
A radioactive spider bit Peter Parker, endowing him with all the power and abilities of a spider: super speed, super strength, the ability to climb walls, and an uncanny "spider sense." But how truly similar to a spider is Spider-Man?

• **Spider Strength:** Spiders aren't really all that strong. Many insects, such as ants, can carry as much as 60 times their own weight, but spiders, which are arachnids, can't.

• **Spider Speed:** Spiders are not particularly fast for their size. Trying to keep track of eight legs at once, without tying themselves in knots, limits their speed and coordination.

• **Spider Sense:** Spiders are covered with *setae*—stiff hairlike structures that collect sensory information and relay it to the brain. But while setae can detect slight air movement (to determine if captured prey is edible), they can't warn a spider of imminent danger.

• **Wall Climbing:** Only a few of the world's 35,000 species of spiders have the ability to walk up walls and cling to ceilings. Hunting spiders have a group of hairs, called *scopula*, located between their claws. The multi-stranded hairs are covered with moisture, which allows them to stick to slick surfaces. This is the only one of Spider-Man's powers that is directly related to spiders.

• **Web Spinning:** In the movies, Spidey shoots webs from his wrists as a natural part of his powers, but in the original comic book, Peter Parker invented his web-shooters and web formula. So far, science hasn't been able to create a compound that sprays out as a liquid and instantly hardens into a silken rope, sticks to walls (but not hands), or can be formed into a net for capturing criminals.

Spiders produce the silk for their webs in their abdomens, so if Peter had developed *real* spider powers, his silk probably would not have come from his wrists. Where would it come from? Well...let's just say the Spider-Man movies would have lost their PG-13 rating.

Dirty movie: Tom Cruise went weeks without bathing while filming *The Outsiders*.

THAT '70s BATHROOM

Step into Uncle John's Groovy Time Machine and we'll travel
back the 1970s, when no bathroom was complete without...

R UBBER DUCKIES. After muppets Bert and Ernie first
sang the song "Rubber Duckie" on *Sesame Street* in 1970
the little, yellow ducks became a bathroom fixture.

AQUA VELVA. "There's something about an Aqua Velva man,"
said the beautiful blond woman in the commercial, and millions of
men believed her.

JOHNSON'S 'NO MORE TEARS' SHAMPOO. It hit the market in 1954, but it wasn't until the '70s that No More Tears
became the best-selling American shampoo.

AN EARTH TONE BATHROOM SUITE. "Earth tones" were
in. Green wasn't green—it was *avodado green*. Yellow wasn't yellow—it was *harvest gold*. Brown wasn't brown—it was *chocolate*. By
today's standards, they're hard to look at (especially in combinations), but were all the rage in the 1970s.

FLOWER-SHAPED NON-SLIP BATH DECALS. The last
remnants of the 1960s Flower Power fad ended up keeping people
safe when getting in and out of the tub.

THE SHOWER MASSAGE. German company Hansgrohe introduced the first hand-held, adjustable showerhead, the *Selecta*, in
1968. Soon they were everywhere. In 1974 Teledyne came out
with probably the most famous one, The Original Shower Massage.

A FUZZY TOILET SEAT COVER. Basically shag carpets on
top of the toilet seat covers, they had one major drawback: when
guys used the toilet, the thick cover would make the seat fall
down...mid-stream, so to speak.

TIDY BOWL. In the 1970s, blue toilet water was clean toilet
water. And then there was the Tidy Bowl Man, that little guy in
the captain's suit in the boat inside the toilet tank.

AND TO READ? Sadly, there were no good books made especially for the bathroom...yet.

THE LOST *STAR WARS*

Think you've seen every Star Wars *movie? Wrong!*

C LONE WARS
Released in May 1977, *Star Wars* was one of the highest grossing movies of all time. Cast members became instant stars and any toy or product with the *Star Wars* logo flew off store shelves. Fans couldn't get enough. Still, the producers were worried. The sequel wouldn't come out for three more years. How could they make sure fans wouldn't lose interest?

Director George Lucas came up with an idea: "The *Star Wars* Holiday Special," a two-hour TV show to air near Thanksgiving, 1978. Lucas wrote a story about how the *Star Wars* characters celebrated Christmas, or "Life Day," as they called it. The plot of the program would follow Chewbacca's family (his wife Malla, son Lumpy, and elderly father Itchy) as they awaited Chewbacca's return home for the holiday. But Han Solo and Chewbacca would be held up by Darth Vader, bent on ruining Life Day for the entire universe. They'd fight him off and make it home to Wookie world...just in time for "Life Day!"

THE SAGA BEGINS
Lucas sold the idea to ABC. Who wouldn't want a chance to take on *Star Wars*? It might have been a Christmas classic, but by the time production was scheduled to start, Lucas was too busy with the early stages of making *The Empire Strikes Back*. ABC left the Holiday Special in the hands of a team of novice staff writers who had worked mostly on short-lived TV variety shows.

Early on, it looked like the show might be pretty good. Almost all of the original cast agreed to appear. The production team behind *Star Wars* was on board for special effects and makeup. There would be cameo appearances from some of TV's biggest stars—Harvey Korman (*The Carol Burnett Show*), Diahann Carroll (*Julia*), and Beatrice Arthur (*Maude*). Advertisements promised never-before-seen action sequences of Han Solo and Chewbecca flying through space fighting Darth Vader's spaceships. It looked like a surefire winner.

Q: What do your coccyx and appendix have in common? Nobody knows what they're for.

THE MEDIOCRE STRIKES BACK
The Star Wars Holiday Special aired at 8 p.m. on November 17, 1978. All expectations instantly evaporated during the first fifteen minutes, which consisted of Chewbacca's family arguing in Wookie language...without subtitles. That foreshadowed the rest of the program: a tacky variety show with a *Star Wars* theme. It had no plot. It mostly showed Chewbacca's whining, grunting relatives watching 3-D television, with sequences that included Beatrice Arthur in an off-key song-and-dance number; a virtual reality erotic dance from Diahann Carroll; a performance of "Light the Sky on Fire" by Jefferson Starship; and a cooking show with a six-armed Harvey Korman in drag. It all concluded with a "Life Day" carol sung by Princess Leia—to the tune of the *Star Wars* theme song. (Actress Carrie Fisher later confessed that she was "highly medicated" during filming.) As the show progressed and each sequence became more outlandish than the last, most of the 20 million viewers flipped over to *Wonder Woman*.

REBEL FIGHTERS
Today, anybody with a DVD player can see any classic movie anytime. In 1978, however, the prospect of seeing *Star Wars* in your own home was irresistible, which explains why ratings were so high, but despite the initially large audience, reviews were awful and true fans hated it.

So did George Lucas.

He was furious that the special had corrupted his beloved characters. Because of his anger (and his clout), Lucas managed to prevent *The Star Wars Holiday Special* from ever airing again. He assumed that the show would be an unfortunate, but quickly forgotten misstep in his career. But that's not what happened. 1978 was the beginning of the VCR revolution, so many viewers taped the show, which set into motion a vast bootlegging network that widely distributes this otherwise forgettable flop to this day. Though most copies are of very poor quality, they can still be obtained cheaply over the Internet. Lucas was forced to give up on his goal of cleansing his reputation by erasing the *Holiday Special* from existence. "If I had the time and a sledgehammer," he once commented, "I would track down every bootlegged copy of that program and smash it."

Makes sense: Streetlamps in Hershey, Pennsylvania, are shaped like chocolate kisses.

NO WHISTLING!

Actors are a superstitious lot. For example, productions of Macbeth *have a history of injuries and deaths, so to ward off bad luck, actors usually refer to it as "the Scottish play." Here are some other theater superstitions.*

L EAVE THE LIGHT ON
Some theaters are old and dingy places, perfect haunts for ghosts. So it's become standard practice to have at least one light glowing onstage around the clock, even when the theater is empty. This "ghost light" is meant to ward off bad spirits. Some theater companies use an old floor lamp with a bare bulb (which, in a way, casts exactly the eerie feeling it's meant to dispel).

GOOD DRESS REHEARSAL, BAD LUCK

A perfect dress rehearsal is an omen that a play will have a short run. That's because the cast and crew tend to feel prepared after a good final rehearsal. If they're too confident, they might lose their nervous edge and goof up. So to avoid a completely perfect final rehearsal, the last line of the play isn't spoken until the actual performance. If it's omitted, the rehearsal isn't "perfect."

OLD GEEZERS, GOOD LUCK

The "front of the house"—the box office and the lobby—has its own superstitions. One of them is that if the first person to purchase a ticket for a play is an old man or woman, it means the play will have a long, profitable run. But if a young person is the first ticket buyer, the play is doomed to close quickly.

DON'T WHISTLE BACKSTAGE

Theater people believe that whistling backstage brings bad luck to a production. Like most superstitions, there's no definitive explanation for the origin—it may date back to when sailors were hired to run the rope system that lowered and raised curtains and scenery. Sailors were a good choice, given their skill with knots and manning sails, but they were used to receiving orders via a bosun's whistle. Thus, the backstage worry: if a sailor heard a whistle, he might lower a heavy curtain or piece of scenery at the wrong time, injuring the actors onstage.

Storage unit: You can fit 600,000,000,000,000,000,000,000 atoms in a thimble.

STAGECOACHES

Stagecoach travel has been glamorized by Hollywood: a handsome hero in an immaculate white shirt and string necktie, and a neatly coiffured heroine swaying gently as the stage races across the prairie. Romantic? Yes. Truthful? No. Stagecoaches didn't race—good drivers averaged 5 mph. And passengers arrived covered with dust and aching from the bone-rattling journey. These rigorous conditions created discord, so at every station, Wells Fargo posted this list.

Stagecoach Riders' Nine Commandments

1. Abstinence from liquor is requested. If you must drink, share your bottle; otherwise you will appear to be selfish and unneighborly.

2. If ladies are present, gentlemen are urged to forego smoking pipes or cigars, as the odor is repugnant to the gentle sex. Chewing tobacco is permitted, but spit with the wind, not against it.

3. Gentlemen must refrain from using rough language in the presence of ladies and children.

4. Buffalo robes are provided for your comfort during cold weather. Hogging robes will not be tolerated and the offender will be made to ride with the driver.

5. Don't snore loudly while sleeping or use your fellow passenger's shoulder for a pillow. He (or she) may not understand and friction may result.

6. Firearms may be kept on your person for use in emergencies. Do not fire them for pleasure or shoot at wild animals as the sound riles the horses.

7. In the event of runaway horses, remain calm. Leaping from the coach in panic will leave you injured, at the mercy of the elements, hostile Indians, and hungry coyotes.

8. Forbidden topics of discussion are stagecoach robberies and Indian uprisings.

9. Gents guilty of unchivalrous behavior toward lady passengers will be put off the stage. It's a long walk back. A word to the wise is sufficient.

WEIRD CANADA

Canada: land of beautiful mountains, clear lakes, bustling cities…and some really weird news reports. Here are some of the oddest entries in the BRI news files.

DON'T EAT THE YELLOW SNOW—IT'S ART

In 1991 British artist Helen Chadwick came to Canada to create a series of 12 artworks: bronzed "urine flowers." She formed round piles of densely packed, fresh snow, and peed on them (to turn them yellow). Then she had a male friend "draw" (pee) a circular pattern on it. The combined result looked something like a daisy. Then, before it could melt, Chadwick made a bronze casting of the snow, to create a lasting, one-of-a-kind sculpture. (She sold all 12 for $2,000 each.)

STICKY SUBJECT

Jason Kronenwald of Toronto makes busts of celebrities for a living. He doesn't use stone or clay—his artworks are made out of chewing gum. (Kronenwald actually hates to chew gum, so he has a friend chew it for him.) His most recent works: portraits of "Gum Blondes," including Britney Spears and Pamela Anderson.

DIRT DU JOUR

Canadian research scientists have developed a program called Instrumental Neutron Activation Analysis, used to determine the nutritional value of rural Ontario dirt. Their finding: the average scoop of soil contains many essential vitamins and minerals needed for a healthy body, including iron, calcium, magnesium, and potassium. But if the thought of eating dirt makes you sick, don't worry—it also contains the mineral kaolinite, which can soothe an upset stomach.

MISFORTUNE BAY?

Fishermen in Fortune Bay, Newfoundland, recently found something washed up on the beach: a "sea monster" measuring 22 feet long and smelling so foul that even seagulls would not go near it. Locals think it's the body of the St. Bernard's Monster, a mythical creature that supposedly inhabited Fortune Bay. Marine biologists say it's more likely the decomposed remains of a basking shark or an oarfish.

GOAL!

Corey Hirsch, goalie for the 1994 Canadian Olympic hockey team, threatened to sue the Swedish government in 1995. Sweden planned to issue a postage stamp commemorating the Swedish hockey team's come-from-behind defeat of Canada to win the gold medal at the 1994 Winter Olympics. Hirsch's objection: The stamp would depict Peter Forsberg scoring the game-winning goal—against Hirsch. That, said Hirsch, is "not the way I want to be remembered." (Sweden issued the stamp anyway.)

EAT MY SHORTS

Alberta police stopped David Zurfluh for driving erratically, suspicious that the teenager was drunk. But before he could be given a breath analysis, Zurfluh, who was sitting in the back of the squad car, ate his own underwear. Questioned in court, Zurfluh later admitted that his intention was to eat enough cotton so that it would absorb the alcohol in his system. Amazingly, it may have worked: the breath test showed his blood alcohol level to be at the legal limit. Zurfluh was acquitted of all charges.

DRILLED TO MEET YOU

Donald Wright was installing a sliding glass door in his Toronto apartment building when he fell off a stepladder and knocked himself unconscious. When he woke up, he discovered that he'd fallen head first onto a power drill, which had bored three inches into his right temple. He tried to pull the drill out, but it wouldn't budge, so he set it on reverse, turned it on...and removed it from his head. (Doctors later removed bone fragments from Wright's brain.)

BUT OFFICER, IT WAS A MOOSEUNDERSTANDING

Police in Bonavista-Clarenville, Newfoundland, stopped a driver and gave him a ticket for having an illegal radar detector. His explanation: the black box on his dashboard wasn't a *radar* detector—it was a *moose* detector.

NIZE GUYZ FINISH LAZT

By adding another "z" to his last name, Zeke Zzzyzus (formerly Zzyzus) regained his status as the last name in the Montreal phone book. His competition for the honor: "Pol Zzyzzo" and "Zzzap Distribution."

Charles Dickens accurately described dyslexia 40 years before it was officially recognized.

THE WHO?

*Ever wonder how bands and recording artists
get their names? After some digging around, we
found the stories behind these famous names.*

CHEAP TRICK. While fooling around with a Ouija board, the band asked it what they'd be having for dinner. The board spelled, "cheap trick."

BREAD. The group picked the name when they got struck in traffic behind a Wonder Bread truck.

MARILYN MANSON. A combination of Marilyn Monroe and Charles Manson.

ALICE IN CHAINS. One day band members were watching an episode of *The Honeymooners*. Ralph Kramden said he'd like to see his wife, Alice, in chains.

SOUNDGARDEN. In the band's hometown of Seattle, there's a modern art structure called *A Sound Garden* that creates a low hum when the wind blows through its many pipes and hollows.

RIGHTEOUS BROTHERS. The duo got their name when an audience member shouted, "Hey, that's really righteous, brothers!"

DEEP PURPLE. Named for the favorite song of guitarist Richie Blackmore's grandmother, the 1963 hit "Deep Purple" by April Stevens and Nino Tempo.

HOOTIE AND THE BLOWFISH. Singer Darius Rucker had two friends in his college choir with odd nicknames. Hootie (he had wide eyes like an owl) and Blowfish (he had puffy cheeks). Neither of them are in the band.

FLEETWOOD MAC. A combination of the last names of the band's founding members, Mick Fleetwood and John McVie.

MOBY. The singer sometimes claims to be a descendant of Herman Melville, author of *Moby Dick*, but other times insists Moby is an acronym for "master of beats, y'all."

DOBBYLOOM CHAINPEGGER

Ever heard of the Dictionary of Occupational Titles? *It's a product of the U.S. Department of Labor, listing more than 25,000 real job titles. In search of a new trade? Uncle Sam's got some suggestions:*

Flocculator Operator

Ripening-Room Attendant

Milk-of-Lime Slaker

Round-up-Ring Hand

Kier Dryer

Bed Rubber

Bologna Lacer

Bosom Presser

Bottom Buffer

Crown Pounder

Egg Smeller

Frickerton Checker

Nibbler Operator

Dog-Food Dough Mixer

Pickle Pumper

Retort Forker

Mutton Puncher

Queen Producer

Human Projectile

Subassembly Assembler

Animal Impersonator

Lap Checker

Hand Former Helper

Pantyhose-Crotch-Closing Machine Operator

Blind Hooker

Dead Header

Gore Inserter

Fish Flipper

Road-Hogger Operator

Dobbyloom Chainpegger

Cheese Cutter

Easter Bunny

Automatic Lump-Making Machine Tender

Boring Machine Setup Operator

Upsetter Setter-Up

Brain Picker

Fur Beater

Soiled Linen Distributor

Buzzle Buffer

Head Chiseler

Jawbone Breaker

End-Touching Machine Operator

Toe Puller

Tumor Registrar

Muck Boss

Guillotine Operator

Take-Down Inspector

Bean Dumper

Slubber Doffer

Gas Dispatcher

Largest fruit crop on Earth: Grapes (bananas are second).

THE MAN INSIDE
THE TERMINAL

*Need proof that truth is stranger than fiction? It's
still sitting on a red bench in Terminal One of
France's Charles de Gaulle Airport.*

STUCK AT THE AIRPORT

In 1974 an Iranian student named Merhan Karimi Nasseri went to Great Britain to attend graduate school. There he demonstrated against the shah of Iran, and when he returned to Iran in 1977, he was thrown in jail. Later that year he was expelled from the country and told never to return. He bounced around Europe until 1981, when he was granted permanent refugee status by the United Nations High Commission for Refugees. After that he settled in Belgium.

Nasseri made his first big mistake in 1986, when he inexplicably mailed his refugee card (similar to a passport) back to the United Nations, thinking he didn't need it anymore. He made his second mistake two years later, when, following a mugging on a Paris subway during which the rest of his travel documents were stolen, he decided to fly to London, even though he no longer had papers to prove who he was or that he had a right to travel in Europe.

Somehow Nasseri managed to talk his way onto a plane, but as soon as he arrived in London, British immigration officials sent him back to Paris. Police at Charles de Gaulle Airport arrested him for entering the country illegally. They couldn't let him in the country, but since Nasseri didn't have any papers, they couldn't deport him, either. What could they do? Here's what they decided to do: nothing. So Nasseri's been at Charles de Gaulle airport ever since. His story is the inspiration for the film *The Terminal*.

KING OF THE FOOD COURT

For more than 15 years, Nasseri has made his home on a red plastic bench near the fast food restaurants and retail shops in the underground level of De Gaulle's Terminal One. In some ways he looks

In six moon missions, American astronauts brought home 843 pounds of lunar rock and soil.

like any other traveler—he dresses neatly and has his clothes dry-cleaned once a week. But he's thin, his skin is pale, his eyes are sunken, and his cheeks are hollow. He looks like what he is: a guy who never gets any sunlight and has been living on airport food for years. In fact, the closest Nasseri ever gets to the great outdoors is when he stands next to the entrance, breathing in fresh air as the automatic doors open and close. He never steps beyond the doors.

RED TAPE

For the first few years in the airport, Nasseri was at the mercy of forces largely beyond his control. He couldn't leave the airport and didn't speak French—how was he going to replace his papers? A famous French human rights lawyer named Christian Bourget eventually took up his case, and in 1992 got a French court to rule that since Nasseri had entered the airport legally as a refugee, the French government couldn't expel him from it. But the court did-n't have the power to force the government to let Nasseri step outside onto French soil, so he was still stuck.

That year Bourget also got U.N. officials in Brussels to issue Nasseri a new refugee card. But there was a hitch—the officials wanted Nasseri to appear in person to collect his card, so they could verify that he was who he said he was. But he couldn't. For whatever reason, the Belgian government refused to let him in.

HIS OWN WORST ENEMY

In 1995 Belgian authorities finally relented and agreed to allow Nasseri to enter the country to pick up his documents from the United Nations, but it set two conditions: 1) Nasseri had to agree to move back to Belgium, where he'd lived in the 1980s, and 2) he had to agree to regular supervision by a Belgian social worker. After seven long years, Nasseri finally had a way out of the airport. So did he go to Belgium? No, he refused: he wanted to live in Great Britain, he explained, and no place else.

Four years later, the U.N. officials in Brussels bowed to the inevitable and mailed Nasseri's new refugee card to him. That year the French also issued him identity papers, which gave him the right to live in France (or at least to step out of the airport). Again, Nasseri refused. He wouldn't even *sign* his French papers, let alone use them. Why? For one thing, the papers listed his nationality as Iranian (and he had disowned his country for throwing him out). For another, they identified him as Merhan Nasseri (and he had adopted the nickname given him by the airport staff—Alfred Sir).

Why is Nasseri being so stubborn when his freedom is so near? His years at the airport have taken their toll on his mental health. Bourget says Nasseri is "extremely paranoid and confused," and the airport's medical chief, Dr. Phillipe Bargain, agrees. "He has a fragile psychological balance," Bargain reports. Both men predict that Nasseri will live at the airport until he dies.

HOME SWEET HOME

Nasseri's schedule hasn't changed much over the years. He rises at about 8:00 a.m. and showers, shaves, and brushes his teeth in the men's room. Then he goes to McDonald's or one of the other restaurants and has breakfast. Afterward he sits on his red plastic bench, reading, smoking cigarettes, and listening to his radio (he's picked up a little French by listening to announcements over the airport's public address system).

Nasseri visits with anyone who wants to talk to him and records each encounter in his journal, now more than 8,000 pages long. He either has fast food for dinner or buys his own food at the airport minimart. "I suppose it's not very healthy to live on burgers, pizzas, and sandwiches all the time," he says. At 9:00 p.m. he curls up on his plastic bench and goes to sleep.

BIG MAN ON CAMPUS

Nasseri used to rely on the kindness of airport staff and strangers for clothing, meal vouchers, and pocket change. Now that DreamWorks—producers of *The Terminal*—has paid him for his story (a rumored $275,000), he can buy things himself. He has been the subject of countless articles, two documentaries, and two feature films over the years. Maybe that's why he stays. "After 15 years, with financial success, I'm happy," he told *Premiere* magazine in 2004. "This is my dream world. I don't have any worries."

*   *   *

"Better to be alone than in bad company."

—Thomas Fuller

Camels have three eyelids.

BASKETBALL 101

*College athletes have to pass their classes or they're not
allowed to play sports. In 2001 the University of Georgia devised a
course to ensure that their basketball players got at least one A:
"Coaching Principles and Strategies of Basketball," taught
by Assistant Coach Jim Harrick, Jr. The following
questions are from the actual final exam.*

1. How many goals are on a basketball court?
a) 1   b) 2
c) 3   d) 4

2. How many players are allowed to play on a team at one time?
a) 2   b) 3
c) 4   d) 5

3. How many halves are in a basketball game?
a) 1   b) 2
c) 3   d) 4

4. How many quarters?
a) 1   b) 2
c) 3   d) 4

5. How many points does a 3-point field goal account for in a basketball game?
a) 1   b) 2
c) 3   d) 4

6. Draw the half-court line.

7. What is the name of the exam which all Georgia high school seniors must pass?
a) Eye Exam
b) How Do the Grits Taste Exam
c) Bug Control Exam
d) Georgia Exit Exam

8. If you go on to become a huge coaching success, to whom will you tribute the credit?
a) Mike Krzyzewski
b) Bobby Knight
c) John Wooden
d) Jim Harrick, Jr.

9. Who is the best assistant coach in the country?
a) Ron Jursa
b) John Pelphrey
c) Jim Harrick, Jr.
d) Steve Wojciechowski

10. Draw the 3-point line.

Answers (if you really need them) are on page 513.

IRREGULAR NEWS

More proof that truth really is stranger than fiction.

SORRY ABOUT THE PAPER

"A tree has been sent a letter—to reassure it that it is safe from being cut down. The two-page message, headed 'Dear The Tree,' was stuck to its trunk. It followed concerns from environmental campaigners that the 60-year-old lime on University Road, Southampton, was about to be cut down. It assures the tree that there is a six-month temporary preservation order on it and goes on to say that if the tree would like to make further comments, it should make them in writing to the local council. A spokesman for Southampton City Council said addressing the tree was a 'standard legal device.'"

—*Metro* (U.K.)

EARS TO YOU!

"A Turkish bus driver glued part of his ear back on after it was cut off by thieves. Recep Yavrucu refused hospital treatment and bought a tube of super glue instead. He said he was scared of doctors and needles and preferred to treat his own wounds. Four youths attacked him on his regular run at Antalya. They also stole around £100. The injured man helped police with their inquiries but refused their offer to take him to the hospital. 'I've never been to a doctor, and I'm not starting now,' Mr. Yavrucu said. 'Having a piece of my ear cut off was not that serious. I fixed it myself.'"

—*Hurriyet* (Turkey)

MISS OTHER UNIVERSE

"In January, sponsors of a Bangkok 'beauty' pageant selected 40 contestants out of about 200 semi-finalists to vie for the title of Miss Acne-Free 2001. The 40 were selected actually on the basis of how severely pimpled and pock-marked their faces were, with the eventual winner to be the woman who, with treatment, clears up the most. Said one eager contestant, 'It is not often that I can step into the limelight because of my acne.'"

—*The Nation* (Thailand)

Pope John Paul I once wrote a fan letter to Pinocchio.

AWW, SHOOT

"Have you ever wondered what it would feel like to be shot? Phil Horner of Philadelphia, Pennsylvania, did, so he took a gun and shot himself in the shoulder. While this may sound odd, it gets even more weird. Recently a 911 call came in and an ambulance was once again sent to the Horner residence. It seems that he shot himself one more time. The reason? In his own words, 'I wanted to see if it hurt as much as it did the first time.'"

—*Bizarre News*

THE HOLE STORY

"Forty-one-year-old Romanian Cornel Pasat has been living for the last year—stark naked—at the bottom of a 30-foot hole dug in his living room, because he can't face people since his girlfriend left him. Relatives, tired of supplying food and water and emptying the bucket he uses as a toilet, called in the authorities for help. Says police chief Marcu Marian: 'I don't know how we can persuade him to come out—he seems quite happy down there.'"

—*The Dispatch* (South Africa)

FULL HOUSE

"A couple in Australia named their three children Kitchen, Bedroom, and Garage after the rooms where they were conceived."

—"The Edge," *The Oregonian*

THAT'S FUNNY

"German authorities have fined a woman for laughing too loudly. Officials in Berlin took action against the 47-year-old, named only as Barbara M. in court papers, when her neighbor complained her giggling was disturbing the peace. The neighbor said Ms. M. frequently invited people round and they would laugh the night away. 'It is against the law in Germany to make noise after 10 p.m.,' he complained. She claims he was exaggerating. 'I invited some colleagues to dinner on one occasion and after a couple of glasses of wine we started to enjoy ourselves.' She said the next thing she knew the police were knocking on her door and a few days later she received a fine for 25 euros. 'It was laughable,' she said."

—*Ananova*

WEARABLE ELECTRONICS

Finally, technology merges with fashion.

THE "NO-CONTACT" JACKET: Inventors hope to challenge the "existing power landscapes between men and women" by delivering 80,000 volts of electricity to the initiator of any unauthorized contact. Turning a key on the left sleeve arms the battery-powered garment. If the wearer is touched anywhere on the upper body, the toucher gets a shock equal to inserting his finger in an electrical socket.

IMAGEWEAR: Designers at Nokia have created necklaces that can store and display up to eight digital images. The images are transferred wirelessly from a mobile phone or computer. The idea behind these techno medallions: "To display images that reflect the individual style or emotion of the wearer."

COMPUTER JACKET: Pioneer Electronics came up with a wearable computer designed "for people on the go." It has an Organic Electro-luminescent flat-panel display screen built into one sleeve, a keypad on its cuff, and speakers in the collar. It's based on the same technology that Pioneer currently uses in their car stereo systems.

AMERICAN SIGN LANGUAGE GLOVE: This glove (which looks more like a robotic arm) translates sign language into spoken word or text. Sensors inside the glove map the wearer's hand and finger movements. A microcontroller analyzes the information to find the correct letter, word, or phrase associated with the movement, then converts them into text or speech.

9-1-1-DERWEAR: German scientists have developed electronic underwear that not only monitors your vital signs, but can also call emergency services when help is needed. The bra and underpants have sewn-in sensors that look for dangerous heart rhythms. When trouble is detected, the sensor will automatically call a number for medical assistance. (They're also machine washable.)

High cost of medicine: Gold was once used to treat lung disease.

BEG YOUR PARTON

Here at the BRI when we think of Dolly Parton we
think of two things: her wit and her wisdom.

"I hope people realize that there is a brain underneath the hair and a heart underneath the boobs."

"I believe in my cosmetics line. There are plenty of charities for the home*less*. Isn't it time somebody helped the home*ly*?"

"What people do behind closed doors is certainly not my concern unless I'm behind there with them."

"I would only set foot on the street without all this makeup if my husband was dying of a heart attack. He'd have to be really sick."

"I'm a very open person. One reason I'm a good boss is 'cause you always know what I'm athinkin'. I won't treat you bad. I'll just say, 'Hey, Joe, there's somethin' that's really been buggin' the s#@* outta me."

"After Mama gave birth to 12 of us kids, we put her up on a pedestal. It was mostly to keep Daddy away from her."

On her namesake, Dolly the cloned sheep:
"Even though it's controversial, I'm honored. There's no such thing as baaaad publicity."

"It's a good thing I was born a girl, because if I'd have been a boy, I'd have been a drag queen."

"I have to honestly say that most of the stuff the tabloids write has a little grain of truth. They've told a lot of stuff about me that's true. They've told a lot of stuff about me that ain't true. And I don't admit or deny any of it, because what I ain't done, I'm capable of doing."

"I'm more apt to count my blessings than my money."

"I think the fact that I look totally artificial, but I am totally real, has its own kind of magic in it."

"I want to be an 80-year-old lady whose sex life they're still wondering about."

Pizza Hut uses 80 million pounds of tomatoes each year.

FOUNDING FATHERS

You already know the names—here are the people behind them.

EDWARD BAUER

EDWARD BAUER
Background: In 1920, at age 20, Bauer used his last $25 to open his own tennis shop. One day while using goose feathers to make badminton shuttlecocks, it occurred to him that goose down might be good insulation material for clothing...and the down jacket was born.

Famous Name: Bauer landed a government contract to provide down jackets for World War II pilots. After the war, pilots remembered the "Eddie Bauer" label and wrote to his Seattle store, prompting him to start a mail-order business. Bauer retired in 1968, still with just one store. But in 1988 the Chicago-based catalog merchant Spiegel bought the business and expanded it to 500 locations, making "Eddie Bauer" a household name.

CLIFF HILLEGASS

Background: Bedridden as a child, Hillegass passed the time reading classic literature. While attending the University of Nebraska, he parlayed his knowledge of books into a job as a buyer for the college bookstore. Through the job, he met Jack Cole, who produced Cole's Notes, a Canadian line of literary study guides. Cole suggested Hillegass do the same thing in the United States.

Famous Name: In 1958 he took out a bank loan and started writing and printing Cliffs Notes—plot and character summaries of classic works of literature—from his basement. He began with 16 Shakespeare titles. Today Cliffs Notes is owned by John Wiley & Sons, publishers of the *For Dummies* guides. It sells more than five million study guides a year for everything from *Beowulf* to trigonometry. All-time bestseller: *Great Expectations*.

LIZ CLAIBORNE

Background: Belgian-born Claiborne's family moved so often that she never finished high school. They eventually settled in the United States, but Claiborne studied art in Europe (her father wouldn't let her study fashion design). She won a *Harper's Bazaar* design contest in 1950 and moved to New York, where she worked for Jonathan Logan, a major clothing designer in the 1950s. For the next two decades, Claiborne tried, unsuccessfully, to persuade Logan to let her design fashions for the newly emerging class of working women.

Famous Name: In 1976 Claiborne started the Liz Claiborne Company and produced the first line of office-suitable clothing for women. Within two years, she was earning $23 million a year. When the company went public in 1981, it had annual sales of $2 billion. By the end of the decade, 60% of working women were wearing Liz Claiborne designs.

IGNAZ SCHWINN

Background: Schwinn left school in 1871 at the age of 11 to become a mechanic's apprentice. He soon went to work for himself, traveling the German countryside fixing bicycles by day, working on his own designs at night. When he showed them to Heinrich Kleyer, an established bicycle maker, Kleyer hired Schwinn to design and build a new line of bicycles.

Famous Name: In 1895 Schwinn formed his own company in the United States. Early bicycles were labor-intensive to build, which made them expensive. But Schwinn found ways to lower the cost, making them available to more people, especially children, who would become their biggest consumer. Schwinn basically created a classic association of American kids and bikes. His company's most popular model, the Sting-Ray, came out in 1963 and is the bestselling bike ever.

THOMAS J. LIPTON

Background: At age 15, Lipton scraped together $18 to take a boat from his native Glasgow, Scotland, to New York City. He worked odd jobs ranging from picking rice to fighting fires until he saved up $500, which he used to return to Glasgow and open a cafe in 1870.

Famous Name: Tea had been popular in the British Isles for 200 years, but it was expensive and unwieldy, sold loose from large chests. Lipton transformed the way tea was sold: he popularized the tea bag and turned tea into a branded product. Today, his company distributes half the tea in the United States.

Acupuncture uses 388 sites on the body, including 26 just for toothaches.

MYTH-CONCEPTIONS

"Common knowledge" is frequently wrong. Here are some examples of things that people believe, but according to our sources, just aren't true.

Myth: There are no straight lines in nature.
Fact: Sure there are. Hundreds, in fact, most notably in crystal formations and snowflake patterns.

Myth: Don't read in dim light—you'll hurt your eyes.
Fact: According to the American Academy of Ophthalmology, while reading in good light makes reading easier and limits eye strain, using poor light "causes no permanent eye damage."

Myth: There are hundreds of different words in the Eskimo language that mean "snow."
Fact: First of all, there is no Eskimo language, because there is no one group of people called "Eskimos." The word misleadingly refers to dozens of tribal groups living in the northern parts of North America. Most speak different languages, and they typically have less than a dozen words that mean snow.

Myth: Monkeys and apes groom each other by picking off fleas and ticks. And then they eat them.
Fact: They're actually removing dead skin (but they do eat it).

Myth: More suicides occur during the Christmas season than at any other time of year.
Fact: Suicides are pretty evenly dispersed throughout the year, but springtime actually has the most occurrences.

Myth: Bats are rodents.
Fact: Although bats are similar to rodents, they have more in common with primates (which include us) than they do with rodents.

Myth: If you get arrested, you're entitled to make one phone call.
Fact: There's no law anywhere that guarantees this. It's just a courtesy or privilege offered, not a legal right. (Some jurisdictions might even let you make a second phone call.)

Approximately 50 million Americans snore.

THE HISTORY OF CIVILIZATION

Who invented the wheel? When were the Dark Ages? Who came first, Jesus or Buddha? What the heck is the Fertile Crescent? We decided to try to answer these and some other basic questions about history with this timeline of civilization. Ground rules: 1) Obviously, we couldn't include everything; 2) Many of the dates are approximate, but close enough for bathroom reading; and 3) You're bound to learn something. Enjoy!

PART I: FROM FARMS TO EMPIRES

• **10,000 to 8000 B.C.** As the last Ice Age ends and the Earth grows warmer, *Homo sapiens* make a revolutionary technological leap: after more than 100,000 years in small nomadic tribes of hunter-gatherers, people discover farming. By domesticating plants and animals, they can now grow and store food. Having surplus food means being able to establish permanent, year-round homes. It also means the ability to support larger populations, and not all of those people have to work at acquiring food. This, in turn, leads to the development of other skills such as arts and crafts, sciences, politics, and religion. And then what happened? Towns and cities were built, and all the necessities and inventions that go with them. The Agricultural Revolution is known as the seed of human civilization.

• **8000 B.C.** The world's first known permanent settlements are founded in the Fertile Crescent, a semi-circular area of land in the Middle East that stretches from present-day Iraq to Egypt. The regular floods of the great rivers there—the Tigris, the Euphrates, the Jordan, and the Nile—create fertile lands that are perfect for farming. The settlements are built around the cultivation of wheat, barley, lentil, and peas, and the domestication of sheep, goat, cattle, and pigs. The world's oldest known settlement, Jericho, is founded at this time in the Jordan Valley. Tools are still made of stone. World population: about 5 million.

• **7000 B.C.** There is extensive trade and transfer of knowledge between the growing settlements in the Fertile Crescent. Catal Huyuk, possibly the first walled town (rather than a scattered collection of huts), is founded in modern-day Turkey, with irrigated crops. Pottery, an important invention for the storage of food, is now being made in many parts of the world.

• **6000 B.C.** The people in the Fertile Crescent weren't the only ones to discover farming. Farming-based settlements now spring up independently in China, the Americas, and sub-Saharan Africa.

• **5000 B.C.** Large towns are flourishing in the world's great river basins: the Tigris and Euphrates (the Middle East), the Nile (North Africa), the Indus (southern Asia), and the Yellow River (eastern Asia). Permanent farming settlements now exist on every continent except Antarctica and Australia (where they won't appear until Europeans arrive there in the 1800s A.D.). Corn is cultivated in Mexico, mangoes in Southeast Asia.

• **4000 B.C.** In Mesopotamia (the Tigris-Euphrates river valley) copper begins to replace stone in tool making. The first plow is invented, greatly increasing crop output. Advances in food production cause a huge spike in world population growth. Agriculture spreads throughout Europe.

• **3500 B.C.** Sumer civilization begins in Mesopotamia with city-states ruled by kings worshiped as gods. Trade and warfare between them spurs great leaps in technology, such as the potter's wheel and cuneiform script, the first known system of writing. The sail is invented in Egypt, further increasing travel and the transfer of knowledge within and beyond the Fertile Crescent.

• **3200 B.C.** King Menes unites the city-states along the Nile and becomes Egypt's first pharaoh. Slightly south, Nubian Kush culture in northern Sudan, one of the earliest known black African civilizations, develops on the upper Nile River, trading gold, ivory, and ebony with Egypt. Sumerians invent the wheel. They also mix tin with copper to invent a new, harder metal—bronze—improving tool and weapon making. Sumerians and Egyptians develop number systems, mathematics, and astronomy.

• **3000 B.C.** Egyptians develop hieroglyphic writing. And they brew beer. Sumerians invent glassmaking; Chinese invent silk. Sumerian mathematicians divide the day into 24 hours and hours into 60 minutes. Construction begins on Stonehenge (southern England) by an unknown people. World population: about 14 million.

Dachshunds were originally bred to hunt badgers.

- **2500 B.C.** Hebrew civilization is developing in the Middle East, Olmec civilization in southern Mexico and Central America. The Chinese invent a potter's wheel. The Egyptians build the Great Pyramid. Sumer has the first standing professional armies.

- **2300 B.C.** After years of war, King Sargon of Akkad (in northern Iraq) succeeds in conquering Sumerian city-states to the south, then conquers his neighbors to the north and west. Result: The world's first empire (or multiethnic state). The Akkadian Empire will eventually stretch from Mesopotamia to present-day Turkey and Lebanon. The Egyptians invent paper, using the papyrus plant.

- **2000 B.C.** The height of Minoan civilization on Crete (in the Greek Islands). The Minoans are very prosperous, with the world's first "leisure society": a large part of even the common person's time is focused on leisure activities, such as sports. They're also the first to have indoor plumbing and flush toilets. The Phoenicians are now the primary traders in the region, carrying news of the latest technology from port to port, which makes them instrumental in the spread of civilization. Europe's Bronze Age begins.

- **1800 B.C.** The Babylonians have conquered and assimilated the Akkadian Empire. Among their achievements: they develop multiplication tables; invent the first windmills (to pump water for irrigation); and create the world's first written laws, Hammurabi's Code. Judaism is founded around this time by Abraham. Horse-drawn chariots are used in Egypt. The Chinese become the first civilization to record an eclipse.

- **1600 B.C.** As traders, the Phoenicians need a better record-keeping system, so they develop a phonetic alphabet, for the first time using written characters to represent sounds, rather than objects and concepts. It is the basis of our modern alphabet.

- **1500 B.C.** The earliest known medical textbook is written in Egypt. The *Vedas*, four collections of hymns that will become part of the basis for Hinduism, are written in India. Massive earthquakes and tidal waves in the Mediterranean destroy Minoan cities, ending that civilization. Hatshepsut becomes pharaoh of Egypt, the first woman known to rule an empire.

And then what happened? *Turn to page 228.*

Light snack: Americans eat about 95 million pounds of marshmallows every year.

THE LYIN' KING

*Over the years we've reported how Disney animators
massaged, rewrote, censored, and sanitized classic fables
and fairy tales for mass audiences. But this is the first time
we've ever heard of them "borrowing" so much of another
artist's work. Did they? Or was it just a coincidence?*

INSPIRATION

In 1950 a Japanese artist named Osamu Tezuka created *Jungle Taitei* (*Jungle Emperor*), a story about an orphaned lion cub who is destined to rule the animals in Africa. From 1950 to 1954 it was a Japanese comic book series, and in 1965 Tezuka turned it into Japan's first color animated television series. The following year, all 52 episodes were released in the United States under the name *Kimba the White Lion*. Over the next few years, *Kimba* enjoyed some success in syndication, mostly on local or regional TV stations, and Tezuka freely acknowledged that the work of Walt Disney—*Bambi* in particular—was an inspiration for the story of his lion hero.

In 1994, nearly 30 years after the creation of *Kimba* and five years after Tezuka's death in 1989, Disney released its feature-length animated film *The Lion King*—about an orphaned lion cub destined to rule the animals in Africa.

FALSE PRIDE

Officially, the executives and animators at Disney denied they had ever even heard of *Kimba*. But fans of the original *Kimba the White Lion* were incensed with the many similarities they found between the two projects. A group of more than a thousand animators in Japan sent a petition to Disney asking the studio to acknowledge its debt to the original series. Disney refused, citing only *Bambi* and Shakespeare's play *Hamlet* as influences.

Walt Disney reportedly met Tezuka at the 1964 New York World's Fair and mentioned that he someday hoped to make something similar to Tezuka's earlier creation, *Astro Boy*. But Disney died in 1966, 28 years before *The Lion King* was made. If he really was a fan of Tezuka's work, would he have approved of the project?

COPYCAT

Some of the most striking similarities between *The Lion King* and *Kimba the White Lion*:

• The main characters' names are remarkably similar: Simba and Kimba.

• Both are orphaned as cubs and destined to become rulers.

• Each lost their father in treacherous circumstances.

• In *The Lion King*, Simba turns to a wise but eccentric baboon (named Rafiki) for guidance. In *Kimba the White Lion*, Kimba turns to a wise but eccentric baboon (named Dan'l Baboon) for guidance.

• One of Simba's friends is a hysterical yet comical bird (named Zazu). One of Kimba's friends is a hysterical yet comical bird (named Polly).

• Simba has a cute girlfriend cub named Nala. Kimba has a cute girlfriend cub named Kitty.

• Simba's chief nemesis is Scar, an evil lion with a scar over his left eye. Kimba's primary nemesis is Claw, an evil one-eyed lion with a scar over his blind left eye.

• In *The Lion King*, Scar enlists the aid of three hyenas (Shenzi, Banzai, and Ed). In *Kimba the White Lion*, Claw enlists the aid of two hyenas (Tib and Tab).

• Kimba and Simba each speak to the spirit of their father, who appears in the clouds.

• The image of Simba standing on Pride Rock in *The Lion King* is almost identical to an image of Kimba as a grown lion, standing on a jutting rock surveying his kingdom in *Kimba the White Lion*.

CAT FIGHT

Disney may have "borrowed" the idea, but they were legally protected. Mushi Productions, the company that made *Kimba the White Lion*, went bankrupt in 1973 and U.S. rights to the show ran out in 1978. That means *Kimba* was in the public domain. Someone tried to release it to home video in the U.S. in 1993, but was delayed by a lawsuit from an undisclosed company. At the same time, details of Disney's new movie began to surface. In an online chat in 1993, Roy Disney mentioned Kimba, the lead character in Disney's next animated film, *The Jungle King*. (*Kimba*'s original English title was *The Jungle Emperor*.)

UNCLE JOHN'S PAGE OF LISTS

Random bits of interesting information from the BRI files.

10 Highest-Scoring Words in Scrabble
1. Bezique
2. Cazique
3. Jazzily
4. Quartzy
5. Quetzal
6. Quizzed
7. Zephyrs
8. Zincify
9. Zinkify
10. Zythums

6 Things That Can Kill Dracula
1. Sunlight
2. Garlic
3. Crucifix
4. Holy water
5. Wooden stake
6. Silver

9 Most Common U.S. Town Names
1. Fairview
2. Midway
3. Oak Grove
4. Franklin
5. Riverside
6. Centerville
7. Mount Pleasant
8. Liberty
9. Salem

7 Things Invented by Canadians
1. Snowmobile
2. Washing machine
3. Zipper
4. Plastic garbage bag
5. Foghorn
6. Electric range
7. Paint roller

5 Songs About Fruit
1. "Banana Boat Song" (Harry Belafonte)
2. "Blueberry Hill" (Fats Domino)
3. "Cherry Cherry" (Neil Diamond)
4. "Lemon Song" (Led Zeppelin)
5. "Little Green Apples" (O.C. Smith)

6 Vegetables That Are Really Fruits
1. Cucumber 2. Okra
3. Eggplant 4. Tomato
5. Pumpkin 6. Squash

4 Horsemen of the Apocalypse
1. Pestilence 2. War
3. Famine 4. Death

9 Jackson Siblings
1. Michael 2. Janet
3. LaToya 4. Rebbie
5. Marlon 6. Randy
7. Tito 8. Jackie
9. Jermaine

7 Types of Triangles
1. Equilateral
2. Isosceles
3. Scalene
4. Right
5. Acute
6. Obtuse
7. Oblique

11 Wars Involving U.S.
1. Revolutionary War
2. War of 1812
3. Mexican War
4. Civil War
5. Spanish-American War
6. World War I
7. World War II
8. Korean War
9. Vietnam War
10. Persian Gulf War
11. Operation Iraqi Freedom

Dromomania **is an abnormal impulse to travel.**

THE *OTHER* MR. COFFEE

Does the name Howard Schultz ring a bell? He's the guy who figured out how to get you to pay $4.50 for a 75¢ cup of coffee.

TALL ORDER

In the early 1980s, a Swedish plastics company called Hammarplast sold plastic coffee filters that fit over a thermos. One day in 1981, one of the company's salesmen, 27-year-old Howard Schultz, happened to notice that a small Seattle coffee roasting company called Starbucks Coffee, Tea and Spice bought more of the filters than the entire Macy's department store chain did. Why?, Schultz wondered. And who would bother making coffee using such a tedious method when an automatic drip coffeemaker could do it all at the push of a button?

Schultz was so intrigued that he made a trip out to Seattle just to have a look at the company. He visited Starbucks' retail store in the historic Pike Place Market, where they sold fresh-roasted coffee beans by the pound and coffee-making supplies...but no coffee drinks or any other beverages by the cup. Schultz took a tour of the roasting plant and met the company's co-founders, Jerry Baldwin and Gordon Bowker. He also drank some of the darkest, strongest, best-tasting coffee he'd ever had.

A FRESH START

Schultz decided right then that he wanted to work for Starbucks; but convincing Baldwin and Bowker to hire him took a little more time. It wasn't until about a year later, when they were planning to open the company's sixth store and the first one outside of Seattle, that they agreed to take Schultz on as director of retail operations and marketing. Even then he had a vision of building Starbucks into a regional and later a national chain, but like Baldwin and Bowker, he saw the company as a retailer of coffee *beans* that people would buy to make coffee in their own homes.

Then in the spring of 1983, Schultz made a trip to Milan, Italy, to attend an international housewares convention. He decided to

---

Number of Starbucks in Chicago's O'Hare Int'l Airport (2004): 15. In all of South Dakota: 6.

walk from his hotel to the convention center. On the way he passed four coffee bars, each one of them overflowing with people who were lined up to buy espressos, cappuccinos, lattes, mochas, and other exotic drinks.

SOMETHING BREWING

Schultz had already noticed that customers who were new to premium coffee got intimidated just standing in a Starbucks store—how many people could tell the difference between Sumatra coffee and Arabian mocha java, between Italian roast and French roast? Even Schultz was a newcomer. In the week he spent in Milan he drank his very first espresso and his very first latte.

Schultz came to realize that espresso bars were the means by which he could reach beyond Starbucks' traditional, narrow clientele of coffee connoisseurs to a much larger customer base: people who'd never tasted really good coffee before and had no idea what they were missing. By serving *cups* of coffee and giving people a place to drink it, Starbucks stores could become a lot more than just a place to buy coffee beans. They could serve as a "third place," as Schultz liked to call it, a place outside of the home and the workplace or school, where people could hang out and enjoy a coffee just as if they were in an espresso bar in Italy.

If Shultz had a hard time convincing Baldwin and Bowker to hire him, convincing them to sell coffee by the cup was an even bigger challenge. It took him a year just to get them to put a single espresso machine in the company's sixth store when it opened for business in downtown Seattle in April 1984. By June that store was averaging 800 customers a day compared to 250 a day at the other Starbucks locations; but even then Baldwin and Bowker refused to sell ready-to-drink coffee from the other stores. "We're coffee roasters," Jerry Baldwin told him. "I don't want to be in the restaurant business."

IL GIORNALE

In late 1985 Schultz quit his job at Starbucks and founded an espresso bar chain called Il Giornale, which he named after an Italian newspaper. The first Il Giornale opened for business in Columbia Center, Seattle's tallest skyscraper, in April 1986.

So why isn't the world's largest espresso bar chain called Il

---

The South American basilisk lizard can run up to a quarter mile across the surface of water.

Giornale? Because in 1987 Jerry Baldwin and Gordon Bowker decided to sell Starbucks. Schultz, who by now had opened three Il Giornales of his own, managed to raise the $3.8 million he needed to buy the six Starbucks stores and the roasting plant. He had a decision to make: Should he keep the Il Giornale name, or go back to Starbucks? He asked around for advice. Nobody knew how to pronounce Il Giornale, people told him, and they didn't know how to spell it, either. Starbucks it was.

COFFEE BUZZ

Starbucks grew exponentially in the years that followed. By 1990 it had grown to 55 locations. The company went public in 1992, and by the end of the year it had 165 locations. Five years later it had 1,412 stores, and by the end of 2002 it had more than 5,800. As of September 2004 Starbucks has 7,569 stores in 31 different countries around the world. It made nearly $268 million in profits in 2003.

How fast is the company growing today? Every time a Starbucks barista finishes working an eight-hour shift, a new Starbucks has opened somewhere in the world, and the rate of growth is increasing. The company hopes to grow to 25,000 locations around the world in the next decade. Is that kind of growth even possible? Here's a clue: Italy has a population of just under 58 million people or about one fifth the population of the United States. It has more than 200,000 coffee bars.

In 1981 a cup of coffee cost 75¢, tops. Today a Starbucks Venti Java Chip Frappuccino will taste a lot better than that cup of coffee did back in 1981, but it'll set you back as much as $4.50.

Now you know who to thank...or to blame.

*   *   *

IT'S A WEIRD, WEIRD WORLD

In 2004 the U.S. Postal Service allowed Internet users to make their own postage stamps featuring pictures of anything they wanted. The program was a success: 2 million stamps were printed in the first six weeks. Then it was terminated. Why? As a joke, some pranksters printed stamps with a picture of Ted Kaczynski (the "Unabomber"), the man who used the Post Office to mail letter bombs in the early 1990s. The USPS didn't think it was funny.

Eye Opener: The original Starbucks logo featured a mermaid with naked breasts.

THE GREAT WALL OF FLORIDA

Why go all the way to Paris, France, to see the Eiffel Tower when you can visit Paris, Texas, and admire a 50-foot replica...wearing a bright red cowboy hat?

MONUMENT: Statue of Liberty, New York City
REPLICA: Paris, France
STORY: France gave the original statue to the United States in 1886 to honor the friendship between the two countries. To show their appreciation, Americans living in Paris built a 35-foot replica in 1889. It stands on the Isle de Grenelle in the middle of the Seine River. But there's more: Between 1949 and 1951, the Boy Scouts of America donated about 200 eight-foot-tall copper Statue of Liberty replicas to towns across the U.S. (San Juan, Puerto Rico, and Cheyenne, Wyoming, each have one). The French have some as well: one in Barentin, made for a film; one in Colmar, birthplace of the original statue's designer, Frédéric Auguste Bartholdi; and one in Bordeaux.

MONUMENT: Great Wall of China
REPLICA: Kissimmee, Florida
STORY: The original is 4,163 miles long and is considered one of the Seven Wonders of the World. The one in Florida isn't. This half-mile recreation is located at the Florida Splendid China Theme Park, built in 1993. It took 6.5 million bricks to construct.

MONUMENT: Leaning Tower of Pisa, Italy
REPLICA: Niles, Illinois
STORY: Industrialist Robert Ilg constructed the 94-foot "Leaning Tower of Niles" in 1934 to honor the Italian "Father of Modern Science"—Galileo. Only half the size of the original, it matches the exact angle of the Pisa tower's distinctive tilt. Do the Italians approve? Yes—Niles and Pisa officially became "sister cities" in 1991.

Sacre bleu! The busiest Pizza Hut in the world is located in Paris, France.

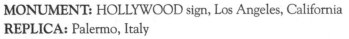

MONUMENT: HOLLYWOOD sign, Los Angeles, California
REPLICA: Palermo, Italy
STORY: In 2001 Italian "post-studio" artist Maurizio Cattelan oversaw the installation of a giant, oversized replica of the famous Hollywood sign. "I had been working on icons," Cattelan explained of the piece. "The Pope, Adolf. I wanted to use one that would not be an icon, but a word. A word has more faces." Each of the nine letters is 75 feet high, and the sign measures 557 feet across (the original is only 450 feet across). It sits on Bellolampo Hill, overlooking Palermo's garbage dump.

MONUMENT: Easter Island statues, South Pacific Ocean
REPLICA: Hunt, Texas
STORY: Located in a field off Texas State Highway 39, these dimensionally accurate re-creations of the facelike statues of Easter Island were built by local artisans Doug Hill and Al Sheppard. Bonus: If you visit, you'll get two for one—the statues share their space with a replica of another ancient monument, Stonehenge.

MONUMENT: Washington Monument, Washington, D.C.
REPLICA: Pope's Creek, Virginia
STORY: It's less than an hour from the actual Washington Monument, but if you're tired of the real thing you can always go here. It's part of the George Washington's Birthplace National Monument—Pope's Creek is where George was born—and although it doesn't have many relics from his childhood, it does have this 56-foot recreation of the monument (the actual one is 555 feet tall).

MONUMENT: Eiffel Tower, Paris, France
REPLICA: Paris, Texas
STORY: Paris, Texas, erected a 55-foot Eiffel Tower in 1993 in honor of its French namesake. When officials in Paris, Tennessee, heard about it, they built one 60 feet tall. Paris, Texas, fought back and made theirs five feet taller. Then, Paris, Tennessee, made *theirs* five feet taller. In 1998 Paris, Texas, put a bright red cowboy hat on their tower, making it a few inches taller. But neither beats the 540-foot replica in Las Vegas (or the 1,052-foot original in Paris, France).

Your heart beats faster during a heated argument than during sex.

SELLOUTS?

It can be quite unsettling when you hear your favorite song being used to sell hemorrhoid medicine. Sometimes artists sell out for a good reason; other times they simply see dollar signs.

Artist: The Who

Background: In 1967 they released an album called *The Who Sell Out*, a sarcastic take on commercialization. The album cover featured poses of band members Pete Townshend and Roger Daltrey in fake ads for deodorant and baked beans.

Cashing In: Turns out they were being prophetic. Thirty years later, Townshend allowed his classic rock anthems "Baba O'Riley," "Bargain," "Won't Get Fooled Again," and "Happy Jack" to be used to sell Nissans and Humvees, while music from the rock opera *Tommy* helped push allergy medicine. And there was more for sale: Their 1978 hit "Who Are You" became the theme for the TV show *CSI* and "Won't Get Fooled Again" became the theme for *CSI: Miami*.

Artist: Sir Laurence Olivier

Background: Actors often appear in commercials, but for someone like Olivier—perhaps the finest actor of his generation—to appear in a commercial was unthinkable.

Cashing In: In 1972 the unthinkable happened—the classically trained Olivier became the first TV spokesman for Polaroid cameras. But Olivier had a good reason: he'd just been diagnosed with a serious muscle disorder and was afraid he might die at any time. Result: He took every job offered to him so that his family would be financially secure after he was gone. Olivier even mocked his selling out by appearing in Paul Hardcastle's 1986 music video "Just for Money." He also acted in some of the worst movies ever made, including *Clash of the Titans* and *Inchon*.

Artist: Folk-rock singer Jewel

Background: She began her career with the image of a sensitive singer-songwriter. She seemed like the real deal; unlike other female pop stars, Jewel wrote her own songs, played an instrument, wrote poetry, and refused to play up her looks. "I'm not slick. I don't have a big image thing," Jewel told *People* in 1997.

Cashing In: In 2003 she began wearing provocative clothes, gyrating in music videos, and singing radio-friendly dance music on her album *0304*. The switch was so startling, some thought her new image was a joke. But it wasn't. And the first single off the album, *Intuition*, was used in an ad for Schick's razor for women called…Intuition.

Artist: Jerry Rubin

Background: Rubin was a different kind of artist—he was one of the most vocal, aggressive, and influential figures of the 1960s counterculture movement. Along with Abbie Hoffman, he organized street theater, demonstrations, and protests for political causes, most often to oppose the Vietnam War. Rubin and Hoffman formed the Youth International Party (the "Yippies") and were among the Chicago Seven, indicted for their part in organizing the protest demonstrations at the 1968 Democratic National Convention.

Cashing In: In the 1970s, Rubin abruptly changed everything. He abandoned activism to become a stock trader and businessman, making a fortune off the '70s health food craze. Former Yippies lambasted him, labeling Rubin a sellout and coining the term "yuppie" (from "young urban professional") specifically to mock him.

Artist: Orson Welles

Background: In the early 1940s, Welles was considered a creative genius. RKO Studios gave him unprecedented full control over the movies he directed. Critics call his films—*Citizen Kane* (1941), *The Stranger* (1946), *The Lady from Shanghai* (1947) and *A Touch of Evil* (1958)—among the best ever made.

Cashing In: Welles gave up directing and became an actor-for-hire, appearing in a few classics (*The Third Man*, *Catch-22*). But as he got older, his lifestyle, not to mention his appetite, got more extravagant…and expensive. "Ask not what you can do for your country," Welles said. "Ask what's for lunch." So he became a voice actor and took any work at all, ranging from TV commercials for California wine ("We will sell no wine before its time") to forgettable animated movies, including *The Enchanted Journey* (as a chipmunk) and *Transformers: The Movie* (as a giant robot from outer space).

NEWS OF THE WILD

Some news that will make you go ape.

L OCK-JAWS
"A man attacked by a shark while snorkeling had to swim back to shore, walk to his car, and then drive to a surf club for help—with the shark still attached to his leg. Lifeguards at a beach near Sydney, Australia, were stunned when the man walked in with the two-foot carpet shark biting his leg and refusing to let go. Once he reached shore, people tried to help, but couldn't remove the shark. Lifeguards flushed its gills with fresh water, forcing it to loosen its grip. The man had 70 needle-like punctures; the shark later died."

—Edmonton Sun

CHIMP CHANGE

"Police in the Colombian capital of Bogota say they have caught a monkey which had been trained to pick pockets. The monkey was captured following complaints from locals who said it had stolen wallets, mobile phones, and other valuables.

"Officials say that after the creature returned home with the stolen goods, it was rewarded with bananas by its owner. Bogota police say the monkey has now been taken to an animal rehab center."

—BBC News

BREATHTAKING

"Scientists at the Lawn Hill National Park in Queensland announced in 2003 that they had found a male Lavarack's turtle, which was thought to be extinct but has apparently survived relatively unchanged for thousands of years. The turtle's primary distinction is that its sex organs and breathing apparatus are both located in its rear end."

—The Australian

SUMO SNORING COMPETITION

"A Romanian man has been sued by his apartment neighbors because his dog snores so loudly that they can't sleep at night. The

Look out! Snakes can continue to bite after they're dead.

dog, named Sumo, is a Neapolitan mastiff. Neighbors say they can't get any peace when Sumo falls asleep because his snoring can be heard in every apartment. One of the neighbors says the dog snores so loud that it interferes with his alarm system."

—*Ananova*

THE GORILLA CHANNEL

"Gorillas in the Moscow Zoo will soon watch TV programs, says zoo director Vladimir Spitsyn. The animals will be able to watch videos about the life of monkeys in the wilderness. Spitsyn thinks these programs are important for the intellectual progress of anthropoids. 'We want them to pick their noses less and think more.'"

—*Pravda*

WE WOULDN'T SHIH TZU

"National Geographic TV recently reported on designer-breeding of dogs, with emphasis on the not yet officially recognized species of *Labradoodle*. Breeding decisions must be carefully made, say experts, because some interspecies pairings create unhealthy off-spring. For example, mating a pug with a Pekingese might create a dog whose eyes would fairly easily dislodge from their sockets. *Yorkipoos* and *schnoodles*, on the other hand, appear to be safe."

—*National Geographic*

THAR SHE BLOWS!

"In August 2003, scientists from the Australian Antarctic Division, traveling by boat on a research mission to attach satellite-tracking devices to whales to study their habitats, managed to capture what they believe is a historical first photo: the water pattern that results from the bubble when a huge whale releases flatulence. Said researcher Nick Gales, 'We got away from the bow of the ship very quickly.'"

—*The Australian*

*   *   *

"Man is an animal that makes bargains: no other animal does this—no dog exchanges bones with another."

—**Adam Smith**

THE GIMLI GLIDER, PT. I

Statistically, airplanes are the safest form of long-distance travel available. So why would anyone be afraid to fly? This article answers that question. (Warning: *If you're reading this on an airplane, you might want to save it until you're back on the ground.*)

JUST ANOTHER FLIGHT

Air Canada Flight 143 on July 23, 1983, started out like any other flight. Captain Robert Pearson and First Officer Maurice Quintal had arrived ahead of time to go over the aircraft and prepare it for departure. The flight was scheduled to depart Montreal shortly before 6:00 p.m. They were going to make a quick, 19-minute hop to Ottawa to pick up more passengers before flying 1,700 miles across Canada to Edmonton, Alberta.

The plane was a twin-engine Boeing 767, one of the most sophisticated commercial aircraft of its day. It was also one of the first commercial jets with a "glass cockpit"—meaning that nearly all of the standard instruments and gauges had been replaced with a bank of computer screens displaying the same information in a digital, graphic format. (Kind of like trading up from a pinball machine to a video game.)

NEW AND IMPROVED

The 767 was so new that Air Canada owned only four of them, none of which had been in service for more than a few months. Captain Pearson, who had more than 26 years on the job, was one of only a handful of Air Canada pilots qualified to fly the plane.

The glass cockpit offered numerous advantages over traditional instruments: Fewer moving parts meant fewer instrument failures. That translated into fewer flight delays, lower operating costs, and higher profits for the airlines. And because so much information was condensed and presented in easy-to-read displays, it eliminated the need for the pilot to scan numerous tiny gauges all over the cockpit, which reduced eyestrain and fatigue.

The new 767s were so sophisticated, in fact, that only two people—the pilot and first officer (co-pilot)—were needed to fly it, instead of the usual three. The position of flight engineer had been

---

Is this a good thing? Helen Keller could identify her friends by their odors.

eliminated, and the job had been divided between the onboard computers, the ground crew, the pilot, and the first officer. Every task had been accounted for.

Or so everyone thought.

A BAD OMEN

As soon as Pearson and Quintal stepped onboard, the ground crew told them that something was wrong with the "fuel quantity processor"—the instrument that measures the available jet fuel and displays the amount on the computer screen. Result: The fuel gauge display was blank. And no spare fuel quantity processors were available on such short notice—the planes were too new. Captain Pearson would have to fly the plane without any fuel gauges.

But was that even permitted? In a traditional jumbo jet the answer was no, but the 767's fuel management system was much more sophisticated than a traditional mechanical fuel gauge. It could measure the rate at which the fuel was being consumed, something that had never been possible before. That meant if you manually told the computer how much fuel was in the tanks at the start of the flight, it could automatically subtract the amount consumed to give a precise estimate of how much fuel was left. It would even display the quantity in the form of a digital "estimated fuel" gauge.

But these were only *estimates*, and they only worked if the pilot entered the correct fuel load into the computer at the start of the flight. If the pilot miscalculated, the information displayed in the estimated fuel gauge would be totally off.

NOT BY THE BOOK

Understandably, Captain Pearson had reservations about flying a jumbo jet without any working fuel gauges. Who wouldn't? So he consulted the 767's official Minimum Equipment List, or MEL, to see if the plane would even be cleared to fly with its fuel gauges out. It wasn't.

But when Pearson pointed this out to one of the mechanics, the mechanic assured him that the plane had been cleared to fly by Air Canada's Maintenance Control division, which has the final say—even over the MEL—as to whether an airplane is safe. Captain Pearson still had misgivings—he didn't like reading one thing in the MEL and hearing something else from the airline. But

---

The first crossing of the United States by automobile took 52 days in 1903.

the 767 *was* a sophisticated plane, so he figured that if Air Canada said it was safe to fly, it was.

MEASURE FOR MEASURE

Air Canada's four 767s were unique in another way, too: they were the first jumbo jets in the entire fleet to use the metric system instead of the traditional British "imperial" system of weights and measures. Canada began phasing in the metric system in 1979, and now Air Canada's air fleet was beginning to make the switch.

This 767's fuel was measured in kilograms, not the imperial pounds that Air Canada pilots were used to dealing with. Adding to the confusion, while the plane measured its fuel by *weight*—kilograms—the fuel truck measured its by *volume*—liters. And with the fuel quantity processor broken, all the calculations—normally done by computers—now had to be done by hand.

But whose job was it to do the math? On an ordinary jumbo jet it was the flight engineer's job to calculate fuel load. But on the 767, that position had been eliminated. As an investigation later revealed, the pilots had been told that fuel calculations were now the job of the ground crew, but since the ground crew hadn't been trained to do the calculations, then either the captain or the first officer had to be responsible for them now.

MATH PROBLEM

Captain Pearson knew that 1) he needed 22,300 kilograms of jet fuel to get to Edmonton, and 2) there were 7,682 liters of fuel in the tanks. So how many liters of additional fuel did he need to get to 22,300 kilograms? More simply put, how many liters of jet fuel are there in a kilogram? That was the question.

Pearson was used to thinking in terms of gallons and pounds, and his knowledge of the metric system was a little rusty. So he asked the guy on the refueling truck how many liters were in a kilogram. "One point seven seven," the guy answered. That sounded about right; First Officer Quintal thought so, too.

PROBLEMS MULTIPLY

How hard was it to do the math? See if you can follow along:

• If there were 7,682 liters of fuel in the tanks and 1 liter is equal

---

Stenophobia is the fear of narrow spaces.

to 1.77 kilograms, that meant the tanks contained nearly 13,600 kilograms of fuel. Thus, they had to add 8,700 kilograms to get the 22,300 kilograms they needed.

• Dividing 8,700 by 1.77 to convert back to liters, the fuel truck had to add a little over 4,900 liters of fuel to fill the tanks to roughly 12,600 liters.

• Multiply 12,600 by 1.77 and you get 22,302 kilograms—more than enough fuel to get to Edmonton.

Simple, right? Well, it's a little confusing in the best of circumstances, harder if you're just learning to master the metric system, and worse still if there's a plane full of people waiting for you to finish the math and take them where they want to go.

But just to be on the safe side, Pearson and Quintal checked and rechecked their math. Sure enough, every time they multiplied 12,600 by 1.77, they got 22,302. According to their calculations, they had enough fuel on board to make the flight, with plenty to spare.

AND AWAY WE GO

Finally satisfied, they programmed their fuel load into the computer manually, then finished their preflight checks and made the 19-minute flight to Ottawa.

During the 43-minute stopover, they had the ground crew check the fuel levels again. Pearson multiplied the remaining liters by 1.77 and concluded that he still had more than 20,000 kilograms of fuel onboard. He entered this estimate into the computer to get the estimated fuel gauge, finished his preflight procedures, and at 7:05 p.m. was cleared for takeoff.

A few minutes later, the Boeing 767 lifted into the air with 61 passengers and 8 crew members aboard. In their wildest dreams, none of them could have imagined what was about to occur.

For Part II of the story, turn to page 319.

*   *   *

SOARING COSTS

A used DC-9 airplane costs more today than it did when it was new in the 1970s.

An eagle's bones weigh half as much as its feathers.

I HEARD IT IN THE BATHROOM

We here at the BRI love rumors and urban legends.
Especially when they involve our favorite room.

RUMOR: To clean a toilet, pour a can of Coca-Cola into the toilet bowl. Let the "real thing" sit for one hour, then flush clean.

BACKGROUND: The Coke-as-bowl-cleaner story was spread as one item on an e-mail list of "household hints." Other items on the list: the "facts" that Coke is so highly acidic a human tooth or a T-bone steak soaking in it will dissolve completely in two days (a steel nail will dissolve in four); Coca-Cola trucks must display "hazardous material" placards when transporting Coca-Cola syrup; and several state highway patrols carry gallons of Coke in their trunks to clean the blood off the highway following auto accidents.

THE TRUTH: Carbonated beverages do contain carbonic acid, and Coke also contains small amounts of citric acid and phosphoric acid. But overall, it's less acidic than many fruit juices. Coke can't dissolve teeth, nails, steaks, or anything else, and it's not considered a hazard...or a toilet cleaner. Any commercially available cleaning product with a picture of a toilet on the label will probably do the job better than Coke. And there's always soap and water.

RUMOR: Microsoft is developing a combination toilet/computer called the "iLoo."

BACKGROUND: In April 2003, someone purporting to be a representative from the software giant's U.K. office issued a press release describing the project, and the story was picked up by newspapers all over the world. The "iLoo," they claimed, would have a built-in computer, complete with wireless keyboard and monitor, making it possible for "end users" to surf the Web while doing their business.

THE TRUTH: The iLoo was indeed a project of Microsoft U.K. ...but somebody forgot to tell the home office. Microsoft's U.S. headquarters immediately issued its own press release calling the

---

British government toilet paper used to read, "Govt. Property, Now Wash Your Hands."

iLoo story a hoax. "This iLoo release was not a Microsoft-sanctioned communication," a spokeswoman told reporters. "We apologize for any confusion or offense it may have caused."

The following day, Microsoft issued a second press release admitting that they had probably "jumped the gun." Microsoft bigwigs apparently learned about the iLoo just like everyone else—by reading about it in the newspaper. They promptly canceled the program because Web-surfing toilets "aren't the best extension of our brand."

RUMOR: Check all shampoo bottles and toothpaste tubes! Your brands may contain *sodium lauryl sulfate*, which causes cancer.

BACKGROUND: This story has been circulating on the Internet since the late 1990s. Supposedly, when the e-mail's author asked a shampoo manufacturer why their product contains a cancer-causing ingredient, an executive replied, "There's nothing we can do about it—we need it to produce the foam."

THE TRUTH: In fact, many shampoos and toothpastes do contain the foaming agent sodium lauryl sulfate. It has been extensively tested and has not been found to cause cancer. However, if you get it in your eyes it will sting, and if you eat it you can get diarrhea. So, learn from Uncle John's mistakes: don't eat shampoo, and don't rub toothpaste in your eyes.

RUMOR: Thanks to the huge wildfires that hit southern California in 2003, the United States is just days away from a severe toilet paper shortage.

BACKGROUND: Someone may have e-mailed you an "article" written by news reporter Jerry Simonreid, apparently based on information given to him by the San Bernardino Fire Department. According to the article, an enormous paper factory located near the U.S.-Mexico border makes 97% of the T.P. for the United States, Mexico, and Canada, and it burned down in the recent wildfires, leaving all of North America with about a three-day supply of toilet paper.

THE TRUTH: The whole story is bogus. Yes, there were fires in southern California, but there aren't any giant toilet paper factories, burned down or otherwise. Your toilet paper supply is safe...for now.

YOUR GOVERNMENT AT WORK

*Rest easy—we've discovered proof that your
tax dollars are being well spent on...*

STRESS REDUCTION

In an effort to reduce stress levels and improve the self-esteem of public housing tenants, the Department of Housing and Urban Development spent $860,000 on a "Creative Wellness" program. The plan: The government was paying to enhance the tenants' lifestyles through "aromatherapy, color therapy, and 'gemstone support' (tapping the healing powers of precious stones)."

GOVERNMENT PENSIONS

• In 1995 Illinois assemblyman Roger P. McAuliffe introduced legislation allowing police officers-turned-state representatives to collect pensions from both fields of employment. The sole beneficiary of the bill: former police officer Assemblyman Roger P. McAuliffe.

• Rhode Island state senator John Orabona claimed an annual pension of $106,000 when he retired in 1995, based on 79 years' worth of state service. The problem: He was 51 years old. So how did he acquire more years in pension credits than he'd been alive? Easy. He found (and exploited) a loophole in the state's pension legislation that made it possible for him to combine benefits from various jobs. (Another Orabona scam awarded government insiders pension credit toward summer jobs, such as lifeguarding.)

UNCOVERING FRAUD

A recent review of the Defense Contract Audit Agency revealed that in 2001 the agency fabricated (and destroyed) documents in order to receive a passing grade from the IRS. The DCAA, which is responsible for auditing government contracts, blew 983 hours and $63,000 creating the fraudulent documents. The task was so difficult that they had to call in additional auditors—for which they billed the American taxpayers $1,600 in travel expenses.

ACCURATE CENSUS REPORTING

In 2003 the U.S. Census Bureau reported that according to statistics compiled by their researchers, more than 200 people living in Indianapolis, Indiana, traveled to work by subway or ferry. However, there are no subways or ferries in Indianapolis.

GI BILLS

In 2002 the General Accounting Office reported finding that at least 200 Army personnel spent $38,000 on personal expenses using Defense Department-issued credit cards. According to reports, many of the charges (including "lap dancing") were made at strip clubs near military bases. Other charges: mortgage payments, racetrack betting, Internet gambling, and Elvis photos from Graceland. Further investigation revealed that many government offices abuse charge card programs. Some examples cited by the GAO: laptop computers, pet supplies, DVD players, pizzas, and $30,000 worth of Palm Pilots.

THE DEPARTMENT OF DUMPSTER DIVING

Before approving benefits, the Oregon Department of Human Services requires all welfare applicants to take an informational workshop on saving money. As part of the program, attendees in 2001 received a list of 17 suggested "saving" techniques, one of which was to "check the dump and residential or business dumpsters."

PROVIDING ROLE MODELS

In April 2000, during the late hours of an all-night session of the Massachusetts legislature, a representative in the middle of a passionate speech on gun control asked members, "Are you leaders or followers?" A chant of "We lead!" erupted from the floor, followed by shouts of "Toga! Toga!" Assistant Majority Whip Salvatore DiMasi (D-Boston) responded with a call for "order in the Animal House." How did things get so out of control? Apparently, a member of the House had sponsored a wine and beer tasting in conjunction with a vote on the state budget. When voting took place, many members were drunk. One representative was rumored to have had his legs shaved by his colleagues while he was passed out.

Q: What is a *natal cleft?* A: The medical term for butt-crack.

PUTTING REVENGE ON THE MAP

*Here's a look at four towns that got their names
from folks who didn't get mad...they got even.*

BILLINGS, MONTANA
The Northern Pacific Railroad Company hoped to run its
railroad tracks through the town of Coulson in the early
1880s, but the three men who owned most of the surrounding land
wanted more money than the railroad was willing to pay. So
Northern Pacific moved the tracks and built its own town, which it
named after the railroad's president, Frederick Billings. Coulson was
a ghost town by 1885; today Billings is the largest city in Montana.

FREEPORT, ILLINOIS
Founded in 1835, the town was named by the wife of William
"Tutty" Baker, who operated a trading post and a ferry across the
Pecatonica River. Mrs. Baker was mad at her husband for turning
their house into a "free port" by taking in any stranger who came
to town.

TOMBSTONE, ARIZONA
When prospector Ed Schieffelin told a soldier that he wanted to
prospect for silver in an area controlled by Apaches, the soldier
laughed and told him the only thing he'd find there was his own
tombstone. When he found a giant vein of silver in 1878,
Schieffelin named the mining camp Tombstone to spite the soldier.

WORCESTER, MASSACHUSETTS
The village was named Quinsigamond until 1684, when England's
King Charles II cancelled the charter of the Massachusetts Bay
Colony, one of the original English settlements in what is now the
state of Massachusetts. The citizens of Quinsigamond were so mad
they renamed their village after the Battle of Worcester in the
English Civil War (1651), which Charles (then King of Scotland)
lost to Oliver Cromwell, forcing him to flee to France.

DUMBERER CROOKS

Our favorite crooks are the ones who do something
dumb, and then do something even dumber.

EMPTY YOUR BRAINS IN THIS TRAY

"Clyde Lamar Pace II made two mistakes. The first, Polk County sheriff's deputies say, was when he emptied his pockets to pass through a courthouse metal detector and apparently forgot about the small bag of marijuana. He threw it in a baggie without realizing it, and the person working the security post said, 'Hey, what's this?' Chief Deputy Bill Vaughn said. 'He gave that old "uh-oh, I've-been-caught" look, and the chase was on.' The second mistake was when he ran away from deputies, directly into a locked revolving door. Pace, 18, was arrested for drug possession and resisting arrest."
—*The Des Moines Register*

THANKS, MOM

"Trilane A. Ludwig, 24, of Vancouver, was arrested after a traffic stop early New Year's Day. At 5:30 a.m. he called his mother, Angela Beckham, and asked her to bail him out with the money in his wallet. She handed $500 to a clerk, who suspected the money was phony and called police. The police report described the counterfeit bills as bad copies that were the wrong size. Beckham said she wasn't going to shell out any real cash to bail him out. The case has been referred to the Secret Service."
—*Kansas City Star*

THEY'LL NEVER FIND ME HERE...OR HERE

"In December 1999, Christopher S. Newsome broke into the Randolph County Courthouse in Muncie, Indiana, and stole $25 from the receptionist's desk. He then hid in a closet, where a janitor found him. When the janitor went to call authorities, Newsome sprinted out of the courthouse, through a parking lot, and toward a nearby building. Unfortunately for Newsome, that building was the county jail. Moments later, the 26-year-old was in handcuffs."
—*Realpolice.net*

The president and vice president of the United States are not allowed to travel together.

HOW'D YOU GUYS FIND ME?

"Police didn't have much trouble finding Joshua W. Kochell, 27, who they say robbed two Lafayette, Indiana, gas stations. They tracked him through the monitoring device he was ordered to wear on a 2001 sentence for theft and habitual offense. Kochell was being held in Tippecanoe County Jail on $60,000 bond."

—**Associated Press**

GUILTY AND GUILTIER

"A New York woman who was given probation for robbery faces four years in jail after punching a juror outside the court. Octavia Williams came face-to-face with juror Geraldine Goldring just after Goldring and the other jurors found her guilty of stealing $160 from a woman in Times Square. Williams ran off after the assault but was caught and returned to the courtroom, where she was charged with assault and contempt of court for ignoring the judge's instructions to report to probation immediately after the verdict."

—*New York Daily News*

NOTE TO SELF...

"Police in Hillsborough, North Carolina, responded to a call from a bank about a man who was acting suspiciously. Capt. Dexter Davis confronted the man and asked if he had a weapon. 'He pulled his book bag off his shoulders, opened the bag up and held it open to me to show he didn't have a gun,' Davis said. When Davis looked inside, there was a note in clear view. It read, 'I want $10,000 in $100 bills. Don't push no buttons, or I'll shot [sic] you.' Davis laughed out loud, and then arrested Christopher Fields (who also was carrying a 10-inch knife) and turned him over to the FBI."

—*Durham Herald-Sun*

CRASH TEST DUMMY

"In Springfield, Illinois, Zachary Holloway, 20, and a pal were arrested and charged with breaking into one car and stealing, among other things, a motorcycle helmet, then attempting to break into another car. To try to get into the second car, Holloway put on the helmet, stood back from the car and charged into it, head-butting a window, unsuccessfully, twice."

—*"The Edge," The Oregonian*

KNOW YOUR GLOBE

Okay, class—time for a pop geography quiz. This one was sent in by BRI member Matthew Rosenberg, author of The Handy Geography Answer Book. *(Answers on page 513...but NO CHEATING!)*

1. Most states in the United States are divided into counties—but one state is divided into parishes instead. Which state?

    a) Louisiana   **b)** Utah
    c) Pennsylvania   **d)** Georgia

2. The Andes Mountains extend the entire length of South America. What city, located in the Andes, is the world's highest capital?

    a) Lima, Peru   **b)** Santiago, Chile
    c) La Paz, Bolivia   **d)** Asunción, Paraguay

3. The Walloons, who speak French, and the Flemings, who speak Flemish, are the two cultural groups that make up what country?

    a) Algeria   **b)** Belgium
    c) Cyprus   **d)** Equatorial Guinea

4. The Amazon is the largest river by water volume, but not by length. What is the longest river in the world?

    a) Nile   **b)** Mississippi
    c) Yangtze   **d)** Danube

5. At 14,494 feet, Mount Whitney is the highest point in the continental United States. Where is the lowest point?

    a) Grand Canyon   **b)** Bonneville Salt Flats
    c) Everglades   **d)** Death Valley

6. The world's largest monolith, Ayers Rock (1.5 miles wide and 1,100 feet high), is in Australia. What do the Aborigines call it?

    a) Azores   **b)** Uluru
    c) Azimuth   **d)** Illuka

7. A desert is an area with little precipitation and few plants. What is a semi-arid grassy area on the periphery of a desert called?

    a) Steppe   **b)** Strath

    c) Fallow   **d)** Drumlin

8. A small, steep-sided hill with a flat top is a pinnacle; a medium-sized one is a butte. What is a large one called?

    a) Mesa   **b)** Arroyo

    c) Piedmont   **d)** Atoll

9. *Tsunami* is a Japanese term used to describe tidal waves that are triggered by what?

    a) Oil drilling   **b)** Whale migration

    c) El Niño   **d)** Underwater earthquakes

10. English is the second most commonly spoken language in the world. Hindi is the third. What's the first?

    a) Spanish   **b)** Russian

    c) Arabic   **d)** Mandarin

11. Since Australia is considered a continent, not an island, what is the largest island in the world?

    a) Greenland   **b)** Great Britain

    c) Cyprus   **d)** Madagascar

12. A landlocked country is one that has no sea coast. Which of these countries is landlocked?

    a) Botswana   **b)** Ghana

    c) Kenya   **d)** Mauritania

13. Granite is a type of rock formed from cooled magma. What is the geologic term for this type of rock?

    a) Metamorphic   **b)** Sedimentary

    c) Stratus   **d)** Igneous

14. The international date line is bent in several locations, but it generally runs along which line of longitude?

a) 0 degrees
b) 45 degrees
c) 90 degrees
d) 180 degrees

15. California is the most populous state in the United States. What's the least populous?

a) Wyoming
b) Rhode Island
c) Montana
d) North Dakota

16. There are four main islands that make up the country of Japan. Which of these is not one of them?

a) Honshu
b) Shikoku
c) Sapporo
d) Hokkaido

17. The Earth's 23.5-degree tilt causes the sun's rays to hit the northern and southern hemispheres differently. What is the result?

a) Time zones
b) Seasons
c) Ice ages
d) Day and night

18. South Africa has three capitals. Cape Town is the legislative capital; Bloemfontein is the judicial. What is the administrative capital?

a) Pretoria
b) Durban
c) Johannesburg
d) Gaborone

19. What is the only country in the world that has no official capital?

a) Nauru
b) Palau
c) Kiribati
d) Marshall Islands

20. In 1887 L. L. Zamenhof developed a new language to solve communication problems between different cultures. What was it?

a) Pidgin
b) Creole
c) Esperanto
d) Pig Latin

VIDEO TREASURES

Ever been in a video store with no idea what to rent? It happens to us all the time. So we decided to offer a few recommendations.

BOB ROBERTS (1992) *Comedy*
Review: "Smart, funny political satire about a right-wing, folk-singing senatorial candidate who knows how to manipulate an audience—and the media." (*Leonard Maltin's Movie & Video Guide*) *Director/Star:* Tim Robbins.

THE TRIPLETS OF BELLEVILLE (2003) *Foreign/Animated*
Review: "This animated film doesn't need subtitles to tell a story that unfolds in a series of extraordinary images involving a boy, a dog, the Tour de France, the French mafia, and jazz-playing triplets. It's comic, touching, and a visual knockout." (*Rolling Stone*) *Director:* Sylvain Chomet.

PARENTS (1989) *Horror/Comedy*
Review: "Dark satire of middle class suburban life in the '50s, centering on a young boy who discovers that his parents aren't getting their meat from the local butcher. Gives new meaning to leftovers and boasts a very disturbing barbecue scene." (*Videohound's Golden Movie Retriever*) *Stars:* Randy Quaid, Mary Beth Hurt. *Director:* Bob Balaban.

PI (1998) *Thriller*
Review: "An obsessive mathematician seeks to find a number that will explain the universe. Gripping, clever theological and psychological thriller." (*Halliwell's Film and Video Guide*) *Stars:* Sean Gullette, Ben Shenkman. *Director:* Darren Aronofsky.

MICROCOSMOS (1996) *Documentary*
Review: "What *Winged Migration* did for birds, this film does for the insect world. An astonishingly up-close and personal look at an infinitesimal world as alien as anything captured by the Hubble telescope—but also a world of strange and unexpected beauty." (*Decent Films Guide*) *Directors:* Claude Nuridsany, Marie Perennou.

The crew of the *Enterprise* under Captain Kirk's command: 430. Under Picard: 1,012.

WELCOME TO THE DOLLHOUSE (1996) *Comedy/Drama*
Review: "Intensely personal tragicomedy about an 11-year-old girl facing vicious ridicule in junior high is an often somber (and more often hilarious) look at pre-teen 'society.' Winner of the Grand Jury Prize at the Sundance Film Festival." (*Filmcritic.com*) *Stars:* Heather Matarazzo, Brendan Sexton, Jr. *Director:* Todd Solondz.

HAPPY ACCIDENTS (2000) *Romance*
Review: "Ruby is a magnet for men with issues. Just when she thinks Sam is normal and romantic, he drops a bombshell—he claims he's a time-traveler from the year 2470. It's fun to speculate all through the movie whether he's crazy or telling the truth." (*themoviechicks.com*) *Stars:* Marisa Tomei, Vincent D'Onofrio. *Director:* Brad Anderson.

MY DOG SKIP (2000) *Family*
Review: "Sweet (but not cloying) family film of author Willie Morris' memoir of growing up in the 1940s with his beloved English fox terrier, who helps him through childhood and adolescence. Warm and winning for grownups as well as children...but have a handkerchief handy!" (*Leonard Maltin's Movie and Video Guide*) *Stars:* Frankie Muniz, Diane Lane, Kevin Bacon. *Director:* Jay Russell.

HEAVENLY CREATURES (1994) *Drama*
Review: "Two New Zealand schoolgirls conspire to murder one girl's mother when parental concerns about their obsessive friendship threaten to separate them forever. Surreal scenes featuring unicorns, giant butterflies, castles, and claymation knights express the teens' emotional slide into chilling actions." (*Video Movie Guide*) *Stars:* Kate Winslet, Melanie Lynskey. *Director:* Peter Jackson.

THE GAME (1997) *Thriller*
Review: "A mysterious company specializes in a tailor-made game. The player doesn't know its point, purpose, or overall design until it's over. An unusually imaginative thriller that bends its offbeat plot into so many twists that you actually have to pay attention." (*Christian Science Monitor*) *Stars:* Michael Douglas, Sean Penn. *Director:* David Fincher.

On average, Hawaiian residents outlive those of all other U.S. states.

BEST PRANKS EVER

Don't look now, but your fly is open. Ha ha—made you look!

G IVE ME TACOS OR GIVE ME DEATH!
Prank: In 1996 the fast-food chain Taco Bell issued a brief statement announcing its purchase of the Liberty Bell. According to the press release, Taco Bell was responding to an inquiry from the U.S. government about the possibility of reducing the national debt by selling off its national treasures to corporations. Taco Bell thought the Liberty Bell would make the ideal company logo. In fact, they planned to rename it the Taco Liberty Bell.

Reaction: Then, just a few hours after the announcement, Taco Bell quietly issued a retraction, saying the whole thing had been a big joke. But by that time, the story had been widely reported by the news media. At a press briefing the next day, White House press secretary Mike McCurry was bombarded by hostile reporters who hadn't yet heard the whole thing was a hoax. "We will also be selling the Lincoln Memorial to Ford Motor Company," McCurry said, "and renaming it the Lincoln-Mercury Memorial."

PAPER TRAIL

Prank #1: The English paper manufacturer Donside holds an annual contest for graphic design students. The theme of the contest in 2000 was "Tell a Lie Convincingly," using paper in some way. After hundreds of entries had been sent in, the participating schools received a letter from Donside Paper stating that the contest had been called off. Disappointed design students all over England began calling Donside to complain. But it turned out Donside hadn't cancelled the contest. The letter was a prank...or a very clever contest entry.

Prank #2: Just as Donside scrambled to get the contest back underway, students received another notice: the final deadline had been moved up. Entrants rushed to get their projects in on time, completely unaware that they'd been fooled again. Who sent the letters? No one knows.

Reaction: Despite the fact that the Donside Paper Company announced that they wouldn't punish the culprits and even offered

---

A newborn baby's heart has the same number of cells as an adult's.

to judge the pranks as contest entries, nobody ever came forward to claim responsibility for them.

A MONUMENTAL HOAX

Prank: Every student election seems to have a joke candidate, and the 1979 student body president election at the University of Wisconsin was no exception. Jim Mallon and Leon Varjian campaigned on a unique platform: to purchase and relocate the Statue of Liberty to Madison, Wisconsin.

Amazingly, they won. But voters didn't take the pledge seriously—Mallon and Varjian couldn't actually pull the stunt off. Or could they?

One winter morning, the instantly recognizable head and torch of the Statue of Liberty appeared, poking out from nearby Lake Mendota. Varjian told the UW student paper that he and Mallon tried to fulfill their campaign promise—but the cable transporting the statue via helicopter broke and, tragically, dropped the statue, partially submerging it. It wasn't the real statue, of course—it was plywood papier-mâché and chicken wire; Mallon and Varjian had been secretly overseeing its construction for months. (The two insisted that it was the real Statue of Liberty.)

Aftermath: The student newspaper later revealed that $4,500 of student money had been used to make the statue. Mallon and Varjian's response: they offered to write a check to any interested student for their individual share of wasted funds—10¢ each. The statue was destroyed by unknown arsonists three weeks later, but the prankster duo won again next year and rebuilt the statue (this time they spent $6,000). That one was removed by the Wisconsin Department of Natural Resources. It now lives in a shed on campus.

* * *

IRONIC, ISN'T IT?

In 1976 Supreme Court Justice William J. Brennan, Jr. co-authored the landmark "Buckley Decision," striking down all limits on spending for political campaigns. In 1995 a powerful group of lawyers and political players in New York began working to get the controversial law overturned. The group: The William J. Brennan, Jr. Center for Justice, made up of family, friends, and former law clerks of the late Justice Brennan.

Hidden meaning? A man's brain is 2% of his body weight, a woman's is 2.5%.

YOU'VE GOT MAIL!

*Like anyone with an e-mail address, we at the BRI get a
lot of unsolicited e-mail that seems too good—or bad—
to be true. We looked into claims made by some
of them, and here's what we found.*

E-MAIL MESSAGE:

> **To:** YOU
> **From:** Illegal_Downloads_Division@FBI.GOV
> **Subject:** Illegal File Downloading
> Ladies and Gentlemen: Downloading of Movies, MP3s
> and Software is illegal and punishable by law. We hereby
> inform you that your computer was scanned and the
> contents have been confiscated as evidence. You will be
> indicted. In the next few days you will receive the charge
> in writing. —Illegal Downloads Division, FBI

ORIGIN: This e-mail has been circulating at least since 2003
and probably longer than that.

THE TRUTH: Relax. Yes, downloading copyrighted material is
illegal, but the FBI didn't send this e-mail. If you received it, your
files haven't really been scanned or confiscated, and you won't
really be indicted...at least not as a consequence of this e-mail.

E-MAIL MESSAGE:

> **To:** eBay user
> **From:** eBay Accounts Management@ebay.com
> **Subject:** Your Billing Information
> We at eBay are sorry to inform you that we are having
> problems with the billing information of your account. We
> would appreciate it if you would visit our website, eBay
> Billing Center, and fill out the proper information that we
> need to keep you as an eBay member.

ORIGIN: This particular e-mail started circulating in 2004, but
similar ones have been floating around the Internet for about as

---

The surface of Venus has been better mapped than the sea beds of Earth.

long as eBay has been in business.

THE TRUTH: E-mails like these are known as "phishing." They imitate legitimate businesses to con people into revealing sensitive financial information, such as credit card and Social Security numbers. eBay gets hit so often, it has set up a special e-mail address, spoof@ebay.com, so that anyone who receives an eBay spoof can report it. Rule of thumb: Legitimate businesses will never e-mail you with a request to send them your personal information. No matter how legitimate the e-mail looks, ignore it.

E-MAIL MESSAGE:

> **To:** The American Taxpayer
> **From:** Outraged Citizen@yahoo.com
> **Subject:** Politicians' Golden Retirement Plan
> Our Senators and Congressmen don't pay into Social Security, and, of course, they don't collect from it. The reason is that they have a special retirement plan that they voted for themselves many years ago. It works like this: When they retire, they continue to draw their full pay until they die, and they get cost-of-living adjustments too. This would be well and good, except that they paid nothing in on any kind of retirement. This money comes right out of the General Fund—in other words, our tax money.

ORIGIN: This e-mail began circulating in April 2000. The full version claims that senators with the most seniority can expect to collect nearly $8 million over their lifetimes without contributing a cent of their own money. And when they die, their widows collect $275,000 per year until *they* die.

THE TRUTH: Say what you want about elected officials, but nearly every "fact" cited in this e-mail is false. Senators and congressmen *do* pay Social Security taxes and are required to contribute to the Federal Employees Retirement System. At last report the average retired member of Congress collected just under $47,000 a year in retirement. At that rate, it would take them 160 years to collect the $8 million claimed here.

THE WORLD'S WORST POET

Great poetry must be considered art—
It tickles the brain and stabs at the heart.
Could there be a worse poet than Uncle John?
It's all in the story that follows; read on.

ALL FIRED UP

One afternoon in June 1877, an impoverished Scottish weaver named William McGonagall fell into a funk. McGonagall was depressed because he wanted to escape the gritty industrial city of Dundee for a few days in the countryside, but he couldn't afford a train ticket. He was stuck at home, and to make matters worse, he was starting to feel a little funny. Was it a cold? The flu?

Hardly. As McGonagall later wrote in his autobiography, it was something else entirely: Divine Inspiration.

> I seemed to feel as it were a strange kind of feeling stealing over me. A flame...seemed to kindle up my entire frame, along with a strong desire to write poetry. I began to pace backwards and forwards in the room, trying to shake off all thought of writing poetry; but the more I tried, the more strong the sensation became. It was so strong, I imagined that a pen was in my right hand, and a voice crying, "Write! Write!"

So McGonagall wrote. His first poem was a tribute to his friend, the Reverend George Gilfillan:

> The first time I heard him speak,
> 'Twas in the Kinnaird Hall,
> Lecturing on the Garibaldi movement,
> As loud as he could bawl.
>
> My blessing on his noble form,
> and on his lofty head,
> May all good angels guard him while he's living,
> And hereafter when he's dead.

A female lobster is called a *hen* or a *chicken*.

A BARD IS BORN

McGonagall showed the poem to Reverend Gilfillan, who remarked diplomatically, "Shakespeare never wrote anything like this!" Encouraged, McGonagall dropped a copy into the mailbox of the *Weekly News*, hoping they might print it. They did...and he was off on a new career.

McGonagall already had a reputation for being an eccentric: His impromptu performances of Shakespeare's plays at the factory where he worked were so bad they were funny, and his co-workers once rented a theater to watch him make a fool of himself alongside professional actors.

But it was McGonagall's poetry that cemented his fame as a local nut. He sold his poems on the street and gave readings at local pubs. And as with his Shakespeare performances, his readings were so funny that people rented halls and subsidized his performances just so they could laugh at his work. Unfortunately, they also pelted him with pies, wet towels, rotten eggs, and garbage while he read his poems. It got so bad that McGonagall refused to perform unless a clergyman sat next to him onstage to keep people from throwing things.

OUCH!

How did McGonagall cope with the abuse? Though his poetry was awful, he never doubted his own talent and refused to believe that his audiences were there to laugh at him. But it was so unrelenting that, by the early 1890s, McGonagall began threatening (in verse) to leave the city forever. Would he really leave? In 1892 the *Scottish Leader* speculated that "...when he discovers the full value of the circumstance that Dundee rhymes with 1893, he may be induced to reconsider his decision and stay for yet a year." McGonagall stayed until 1894, when he moved to Edinburgh. There he continued writing poetry until ill health forced him to lay down his pen forever. McGonagall passed away in 1902, at the age of 77, and was buried in an unmarked pauper's grave in Greyfriars Kirkyard. The grave remained unmarked until 1999, when the city of Edinburgh finally erected a plaque at the cemetery. The *Oxford Companion to English Literature* says he "enjoys a reputation as the world's worst poet," and more than a century after his death, his poems are still in print.

See for yourself: Virginia extends 95 miles further west than West Virginia.

A MCGONAGALL SAMPLER

*So is William McGonagall the worst
poet ever? Here are selections from
his poetry to help you decide.*

ALAS! Sir John Ogilvy is dead,
aged eighty-seven,
But I hope his soul is now in
heaven;
He was a public benefactor in
many ways,
Especially in erecting an asylum
for imbecile children to spend
their days.
—*The Late Sir John Ogilvy*

And from the British battleships
a fierce cannonade did boom;
And continued from six in the
morning till two o'clock in the
afternoon.
And by the 26th of July the guns
of Fort Moro were destroyed
And the French and Spaniards
were greatly annoyed.
—*The Capture of Havana*

ALAS! Lord and Lady Dalhousie
are dead, and buried at last,
Which causes many people to feel
a little downcast.
—*Death of Lord & Lady
Dalhousie*

Ye sons of Great Britain, I think
no shame
To write in praise of brave
General Graham!
Whose name will be handed down
to posterity without any stigma,
Because, at the battle of El-Teb,
he defeated Osman Digna.
—*The Battle of El-Teb*

Arabi's army was about seventy
thousand in all,
And, virtually speaking, it wasn't
very small.
—*The Battle of Tel-el-Kebir*

Beautiful city of Glasgow,
I now conclude my muse,
And to write in praise of thee
my pen does not refuse;
And, without fear of contradic-
tion, I will venture to say
You are the second grandest city
in Scotland at the present day!
—*Glasgow*

The New Yorkers boast about
their Brooklyn Bridge,
But in comparison to thee it
seems like a midge.
—*To the New Tay Bridge*

And when life's prospects may at
times appear dreary to ye,
Remember Alois Senefelder, the
discoverer of Lithography.
—*The Sprig of Moss*

He told me at once what was
ailing me;
He said I had been writing too
much poetry,
And from writing poetry I would
have to refrain,
Because I was suffering from
inflammation of the brain.
—*A Tribute to Dr. Murison*

The Roman poet Virgil spent the equivalent of $92,000 on a funeral for his pet fly.

FOOD FOR THOUGHT

You know what these foods taste like, but have you ever wondered how they got their names? For that matter, how did the word food *gets its name?*

Whiskey. This word is from the Gaelic *usquebaugh*, meaning "water of life."

Lasagne. Ancient Greeks used chamber pots called *lasanons*. So the Romans jokingly called any flat cooking pots *lasasum*. The food took on the name of its container.

Albacore. From the Arabic *al-bakrah* (young camel). That's how it tasted to some people.

Tutti-frutti. Ice cream made with several fruits. "Tutti frutti" is Italian for "all fruits."

Food. The word was *foda* ("sustenance") in Old English, *fode* in Middle English, and *food* in Modern English.

Pudding. From *boudin*, a gooey French dish of sausage encased in the intestines of animals.

Pinto beans. *Pinto* is "painted" in Spanish. The beans were so named for their mottled skins.

Rutabaga. The name comes from an Old Norse word meaning "baggy root."

Crawfish (or crayfish). Either way you pronounce it, this lobster-like critter got its name from the Old French word *crevisse*, meaning "crab."

Butterscotch. It doesn't contain any scotch or have any affiliation with Scotland—while the candy is cooling, it is "scotched" into squares. ("To scotch" something used to mean "to score" it.)

Corned beef. The "corn" in this dish refers to the corns of salt used to make salted beef.

Au gratin. From the French, this cooking method becomes "with scrapings." A dish served *au gratin* includes dried bread crumbs mixed with grated cheese and browned on top.

Ginger. Originating in India, this spice's name is from the Sanskrit *singabera* ("horn shaped") because of the roots.

Junk food. From the Dutch *jonket*. These were dried fish and salted meat rations fed to sailors on long voyages.

GOOOOOOOOOOOOOAL!

Weird tales from the world of football...no, soccer...no...

POT SHOTS. Newspapers reported in 2004 that Portuguese police were turning a blind eye to marijuana-smoking among fans at soccer matches—especially if they were English. A police spokesperson said they hoped it would keep the notoriously rowdy fans calm.

PIN-UP GUY. Swiss newspapers featured cut-out voodoo dolls of English soccer star David Beckham before the Switzerland/England match in the Euro 2004 games. "Let's all rip this page out, pin it on the wall and stick in nails, needles and staples," read the caption. "If we believe it will work, then it will." (It didn't.)

TASTES GREAT. LESS WINNING. The Bernard brewery offered Czech Republic football coach Karel Bruckner 60 liters of beer per year for the rest of his life if the team won the Euro 2004 competition. They also promised 160 liters to every player on the team. "While they will earn a lot of money if they win," said a brewery spokesman. "We think the offer of free beer is extra motivation and will inspire the team to go for gold." (They didn't win.)

KILL YOUR TELEVISION. Police in a Romanian town received several phone calls after explosions were heard all over town. Explanation: the Romanian team had just been knocked out of the Euro 2004 and several fans had thrown their TV sets out of their windows.

WARDROBE MALFUNCTION. During a game between two teams in the Belgian Football Association, a man ran onto the field and pulled the referee's pants and shorts down. Ref Jacky Temmerman said, "I looked very nice in front of a few hundred supporters. That man made a fool of me." The fan faces a lifetime ban from Belgian soccer games.

BLACK MAGIC WOMAN. An award winning Romanian sports photographer was banned from flying with the Romanian soccer team in 2003 because she's female—and women bring bad luck. The Romanian team is notoriously superstitious: Women aren't allowed on the team bus, players can't whistle on the bus, and the bus isn't allowed to drive in reverse while players are aboard.

DID THEY WEAR TRUNKS? Prison officials in Thailand wanted to avoid gambling and rivalry troubles during the Euro 2004 tournament. So they scheduled an actual game—inmates versus non-inmates. The non-inmates were trained soccer-playing elephants. They played to a 5-5 tie.

BRING IT ON! Turkish soccer commentator Ahmet Cakar is well-known as an outspoken critic of officials, coaches, players, fans, the game, his fellow Turks, and just about everyone in general. When asked in 2004 if he would enrage someone, he said, "Whoever dares can come and try and take my life." In March, 2004, an angry fan shot him five times in the stomach and groin. (He survived the attack.)

HE HAD A DREAM. In January 2004, nine-year-old English soccer fan Billy Harris had a dream: Middlesbrough would beat the Bolton Wanderers 2–1 to win the English League Cup...AND Boudewijn Zenden would score the winning goal. So his dad, who had never bet on a game before, put a £15 ($27) wager on the team. On February 29, Middlesbrough, a 60 to 1 long shot, beat the Bolton Wanderers and won the cup. The score was 2-1...and Boudewijn Zenden scored the winner. Dad won £900 ($1,600). "It was unbelievable," said Billy. "Now my mum's given me a notepad to write down all my dreams."

AIN'T THAT A KICK IN THE HEAD. "The wind tunnel we've developed enabled us to analyze David Beckham's sensational goal against Greece in the World Cup," said physicist Dr. Matt Carré of England's University of Sheffield. "We know that the shot left his foot at 80 mph from 27 meters out, moved laterally over two meters during its flight due to the amount of spin applied, and during the last half of its flight suddenly slowed to 42 mph, dipping into the top corner of the goal. The sudden deceleration happens at the moment when the airflow pattern around the ball changes, increasing drag by more than a hundred percent. This crucial airflow transition is affected both by the velocity and spinning rate of the ball and by its surface seam pattern. Beckham was instinctively applying some very sophisticated physics calculations in scoring the goal."

I SCARE NOTHING! EVEN YOU BECOME NAPKINS!

Here are some actual English subtitles from movies
made (and translated) in Hong Kong.

"Fat head! Look at you! You're full of cholesterol."

"The tongue is so ugly. Let's imagine it to be Tom Cruise."

"It took my seven digestive pills to dissolve your hairy crab!"

"Dance the lion for others for just some stinking money! It's like razing my brows with the kung-fu I taught you."

"Alternatively, you must follow my advice whenever I say 'maltose.'"

"If you nag on, I'll strangle you with chewing gum."

"A red moon? Why don't you say 'blue buttocks?'"

"Let us not forget to form a team up together and go into the country to inflict the pain of our karate feets on some ass of the giant lizard person."

"Catherine is a nasbian!"

"A poor band player I was, but now I am crocodile king."

"Aha! I forget nothing. Elephant balls!"

"Watch out! The road is very sweaty."

"The wet nurse wants rock candy to decoct papayas."

"Cool! You really can't see the edges of the tea-bag underwear."

"Beauty and charm is yours, to you I run. I'd never leave, even forced by gun. I'd always want you, even if you were a nun."

"I scare nothing! Even you become napkins!"

"Your dad is an iron worker, your mom sells beans!"

"Same old rules: no eyes, no groin."

"I'm Urine Pot the Hero!"

AMAZING LUCK

*Sometimes we're blessed with good luck, sometimes we're cursed
with bad luck, sometimes we get a little of both. Here are some
examples of people who lucked out...for better or worse.*

THAT SINKING FEELING

While on vacation in Orange Beach, Alabama, Mark Waters accidentally locked himself out of his condo. His solution: to go through his neighbor's apartment, climb out the window, scale the balcony, leap next door onto his balcony, and climb in his own window. The only problem: his condo was on the 14th floor. While he was climbing out of his neighbor's window, Waters slipped and fell. As he plummeted 14 stories, Waters was certain he faced imminent death. Instead, he landed in the condo swimming pool below. Suffering only a few broken ribs and a collapsed lung, Waters said, "I'm very convinced there is a God."

HE WAS STUNNED

In the summer of 2000, Laurence Webbler took his eight-year-old grandson Josh on a fishing trip. The Texas native was looking forward to relaxing and spending some quality time with his grandson, but unfortunately, while they were out, he suffered a heart attack. As Webbler lost consciousness, Josh sprang into action. He picked up the electronic fish stunner his grandpa had brought and jabbed him with 5,000 volts. "That was enough to get the old ticker going again," Webbler later commented.

LA BOMBA

Doctors at a military hospital in Bogota, Colombia, took off their surgical robes and put on bulletproof vests when Nicolas Sanchez was wheeled into the operating room. Why? Another soldier accidentally fired a grenade launcher at him and he had a live grenade embedded in his left thigh. It took the surgeons only three minutes to expose the device before a police bomb expert removed it from his leg and detonated it in an empty lot near the hospital. Pressed directly against Sanchez's femur, the explosive had failed to detonate.

Bummer! Over 4 million Americans suffer from chronic constipation.

TOUGH GUY

Donald Morehouse was shot in combat seven times during his service in the Korean War. Six rounds never made it past his bulletproof vest, but one slug entered through his left shoulder and lodged in his right side. The wounded Morehouse hiked to a M.A.S.H. unit, where medics successfully removed the bullet. Forty-eight years later, as Morehouse was undergoing routine bypass surgery in 2001, doctors made a startling discovery: Calcified scars showed that the .29-caliber bullet removed from his side in 1953 had in fact *passed through his heart.* Most people would have died minutes after sustaining such an injury; Morehouse walked three miles…and lived.

HANGNAIL

Jan Madsen was fixing the roof of his home outside of Berlin when he tripped and started sliding toward the roof's edge. As he scrambled to grab onto anything that might prevent his fall, Madsen's nail gun accidentally went off and shot him through the knee. It was excruciatingly painful, but the nail pinned his leg to a wooden support beam and held him there until rescue workers arrived an hour later and freed him.

BABY SAVES THE DAY

One afternoon in 1995 at the Kiddie Kove Nursery in Chicago, two-year-old Kolby Grinston reached up and innocently pulled the school's fire alarm. Teachers calmly filed their students outside as they had practiced many times before. Minutes later, as the children were waiting to return to their classroom, a car barreled through a red light and struck another vehicle, sending it across the nursery playground and crashing into the school. The car landed on top of a row of lockers, where the children would have been standing, hanging up their jackets and sweaters before their afternoon nap had Kolby not pulled the fire alarm.

*   *   *

SOMETHING TO LOOK FORWARD TO

Between the ages of 30 and 70, a person's nose may lengthen and widen by as much as half an inch.

Could it be true? Donkeys have the loudest farts in the animal kingdom.

THAT'S ABOUT THE SIZE OF IT

Most people never give a second thought to life's most important questions, such as: How tall should a bowling pin be? Fortunately for them, Uncle John does. Here's a look at the standard sizes of everyday objects.

Soccer Ball: Must measure between 27 and 28 inches in circumference and weigh 14 to 16 ounces.

Napkin (dinner): Should be no less than 183 square inches, unfolded. (A cocktail napkin should be no larger than 100 square inches, unfolded.)

Boulder: An "official" boulder must be at least 256 millimeters (10.07 inches) in diameter.

Pebble: A pebble must be no smaller than 4 millimeters (0.16 inch) and no larger than 64 millimeters (2.51 inches) in diameter.

Bowling ball: Should be 27 inches in circumference and weigh no more than 16 pounds.

Bowling pin: Should weigh between 3 pounds, 2 ounces and 3 pounds, 10 ounces and should be exactly 1 foot, 3 inches tall.

Dart: Cannot be more than 1 foot in length, or weigh more than 50 grams.

Dartboard: Must be hung so that the bull's-eye is 5 feet, 8 inches above the floor. The person throwing the dart must stand 7 feet, 9 1/4 inches from the board.

Wash cloth: Should be a square of cloth no smaller than 12 by 12 inches and no larger than 14 by 14 inches.

Compact car: Must weigh at least 3,000 pounds, but no more than 3,500.

Parachute: To slow a 200-pound person to a landing speed of 20 feet per second, a parachute must be 28 feet in diameter.

Golf ball: Must weigh no more than 1.62 ounces, with a diameter no less than 1.68 inches. (A standard tee is 2-1/8 inches long.)

King mattress: Must be no smaller than 80 inches long and 76 inches wide.

Jumbo egg: One dozen jumbo eggs should weigh no less than 30 ounces.

What fore? Americans spend over $630 million a year on golf balls.

THE CIA'S FIRST COUP, PART I

Few Americans know much about a secret coup orchestrated by the CIA in Iran in 1953. Yet it is one of the most important moments in the history of U.S. relations with the Muslim world. Here's the story.

LIVE FROM BAGHDAD

L In March 2003, the United States invaded Iraq, overthrew the dictatorship of Saddam Hussein, and began working toward the day when U.S. administrators would turn over control of the country to a new elected government in Iraq.

The war in Iraq was easily the most thoroughly documented "regime change" ever. CNN covered developments live, 24 hours a day. So did Fox News, MSNBC, the BBC, Deutsche Welle, Al-Jazeera, and every other news network worldwide. If you didn't have a TV or newspaper, you could follow events on the Internet. Breaking news was never more than a click away.

Compare that to another U.S. attempt at regime change: the 1953 CIA-sponsored coup in Iran, right next door to Iraq. It doesn't sound familiar? That's not surprising—CIA coups are *supposed* to be secret, and for nearly 50 years this one was as secret as the Iraq war was public.

Rumors have been circulating about it since the 1950s, especially in Iran. But it wasn't until April 2000—when the agency's own in-house history of the coup became public—that Americans got the first detailed account of U.S. involvement in the affair. And that only happened because someone leaked the history to the *New York Times*. Had that document not been leaked, much of what we now know about the coup would still be secret today.

DECLARATION OF INDEPENDENCE

Pop quiz: What do Iraq and Iran have in common? Answer: They both have lots of oil. For decades Great Britain had controlled Iran's oil industry, but by the early 1950s, the Iranians were ready for a change. On March 15, 1951, the Majlis (an elected assembly

---

The moon is 2,140 miles in diameter. That's less than the width of the continental U.S.

similar to the U.S. House of Representatives) voted to nationalize their country's oil industry and take it back from Great Britain.

The British government owned a 51% stake in the Anglo-Iranian Oil Company (now known as British Petroleum), a private company that had begun developing the Iranian oil fields in 1908. Iran was home to one-fourth of the world's proven petroleum reserves, and the British-built refinery at Abadan was the largest on Earth, supplying Europe with 90% of its oil. England had no known oil reserves of its own, nor did any of its colonies. If the nationalization of the Iranian oil industry was allowed to pass, Great Britain would be stripped of its most valuable foreign asset and the only source of oil it directly controlled.

And they weren't about to just let it happen.

By May 1952, the British had drawn up plans for invading Iran with 70,000 troops and seizing the oil fields and the Abadan refinery. But they were reluctant to do it without at least the tacit approval of their ally, the United States. President Truman was adamantly opposed and urged the British to resolve the dispute by negotiating with Iran.

BACKUP PLAN

Without U.S. support, the British scrapped their invasion plans. Rather than negotiate, however, they started planning a coup against Iran's nationalist prime minister, Dr. Mohammed Mossadegh. Truman refused to support the coup, too. When Mossadegh caught wind of it in October 1952, he broke off diplomatic relations with Britain and expelled all British diplomats from the country.

The coup had been thwarted, and Great Britain was even worse off than before. President Truman had no sympathy—he blamed the British government for refusing to negotiate. "We tried to get the block-headed British to have their oil company make a fair deal with Iran," Truman wrote in disgust to his former ambassador to Iran, Henry Grady. "No, no, they could not do that."

NASIR AL-DIN

President Truman *did* have sympathy for the Iranians as they struggled to gain control of their own natural resources. He was no fan of European colonialism, and British relations with Iran smacked of exactly that. They and the Russians had dominated and exploited Iran since the 1840s, when the country was ruled by an incompetent, despotic shah, Nasir al-Din.

The court of Nasir al-Din was something to behold: He had a harem of more than 1,000 wives and concubines, and through them had fathered hundreds of princes and princesses. Each one was a drain on the national treasury, so to support them Nasir al-Din set taxes exorbitantly high, raided the fortunes of Iran's wealthiest citizens, and sold government offices to the highest bidder.

After a while even these measures didn't generate enough cash, so Nasir al-Din began selling "concessions"—exclusive rights to build railroads and streetcar lines, irrigate farmland, buy and sell tobacco, mine for minerals, print the national currency, and anything else he could think of—to foreign businesses, for a pittance.

Nasir al-Din's successors continued the practice, and in 1901, his son Muzaffar al-Din sold what would turn out to be the biggest concession of all: the right to explore the southern part of the country for petroleum and natural gas. He sold Iran's most valuable natural resource to a British businessman named William Knox D'Arcy for £20,000, plus 16% of profits realized from the sale of any oil that was discovered.

ENOUGH IS ENOUGH

The D'Arcy concession, which was later purchased by the Anglo-Persian Oil Company (later changed to "Anglo-Iranian"), didn't attract much opposition at the time because oil had not been discovered yet in that area. What made Iranians *really* angry was when the shah tried to raise the price of sugar in 1905.

After decades of being sold out by their leaders and exploited by foreigners, Iranians decided they'd finally had enough when the price of sugar went up. Riots broke out in Tehran, and when a nationwide revolt seemed imminent, Muzaffar al-Din cancelled the sugar price increase and even agreed to a written constitution that would limit his power, as well as to an elected assembly (the *Majlis*) that would share power with him.

DEMOCRACY AT LAST?

The wholesale looting of Iran appeared to be over...but it wasn't. For one thing, Muzaffar al-Din died a week after he signed the new constitution, and his son and successor, Muhammad Ali, was openly hostile to democratic reforms. For another, the British and the Russians profited handsomely when Iran was for sale, so they had a lot to lose if the monarchy gave way to a constitutional democracy. In 1907 the two powers signed an agreement dividing the country into Russian and British spheres of influence. Then, together with Muhammad Ali, they began to fight back.

In 1908 they attempted to disperse the Majlis by force. The plan backfired, and Muhammad Ali was forced to abdicate in favor of his 12-year-old son, Sultan Ahmad. Then in 1911, the Majlis did the unthinkable—they hired an American banker named W. Morgan Shuster to be Iran's treasurer-general. Shuster immediately went to work straightening out the country's finances and reforming its corrupt tax system, a job that included exposing many of the secret deals that the British and Russians had used to exploit the country. That of course, was intolerable. In late 1911, Russia invaded Iran, overthrew the Majlis, and forced Shuster to resign.

DIVIDE AND CONQUER

The Iranian democratic experiment was over for now, but foreign manipulation of the Iranian government was only beginning:

• When World War I broke out in 1914, Iran declared neutrality but leaned in favor of the Germans (who were fighting the British and Russians). That prompted the latter two to send troops into Iran, and by the end of the war they occupied nearly the entire country—the Russians in the north and the British in the south.

• Following the Russian Revolution of 1917, the Russians withdrew from northern Iran, leaving the country wide open to the British. In 1919 they drafted a document called the Anglo-Persian Treaty and forced it on the shah. In effect, the "treaty" gave the British outright control of the Iranian army and treasury, as well as the country's transportation and communication systems. Then, to quell any dissent, the British declared martial law. With the stroke of a pen, Iran was reduced to little more than a British protectorate and the gas pump of the Royal Navy.

• By 1921 the country was on the verge of splitting apart, so the British encouraged a strong-willed army officer named Reza Khan to seize control of the government. In February 1921, Reza led 3,000 troops into Tehran and forced the shah to appoint him commander of the armed forces. In 1923 he became prime minister and in 1925 overthrew the shah. The following year he crowned himself shah and changed his name to Reza Pahlavi.

• Reza Pahlavi lasted until 1941, when the British and Russians overthrew him for leaning in favor of the Germans during World War II. They installed his 21-year-old son, Mohammed Reza Pahlavi, in his place.

CRUDE PLANS

Getting rid of Reza Pahlavi solved one problem, but it created another—Mohammed Reza was nothing like his iron-fisted father. Weak, fearful, and indecisive, he wasn't strong enough to impose his will on the country when nationalist sentiment came roaring back after the war.

The Majlis, which had been powerless during the reign of Reza Pahlavi, began to reassert itself. In 1947 it passed a law requiring the government to renegotiate the petroleum concession with the Anglo-Iranian Oil Company. And it really needed renegotiating.

After 40 years, Anglo-Iranian still had no Iranians on its board of directors. It had no Iranians in management positions and hadn't trained a single Iranian technician to help run the refinery at Abadan. British employees lived in spacious homes in a tidy company town with social clubs and a swimming pool; Iranian employees lived in rat-infested shanty towns with no indoor plumbing or electricity. Iran was supposed to receive 16% of the profits generated from the sale of crude oil, but Iranians weren't allowed to audit the company's books. And Iran was only entitled to a share of profits from the sale of *crude* oil—Anglo-Iranian kept the profits from refining and marketing the oil around the world.

Although Iran had a quarter of the world's proven oil reserves, the concession with the Anglo-Iranian Oil Company was so biased in favor of the British that Iran was making more money from exporting carpets than from exporting oil.

For more of the CIA's First Coup, turn to page 303.

NUDES & PRUDES

*Nudity can be shocking...and so can prudery. But these
characters demonstrate that whether you're dressed
or naked, you can still be dumb (and funny).*

NUDE...On Christmas Day 2003, Minneapolis firefighters
with sledgehammers knocked down the chimney of Uncle
Hugo's Bookstore and rescued a naked 34-year-old man
who was trapped inside. The man claimed he had stripped naked in
order to fit down the 12-by-12-inch chimney, and that he was looking for some keys he had accidently dropped down the shaft. Police
didn't buy it—and planned to charge him with attempted burglary.
"He doesn't appear to be a hard-core criminal," said Lieutenant
Mike Sauro, "just stupid."

PRUDE...Acting on a neighbor's complaint, in May 2004, police
in Barnsley, England, ordered a local man named Tony Watson to
do something about the naked lawn gnomes in his front yard or
face arrest for "causing public offense." Watson, an ex-army sergeant, complied by painting bathing suits on the gnomes. "We
have to take complaints from members of the public seriously," a
police spokesperson told reporters.

NUDE...In April 2004, a woman parking her car in Göttingen,
Germany, was confronted by a man who complained that she did a
bad job parking her car. According to police, the man was completely naked and ran after her "to communicate his displeasure
about the noise and time she had taken to park." The woman
swore at the man, then ran into her house and called authorities.

PRUDE...In 1998 the Navy charged a career officer with indecent exposure and conduct unbecoming an officer following an
incident at the Pensacola Naval Air Station in Florida. The incident: Lieutenant Patrick Callaghan, 28, had mooned a friend while
jogging on the base. "There are people who are real offended when
you take your pants down in a public street," Callaghan's commanding officer, Captain Terrence Riley, explained. At first,

Callaghan faced dismissal from the Navy for the prank, but officials let him off with only a letter of reprimand in the end.

NUDE...In January 2004, a businessman named Bill Martin bought a run-down nudist colony outside of Tampa, Florida, for $1.6 million and made plans to open a new business on the site. What kind of business? A *Christian* nudist colony. "The Bible very clearly states that when Adam and Eve were with God, they were naked," says executive director David Blood. "When people are right with God, they do not have to fear nudity."

PRUDE...A 51-year-old woman returning home from a date in 1991 kissed her friend goodnight and went inside her condo. The next day she received a notice from the homeowners association threatening her with a fine. The complaint read: "Resident seen kissing and doing bad things for over one hour." Kim Garrett insisted she only kissed her date once, then got out of his car and was back in the condo in less than a minute. "If they can judge my morals, which are not wrong, they can just keep passing rules," she said. "It will be just like living in Russia."

NUDE...In January 2004, Stephen Gough, 44, known as the "Naked Rambler," accomplished his goal of walking the length of the United Kingdom wearing only socks, walking boots, and a hat. His purpose: To encourage greater acceptance of the naked body. The 900-mile trip took a long time—seven months. Gough was arrested 16 times along the way and served two stints in jail for indecent exposure.

PRUDE...Mel Culver, a teacher in Waukesha, Wisconsin, asked the school district to remove the 2001 *Guinness Book of World Records* from all 17 elementary schools in the district. The book contains photos of models wearing "the world's most valuable bikini" and "the world's most expensive bra and panties." "Boys are asking to go to the library for the sole purpose of looking at these pictures," Culver wrote in her complaint. "The news of the pictures is spreading like wildfire." (The review committee voted 9–0 to reject her request.)

A GREAT APE

The United States has McGruff the Crime Dog. But what about the rest of the world? Well, South Africa has Max the crime-fighting gorilla—and he's real, not a cartoon.

PIT STOP

In 1997 an armed criminal named Isaac Mofokeng tried to break into a house near the Johannesburg Zoo. The homeowner caught him in the act and called police. Mofokeng fled into the zoo, jumped down into the gorilla pit and he found himself face to face with two gorillas: a 400-pound male named Max, and a smaller female named Lisa.

Max had lived almost all of his 26 years in the zoo, so he was used to humans, but he'd never been confronted like this before. Sensing that he and his mate were threatened, he grabbed Mofokeng in a giant hug, then bit him on the butt and slammed him against the wall of the enclosure. Terrified for his life, Mofokeng fired three shots from his .38, hitting Max in the neck and chest.

By then Max was pretty agitated. He attacked police officers as they entered the enclosure to arrest Mofokeng, and zoo officials had to subdue him with a tranquilizer dart. Max was rushed to a nearby hospital and registered under the name "Mr. M. Gorilla." Surgeons successfully removed the bullet from his neck but decided it was safer to leave the one in his shoulder. Luckily Max made a full recovery. A month later he received an apology from Mofokeng. "I wanna say I'm sorry to the gorilla," the burglar told reporters as he was being led from court. "I was just protecting myself."

PRIME PRIMATE

Max became the star attraction of the Johannesburg Zoo, as well as a national hero and a symbol of defiance to South Africans frustrated by the country's high crime rate. For his courage under fire he was awarded a bulletproof vest and named an honorary officer by the Johannesburg police force. Max lived out the rest of his life in peace and quiet, enjoying his favorite snacks of garlic, onions, and the occasional beer before dying in his sleep of old age in May 2004. He was 33.

Barnum's Animal Crackers celebrated their hundredth anniversary by adding koalas.

UNINTENDED CONSEQUENCES

Sometimes when a plan is put into action, the result can be something that no one could have predicted. But, hey—that's what makes life interesting.

WHAT HAPPENED: The approval of the drug Viagra by the FDA in 1998

INTENDED: Improved sexual performance in men and, thus, better physical relationships between couples

UNINTENDED: A sharp rise in the divorce rate among the elderly. Reports released between 2001 and 2003 dubbed the problem the "Viagra divorce." *USA Today* reported that "husbands previously unable to perform now confront 'Viagra wives' not excited to be asked once again for sex." This, according to the reports, often led the men to have affairs, which often resulted in divorce.

WHAT HAPPENED: The Roman army's victories in Asia Minor between 161 and 166 A.D.

INTENDED: Armenia, Syria, and Mesopotamia were annexed to the Roman Empire

UNINTENDED: The plague. Returning soldiers brought it back with them, and as much as half the entire population of Rome was decimated by the disease.

WHAT HAPPENED: The invention of "text messaging" on cell phones

INTENDED: Cell phone users can easily and silently send written messages

UNINTENDED: Cheating husbands and wives can more easily get caught by their spouses. A 2003 survey by a private investigation firm in Italy, the most cell phone–saturated country in Europe, found that nearly 90% of all cheaters who were caught, were caught because of their cell phones. Private eye Miriam Tomponzi told reporters that being able to send silent messages from anywhere had increased contact between illicit lovers. But it

---

Chock full o' nuts! The Old Testament mentions almonds 73 times.

also meant that saved "love letters" could be found by a suspicious spouse. She also said that since the advent of text messaging, her business was booming.

WHAT HAPPENED: A ban on smoking in bars in Winnipeg, Manitoba

INTENDED: A decrease in the health risks of cigarette smoke to bar-goers and workers in the city

UNINTENDED: The discovery of a mummified body in the wall of a bar. In December 2003, police found the body of Eduardo Sanchez, 21, behind a wall in the Village Cabaret. The club's owners said they had been aware of an offensive smell for a year but thought it was just normal bar odors: stale beer and cigarettes. When the smoking ban went into effect, the odor stood out and neighbors called police. Sanchez was a DJ at the club; police had been unable to solve the mystery of his disappearance in October 2002. They said it now appeared that Sanchez had crawled into a gap between two walls in the basement—for an unknown reason—and gotten stuck.

WHAT HAPPENED: The U.S. government's $1.3 billion "War on Cocaine" in Colombia

INTENDED: A decrease in cocaine use in the United States

UNINTENDED: An increase in heroin use in the United States. In 2001 the *Chicago Sun-Times* reported that under the U.S. plan, Colombian planes and helicopters were being used to go after coca plantations. Those aircraft had previously been used to search for poppy plantations. Poppy growers took advantage of the sudden freedom and started making record amounts of heroin…and shipping it to North America.

WHAT HAPPENED: America Online banned the word "breast" from its service in 1995

INTENDED: A decline in "cybersmut"

UNINTENDED: Breast cancer patients lost the ability to communicate vital information online. One subscriber even had her personal profile completely deleted. She tried to create a new one, but got a message from AOL saying she couldn't use "vulgar" words on their service. "I don't have any problem with

AOL trying to keep dirty words off their service," the American Cancer Society's Barbara LeStage told the *Boston Globe*, "but I don't consider 'breast' a dirty word." After a deluge of angry e-mails, AOL quickly allowed the word back on.

WHAT HAPPENED: The use of salicylic acid as early as the fifth century B.C. and its modern form, acetylsalicylic acid—better known as aspirin
INTENDED: Pain relief
UNINTENDED: The prevention of countless heart attacks and strokes. British scientist John Vane showed in 1971 that aspirin suppresses the production of hormones known as *prostaglandins*. They not only suppress the transmission of pain signals to the brain and reduce inflammation and fever, they also affect the blood's ability to clot. Blood clots are the leading cause of heart attacks and strokes—the leading cause of death in the Western world. Vane's research showed that small regular doses of aspirin could prevent their occurrence, for which he won a Nobel Prize.

WHAT HAPPENED: The creation of the DMZ (Demilitarized Zone) between North and South Korea at the end of the Korean War in 1953
INTENDED: The barbed wire–enclosed 2.5-by-150-mile strip of land would help preserve peace between two nations that, since 1953, have been officially "at war."
UNINTENDED: The DMZ is an environmental paradise. It's been virtually human-free for more than 50 years. Result: According to scientists, nearly 3,000 species of plants and animals thrive in the zone today—many that no longer exist in either country. That includes several severely endangered animals, such as Asiatic black bears, Siberian tigers, and two of the most endangered birds in the world: the white-naped crane and the red-crowned crane. In 1999 environmental leaders created a group called the DMZ Forum, which is trying to convince the two countries to turn the strip into a permanent nature reserve.

*　　　*　　　*

A Groaner: Birds are sad in the morning. Why? Their bills are over dew.

One reason cats scratch furniture: they have scent glands in their paws.

OL' JAY'S
BRAINTEASERS

BRI members enjoy trying to stump us with brainteasers and riddles. Now we try to stump you back. Answers are on page 515.

1. One morning while she was eating breakfast, Laura's diamond ring slipped off her finger and fell into a full cup of coffee, but the ring didn't get wet. Why not?

2. Sam's father is five years older than Sam's grandfather. How can this be?

3. What grows down while it grows up?

4. Five hundred begins it,
 five hundred ends it,
Five in the middle is seen.
The first of all letters, the first
 of all people,
Take their places in between.
Combine them all to make
 the name of a famous king.

5. What is the only professional sport in which neither the players nor the spectators know the score until the match is over?

6. What ship has two mates but no captain?

7. What is it that turns everything around but does not move itself?

8. What is the greatest worldwide use of cowhide?

9. I know a man who can shave 10 times a day and still have a full beard. Who is he?

10. My friend Julia was walking down Fifth Street when she found something that had no bones and no legs. She brought it home and put it on her windowsill. A week later, it walked away. What did Julia find?

11. I can sizzle like bacon,
I am made with an egg,
I have plenty of backbone, but
 lack a good leg.
I peel layers like onions, but
 still remain whole;
I can be long, like a flagpole,
 yet fit in a hole.
What am I?

12. Hi there! Ma and Pa told

The word *anthology* is Greek for "a collection of flowers."

me I'd better tell you that all the two-letter words in this paragraph have something in common—or else! What's the deal?

13. The first man is the master of priceless gems;
The second man is the master of love;
The third man is the master of shovels;
The fourth man is the master of big sticks;
Who are they?

14. What well-known object is described in this poetic riddle by the 19th-century English poet Sir Edmund Goss?

My love, when I gaze on they beautiful face,
Careering along, yet always in place,
The thought has often come into my mind
If I ever shall see thy glorious behind.

*　　*　　*

ROYAL SHAFT

In 2003 the British government leaked to the media a list of 300 artists, actors, and others who had refused knighthoods or titles such as Commander of the Order of the British Empire. Some examples:

• Winston Churchill declined a knighthood in 1945 because he was embarrassed after being voted out as prime minister. He finally accepted the honor in 1953—when he became prime minister again.

• Actress Helen Mirren turned down a Commander of the Order of the British Empire title in 1996 because she opposed the conservative government. When the liberal Labor party returned to power in 2003, Mirren happily accepted the title of Dame Helen.

• Poet Benjamin Zephaniah publicly rejected an Officer of the Order of the British Empire award because the title reminded him of "thousands of years of brutality" and English imperialism.

• Actor Albert Finney declined knighthood in 2000 because he felt the awards system contributed to the stereotype that the British are snobs.

Your eye muscles move an average of 100,000 times a day.

BEHIND THE HITS

*Ever wonder what inspired your favorite songs? Here
are the inside stories of some popular tunes.*

The Artist: Rick Nelson
The Song: "Garden Party" (1972)
The Story: Nelson was a teen idol in the early days of television, performing rock 'n' roll songs weekly on *The Adventures of Ozzie and Harriet* from the mid-1950s until the show was cancelled in 1966. In 1971 Nelson played a nostalgia show at New York's Madison Square Garden. The audience came to hear his hits ("Poor Little Fool," "Travelin' Man," etc.), so when Nelson played a set of new songs, he was booed off the stage. The next act, Chuck Berry, played only his hits ("Johnny B. Goode," "Maybelline," etc.) and the audience loved it. Frustrated and hurt, Nelson wrote "Garden Party" about the experience, with bitter lyrics like "if memories were all I sang I'd rather drive a truck." Ironically, Nelson's song about being rejected by audiences was embraced by those same audiences and became a top 10 smash. But he never had another hit.

The Artist: Red Hot Chili Peppers
The Song: "Under the Bridge" (1991)
The Story: After a decade as a punk-funk band little known outside Los Angeles, the Chili Peppers were possibly the unlikeliest group to score a pop hit, especially with a ballad. While recording the album *Blood Sugar Sex Magik*, the group was grasping for ideas when producer Rick Rubin discovered Anthony Kiedis's notebook and was moved by an unfinished poem the singer had written about his days as a homeless drug addict. He thought "Under the Bridge" would make a great song. Kiedis agreed to record it, figuring it would go nowhere. The album went on to sell 7 million copies, reach #2, and help make the Chili Peppers one of rock's biggest acts.

The Artist: Kyu Sakamoto
The Song: "Sukiyaki" (1963)
The Story: Sakamoto had Japan's biggest hit of 1962 with "Ue O Muite Aruko" ("I Look Up When I Walk"). Louis Benjamin, a

---

KISS bassist Gene Simmons speaks four languages and has a B.A. in education.

British record executive, heard the song while on vacation in Japan and brought it to an English musician, Kenny Ball, who'd had a hit with the import "Midnight in Moscow." Figuring DJs wouldn't be able to pronounce the title, Benjamin renamed it after the only Japanese word he knew, a beef-and-noodle dish called *sukiyaki*. Ball's version was a minor hit, and that prompted a DJ in Pasco, Washington, to play Sakamoto's original version. Listeners loved it. It gradually picked up steam, and was released by Capital Records under the name of the British version, "Sukiyaki." It is the only song sung in Japanese ever to hit #1 on the U.S. charts.

The Artist: Daryl Hall and John Oates
The Song: "Rich Girl" (1977)
The Story: Despite many years of hard work touring and recording, commercial success eluded Hall and Oates…until 1976, when Daryl Hall wrote this song. The inspiration: He had always despised an ex-boyfriend of his girlfriend: an obnoxious heir to a fast-food fortune who had had everything handed to him but appreciated nothing. Still, Hall thought "rich boy" might not sound right to record buyers, so he made the subject a "rich girl." The song was the breakthrough hit they had been waiting for, going to #1 in March 1977. The group would go on to sell 40 million albums and become the bestselling duo in music history. **Strange fact:** Serial killer David Berkowitz, the Son of Sam, told reporters that his murders were partially motivated by "Rich Girl."

The Artist: Frankie Goes to Hollywood
The Song: "Relax" (1983)
The Story: FGTH were arguably the biggest group since The Beatles to come out of Liverpool. As "Relax" climbed the English charts, a DJ for England's Radio One read the lyrics as the song played. He was appalled and yanked the song off the air, calling it obscene. (The lyrics aren't explicit, just sexually suggestive.) Radio One subsequently banned the song and BBC Television banned the video, but that of course only increased demand—people wanted to hear what the fuss was about. Result: The song hit the top of the charts. It later became popular in American dance clubs and has since become identified as one of the seminal songs of the 1980s.

LAST WORDS

Words associated with death and funerals are kind
of creepy. But they didn't start out that way.

C EMETERY. The Greek verb *koiman*, meaning "to put to sleep," led to the noun *koimeterion*, meaning "dormitory." It was early Greek Christian writers who first used the Latin translation of that word—*coemeterium*—to describe burial grounds.

AUTOPSY. A combination of *auto*, meaning "done by oneself," and *opsy*, meaning "seeing." *Autopsy* literally means "seeing or discovering for oneself," as in the true cause of someone's death.

MORGUE. The origin is French, despite the fact that it sounds like the Latin word *mors*, meaning "death." Initially a *morgue* was a room in a prison where new (live) prisoners were examined so that their bodies could be recognized, if necessary, in the future.

CORONER. From the Latin word *corona*, for "crown." *Coronae* was once the title of an English officer whose duties included collecting the king's income. English law stated that if someone died without a will, that person's property became the king's. It was the coronae's job to investigate deaths and determine whether a will had been written.

EMBALM. Stems from the Latin phrase *in balsamum*, which means "to put into balsam." Ancient cultures used to preserve bodies by rubbing a mixture of aromatic plant resins called balsam on the skin of a corpse.

PALLBEARER. Ancient Romans wore a square piece of cloth called a *pallium* over their shoulders. Over the centuries any covering came to be known as a "pall." Pallbearers—the men who carry a coffin at a funeral—once carried it under a "pall."

HEARSE. In Old French, *hearse* was the word for a harrow, a triangular farming tool. At the time, triangular frames were used to hold candles at the head of a coffin, and so they adopted the same name. Then, because the frame used to transport a coffin from house to church was also decorated with candles, it too came to be known as a hearse. Carriages replaced the need for the frames, but the name stayed.

What do U.S. presidents Theodore Roosevelt, John F. Kennedy, and Ronald Reagan...

UNCLE JOHN'S "CREATIVE TEACHING" AWARDS

If schools handed out degrees for dumb, these
teachers would have earned a Ph.D.

SUBJECT: Biology
WINNER: Miles Dowling, a carpentry teacher at North Shore Technical High School in Massachusetts
CREATIVE APPROACH: Mr. Dowling is also interested in taxidermy, so when he saw a dead coyote in the middle of the road in March 2003, he tossed it in the back of his pickup truck and brought it to school. Later that day he showed his students how animals are skinned; some of them even got to touch the dead coyote.

Dowling's students learned some other lessons when school administrators heard about the impromptu demonstration: 1) touching dead animals potentially exposes you to rabies, which is fatal if left untreated; 2) if the animal has been dead long enough, like the coyote, there's no way to tell if it has rabies; and 3) if you touch the animal, you have to get some really painful rabies shots.
REACTION: Dowling was suspended without pay, and the two students who touched the animal had to get the shots.

SUBJECT: Motivational Speaking
WINNER: Steven Rivers, a 7th-grade teacher in New York State
CREATIVE APPROACH: Mr. Rivers, a teacher for more than 30 years, routinely called his seventh graders "dumb" and "retards" when they misbehaved or answered questions incorrectly, and repeatedly singled out one particular student as a "failure" who "would never do anything in life." But why stop at words? In one incident he grabbed a student by the neck for giving the wrong answer to a math question.
REACTION: After a 17-month investigation, state officials found Rivers guilty of "conduct unbecoming a teacher, administering corporal punishment, and insubordination." He was put on unpaid leave for half a school year.
UPDATE: The local school board appealed the state's decision—

...have in common? They were all members of the NRA—and they were all shot.

they wanted Rivers fired. But at last report, he was planning to return to the classroom. "I'm looking forward to being back on the job," he told reporters.

SUBJECT: Chemistry

WINNER: Karmen Bosma Van Beek, a Talented and Gifted Program instructor at Sheldon High School in Iowa

CREATIVE APPROACH: On a school-sponsored trip to a mock trial competition in Des Moines in 2001, Mrs. Van Beek let some of her students sip from her alcoholic drink at dinner; afterward she shared a case of beer with four of them while they watched movies in her hotel room. When word of the beer bash circulated around school, Van Beek at first lied to cover her tracks and encouraged the students to do the same. She later confessed and attributed her misconduct to "stress from a difficult marriage."

REACTION: The state recommended that Van Beek get counseling and suspended her teaching license indefinitely.

SUBJECT: Fashion

WINNER: The Merriday Montessori School in Florida

CREATIVE APPROACH: The Florida Department of Children and Families launched an investigation into the school after a teacher reported how she dealt with an unruly student: she put the five-year-old boy in a dress and had the other kids laugh at him. (It was a yellow dress with flowers on it.) An investigation revealed that it may have been done to other students, too.

SUBJECT: Invisibility

WINNER: Teachers at Gillepsie Middle School, Philadelphia

CREATIVE APPROACH: In May 2004, 12-year-old Aubrey Wharton and his mother were summoned to appear in court to face truancy charges. The reason: records showed Aubrey had failed to attend class the previous year, and had the bad grades to show for it. Strangely, Aubrey freely admitted to not being at school. He was enrolled in a *different* school. Stranger still, along with two F's, the boy received a D, a C, and even a B at the school he didn't attend—and his behavior was graded as "excellent." The school quickly dropped the truancy charges; how he got grades for those classes is under investigation.

(BAD) DREAM HOUSES

Everyone thinks their own horror stories about buying a
new home are the worst, but they're not—these are. Note:
Some names have been changed to protect the gullible.

Dream House: In 1998 John and Mary Jones found theirs in South Carolina.

From Bad…They didn't get a home inspection before closing. Result: Right after they moved in, problems started. The kitchen sink backed up, the washing machine overflowed, and when the plumber came to fix the leaks, the bathroom floor caved in.

…To Nightmare! Then the air conditioner stopped working. The repairman figured the system was missing a filter, so he went into the attic to explore. But instead of a filter, he found bats—thousands of them. Even worse, over the years hundreds of gallons of bat guano had soaked into the insulation and wood of the structure, rendering the home a health hazard and completely uninhabitable. (Mary Jones developed a rare disease due to exposure from bat guano.)

Dream House: Bill Barnes of southern Maryland was trying to sell his house. Ari Ozman, who claimed to be a traveling salesman who was moving his family into the area, didn't want to buy—he wanted to rent. The market was a little slow, so when Ozman offered six months' rent in advance, Barnes jumped at it.

From Bad…Ozman wasn't a traveling salesman—he was a scam artist. He put an ad in the local paper, offering Barnes' house for sale at a bargain price and—no surprise—had more than 100 calls. And when buyers saw the space, they couldn't resist the deal. Ozman's terms: he'd reserve the house—for a $2,000 cash deposit.

…To Nightmare! He repeated the scam 30 times, collected $60,000, and then took off. Barnes was left with nothing except Ozman's security deposit and 30 angry "buyers."

Dream House: Jack Newman purchased his in Virginia in 2001.

From Bad…A few nights later, Newman was asleep in bed when a squadron of fighter jets tore across the sky. He practically jumped out of his skin. It turned out that there was a military base nearby

---

1957 was the first year Americans ate more margarine than butter.

and flight training took place 15 nights a month. Still, Newman decided to tough it out. Until the house started to smell.

...To Nightmare! Newman couldn't locate the source of the odor, so he called the Department of Environmental Quality, which found the cadaver of a rotting animal in the foundation (the foul smell was filtering in through cracks in the concrete). What else could go wrong? Plenty—the roof structure was caving in; the chimney was disconnected from the house; and the ground under the house was shifting. Newman's recourse: He had none—the builder had long since filed for bankruptcy and disappeared.

Dream House: Alan and Susan Sykes moved into theirs in West Yorkshire, England, in 2000.

From Bad... One evening a few months after moving in, the couple was watching a TV documentary about Dr. Samson Perera, a dental biologist who murdered his 13-year-old daughter and hid her dismembered body throughout his home and garden. Suddenly they recognized the house on TV: it was *their* house. When they got to the part that said the child's body—which had been cut into more than 100 pieces—was never fully recovered, the Sykeses packed their bags, moved out that same night...and never went back.

...To Nightmare! They sold the house (at a loss) and filed suit against the former owners, James and Alison Taylor-Rose, for withholding the house's history. The judge said that since the Taylor-Roses were unaware of the murder when *they* bought the house in 1998 (they only placed it on the market after a neighbor told them about it), they were not liable, so the Sykeses lost the suit.

Dream House: Cathie Kunkel found hers in Ontario, California.

From Bad... In August 2001, four months after she moved in, Kunkel had a pond dug in her backyard. After removing only a foot of earth, workers discovered something putrid. "We thought it was a dead chicken," said Kunkel. "The smell was horrendous." The contractor filled in the shallow grave, but the odor lingered. Kunkel and her three children had to move out.

...To Nightmare! It wasn't a chicken—it was a dead cow wrapped in plastic. The development was built on 18,000 acres of former dairy land...and they still don't know how many dead cows are buried there.

MARATHON OF HOPE

If you're Canadian you've probably already heard of Terry Fox. If you haven't, here's his incredible story.

D ETERMINATION
Terry Fox was born in 1958 and grew up in British Columbia. He was an average kid, with the exception of being very athletic—in high school he played hockey, basketball, lacrosse, and ran track. Then in 1976, shortly after graduating from high school, he was diagnosed with osteogenic sarcoma: bone cancer. A few months later, his right leg had to be amputated and Fox didn't think he'd ever be able to run or play sports again.

The night before the surgery, Fox's former basketball coach brought him a magazine article about an amputee who'd run in the New York Marathon. The story inspired Fox. He determined then and there not to let having an artificial leg prevent him from living the life he wanted to live. Fox decided to raise awareness about cancer and raise money for research by doing something nobody had ever done before: he would run across Canada.

THE RACE IS ON

For nearly two years, Fox prepared for his "Marathon of Hope." First he learned to walk with an artificial leg, then he learned to run, then he built up his endurance. Finally, on April 12, 1980, he flew to St. John's, Newfoundland, dipped his prosthetic leg in the Atlantic Ocean, and began his trek west, expecting that in a few months he'd dip it into the Pacific Ocean on the other side of the country.

The run began with almost no fanfare, but then the press picked up the story. They started detailing Fox's daily progress and suddenly all of Canada was rooting for him and bombarding his family with letters and donations. Fox's pace was staggering: every day he ran an average of 26 miles—the length of an entire marathon. Marathon runners typically train for months and spend weeks afterward recuperating. Fox was essentially running a marathon every day for months on end—with an artificial leg. Had anyone ever done something similar? No. The *Guinness Book of*

During the American Revolution, patriotic brides wore red dresses to symbolize rebellion.

World Records lists Rick Worley as the marathon record holder: he ran 200 straight marathons, but he did it over 159 consecutive weekends, not over days as Fox was trying to do.

Then, on September 1, 1980, the Marathon of Hope ended near Thunder Bay, Ontario. The cancer had come back and spread to Fox's lungs. After running for 143 days straight, through Newfoundland, Quebec, and Ontario—more than 3,300 miles— he had to abandon the quest and return home for treatment. Terry Fox died on June 28, 1981, just shy of his 23rd birthday, but his strength and determination remain beacons for an entire generation of Canadians.

FOX'S LEGACY

• During the actual run, Fox raised $1.7 million for cancer research.

• The day after the run ended, the Four Seasons hotel chain announced plans to sponsor an annual marathon in Fox's honor.

• That same week, a Terry Fox telethon raised $10 million.

• Fox was awarded the Companion of the Order of Canada (similar to a knighthood or a Presidential Medal of Freedom) and the Order of the Dogwood, British Columbia's highest civilian honor.

• In 1980 the Canadian press named him Canadian of the Year.

• An 8,700-foot Rocky Mountain peak was named Mount Terry Fox.

• A stretch of highway near the end of Fox's run was renamed the Terry Fox Courage Highway.

• Fox was memorialized on two postage stamps, had a Canadian Coast Guard ship named after him, and was named Canadian Athlete of the Decade (beating out Wayne Gretzky).

• In 1999 Terry Fox was voted Canada's greatest national hero of all time in a magazine survey.

• As of 2004, annual fund-raising Terry Fox Runs have donated more than $340 million to cancer research.

The Terry Fox Library in Port Coquitlam, B.C., houses 100,000 artifacts from Fox's life and the Marathon of Hope. One room is stacked floor-to-ceiling with boxes of letters and get-well cards. All kinds of people from all walks of life are represented, showing just how far Terry Fox reached. He only made it halfway across Canada, but he touched every corner of the country.

NICE CROOKS

If they were really nice, they probably wouldn't be crooks to begin with. But what else would you call a thief who apologizes?

GIMME TEN

At 5:00 a.m. on November 17, 2003, a man walked into a 7-Eleven in Santee, California, pulled out a gun, and told the clerk to give him $10. The clerk gave the man the money, and the man ran off. At 10:00 a.m. the same man returned to the store, put $10 on the counter, and apologized for the robbery. The clerk didn't wait for the apology—he immediately pressed the "panic" button under the counter. The police arrived and arrested the thief, who explained that he had stolen the money to buy gas for his car.

BEER NUT

Twenty-one-year-old Nicholas Larson stole a cash register from the Bonnema Brewing Co. in the town of Atascadero, California. Apparently he couldn't stand the guilt, because the next day he called the brewery to apologize. The kicker: He turned himself in for the theft—even though the register had been empty.

SHOOTING BLANKS

A man walked into a Kansas liquor store, pulled out a gun, and told the clerk, "Give me everything in the register." The clerk told him that it was empty—there was no money. "That's okay," the robber responded. "There aren't any bullets in the gun. I was just kidding."

CHANGE OF HEART

In January 2002, Ronald Van Allen went into the Savings Bank of Manchester in Manchester, Connecticut, and handed the teller a note. "This is a robbery!!" it read. "All I want is the money from the cash drawer. No one has to get hurt or shot but me. Sorry for your inconvenience." Van Allen left with $2,000, but four days later, he walked into the Manchester police department with a bag full of the money, apologized, and turned himself in. "I wish all of our cases were solved like this," said Detective Joseph Morrissey.

ANCIENT WISDOM

Very little has changed about human nature in the last 2,500 years, which may be why these pearls of wisdom still hold up today.

"A journey of a thousand miles begins with a single step."
—Confucius (551–479 B.C.)

"Let him who would move the world, first move himself."
—Socrates (469–399 B.C.)

"The birth of a man is the birth of his sorrow. The longer he lives, the more his anxiety to avoid unavoidable death. What bitterness! He lives for what is always out of reach! His thirst for survival in the future makes him incapable of living in the present."
—Chuang-Tzu (369–286 B.C.)

"What you cannot enforce, do not command."
—Sophocles (496–406 B.C.)

"The road up and the road down are one and the same."
—Heraclitus (540–480 B.C.)

"Once a word has been allowed to escape, it cannot be recalled."
—Horace (65–8 B.C.)

"Reserve your right to think, for even to think wrongly is better than not to think at all."
—Hypatia (350–415 A.D.)

"Slight not what's near, while aiming at what's far."
—Euripides (480–406 B.C.)

"To know that we know what we know, and to know that we do not know what we do not know, that is true knowledge."
—Copernicus (1473–1543 A.D.)

"After I'm dead I'd rather have people ask why I have no monument than why I have one."
—Cato the Elder (234–149 B.C.)

"It is not the oath that makes us believe the man, but the man the oath."
—Aeschylus (525–456 B.C.)

"Men often applaud an imitation and hiss the real thing."
—Aesop (620–560 B.C.)

"Remember: Upon the conduct of each depends the fate of all."
—Alexander the Great (356–323 B.C.)

"We sit together, the mountain and I, until only the mountain remains."
—Li Po (701–762 A.D.)

WOMEN IN SPACE, PART I

If you're interested in the history of space exploration, you've heard of the Mercury 7. But have you ever heard of their (unofficial) female counterparts, the Mercury 13? Here's their story.

THE RIGHT STUFF

On April 9, 1959, the National Aeronautics and Space Administration (NASA) introduced the seven astronauts who would take part in the Mercury Program. The goal: To put an American into orbit. It was America's first manned space program, and competition for the seven slots had been fierce. An original list of 508 military test pilots was winnowed down to 32 candidates, who were then subjected to a battery of intense medical, psychological, and spacecraft-simulator tests. Eighteen made the final cut, and from these the "Mercury 7"—Alan Shepard, Gus Grissom, John Glenn, Scott Carpenter, Walter Schirra, Gordon Cooper, and Donald "Deke" Slayton—were chosen.

WHY NOT WOMEN?

One of the people who helped design the medical tests was Dr. W. Randolph Lovelace II, a specialist in aviation medicine and chairman of NASA's Life Sciences Committee. Lovelace wondered how well *women* might do if they were subjected to the same tests. He took an even greater interest in the idea in the summer of 1959, when he made a trip to the USSR to study the Soviet space program. There he learned that the Russians were already looking into sending a woman into space. There were even rumors that the very first Soviet cosmonaut might be a woman.

Apparently, the Soviets felt that women had a great deal to offer the space program and that in some ways, they were better suited for space travel than men were. A typical female needed less oxygen, ate less food, and weighed less than a typical male. That would make for a smaller payload; no minor consideration at the dawn of the Space Age, when rockets were smaller and less powerful. Every pound that could be shaved from the total weight was critical. But were women physically and mentally tough enough for spaceflight? The Russians thought so, and so did Dr. Lovelace. But he wanted to test them to find out for sure.

CRITICAL TESTING

The Mercury 7 astronauts had undergone three phases of testing to qualify for the space program. Phase one—medical testing—was conducted at Lovelace's clinic in Albuquerque, New Mexico. Testing women there wouldn't be a problem, since it was a civilian facility, and he could run it as he pleased. But the second and third phases—psychological and spacecraft-simulator testing— were a different matter: For the Mercury 7, the tests had been done at Wright Air Development Center in Ohio. The female test subjects had no official ties to NASA, so the Air Force simply wasn't interested in testing them.

Lovelace decided to conduct phase-one testing at his clinic anyway. Then, if those results were promising, he thought he might be able to convince the Air Force or some other branch of the military to make its facilities available for further tests.

GETTING STARTED

Lovelace established several basic criteria for his subjects: they had to be 35 years of age or younger (he later raised the limit to 40), had to be in good health, and had to have a four-year college degree. They also had to have a commercial pilot's license with at least 1,000 hours of flying experience. That summer he met a 28-year-old pilot named Geraldyn "Jerrie" Cobb at an aviation conference in Florida. Cobb, who had more than 10,000 hours of flying experience and three world aviation records to her name, had just been named Pilot of the Year by the National Pilots Association. Lovelace invited her to be the first woman he tested.

Nothing in Cobb's experience could have prepared her for the grueling week she spent at Lovelace's clinic in February 1960. In one test, she had to swallow three feet of rubber hose so that doctors could study her gastric juices. In another, she had ice water squirted into her ears to knock her off balance and test her equilibrium. She also had colon exams, three barium enemas a day, and countless X-rays. Over a six-day period, she submitted to more than 80 different medical tests.

FLYING COLORS

Cobb tested so well against the Mercury 7 astronauts that Lovelace worried that if he went to NASA with her results alone, they'd dismiss her as a fluke. So he asked Cobb to come up with a list of 24 other female pilots he could test, to be sure that her results weren't an anomaly. Eighteen of the women agreed to come to Albuquerque, and of these, 12 tested well enough to qualify for the next phase...if there was to be a next phase.

The other 12 women:

- Bernice "B" Steadman, 35, commercial pilot and owner of a flight school in Flint, Michigan
- Marion Dietrich, 34, pilot and reporter for the *Oakland Tribune* in California
- Dietrich's identical twin sister, Jan, 34, flight instructor and commercial pilot
- Mary Wallace "Wally" Funk, 21, flying instructor at Fort Sill, Oklahoma
- Jean Hixson, 37, World War II engineering test pilot and flight instructor who'd become a school teacher in Akron, Ohio
- Myrtle Cagle, 36, flight instructor in Macon, Georgia
- Sarah Gorelick, 27, electrical engineer with AT&T in Kansas City, Kansas
- Rhea Hurrle, 30, executive pilot for an aircraft company in Houston, Texas
- Irene Leverton, 34, charter pilot and flight instructor in Santa Monica, California
- Gene Nora Stumbough, 24, flight instructor at the University of Oklahoma
- Geraldine "Jerrie" Sloan, 30, owner of an aviation business in Dallas, Texas
- Jane "Janey" Hart, 40, airplane and helicopter pilot, wife of U.S. Senator Philip Hart, and mother of eight

THE MERCURY 13

Because Lovelace had to fit these tests into the clinic's regular schedule, most of the women were invited to Albuquerque individually as openings became available. And because he insisted on secrecy—he wanted to keep the testing under wraps until he had the results—few of the female pilots even knew who the other members of the group were. In some cases the women did not meet each other until years later—they were a group in name

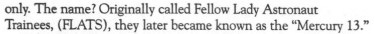

only. The name? Originally called Fellow Lady Astronaut Trainees, (FLATS), they later became known as the "Mercury 13."

Now that Lovelace had a pool of women who had tested well against the results of the men, he was ready to move on to phase two (psychological tests) and phase three (spacecraft-simulators). But where would he conduct these tests?

Cobb found a psychiatry professor at the University of Oklahoma College of Medicine who was willing to conduct the phase-two testing on all 13 women. And the U.S. Naval School of Aviation Medicine agreed to test Cobb in its simulators in Pensacola, Florida. If she tested well, the other 12 FLATs would be invited, too.

COLD WATER

Cobb went through phase-two testing in Oklahoma. Again, she passed. Then she went to Pensacola for phase-three testing...and scored as well as any experienced Navy pilot. That was all the Navy needed—it began making plans to test the rest of the FLAT team. Before it did, however, it contacted NASA to confirm that the space agency actually wanted the women tested.

It didn't. "NASA," the space agency explained, "does not at this time have a requirement for such a program." With that, the Navy backed out. Just six days before the testing was scheduled to begin, each of the Mercury 13 received a telegram from Dr. Lovelace. "Regret to advise that arrangements at Pensacola cancelled," it read. "Probably will not be possible to carry out this part of the program."

For Part II of the story, fly over to page 403.

*   *   *

GOING UP? Elevators are the safest form of transportation: they have the record of only one fatality per every 100 million miles traveled. Stairs, on the other hand, are five times more dangerous. (It's harder to trip in an elevator than on the stairs, and you don't fall as far.)

COMIC BOOK SCIENCE

No one says that science has to make sense in comic books—no one except Uncle John, that is. He wanted to know whether his favorite comic book heroes were using science fact... or science fiction. Here's what we found out.

THE INCREDIBLE HULK

Comic Book Science: In *The Incredible Hulk* #1 (May 1962), Dr. Bruce Banner invents a "gamma bomb." It accidentally goes off. To save his friend, Rick Jones, Banner leaps in front of Jones and takes the full assault of the gamma ray blast. And he pays a terrible price: Whenever he gets angry, he unleashes the monster inside, which is called The Hulk.

Could It Happen? No. Gamma rays are an extremely powerful form of electromagnetic radiation. Given the dosage to which he was exposed, Banner wouldn't have turned into anything except The Incredible Corpse—he would have suffered a painful death from incurable radiation sickness within two days of his exposure.

BATMAN

Comic Book Science: In *Detective Comics* #27 (May 1939), young Bruce Wayne witnesses the murder of his parents by a cheap thug, sparking a quest for vengeance and leading him into a life of crime-fighting as Batman. Since he has no special powers, Batman relies on his intellect, strength, and, later, a battery of mini-gadgets contained in his utility belt to help him wage war on crime. Some of the contents of the utility belt: explosives, fingerprint equipment, oxyacetylene torch, smoke capsule, infrared flashlight, and camera.

Could It Happen? Yes. In a world before computer chips and microcircuitry, most of the items would have seemed very futuristic, but each is scientifically and technologically sound. In fact, many of them are in use today. The Batplane, the Batmobile, and the Bat Cave's crime lab are all feasible as well.

SUPERMAN

Comic Book Science: In *Action Comics* #1 (June 1938), Superman

---

Q: What percentage of the world has type O blood? A: More than 46%.

started life as a baby named Kal-El on the planet Krypton. Shortly before Krypton is destroyed, his father places the infant in a rocket ship and sends him to Earth, where the difference between Earth's gravity and Krypton's give the child super strength and the ability to jump enormous distances (X-ray vision and flying came later).

Could It Happen? No. To account for Superman's amazing strength—easily 1,000 times the average earthling's—the gravity on Krypton would have to be approximately 1,000 times stronger than Earth's. To produce gravity of that magnitude, Krypton would have to be 3,000 times as massive as our sun. And that, according to the basic laws of physics, is impossible.

THE FLASH

Comic Book Science: In *Showcase* #4 (September 1956), a bolt of lighting strikes the laboratory of police scientist Barry Allen, thoroughly drenching him with a wild mixture of electrified chemicals and giving him the power of super speed.

Could It Happen? No. The Flash travels amazing distances in record time: on at least one occasion, he circumnavigated the globe without stopping for lunch. An active 160-pound man normally consumes about 3,000 calories per day. If the Flash were to run 3,000 miles—say, from Los Angeles to New York—it might take him only a few minutes, but he'd burn roughly 375,000 calories doing it. Unless he stopped to eat a meal every second, he'd probably starve to death somewhere around Bakersfield.

DONALD DUCK

Comic Book Science: In Walt Disney Comics #104-02 *"The Sunken Yacht"* (May 1949), Donald and his three nephews, Huey, Louie, and Dewey raise a sunken ship by filling the hold with Ping-Pong balls, something the boys (okay, they're ducks) read in their Junior Woodchuck handbook.

Could It Happen? Yes. In fact, a group of Swedish oceanographers used the technique to salvage a ship in 1964. Nearly all of Donald's comic book adventures were written and drawn by Carl Barks, who never underestimated the intelligence of his audience. Barks was careful to include elements of science in his stories (possibly to compensate for the fact that his main character was a talking duck).

BATHROOM NEWS

*Here are a few fascinating bits of bathroom trivia
that we've flushed out from around the world.*

R ELIEF PLAYER
In April 2004, a minor league baseball player named Jeff
Liefer made history when he got locked in the bathroom
during a game between the Indianapolis Indians and the Louisville
Bats. "The handle didn't work," says Liefer, who plays first base for
the Indians and spent five seasons in the big leagues. Maintenance
workers passed a wrench through a vent in the wall, but all Liefer
managed to do was remove the door handle without unlocking the
door. Then they handed him a hammer and chisel, and he finally
freed himself by prying the hinges off the door. The game resumed
after a 20-minute delay (the Indians lost, 9–0). "I don't want to be
remembered as the guy who got stuck in the bathroom," said
Liefer. "Hopefully, it'll happen to someone else so it won't be such
a big deal."

PLEASE BE SEATED

A German inventor named Alex Benkhardt has created a device
designed to shame men with bad aim into sitting down to pee. The
device, called the WC Ghost, attaches to a toilet seat. Every time
the seat is lifted, a stern female voice says, "Hello, what are you up
to then? Put the seat back down right away, you are definitely not
to pee standing up—you will make a right mess." As of mid-2004,
Benkhardt had sold more than 1.6 million of the devices in
Germany, and plans to expand into Italy, Canada, and England.

NOW, WHERE'D I PUT THAT?

In April 2004, a federal air marshal made a pit stop in the ladies'
room at the Cleveland Hopkins International Airport in
Cleveland, Ohio. A few minutes later the marshal realized she'd
left something behind: her loaded handgun. She apparently had
put the gun on a shelf while she washed her hands, then forgot to
grab it after she finished. A few minutes later someone else using
the restroom saw the gun and, fortunately, alerted airport police.

YOU'VE GOTTA GO

In November 2003, Caterpillar Inc., maker of bulldozers and other heavy equipment, fired an assembly line worker after he failed a company drug test. Tom Smith, 55, suffers from paruresis (also known as "shy bladder syndrome" or "stage fright"). After it took him more than the permitted three hours to produce a urine sample, Caterpillar didn't even bother to test the sample for drugs. They just fired him. Smith is fighting back—in May 2004, he sued Caterpillar, alleging that the time limit violates the Americans with Disabilities Act. "This is supposed to be a country where losing a job for a disorder like this shouldn't be a problem," he states.

PINK POT OF GOLD

Fifteen people hoping to raise money for the American Cancer Society in Whitehouse, Ohio, have come up with a unique way to do it. Every night for more than a month, the fundraisers put a fluorescent pink toilet on a volunteer's front lawn, along with a big sign that read "Help Flush Out Cancer!" At last report neighbors had deposited more than $800 in the pink pot for cancer research.

KABOOM!

Remember the automated, self-cleaning public restrooms we told you about in *Uncle John's Ahh-Inspiring Bathroom Reader*? The city of Stoke-on-Trent in England has six of them...or at least it *had* six. In February 2004, one of them blew up at 4:00 in the morning. The "superloos," as they're known in England, are built like tanks and are virtually indestructible, but the explosion was so powerful that it blew the roof off. (Luckily, no one was inside at the time.) Officials think it was caused by a fault in a high-voltage cable running underneath the restroom. "The toilet just happened to be above it," city council spokesperson Terry James told reporters.

SAVING NEMO

The Singapore International Fish Show introduced a new attraction in 2004: an adoption program to save unwanted pet fish from the usual fate that awaits them—being flushed into oblivion. Any of the show's 80,000 visitors who want to get rid of their fish can drop them off at the show's "orphanage," where other visitors can adopt them. "It's more humane than flushing them down the toilet," says spokesperson Carol Lian.

THUMBERS & MODOCKS

Was your grandma gruntled when she was infanticipating? What are we talking about? You'll have to brush up on your 1930s lingo!

Ackamarackus: Nonsense

Clip joint: A bar that charges outrageously high prices

Ripple: Ice cream with a colorful syrup stirred in, giving it flavor and a rippled appearance

Trafficator: What some 1930s cars had instead of blinkers— "arms" on either side of the car that could be raised when the driver wanted to turn

Thumber: A hitchhiker

That's one for Ripley: In reference to "Ripley's Believe it or Not!" cartoons, meaning anything strange or bizarre

Gruntled: Happy. The word was created by dropping the *dis-* from *disgruntled*

The Magoo: Sex appeal

Superette: A small supermarket, something about the size of a modern 7-Eleven

Glamour boy: Like a pretty boy, but more masculine

Gaff: A building or house

Pen-friend: What pen-pals used to be called

Infanticipate: Pregnant or expecting; *anticipating* an infant. (Why didn't this term survive? One theory: it's too close to "infanticide.")

Shy-making: Embarrassing

Sky-shouting: Sky-writers write messages in the sky with trails of smoke; sky-*shouters* broadcast messages to the ground using loudspeakers

Modock: A man who becomes a military pilot to be glamorous and have sex appeal

Milk bar: Like a regular bar, except that the drinks are made with milk, not alcohol. The milkshake is one of the few such drinks that survives today

Spliff: A marijuana cigarette

Balls-up: Messed up, ruined, confused or disordered

Slim: To lose weight by dieting

Gravel: Sugar

Candy Leg: A rich and popular young man

Melon: A financial windfall

Barnburner: A riotous party

CRAZY EIGHTS

This page originally explained the meaning of life, but our dog eight it.

VEGETABLES IN V-8 JUICE
Tomatoes, Celery
Carrots, Lettuce
Watercress, Beets
Parsley, Spinach

LONGEST RIVERS IN NORTH AMERICA
Missouri
(2,500 miles)
Mississippi
(2,330 miles)
Rio Grande
(1,885 miles)
Colorado
(1,450 miles)
Yukon
(1,265 miles)
Mackenzie
(1,250 miles)
Columbia
(1,152 miles)
Churchill
(1,000 miles)

U.S. PRESIDENTS FROM VIRGINIA
George Washington
Thomas Jefferson
James Madison
John Tyler
James Monroe
Zachary Taylor
Woodrow Wilson
William H. Harrison

MOVIES WITH "8" IN THE TITLE
8-1/2
BUtterfield 8
8 Million Ways to Die
8 Heads in a Duffel Bag
8 Mile, Eight Men Out
8MM, Jennifer Eight

GR8 MUSICIANS WHO NEVER WON A GRAMMY
The Doors
Diana Ross
Led Zeppelin
Jimi Hendrix
Chuck Berry
Patsy Cline
The Beach Boys
Sam Cooke

DEFUNCT OLYMPIC SPORTS
Tug-of-war, Golf
Rugby, Croquet
Polo, Lacrosse
Power boating
Waterskiing

THE PARTS OF SPEECH
Noun, Verb
Adjective, Adverb
Pronoun, Preposition
Conjunction
Interjection

THE KIDS ON *EIGHT IS ENOUGH*
Mary
(Lani O'Grady)
Joanie
(Laurie Walters)
Nancy
(Dianne Kay)
Elizabeth
(Connie Needham)
Susan
(Susan Richardson)
David
(Grant Goodeve)
Tommy
(Willie Aames)
Nicholas
(Adam Rich)

THE IVY LEAGUE
Harvard, Brown, Yale
Cornell, Dartmouth
Princeton, Columbia
University of
Pennsylvania

MOST POPULAR ICE CREAM FLAVORS
Vanilla
Chocolate
Butter pecan
Strawberry
Neapolitan
Chocolate chip
French vanilla
Cookies and cream

The average cat consumes 28 times its weight in food annually.

MUHAMMAD ALI: POET

*Muhammad Ali had a knack for promoting himself and his causes
(and taunting his opponents) with verse. Here are some examples.*

There are two things
That are hard to hit and see,
That's a spooky ghost
And Muhammad Ali.

My face is so pretty,
You don't see a scar,
Which proves I'm the king
Of the ring by far.

I'm a baaad man.
Archie Moore fell in four,
Liston wanted me more,
So since he's so great,
I'll make him fall in eight.
I'm a baaad man,
I'm king of the world!

Keep asking me,
no matter how long,
On the war in Vietnam,
I sing this song:
"I ain't got no quarrel
with them Viet Cong."

I float like a butterfly,
Sting like a bee…
His hands can't hit
What his eyes can't see.

If you ever dream of
beating me,
You better wake up
and apologize.

Stay in college,
Get the knowledge;
Stay there till you are through.
If they can make penicillin
Out of moldy bread,
They sure'll make
Something out of you.

Joe's gonna be smokin'
An' I ain't even jokin',
But I'll be peckin' and pokin'
And pour water on that
smokin'.
Now this might
Astound and amaze ya,
But I will destroy Joe Frazier.

My opponents are like postage
stamps—always gettin' licked.

I done wrestled an alligator,
I done tussled with a whale.
Only last week
I murdered a rock,
Injured a stone,
Hospitalized a brick,
I'm so mean
I make medicine sick.

You don't want no pie
In the sky when you die,
You want something
Here on the ground
While you're still around.

McLEANED

In Uncle John's Ultimate Bathroom Reader, we told you about how the producers of M*A*S*H were so mad that McLean Stevenson was leaving the show that they killed off his character, shocking the cast and audience. The incident spawned a TV industry term: when an actor leaves a show and their character dies, they've been "McLeaned."

McLeaned: Rosalind Shays (Diana Muldaur)
Show: *L.A. Law*
Deadly Plot: Muldaur played cold-hearted, ruthless lawyer Rosalind Shays from 1989 to 1991 on the NBC legal show. Rosalind manipulated her way to controlling the show's law firm, sued her (fictional) co-workers, and was despised by audiences. Writers hated her too—the character was so harsh, she was ruining the show. Their solution: kill her. Rosalind died suddenly—elevator doors opened and she walked in, then plunged to her death down the empty shaft, horrifying and delighting viewers. The title of the episode: "Good to the Last Drop."

McLeaned: Maude Flanders (voice of Maggie Roswell)
Show: *The Simpsons*
Deadly Plot: Roswell had voiced countless minor characters, but her biggest was nosy, righteous Maude Flanders. After 10 seasons, Roswell asked for a raise from the $2,000 she earned per episode. (The main cast was pulling down over $100,000.) On top of that, Roswell was flying to Los Angeles from her Denver home at her own expense to record her scenes. Producers turned her down, so Roswell walked. Producers found a way to get back at her—they killed Maude. She tumbled over the grandstands at an auto race after being hit by a T-shirt fired from a cannon.
Afterlife: Roswell's other characters were subsequently voiced by another actor, Marcia Mitzman Gaven. The new voice proved too jarring, so after three years Roswell was asked back to the show with a significant pay raise. (Maude remained dead, however.)

McLeaned: Valerie Hogan (Valerie Harper)
Show: *Valerie*

Deadly Plot: Harper starred as a wisecracking but tender mother of three on this 1980s sitcom. But in 1987, the beginning of the show's third season, Harper demanded creative control and double her salary. Lorimar, the production company, refused, so Harper didn't show up for work. (The tactic had been successful when she had asked for a raise on *Rhoda* in 1975.) Lorimar ultimately gave in, but when Harper returned to the set, she lashed out at co-stars and producers, accusing them of trying to upstage her with her popular teen co-star Jason Bateman. Harper permanently left the show one week later. She says she was fired; Lorimar says she quit. To end the squabbling, her character was killed off in a car crash and replaced with Sandy Duncan. The show went on for another four seasons, first as *Valerie's Family*, and then as *The Hogan Family*.

McLeaned: Bobby Ewing (Patrick Duffy)
Show: *Dallas*
Deadly Plot: Duffy left *Dallas* in 1985 to pursue a movie career. Producers felt slighted so they killed off his character, Bobby, possibly the only nice guy on the show, by having him get run over by a car after saving his wife Pam from a hit-and-run driver. Duffy's movie career didn't pan out, and when millions of viewers abandoned *Dallas* with nobody to root for, the producers swallowed their pride and asked Duffy to return a year later. But how do you bring back a dead character? At the beginning of the 1986–87 season, Pam Ewing awakes, hears water running, and finds Bobby in the shower. It seems she had only *dreamed* Bobby had died, and as a result, had also dreamed the entire previous season of the show.

McLeaned: James Evans (John Amos)
Show: *Good Times*
Deadly Plot: In 1975 Amos became mired in a contract dispute with the producers of *Good Times*. The argument was primarily about money, but Amos and co-star Esther Rolle complained about the quality of the show and its writers in *Ebony* magazine. Livid about the comments, producers released Amos from his contract in 1976. And to prevent him from returning, his character was killed in a car accident.
Rerun: Twenty-eight years later, Amos would be unceremoniously removed from another TV series when his character Admiral Percy Fitzwallace died on *The West Wing*.

At three weeks, a human fetus is about the size of a sesame seed.

ONE EGG POP, PLEASE

Back in colonial days, folks used to mix some mighty peculiar drinks.
Here are a few favorites from the 17th and 18th centuries.

• **SACK POSSET:** Made by mixing clots of curdled milk into ale or wine

• **EGG POP** (or **Egg Hot**): Eggs, brandy, sugar, and ale

• **ALEBERRY:** Ale boiled with sugar, spices, and sops of old bread

• **METHEGLIN:** Spiced or medicated mead (fermented honey and water)

• **MIMBO:** Rum mixed with water and sugar

• **FLIP:** Mix strong beer with molasses and rum, then take a red hot poker from the fire and thrust it into the mixture to give the flip its characteristic bitter, burnt flavor

• **BELLOWSTOP:** A variation of the flip made with eggs

• **LORD MAY'S FLIP:** Like a regular flip, except you add a two-day-old mixture of sugar, eggs and cream to the beer and rum (leave out the molasses) and then heat it with the hot poker

• **CALIBOGUS:** A straight mix of rum and beer

• **BLACK SAP:** Cold rum and molasses, shipped in barrels and sold at general stores throughout the colonies

• **EBULUM:** A cider-based punch flavored with juniper and elderberries

• **SWITCHEL:** Molasses and water seasoned with sugar, vinegar, and ginger

• **COCK ALE:** A mixture of chicken soup and beer

• **MUMM:** A flat ale brewed from oats and wheat malt

• **WHISTLEBELLY VENGEANCE:** A specialty of Salem, Mass., taverns. Old sour beer, boiled with molasses and rye bread and served hot

• **MARTHA WASHINGTON'S RUM PUNCH:** (Taken from her journals) 3 oz. white rum, 3 oz. dark rum, 3 oz. orange curaçao, 4 oz. simple syrup, 4 oz. lemon juice, 4 oz. fresh orange juice, 3 lemons (quartered), 1 orange (quartered), 1/2 tsp. ground nutmeg, 3 cinnamon sticks (broken), 6 cloves, and 12 oz. boiling water (Yum!)

Q: Name the only three English words that end in "ceed." A: Succeed, proceed, and exceed.

IT WORKED...TOO WELL!

*The old saying "the best-laid schemes of mice and men often go awry"
comes from a line by Scottish poet Robert Burns. It means that no
matter how well a project is planned, something may still go wrong.
In the case of these plans, what went wrong was...they worked.*

THE PLAN: In 1959 a program was started to aggressively
introduce wild turkey populations to California. Officials
hoped having the game birds would mean big revenue from
local and out-of-state hunters.

IT WORKED... By 1969 there were enough turkeys for a regular
hunting season. By the 1980s, there were tens of thousands of
them.

...TOO WELL! In 2003 California officials began introducing
programs to get *rid* of wild turkeys. There were more than a quarter
million of the birds living in the state, and they were wreaking
havoc. Biologists said they were invading habitats of native birds,
consuming endangered species of plants and animals, damaging
crops, ruining gardens, fouling backyards—and sometimes even
attacking children.

THE PLAN: In May 2003, German advertising firm JC Decaux
presented fashion chain H&M with a marketing plan for a new
line of bikini swimwear. The idea was simple: plaster the country
with posters of German supermodel Heidi Klum wearing the sexy
swimsuits.

IT WORKED... The Klum ads became one of the most successful
advertising campaigns in the country's history. H&M reported
huge sales.

...TOO WELL! More than half of the posters were immediately
stolen. Not only that, people smashed display cases to get them.
JC Decaux president Hans-Peter Bischoff said, "We put up 750
small posters, and they were all gone within a few hours. It's mad-
ness." The company had to hire guards to protect the display boxes
while they figured out a solution. The solution: H&M started giving the posters away for free.

Is your second toe longer than the rest? If so, 15% of the population has toes just like you.

THE PLAN: After a hole was discovered in the ozone layer above Australia in the mid-1980s, the government began aggressive ad campaigns to warn people about the risks of getting too much sun. The ozone layer acts as a filter against the dangerous ultraviolet rays in sunlight, and the country already had the highest skin cancer rates in the world. One of the most popular campaigns was "Slip, Slop, Slap": "Slip on a shirt, Slop on sunscreen, and Slap on a hat!"

IT WORKED... National health associations credited the campaign with making sunscreen usage a normal part of life for many Australians, saving countless lives.

...TOO WELL! In 2000 officials announced that nearly 25% of Australian adults were vitamin D deficient. How do you get vitamin D? Primarily by exposure to sunlight—the skin produces it in reaction to the sun's rays. Lack of the vitamin can cause a host of health risks, including osteoporosis, and is believed to be linked to breast, colon, and prostate cancer.

THE PLAN: To get its citizens to spend money, and thus boost the country's faltering economy, in 1999 South Korea instituted a program making it easy for anyone to obtain a credit card.

IT WORKED... The nation's economic growth climbed by 10% in the first year alone.

...TOO WELL! By 2003 the average South Korean worker had four credit cards and consumers had rung up more than $100 billion in debt. There were so many unpaid credit card accounts that the nation's largest credit company had to stop issuing money from their ATMs and had to get an emergency loan just to stay afloat. Credit card debt was also blamed for a rash of suicides, thefts, kidnappings, and prostitution cases. "Koreans ate a poison pill," economist Kim Kyeong Won told *Time* magazine, "It tasted sweet at the time, but was still poison."

* * *

TWO REAL NOTES GIVEN TO TEACHERS

"Dear School: Please excuse John being absent on Jan. 28, 29, 30, 31, 32, and also 33."

"Sally won't be in school a week from Friday. We have to attend her funeral."

Before the Civil War, the average work week was 11 hours a day, 6 days a week.

WHERE'S YOUR MECCA?

You've probably heard of the pilgrimage to the city of Mecca in Saudi Arabia that is a requirement of the Islamic faith. But have you heard about the Kumbh Mela? How about the...

HOLY SITE: Sites around Mecca, Saudi Arabia
THE JOURNEY: The *Hajj* pilgrimage is the duty of all Muslims, if they are physically and financially able to make the journey. It always takes place in the 12th (and holy) month of the Islamic year, *Ramadan*. Some requirements of the Hajj: Pilgrims are not allowed to hunt, wear perfume, have marital relations, or argue; they must walk around the *Ka'aba*—the ancient mosque said to be built by Islam's patriarch, Abraham, and his son Ishmael— seven times. (The *Ka'aba* is the direction that all Muslims face during prayer.) They must also stone the three pillars of *Jamraat*, which represent Satan, symbolizing Abraham's rejection of temptation. More than 2 million people make the Hajj to Mecca every year.

HOLY SITES: Four cities in India
THE JOURNEY: The *Kumbh Mela* is the world's largest religious pilgrimage. It centers around a Hindu myth: Long ago the gods and demons fought a battle over the *Kumbh*, a pitcher containing the nectar of immortality. During the battle, four drops of nectar spilled onto the Earth. Those drops fell in the Indian cities of Allahabad, Nasik, Ujjain, and Haridwar. Every three years a *mela* (fair) is held in one of the cities, rotating so that each is visited every 12 years. *The Guinness Book of World Records* called Allahabad's 1989 gathering "the largest number of human beings to ever assemble with a common purpose in the entire history of mankind." An estimated 25 million people—nearly the population of Canada—attended.

HOLY SITE: Ise Jingu (The Grand Shrine of Ise), Mie, Japan
THE JOURNEY: The Ise Jingu is the Shinto shrine dedicated to Amaterasu Omikami, the Great Sun Goddess and mythological ancestor of the Japanese royal family. In the 600s A.D., Emperor Temmu declared it the most important shrine in Shintoism. At first, only Japanese royalty were allowed in, but it in the 1600s it was opened to the public. Ise Jingu also has the distinction of being

one of the oldest—and newest—pilgrimage sites in the world. Every 20 years it undergoes *shikinen sengu*—all the shrine's buildings are destroyed and rebuilt, using the same construction techniques that were used 13 centuries ago. (The next *shikinen sengu* is in 2013.) Today more than 6 million make the trip every year, with more than a million showing up around New Years Day alone.

HOLY SITE: Chek Chek shrine near Yazd, Iran

THE JOURNEY: Zoroastrianism was founded in the 6th century B.C. and was the official religion of the ancient Persian Empire. Legend says that in 640 A.D. Muslim armies chased the daughter of Persian Emperor Yazdgird III to the mountains near Yazd. There she prayed to the Zoroastrian creator, Ahura Mazda, for her freedom, and the mountain opened up and saved her. A holy spring still runs at the site (Chek Chek means "drip drop"). Every June, thousands of pilgrims make their way up the mountain to a sacred cave, where they pray and drink the water from the spring.

HOLY SITE: Hill Cumorah, near Palmyra, New York

THE JOURNEY: Hill Cumorah is where Joseph Smith had visions in the 1820s, upon which the Mormon faith is based. There, Mormons believe, Smith was visited by the Angel Moroni, who gave him the Book of Mormon—the history of the New World on gold tablets. A huge statue of Moroni stands on the hill, and every July, nearly 100,000 Mormons come for "The Cumorah Pageant: America's Witness for Christ," during which dramatic reenactments of the Book of Mormon are performed.

HOLY SITE: The Saut d'Eau waterfall near Ville Bonheur, Haiti

THE JOURNEY: Many Haitians follow a combination of Voodooism and Christianity. In 1847, believers say, an image of the Virgin Mary was seen in a tree near the falls. In the Voodoo faith, the Virgin Mary is often associated with Erzuli, the Voodoo goddess of love. Every July, pilgrims journey to Ville Bonheur (the Village of Bliss) and the Saut d'Eau falls. There they stand in the falls and sing, chant, and pray to Mary and/or Erzuli and other Voodoo spirits. Anywhere from hundreds to tens of thousands of Haitians (depending on political conditions in the country) make the trip each year.

Pound for pound, the hummingbird has the most powerful muscles of any animal.

WAS IT...MURDER?

A mysterious death reveals a deep, dark secret. Lives are changed forever; the community is shocked. Mrs. Uncle John finds her husband in the arms of—no, wait! That's not part of the story.

L AST NIGHT
On the evening of March 18, 2003, a 75-year-old Tampa, Florida, socialite named Jean Ann Cone drove to the home of friends to help plan the annual benefit gala for the Tampa Museum of Art. She had a few drinks while she was there, and when it came time to leave, another woman, Bobbie Williams, followed behind Cone's Rolls Royce to make sure she got home safely. Cone's husband, Douglas, was away on business, so she appreciated the offer.

When the two women arrived at the Cone residence, Williams watched as Cone pulled into her garage and closed the automatic door behind her; then Williams drove home.

It was the last time anyone saw Mrs. Cone alive.

NOBODY HOME

At 5:00 p.m. the following day, the part-time housekeeper, Norma Gotay, arrived and noticed that Cone's bed was neatly made. That was unusual because it was Gotay's job to make it, but she assumed that Cone must have slept at a friend's house.

A little later, a friend of Cone's came by to take her to a baseball game they had planned to see together. All Gotay could tell the friend was that Cone was not home and that she had no idea where she was. At 7:00 p.m., Gotay finished her work and went home without ever seeing her employer. It wasn't until Cone missed a lunch appointment the next day that people began to worry.

Someone called Cone's daughter Julianne McKeel to ask if *she* knew her mother's whereabouts. McKeel promptly went over and searched the house but couldn't find any sign of her mother—until she checked the garage and saw the Rolls Royce parked in a puddle of green antifreeze. The windows were rolled up, all four doors were locked, and there, slumped in the driver's seat, was Jean Ann Cone. She was dead.

WEIGHING THE EVIDENCE

Considering the unusual circumstances surrounding Mrs. Cone's death and her prominence in Tampa society, the investigation into her death was surprisingly short.

Facts of the case:

✓ There was no indication that Cone was despondent or suicidal in the days leading up to her death.

✓ The garage door was in the closed position when the body was discovered, and so was the door into the house.

✓ Cone was on medication, and the autopsy revealed that her blood-alcohol level at the time of her death was 0.18 percent—twice the legal limit. She had had a history of episodes of light-headedness caused by her medications, something that alcohol might have made even worse.

✓ Her car key was still in the ignition of the Rolls Royce, and it was turned to the on position, even though the engine was not running when she was found.

✓ Julianne McKeel confirmed that her mother was in the habit of pulling into the garage and closing the garage door behind her before shutting off the engine, unlocking the door, and getting out of the car.

The police considered all the evidence and concluded that Cone's death was accidental. They surmised that when she arrived home on the evening of the 18th, she pulled into her garage, closed the door behind her, and then passed out behind the wheel of her car before she could shut off the engine. The victim of too much alcohol and prescription drugs, she did not regain consciousness in time to turn off the ignition, and suffocated on the exhaust fumes that filled the closed garage. The car kept running until it overheated—which explained the puddle of antifreeze—and then stalled.

THE PLOT THICKENS

When Mr. Cone returned home, having heard of his wife's death, he was crying and inconsolable. He behaved just as you'd expect a man to behave after losing the woman he'd loved for 52 years. "He was really depressed," the housekeeper told reporters. "They cared about each other. They had been married for so many years." Nothing Mr. Cone said or did aroused even a hint of suspicion...at first.

Then, just 13 days later, friends of the family happened to read a baffling wedding announcement in the local newspaper. Less than two weeks after his wife's death, Douglas Cone had remarried—and he hadn't bothered to tell his three grown children. Now *that* could be considered suspicious behavior.

Had Mrs. Cone been murdered? Was Douglas Cone her killer? What was going on? Their son Doug Jr. asked the police to take another look into his mother's death.

MYSTERY MAN

The first thing they did was investigate the woman Cone had just married. Here's what they found:

✓ Her name was Hillary Carlson and she was already married.

✓ Few of her acquaintances had ever met her husband, Donald Carlson, who worked for the U.S. State Department and was always traveling.

✓ They had been married for more than 20 years, had two grown children, and lived on a 67-acre gated estate 20 miles north of Tampa.

Then the investigators discovered some bizarre coincidences: The Carlsons and the Cones traveled in the same exclusive social circles. The two families had both sent their children to the same prestigious Berkeley Preparatory School, and Hillary Carlson and Jean Ann Cone had served together on the school's board of trustees. Both families had given lots of money to the school—the library named in honor of Mrs. Cone was just yards away from the baseball field that was named for Mrs. Carlson.

Douglas Cone and Donald Carlson seemed to have less in common than their wives did. Cone didn't travel in diplomatic circles like Carlson—he was in road construction. But had Jean Ann Cone and Hillary Carlson compared notes about their husbands, they might have noticed something unusual: Jean Ann's husband was away on business during the week and home on weekends, while Hillary's husband was away on weekends but home during the week.

And just like Superman and Clark Kent, Douglas Cone and

In 1014 A.D., Viking ships pulled down the London Bridge, apparently on a whim.

Donald Carlson were never in the same place at the same time.

THE JIG IS UP

With the cops (and the newspapers) hot on his trail, Douglas Cone had no choice but to reveal his incredible secret: for more than 20 years, he had been living a double life. On weekends he lived with his wife Jean Ann in town, but during the week he posed as Donald Carlson, living with his mistress, Hillary Carlson, and their two children on their large estate.

He and Hillary had made up the story about the State Department job so they would never have to appear together in public. Douglas Cone's "business trips" were simply a ruse so he could spend the week with Hillary. She knew everything, but Jean Ann Cone apparently died without realizing that her husband had been two-timing her for over two decades.

REST IN PEACE

The police still believe, and the Cone children now accept, that Jean Ann Cone's death was an accident. "The family was only sus-picious because Douglas Cone remarried too quickly," says Tampa Police Sergeant Jim Simonson. "Turns out that can be easily explained; it's not like he met the woman two weeks before."

* * *

RANDOM INSECT FACTS

• The word "bug" started out as the Anglo-Saxon word *bugge* or *bough* meaning a terror, a devil, or a ghost.

• The word "dragonfly" probably originates with the Greek word *drakos* meaning "eye."

• The hairs on the butt of a cockroach are so sensitive that they can detect the air currents made by the on-rushing tongue of a toad.

• The praying mantis is the official state insect of Connecticut.

• Mating soapberry bugs remain locked in embrace for up to eleven days, a period of time which exceeds the life span of many other insects.

The skin on the soles of your feet is called the *stratum corneum* (Latin for "horny layer").

COMIC RELIEF

Great lines from great comedians.

"My doctor told me I had Attention Deficit Disorder. He said, 'A.D.D. is a complex disorder, blah, blah, blah.' I didn't pay attention to the rest."
—**Kyle Dunnigan**

"One night I made love for an hour and five minutes. It was the day they pushed the clock ahead."
—**Garry Shandling**

"Personally, I'm waiting for caller IQ."
—**Sandra Bernhard**

"A relationship is like a full-time job, and we should treat it like one. If your boyfriend or girlfriend wants to leave you, they should give you two weeks' notice...and they should have to find you a temp."
—**Bob Ettinger**

"Penguins mate for life. Which doesn't exactly surprise me that much 'cause they all look alike—it's not like they're going to meet a better-looking penguin some day."
—**Ellen DeGeneres**

"While driving I had an accident with a magician. He came out of nowhere!"
—**Auggie Cook**

"You know the good thing about gangs is, they carpool."
—**John Mendoza**

"I was on the corner the other day when a wild-eyed sort of gypsy-looking lady with a dark veil over her face grabbed me right on Ventura Boulevard and said, 'Karen Haber! You're never going to find happiness, and no one is ever going to marry you!' I said, 'Mom, leave me alone.'"
—**Karen Haber**

"I'm not saying my wife's a bad cook, but she uses a smoke alarm as a timer."
—**Bob Monkhouse**

"I was on the subway sitting on a newspaper, and a guy comes over and asks, 'Are you reading that?' I didn't know what to say. So I said, 'Yes,' stood up, turned the page, and sat down again."
—**David Brenner**

THE BIRTH OF THE MAJOR LEAGUES

Over the years, the BRI has written a lot about the history of the game of baseball. Here's what happened when people began to realize that there was a lot of money to be made in the business *of baseball.*

PROFESSIONAL BASE BALL

On May 17, 1857, the Knickerbocker Club of New York City invited rival clubs from around their region to a meeting. The reason: to draw up a standardized set of rules for the new sport they all played—base ball. Twenty-five clubs attended and by the end of the meeting they had become The National Association of Base Ball Players. The sport had only recently emerged from various similar, traditional games being played around the country—cricket, "rounders," and "townball"—but by 1868 more than 100 teams were members of the National Association.

One of the Association's original principles had been that baseball should remain a purely amateur sport. It didn't. In 1862 Albert Reach of the Brooklyn Eckfords became the first professional player when he was paid $25 to join the Philadelphia Athletics. As the game's popularity grew, rivalries between the different teams became so intense that paying players, though still against the rules, became commonplace. In 1869 the Cincinnati Red Stockings became the first all-professional team, traveling the country challenging—and demolishing—all comers. (They won 65 straight games that year.) Other clubs followed suit and two years later the original organization rewrote its charter to become the first "major league"—The National Association of *Professional* Baseball Players.

THE NATIONAL LEAGUE

As attendance continued to climb and even more teams got into the act, baseball started to generate substantial revenue. And people involved with the sport started to realize that the NAPBP might be more suitably run by *businessmen* than by players. By 1875 many of the teams found themselves in a pickle. Why? That year, seven of the 13 teams in the league ran out of money and were unable to finish the season. The owners had to do something. In December, 1875, they held a secret meeting and formed the National League of Professional Base Ball *Clubs* with rules specifically tailored to benefit the owners, not the players—the era of big-business baseball had begun.

The new League had a board of five directors who were empowered to enforce the new rules and dole out punishments for teams and players that broke them. The reserve clause, prohibiting players from going to another team for better pay, was implemented at this time, and salary caps were put in place. Other rules: both liquor and gambling, which had coexisted with baseball since its early days, were no longer allowed. The board of directors began fining teams and banning players for "conduct in the controversion of the objects of the league."

In 1880 the board of directors ejected the entire Cincinnati Reds team for "the selling of spiritous liquors on league grounds." Cincinnati owner Justus Thorner responded by quitting the league and forming his own: the American Association—and it was a success. By 1883 the National League was forced to deal with them, so the two leagues (along with a third, the Northwestern League) met to draw up a "National Agreement," establishing many of the rules that are still in place today, as well as promoting cooperation between teams and leagues. The American Association wouldn't last (it was gone by 1891; the Reds went back to the National League in 1890), but the National Agreement gave the game a foundation, and business continued to grow.

THE AMERICAN LEAGUE

The players weren't happy with all the new changes in the game. They resented the loss of power that had come with the rise of club ownership and wanted to maintain the right to sell their talents to the highest bidder. So they tried—twice—to start up separate, player-controlled organizations: the Union Association of 1884 and the Player's League of 1890. It didn't work—both folded within a year for lack of finances. Baseball players had become the contracted property of commercial teams. (It wouldn't be until free agency came into being in 1976 that players would regain some control over their fates.)

By 1900 there were 14 leagues signed on to the National

Agreement, with the National League the undisputed leader in terms of prestige and revenue. In 1901 another successful group, the Western League, changed its name to The American League and declared itself the National League's equal. The older league refused to recognize the claim, so the new league withdrew from the National Agreement. They began raiding National League teams for players, luring away top stars with higher salaries, and placing teams in National League cities. The upstarts were gaining popularity; recognition by the National League seemed inevitable.

"THE WORLD CHAMPIONSHIP SERIES"

At the end of the 1903 season the owners of the National League Champion Pittsburgh Pirates and the American League leading Boston team (known variously as the Pilgrims, Puritans, or Red Sox) agreed to compete in a best of nine game inter-league, championship series. After falling behind three games to one, the Boston team came back to win the next four games...and the first "World Championship Series," and the win sent a message to the baseball establishment: The American League was here to stay.

The following year the New York Giants won the NL pennant and refused to play the Red Sox, who had repeated their AL title. The Giants manager, John McGraw, told reporters, "Why should we play this, or any other American League team, for any post season championship? When we clinch the National League pennant, we'll be champions of the only real Major League."

Fans didn't like his attitude, and the next year, when the Giants again won the NL pennant, public demand for the post-season series was so strong that they were compelled to play. But New York owner John T. Brush insisted on crafting a set of rules for post-season play and box office revenues—the same rules that are in use today. It is the "Brush Rules," for example, that established the length of the series at seven games rather than nine.

After this second World Series, the two leagues buried the hatchet for good and drafted a new National Agreement establishing the American and National as the "Major Leagues" and all others as the "Minor Leagues." And compared to most other professional sports, the game of baseball has changed very little since.

Turtles live in the sea, *tortoises* live on land, and *terrapins* live in fresh water.

THE SEARCH FOR THE "AFGHAN GIRL"

Here's the story of one of the most famous photographs of the 20th century.

SNAPSHOT

In December 1984, a *National Geographic* photographer named Steve McCurry visited the Nasir Bagh refugee camp on the Afghan/Pakistan border while covering the war between the Soviet Union and Afghanistan. While there he snapped a photograph of a 12-year-old girl with haunting blue-green eyes. The girl had been living in the camp ever since Soviet helicopters had bombed her village five years earlier, killing both her parents.

McCurry didn't have a translator with him that day, so he never got the girl's name. But the photograph, which appeared on the cover of the June 1985 issue, went on to become the single most recognized photograph in *National Geographic's* 115-year history and one of the most reproduced images in the world.

NO FORWARDING ADDRESS

As the image's fame grew, so did the mystery: Who was the girl? "I don't think a week has gone by for 15 years," McCurry told *National Geographic* in 2002, "that I don't get requests from people trying to get information about her."

McCurry went on assignment to the region 10 more times in the years that followed, and each time he searched for the Afghan girl, but couldn't find her. Then in January 2002, he and a team from *National Geographic* made one more trip to the Nasir Bagh refugee camp to try to track her down. The girl—who by then would have been a woman of about 30—apparently hadn't lived in the camp for several years. But McCurry hoped they might find *someone* who knew her. The camp was scheduled to be demolished, so it was their last chance. Once Nasir Bagh was gone, there would be little hope of ever finding her.

COULD IT BE HER?

At the refugee camp the team pursued several false leads before finally meeting a man who claimed to recognize the girl in the photograph. *This* guy seemed authentic. He said the woman was his neighbor's wife and even offered to go and get her.

Several days later, the man returned with the woman's husband. In Afghanistan, women do not meet men other than family members, so McCurry was not allowed to see her. He sent a female member of the team, Carrie Regan, to photograph her face, so that it could be compared against the photos taken in 1984.

One look at the new photos was all it took. McCurry was certain that this woman, whose name was Sharbat Gula, was the same person he'd photographed 17 years earlier. But to be sure, he had photo analysts compare the irises of the girl in the 1984 photos with those of the woman in the 2002 photos. Result: They were 99.9% certain that Sharbat was the girl (an FBI analysis of her facial features came to the same conclusion). McCurry quickly negotiated with the family and not only received permission to meet Gula, but also to photograph her a second time for the April 2002 issue of *National Geographic*.

UPDATE

So what had happened to the "Afghan girl" in the intervening years? She had lived at Nasir Bagh until 1992 (she returned to Afghanistan during a lull in the fighting between the Soviets and Afghan rebels). She married a baker and had four daughters, one of whom died in infancy. Life for Gula had been hard and it showed in her face. Although only about 30 (she doesn't know exactly when she was born), she looked much older. One thing hadn't changed, though: "Her eyes are as haunting now as they were then," says McCurry. And although Gula is the subject of one of the most famous photographs of the 20th century, it was only in 2002 that she saw the photo for the first time.

Gula has returned to her normal life. *National Geographic* provides medical assistance and other aid, and is seeing that her daughters receive an education. But the magazine will not reveal where she lives, ensuring that the girl with the haunting eyes will likely live out the rest of her life as she wishes—in anonymity, never to be heard from again.

WELCOME TO THE TWILIGHT ZONE

Scientists (and conspiracy theorists) seem to have explanations for everything...except these things.

PLACE: Blind River, Ontario

MYSTERIOUS OCCURRENCE: On June 14, 2004, someone called the local radio station to ask whether anybody knew why their clock had jumped ahead 10 minutes. That didn't seem very interesting...until somebody else called. And then somebody else. Word quickly spread: clocks all over town were going haywire. And it kept on for days. "I thought it was just me," reported city administrator Ken Corbiere, "until I mentioned it at work." But, strangely, it was only specific clocks—digital clocks on stoves, microwaves, and clock radios, and electrically powered dial clocks.

EXPLANATIONS: Since it didn't happen to battery-powered clocks, at first it was thought to be a problem with the local power company. But company spokespeople called that "highly unlikely." A power surge, they said, would burn clocks out, not move them ahead. And besides, any power fluctuations would affect *all* appliances—not just clocks. Other explanations? So far, none.

PLACE: Calgary, Alberta

MYSTERIOUS OCCURRENCE: Scientists at the Alberta Children's Hospital in Calgary recently released the findings of a study confirming what epileptic dog owners have been saying for years: dogs can tell when someone is about to have an epileptic seizure. Nine of the 60 dogs tested were able to show, by licking or whimpering, when a seizure was about to strike.

EXPLANATIONS: They have none. Some researchers believe the body may give off a distinctive smell during a seizure, but it's just a guess. Tests continue.

PLACE: Las Vegas, Nevada

MYSTERIOUS OCCURRENCE: In February 2004, hundreds of people in Las Vegas called locksmiths, towing companies, and auto

---

Sea cucumbers startle their enemies by shooting their digestive organs out their rear ends.

dealerships with the identical problem: the keyless entry devices for their cars didn't work. Many people, locked out of their cars, were stranded. Some resorted to the old-fashioned way of opening doors—keys—but set off their car alarms in the process.

EXPLANATIONS: There have been many. One was solar flares—but local observatories reported low solar activity on the day of the lockouts. Another was a weather-induced static electricity buildup—but researchers said the damp, cloudy weather made that unlikely. Others said it was caused by secret technology at nearby Nellis Air Force Base. (A similar lockout happened in 2001 near a Navy base in Bremerton, Washington.) The Air Force dismissed the idea, saying any equipment they may (or may not) be working on wouldn't affect car remotes. A more exciting explanation: space aliens, and whatever the military was doing at the fabled Area 51, about 100 miles northwest of Las Vegas.

PLACE: Canneto di Caronia, Italy

MYSTERIOUS OCCURRENCE: In January 2004, objects started spontaneously bursting into flames in homes all over this tiny town in Sicily. Fires were reported in refrigerators, microwave ovens, fuse boxes, cars, and more...with no plausible explanation. "With my own eyes I've seen unplugged electrical cables burst into flames, but I just can't explain it," a local policeman told reporters. The situation got so bad that a state of emergency was declared and the town's residents—all 39 of them—were evacuated.

EXPLANATIONS: Local officials decided it must have something to do with the town's power supply, so they cut off all electricity—but the fires kept happening. The town has since been overrun by scientists and paranormalists from all over the world. Some explanations given: volcanic activity from nearby Mount Etna; a surge in electrical energy from the Earth's core; "high amplitude surges of solar wind protons"; and, of course, Satan. An exorcist was called to the town. (The fires persisted.)

*　　　*　　　*

"The most incomprehensible thing about the world is that it is at all comprehensible."

—**Albert Einstein**

THIS *IS* MY OTHER CAR

Every year, BRI member Debbie Thornton sends in a list of
real-life bumper stickers. Have you seen the one that says…

Where am I going, and why
am I in this handbasket?

I love defenseless animals—
especially in a good gravy

I'M MULTITALENTED: I CAN
TALK AND ANNOY YOU
AT THE SAME TIME

Do they ever shut
up on your planet?

THERAPY IS EXPENSIVE;
POPPING BUBBLE WRAP IS
CHEAP! YOU CHOOSE.

I brake for no apparent reason

HONK IF YOU'VE NEVER SEEN AN
UZI FIRED FROM A CAR WINDOW

TRY NOT TO LET YOUR MIND
WANDER—IT'S TOO SMALL
TO BE OUT BY ITSELF

Politicians and diapers
need to be changed—often
for the same reason

Whose cruel idea was it for the
word LISP to have an S in it?

MY WIFE KEEPS COMPLAINING
THAT I NEVER LISTEN TO HER…
OR SOMETHING LIKE THAT

Caution: I drive like you do

I'll bet you a new car that I
can stop faster than you can!

BOYCOTT SHAMPOO!
DEMAND REAL POO!

It's time to pull over and
change the air in your head

Everyone has a right to be stupid.
Some just abuse the privilege.

Bad Cop, No Donut

I'M NOT A COMPLETE IDIOT—
SOME PARTS ARE MISSING

If you don't like the way I
drive, stay off the sidewalk

ON THE OTHER HAND, YOU
HAVE DIFFERENT FINGERS

QUESTION REALITY

PRESERVE NATURE:
PICKLE A SQUIRREL

Four out of five voices in
my head say, "Kill!"

If I throw a stick,
will you leave?

Why Are You Staring At My
Bumper, You Pervert!

Q: What is a *septillion?* A: 1 followed by 24 zeroes.

FOUND AND LOST

If you found a fortune in cash that didn't belong to you, what would you do with it? From our Famous for 15 Minutes file, here's the story of a guy who faced just such a dilemma.

THE STAR: Joey Coyle, 28, an unemployed dockworker
THE HEADLINE: *Nightmare on Easy Street*
WHAT HAPPENED: On February 26, 1981, Coyle was driving through an industrial section of Philadelphia with some friends when he spotted an overturned plastic tub by the side of the road. Thinking it might make a good toolbox, Coyle told his friends to stop the car, got out, and examined the tub. Inside—just like in the movies—there were two canvas bags marked FEDERAL RESERVE BANK containing $1.2 million in cash.

The tub had fallen out of an armored car only minutes before, and the money—bundles of $100 bills collected from an Atlantic City casino—was completely untraceable. Had Coyle simply kept a low profile, he might have gotten away with keeping it. But he didn't—he told everyone he knew and flashed $100 bills all over town. Six days later, the FBI nabbed him at the airport trying to catch a flight to Acapulco with $135,000 stuffed into his shoes. Charged with theft, he pled temporary insanity. That may sound like a dumb idea, but it worked—Coyle was acquitted. He didn't get to keep the money, but he didn't have to do any jail time.

In 1993 Coyle found fame (but no fortune) when his story became the subject of the film *Money for Nothing*, starring John Cusack. So was it worth it? "I wouldn't put nobody in my situation," Coyle told an interviewer. "Everybody's thinking, 'That must have been great.' Little do they know it was nothing but agony and despair. In those six days I must have aged 20 years. You have no idea what money does to you—especially that kind of money."

AFTERMATH: Coyle never even got to enjoy seeing himself portrayed on the silver screen. He had battled drug addiction for years and was awaiting sentencing on his sixth drug conviction when his mother died in the summer of 1993. He committed suicide that August, one month before *Money for Nothing* opened nationwide.

Q: What are *tiercels*, *hens*, and *eyas*? A: Father, mother, and baby hawks.

AMERICA'S FORGOTTEN FOUNDING FATHER

"That the name of George Mason should be acclaimed throughout the Republic whose birth pangs he shared, and indeed throughout the free world, will be agreed, I believe, by all American historians." —Dumas Malone, 1961
...George who?

FAMOUS FIRST WORDS

In May 1776, a wealthy Virginia landowner and outspoken critic of the British government wrote some of the most famous words in American history:

> That all men are by nature equally free and independent and have certain inherent rights...namely, the enjoyment of life and liberty, with the means of acquiring and possessing property, and pursuing and obtaining happiness and safety.

Thomas Jefferson, right? No, those words are from Virginia's Declaration of Rights, written by another wealthy Virginian— George Mason. Jefferson was to borrow and edit Mason's words less than two months later when he wrote the Declaration of Independence. Other parts of Mason's document would later be used for the Bill of Rights. So why isn't Mason as well known as Jefferson, Adams, Washington, and the other Founding Fathers?

CURIOUS GEORGE

George Mason was born to a wealthy Virginia family near the Potomac River in 1725. His father died when George was 10, so he was raised by his mother and his uncle, John Mercer, a prominent lawyer in the colony. Historians agree that young Mason benefited from the move because it provided him with access to his uncle's private library—more than 1,500 volumes, most of them concerning history and the law. Although his future work would influence governments all over the world, Mason had virtually no formal schooling: he taught himself in that library. It was there, biographers say, that he learned and developed his theories about government—that too strong a central government was dangerous and that there must be protected rights for individuals—as well as his lifelong opposition to slavery (although he was, like Jefferson, a slave owner).

THE STRONG, SILENT TYPE

Known as an intensely private man, Mason believed in public service, but had no desire for the limelight and no interest in the "babblers" of national politics (he was elected to the Continental Congress in 1777 but refused the seat). Yet despite his disdain for national politics, his extensive legal knowledge (especially in English law), his strong beliefs in personal freedoms, and his hatred of British tyranny led him to a prominent position in the shaping of the United States.

• In the 1750s, he began a career in local Virginia politics as a trustee of the town of Alexandria and justice for Fairfax County.

• In 1759 Mason was elected to the Virginia House of Burgesses (the colonial legislature), where he first earned his reputation as a fearless critic of the British.

• In 1765 he wrote an open letter condemning and urging resistance to the infamous Stamp Act, Great Britain's first direct tax on the colonies.

• In 1774 Mason and his neighbor, George Washington, wrote "The Fairfax Resolves," calling for a congress of the colonies and a halt of trade with Great Britain. The Resolves were adopted by Virginia that year and by the Continental Congress in 1775.

• In 1776 he was asked to write Virginia's Declaration of Rights (assisted by 25-year-old James Madison). That document is widely considered to be one of the most influential and important papers in the history of modern democratic government. Along with the "pursuit of happiness," the extraordinary declaration also called for a separation of government powers, guaranteed freedom of the press, freedom of religion, and trial by a jury of one's peers. It would soon serve as a model for other state declarations, and eventually for Jefferson's Declaration of Independence, which spurred the American Revolution.

AT THE CONSTITUTIONAL CONVENTION

- In the summer of 1787, Mason, now an elder statesman, was called out of retirement to attend the Constitutional Convention and to assist in writing the new nation's constitution. He took the job seriously, writing that the final work would affect "the happiness or misery of millions yet unborn." He is considered one of the most influential participants—giving more than 136 speeches on the convention floor. But as the work progressed, Mason grew to dislike the direction in which he saw the document headed. On August 31, he announced "that he would sooner chop off his right hand" than see such a constitution passed. In September, Mason passed a list of "Objections to This Constitution of Government" to his colleagues. They outlined 16 points of contention. Among them:

- The working constitution contained no bill of rights for individuals—this was the worst problem, in Mason's view.

- The Supreme Court was given too much power over state judiciaries, "enabling the rich to oppress and ruin the poor."

- The president had excessive pardoning powers "which may be sometimes exercised to screen from punishment those whom he had secretly instigated to commit the crime, and thereby prevent a discovery of his own guilt."

- Slaves were allowed to be imported for another 20 years. Mason wanted to immediately end the importation of slaves and to abolish slavery as soon as possible.

- The proposed constitution threatened to "produce a monarchy, or a corrupt, tyrannical aristocracy."

PAYBACK

The Constitution was signed by the delegates on September 17, 1787—but George Mason was not among them. In the end, after having been so influential in the document's creation, he refused to sign it, and the move is said to have cost him his long friendship with George Washington. Critics said that he had let his ego get the best of him; some even questioned his sanity. But Mason continued to fight for his changes, opposing the document's ratification in Virginia. When the Constitution was formally ratified on July 2, 1788, Mason still opposed it.

As more and more Americans read the Constitution after its initial signing, it became obvious that many people shared Mason's biggest fear: that it contained no bill of rights. In fact, many of the states ratified it only on the promise that such a bill would quickly be added. With pressure mounting from across the new nation, the anti-Bill of Rights contingent finally had to give in. In 1791 Congress made the first change to the U.S. Constitution by ratifying 10 amendments—the Bill of Rights.

The First, Second, Fourth, Fifth, Sixth, Seventh, and Eighth Amendments were all largely borrowed from Mason's Virginia declaration, sometimes using his exact wording. Mason later wrote that "I have received much satisfaction from amendments to the federal Constitution that have lately passed. With two or three further amendments, I could cheerfully put my hand and heart to the new government." (In 1795 the Eleventh amendment was passed, limiting the power of the Supreme Court over the states—another of Mason's ideas.)

George Mason died on October 7, 1792 at his home in Virginia. His refusal to sign the Constitution makes him largely unknown to modern Americans, but his place as the "Father of the Bill of Rights" and one of the most important Founding Fathers is unquestioned. In 2002 he was finally recognized by the nation he helped found when the George Mason National Memorial was formally dedicated near the Thomas Jefferson Memorial in Washington, D.C.

* * *

THANKS, GEORGE

"In giving this account of the laws of which I was myself the mover and draughtsman, I by no means mean to claim to myself the merit of obtaining their passage. I had many strenuous coadjutors in debate, and one most steadfast, able, and zealous. This was George Mason, a man of the first order of wisdom among those who acted on the theatre of the revolution, of expansive mind, profound judgment, cogent in argument, learned in the lore of our former constitution, and earnest for the republican change on democratic principles."

—Thomas Jefferson, 1821

George Washington liked to tell dirty jokes.

LUCKY STRIKES

It may shock you to learn that some people who are struck by lightning live to tell the tale.

SHOCKING STATISTICS

If you're struck by a bolt of lightning, are you more likely to live or die? More likely than not, you'll survive. The National Weather Service estimates that roughly 400 people are struck by lightning each year in the United States. Of these, only 10% are killed—and some of them could have been saved by CPR.

As for the survivors, 70% of them suffer long-term effects, including pain, stiffness, numbness, headaches, insomnia, hearing loss, fatigue, short-term memory loss, depression, and difficulty sitting for long periods of time. The remaining 30% have few or no long-term problems. Here are some folks who got lucky:

EDWIN E. ROBINSON, 62, a former truck driver from Falmouth, Maine, who had lost most of his sight and hearing after suffering a head injury in a 1971 truck accident

The Strike: In June 1980, Robinson was struck by lightning when he went into his backyard during a thunderstorm to look for his pet chicken. "It was like somebody cracked a whip over my head," he told reporters. "I fell right on the ground, face forward." Being struck by lightning would take a lot out of anyone, so after being struck, Robinson got up, went in the house, and took a nap. When he woke up 20 minutes later, he felt a little "rubbery," but other than that he was fine.

Aftermath: Most people would consider themselves lucky just to break even after a lightning strike, but Robinson's health actually improved—somehow the electric shock reversed the brain damage from the 1971 truck accident and caused his hearing and sight to return. Robinson's ophthalmologist has verified the improvement, but other eye specialists speculate that his was a case of "hysterical blindness"—Robinson *wanted* to think he was blind, and now he wants to think he's been cured. Robinson says that's "a load of bull." He gives the credit to God. "He put me with this," he says. "I coped with it, and when the time came, lightning struck me."

JOHN CORSON, 56, of Madison, Maine

The Strike: Corson was struck in July 2004, while working outside on his house just after a thunderstorm had passed by. "It was a whitish-blue, and so bright," he told reporters. "I actually heard the snap, but I was paralyzed. My whole body was vibrating. It was a hell of a sensation."

Aftermath: The lightning strike tripped three circuit breakers in the garage, but Corson—who has had three heart surgeries—was not even knocked down. His knees buckled a little and the bolt left red marks on his shoulders. Otherwise he's fine. In fact, he says he feels better than before. "I'm feeling like my body is light," he says. "It's the best I've felt in ten years."

MARK DAVIDSON, 33, a fisherman from Whitley Bay, England

The Strike: Davison got his jolt while fishing for salmon off the coast. "A lightning bolt hit the antenna mast on top of the wheelhouse, then it went straight through me," he says. "It felt like somebody had whacked me on the head with a hammer." After the strike, Davison's friend fired off a distress flare and the Coast Guard came and took him to the hospital.

Aftermath: Davison was fine—and when he was released a few hours later, he headed right back out to fish. (He figured lightning never strikes the same place twice.)

DANYL LEVIEGE, 44, an ex-preacher from Omaha, Nebraska

Strike: LeViege was standing in the doorway of his porch watching storm clouds when lightning struck him on the neck—right on the spot where he was wearing a cross. "The lightning hit the necklace," he says. "That's where the pain was. I went flying."

Aftermath: The pain is gone, but LaViege still has burn marks. His wife, Sheila, says the bolt was the Almighty's way of telling him to return to the ministry. "It's a miracle," she told *Jet* magazine. "I told him it happened for a reason. 'God's giving you a message. Straighten up.'"

CARRIE KWASNIEWSKI, a constable in West Sussex, England

The Strike: Kwasniewski, who patrols on bicycle, was struck while taking a report from a motorist. "There was an almighty flash, and a bolt shot through my arm, throwing me from my bike," she says. The bolt shot out the handlebar and struck the motorist's car, knocking out its electrical system. "The woman said 'did that really just happen?'" Kwasniewski says. "We just looked at each other and said, 'we've just been struck by lightning.'"

Aftermath: Kwasniewski's arm felt a little tingly, but otherwise she felt fine. So she went on to her next assignment—taking a report from a nearby gas station that had been struck by lightning. "We've dubbed her Superwoman," says her boss, Geoff Charnock.

JIM CAVIEZEL, 35, the actor who played Jesus in the film *The Passion of the Christ*

Strike: Caviezel was filming the Sermon on the Mount scene when a bolt of lightning struck him on the head. "I'm about a hundred feet away from him when I glance over and see lightning coming out of Caviezel's ears," says producer Steve McEveety.

"There was a big flash," Caviezel says. "My hair was up like Bozo the Clown. A giant pressure engulfed my head."

Aftermath: You might expect an actor who is struck by lightning while playing Jesus to wonder if maybe God isn't too crazy about the movie. Caviezel took a narrower view—"I thought, 'Didn't like that take, huh?'"—and then resumed his work on the film.

ROBERT GILMER, 72, a security guard in Jamesville, New York

Strike: Gilmer was sipping iced tea in the company cafeteria when lightning struck the flagpole outside the building, about two feet from where he was sitting. The bolt traveled inside the building, struck Gilmer, and knocked him down. He stood up and saw that his pants were on fire. He put the fire out with his hands. Then, unable to phone for help (the lightning having knocked out the phone system), Gilmer just sat and waited until Phillip Wheeler, the assistant superintendent, found him about an hour and 45 minutes later.

Aftermath: When Wheeler found Gilmer, he was complaining of ringing in his ears and had burns on his left leg, face, and hands. But what made him really mad was his pants. "He was more concerned that he didn't look presentable because of his pants being burnt," Wheeler says. "It burned his undershorts, too."

Want to know how you can avoid a lightning strike? Go to page 439.

Horse meat is more popular in Sweden than lamb.

IRONIC, ISN'T IT?

*There's nothing like a good dose of irony to put the
problems of day-to-day life into proper perspective.*

R ATS!
In 1999 England's *New Scientist* magazine reported that rats
in the United Kingdom were becoming increasingly resistant to rat poison. But owls and other birds of prey, for whom rats
are a natural food source, aren't resistant and were dying after eating poisoned rodents. Result: The poison intended to control the
rat population was actually killing off the rats' natural predators—
resulting in an increase in the number of rats.

TOXIC AVENGER
Legal aide Erin Brockovich made history in 1996 by winning a
class-action lawsuit against a giant utility company, Pacific Gas &
Electric, for toxic contamination of groundwater in a small
California town. The $333 million settlement was the largest to
date and made Brockovich famous—especially after Julia Roberts
played her in a movie about the lawsuit. She got a $2 million
bonus for winning the case and bought her dream house in Agoura
Hills, California, for $600,000. Shortly after moving in,
Brockovich discovered that it was contaminated with toxic mold.
(She sued.)

TOY STORY
On October 30, 2003, the U.S. Congress General Accounting
Office published the results of a study. Finding: There is little evidence to show that toy guns have any relationship to crime. That
same day, the Capitol had to be locked down as SWAT teams conducted a one-hour manhunt for two employees who'd brought
what turned out to be toy guns to work, as part of their Halloween
costumes.

DETAILS, DETAILS...
Florida's secretary of state, Katherine Harris, became famous during
the 2000 presidential election as the person in charge of the dis-

---

In South Korea, a can of Spam is considered a prestigious wedding gift.

puted ballot count. In the 2004 local election in her hometown of Longboat Key, Florida, she was informed that her vote would not be counted because she had turned in an invalid ballot. (She forgot to sign it.)

CUT TO THE CHASE

In 2002 the *Sydney Morning Herald* reported an incident where a 42-year-old man in the town of Kurrajong, Australia, stole a truck and was being chased by the owner's father in a car. As the pursuer got closer, the thief panicked, jumped out of the truck, tried to escape on foot—and was immediately hit by another car. According to witnesses, the driver of that car got out, walked over to the injured thief—and stole his wallet. The truck thief was arrested; the wallet thief got away.

SKIN DEEP

Twenty-six-year-old Samuel Worlin Moore was arrested for attempted armed robbery in Long Beach, California. Witnesses were able to ID him because of the distinctive tattoo on his arm. It read "Not Guilty."

DO UNTO OTHERS...

In 1998 former White House aide Linda Tripp became famous for her part in the Monica Lewinsky scandal. Tripp had secretly taped private telephone conversations, in which Lewinsky revealed details of her affair with President Clinton. Tripp then gave the tapes to the special prosecutor, ultimately leading to Clinton's impeachment. Five years later, Tripp won a $595,000 settlement against the Pentagon—for violating her privacy. Details of her life, including an arrest as a teenager, had been leaked to the media after she turned over the tapes.

MR. SATURDAY NIGHT SPECIAL

In February 2004, 74-year-old James Joseph Minder had to retire as chairman of gun manufacturer Smith & Wesson. A local newspaper had revealed that Minder had a dubious resume: he'd spent 15 years in prison for armed robbery. He said that he hadn't told anybody about it because "nobody asked."

First female passenger on a trans-Atlantic flight: Amelia Earhart.

GETTING THE LAST WORD

These lines were taken from the actual wills of some pretty frustrated, but creative (and slightly looney) people.

DAVID DAVIS (1788): "I give and bequeath to Mary Davis the sum of five shillings, which is sufficient to enable her to get drunk for the last time at my expense; and I give the like sum to Charles Peter, the son of Mary, whom I am reputed to be the father of, but never had or ever shall have any reason to believe."

• JOHN AYLETT (1781): "I hereby direct my executor to lay out five guineas in purchase of a picture of the viper biting the benevolent hand of the person who saved him from perishing in the snow. This I direct to be presented to him in lieu of a legacy of 3,000 pounds which I had, by a former will, now revoked and burnt, left him."

• HENRY, EARL OF STAFFORD (England, 1719): "I give to the worst of women, who is guilty of all ills, the daughter of Mr. Gramont, a Frenchman, who I have unfortunately married, five and forty brass halfpence, which will buy her a pullet for her supper, a greater sum than her father can make her; for I have known when he had neither money or credit for such a purchase, he being the worst of men, and his wife the worst of women, in all debaucheries. Had I known their character, I would have never married their daughter, nor made myself unhappy."

• GARVEY B. WHITE (1908): "Before anything else is done 50 cents is to be paid to my son-in-law to enable him to buy for himself a good stout rope with which to hang himself, and thus rid mankind of one of the most infamous scoundrels that ever roamed this broad land or dwelt outside of a penitentiary."

• ELIZABETH ORBY HUNTER (1813): "I give and bequeath to my beloved parrot, the faithful companion of twenty-five years, an annuity for its life, of 200 guineas a year, to be paid half yearly,

---

At the end of the Civil War, 33% of the circulating U.S. paper currency was counterfeit.

as long as this beloved parrot lives, to whoever may have the care of it; and if the person who shall have the care of it should substitute any other parrot in its place either during its life or after its death, it is my will and desire that the persons doing so shall be refused by my heirs the sum or sums they may have received from the time they did so; and I empower my heirs and executors to recover said sum from whoever would be base enough to do so."

• **PHILIP, FIFTH EARL OF PEMBROKE (England, 1700s):** "I give nothing to my Lord Saye, and I make him this legacy willingly, because I know that he will faithfully distribute it to the poor. I give to the Lieutenant-General Cromwell one of my words which he must want, seeing that he hath never kept any of his own."

• **CAPTAIN PHILIP THICKNESSE (England, 1793):** His will instructed that "my right hand to be cut off after my death and given to my son Lord Audley and I desire it may be sent to him in hopes that such a sight may remind him of his duty to God after having so long abandoned the Duty he owed to a father who once affectionately loved him."

• **FRANCIS H. LORD (Australia, date unknown):** To his wife: "one shilling for tram fare so she can go somewhere and drown herself."

• **JOSEPH DALBY, (England, 1784):** "I give to my daughter Ann Spencer, a guinea for a ring, or any other bauble she may like better. I give to the lout, her husband, one penny, to buy him a lark-whistle; I also give to her said husband of redoubtable memory, my fart-hole, for a covering for his lark-whistle, to prevent the abrasion of his lips; and this legacy I give him as a mark of my approbation of his prowess and nice honour, in drawing his sword on me, (at my own table), unarmed as I was, and he well fortified with custard."

• **WILLIAM RUFFELL (1803):**
> "To employ an attorney I ne'er was inclined.
> They are pests to society, sharks of mankind.
> To avoid that base tribe, my own will I now draw,
> May I ever escape coming under their paw."

Cats have been known to try to seduce dogs. (Few succeed.)

STATUE RATS

They're called "flying carp," "winged weasels," "scum of the sky," "park lice," and "winged infestation." Lawyers? No, pigeons. They don't get much respect, but maybe they should. There's more to them than you might think.

• Pigeons were first domesticated by the ancient Egyptians more than 5,000 years ago.

• Pigeons can see clearly for 25 miles and hear wind changes hundreds of miles away.

• Homing pigeons were used in both world wars to carry messages between troops and headquarters. They had a 98% success rate in missions flown.

• Pigeons mate for life and share parenting duties. The father sits on the eggs during the day, the mother at night.

• Pigeons are the only birds that don't have to lift their heads to swallow water.

• In the 17th century, pigeon droppings were used to tan hides and to make gunpowder.

• Passenger pigeons were once the most numerous birds in the world. Ornithologist John J. Audubon recorded seeing a single flock in 1808 that he calculated to be 150 miles long, numbering over two billion birds. By 1914 hunting and deforestation had led to the total extinction of the birds.

• Ever seen a baby pigeon? You probably have: young pigeons grow extremely fast. They may weigh more than their parents by the time they're only four to six weeks.

• In the late 1800s, a homing pigeon was released in Africa. Fifty-five days later it made it home—to England. It had flown more than 7,000 miles.

• Racing pigeons have been clocked at 110 mph.

• Only mammals produce milk, right? Wrong. Pigeons make "pigeon milk." It's a specially produced, extremely nutritious secretion from the "crop," a chamber at the bottom of the esophagus. Both parents make it and feed their young with it.

• Racing pigeons are bred for speed. In 1992 champion racer *Invincible Spirit* was sold for over $130,000.

• Why do pigeons live in cities? One theory: They are descended from rock doves, cliff dwellers that live near the Mediterranean. Urban structures mimic those ancestral cliffs.

In the 1600s, thermometers were often filled with brandy instead of mercury.

RANDOM ORIGINS

*Once again, the BRI asks—and answers—the
question: "Where did all this stuff come from?"*

CELL PHONES

AT&T first tested mobile phones for use in Swedish police
cars in 1946. To develop the technology in the United
States, they needed approval from the FCC—which controls the
radio waves. The FCC didn't think mobile phones would work and
repeatedly turned down AT&T. They finally agreed to change
their minds in 1968, but only if AT&T could prove that their
technology worked. AT&T's plan: offer phone service via many
low-powered broadcast towers, each covering a "cell" of a few
miles. As the car phone user traveled, calls passed from tower to
tower uninterrupted.

Meanwhile, rival Motorola had secretly developed their own
mobile phone, only theirs was a handheld model. (AT&T had
concentrated on car phones.) In 1973 one of Motorola's engineers,
Dr. Martin Cooper, used a prototype to make the first cell phone
call—to AT&T, to gloat.

But AT&T was the first to get FCC approval, and had a trial
cellular network set up in Chicago by 1978. (Motorola had one by
1981 in Washington, D.C.) The FCC authorized nationwide commercial cellular service in 1982 and just five years later there were
over one million cell phone users in the United States.

SEAT BELTS

Safety belts predate cars. They were originally designed as devices
to secure workmen and window-washers to their equipment when
scaling tall buildings. Although they first appeared in cars in the
1920s, it wasn't until the 1950s that seat belts were offered—and
even then only as *options*—by most car manufacturers. In those
days seat belts were like belts on pants: the strap went around your
waist and buckled in the center of the abdomen just like a belt
buckle. This design was far from perfect: the buckle itself could
cause severe abdominal injuries in a crash, and since there wasn't
any shoulder strap, the upper body was unrestrained. Head, spinal,
and internal injuries were common in serious crashes.

A typical gold brick weighs 27 pounds.

In the 1950s, Volvo experimented with a diagonal seat belt that went across the passenger's chest, but this presented new problems: in a crash the passenger's body tended to "submarine" or slip under the belt, at which point the passenger's neck could catch on the belt, causing severe neck lacerations or even decapitation.

In 1958 a Volvo safety engineer named Nils Bohlin hit on the idea of combining both types of belts—the lap belt and the diagonal shoulder belt—and moving the buckle from the center over to the side. The modern "three-point" seat belt, so called because it is anchored to the car frame on either side of the passenger's waist and over their shoulder, was born. It became standard equipment on all Volvos (front seats only) beginning in 1963; by 1968 all cars sold in the United States were required to have them. Since then they've reduced automobile fatalities by an estimated 75% and have saved more than a million lives.

RESTAURANTS

The oldest ancestor of the restaurant is the tavern, which dates back to the Middle Ages. Typically taverns served one meal at a fixed hour each day, usually consisting of only one dish. According to French food historians, it wasn't until 1765 that someone came up with the idea of giving customers a *choice* of things to eat. A Parisian soup vendor named Monsieur Boulanger is said to have offered his customers poultry, eggs, and other dishes, but it was his soups, also known as "restoratives" or *restaurants* in French, that gave this new type of eatery its name.

THE NICOTINE PATCH

In 1979 Dr. Frank Etscorn, a psychologist studying addictive substances, was experimenting with liquid nicotine when he accidentally spilled some of it on his arm. A little while later he felt the telltale effects of a nicotine buzz. Nicotine is the most addictive drug in tobacco, but its health risks are far lower than that of the tars and carbon monoxide ingested from smoking. Etscorn's nicotine buzz gave him the idea that people trying to quit smoking could be given, through the skin, gradually decreasing doses of nicotine as they tried to quit smoking. The first nicotine patches hit drugstore shelves in 1992.

TAXI DRIVER, STARRING NEIL DIAMOND

Some roles are so closely associated with a specific actor that it's hard to imagine he or she wasn't the first choice. But it happens all the time. Can you imagine, for example...

KEVIN KLINE AS BATMAN (*Batman*—1989) Many fans were puzzled when Michael Keaton was cast as Batman, but it could have been stranger: Kline was the first choice. Lacking confidence in his action-star abilities, Kline passed on the role and made *A Fish Called Wanda* instead, for which he won an Academy Award. Other actors offered the role of Batman: Alec Baldwin, Charlie Sheen, Pierce Brosnan, Mel Gibson, Bill Murray, and Tom Hanks.

WILL SMITH AS NEO (*The Matrix*—1999) After *Independence Day* and *Men in Black*, Smith was Hollywood's biggest action star. He was offered the lead role in a new action-adventure series called *The Matrix*, but turned it down. Why? Smith didn't want to be involved in an obscure, dense, low-budget science-fiction mess. Instead, he chose to make *Wild Wild West*, which bombed.

GWYNETH PALTROW AS ROLLERGIRL (*Boogie Nights*—1997) Director Paul Thomas Anderson liked Paltrow's performance in his first film, *Hard Eight*, so much that he considered her for the part of Rollergirl in *Boogie Nights*, a movie about the 1970s adult film industry. Paltrow was still relatively unknown and was picking her roles with care. She turned *Boogie Nights* down because of the sex scenes and nudity. Heather Graham got the part.

NEIL DIAMOND AS TRAVIS BICKLE (*Taxi Driver*—1976) When Brian De Palma planned to direct the film, he almost cast Diamond, at that time a very successful singer. Producers thought *Taxi Driver* would be an ideal debut for Diamond. His dismal screen test proved otherwise. De Palma dropped out and was replaced by Martin Scorcese who chose Robert De Niro to star.

ERIC STOLTZ AS MARTY MCFLY (*Back to the Future*—1985) Michael J. Fox was the first choice to play Marty McFly, but he said he was too busy filming the TV series *Family Ties*, so the producers cast Eric Stoltz (*Mask, Some Kind of Wonderful*). When Fox had a change of heart, they fired Stoltz even though they'd already filmed several scenes.

MEG RYAN AS VIVIAN (*Pretty Woman*—1990) Ryan was the queen of romantic comedy in the late 1980s, and the first choice for *Pretty Woman*. But producers didn't think audiences would find her believable in the role of a prostitute, so they went with a relatively unknown actress instead. The role made Julia Roberts a superstar. (1980s teen movie star Molly Ringwald was also considered.)

WARREN BEATTY AS BILL (*Kill Bill*—2003/2004) Quentin Tarantino wrote the Bill character with Warren Beatty in mind, but when discussing the character with Beatty, Tarantino repeatedly insisted he play the part "more like David Carradine." Beatty finally suggested that Tarantino just cast David Carradine. After nearly going with Kevin Costner, Tarantino took Beatty's advice and hired Carradine.

BILL MURRAY AS FORREST GUMP (*Forrest Gump*—1994) Murray was strongly considered for the role, but lost it to Tom Hanks, whose work in *Philadelphia* proved he was capable of drama. Murray, on the other hand, was still considered a comic actor.

ROD STEWART AS THE PINBALL WIZARD (*Tommy*—1975) Stewart declined the chance to appear in the film version of The Who's rock opera. Why? His friend Elton John convinced him he'd look ridiculous in the garish costumes and psychedelic musical numbers. Plus, said John, the movie was sure to bomb and would ruin Stewart's career. So who ended up playing the Pinball Wizard? Elton John. He'd wanted the role all along and purposely talked Stewart, the producers' first choice, out of taking it.

AMAZING ANAGRAMS

We're back with another installment of anagrams—words or phrases whose letters are rearranged to form new words or phrases. We don't know who writes these things, but we love 'em.

THE AMERICAN REVOLUTION *becomes...* **UNITE TO REVILE A MONARCH**

JAY LENO *becomes...* **ENJOY L.A.**

THE LEANING TOWER OF PISA *becomes...* **WHAT A FOREIGN STONE PILE**

BRUCE SPRINGSTEEN *becomes...***BURSTING PRESENCE**

EXCLAMATION! *becomes...* **NOTE: A CLIMAX**

FRANCIS FORD COPPOLA *becomes...***COLD POPCORN AFFAIRS**

MUSIC TELEVISION *becomes...* **SIT, VOLUME IS NICE**

WILLIAM SHAKESPEARE *becomes...***I'LL MAKE A WISE PHRASE**

LOVE IS BLIND *becomes...* **BLOND IS EVIL**

ALIEN ABDUCTIONS *becomes...* **TABLOID NUISANCE**

A CASE OF MISTAKEN IDENTITY *becomes...* **TESTIMONY INDICATES A FAKE**

HELLO KITTY *becomes...* **KILL THE TOY**

MEDIOCRITY *becomes...* **ME CRY "IDIOT"**

THE UNITED STATES OF AMERICA *becomes...* **THE DREAM: FINE CAUSE—TOAST IT.**

BETTE MIDLER *becomes...* **DIET? TREMBLE!**

ARNOLD SCHWARZENEG GER, THE GOVERNOR OF CALIFORNIA *becomes...* **AFTER RECALL, SIGH, AN OVER GROWN NERD IN CHARGE OF ZOO**

ADIOS, AMIGOS *becomes...* **I GO, SO I AM SAD**

60% of women and 49% of men receive at least 11 e-mails per day.

AND THEN WHAT HAPPENED?

Our next installment of the history of (almost) everything that ever happened. (Part I is on page 110.)

PART II: FROM MOSES TO CLEOPATRA

• **1479 B.C.** Egypt conquers modern-day Israel and Syria, and becomes an empire.

• **1300 B.C.** Moses leads the Jewish slaves from Egypt. The Ten Commandments are codified. The Hittites (in Turkey) develop iron smelting, improving tools and weaponry—the Near Eastern Iron Age begins.

• **1235 B.C.** Athens is founded.

• **1200 B.C.** The Olmecs in southern Mexico now have a calendar, hieroglyphic writing, and the first urban centers in the Americas. The culture will disappear by 400 B.C., but they are believed to be precursors of the Mayan and Aztec cultures.

• **1100 B.C.** The first books of the Bible are written. The Zhou dynasty begins in China. It will last almost 900 years and become one of the most advanced civilizations on Earth, making huge advances in metallurgy, mathematics, astronomy, medicine, art, and architecture. Iron smelting begins in Mesopotamia.

• **1000 B.C.** King David rules Israel; his son, King Solomon, will soon begin work on the Great Temple of Jerusalem. The first Latin tribes settle in central Italy. The Bantu people of western Africa begin the Bantu Migrations, spreading agriculture over much of sub-Saharan Africa. World population: about 50 million.

• **814 B.C.** Phoenicians establish the city of Carthage on the northwest African coast (Tunisia). For 400 years, it will be the primary trade center for the Mediterranean.

• **776 B.C.** The first Olympic Games are held in Greece.

- **753 B.C.** Traditional date for the founding of Rome; approximate time of the writing of the *Iliad* and the *Odyssey* by Homer in Greece.

- **700 B.C.** The Nubians (black Africans from northern Sudan) conquer Egypt; their leaders become pharaohs. Led by King Sargon II, the Assyrian Empire conquers Israel and expels the Jewish people, the basis of the legendary lost tribes of Israel. Musical notation is first used in India.

- **660 B.C.** Jimmu establishes the first Japanese empire. Greeks use standardized coins, initiating the idea of government-sanctioned money to be used in trade.

- **600 B.C.** The next century will see the start of several of the world's great social and religious philosophies: Zoroastrianism is founded by Zoroaster in Persia (it is the first monotheistic religion and the first to define the concepts of good and evil); Taoism is founded by Lao Tzu in China; Buddhism is founded in India by a former prince, Siddhartha Gautama; Confucius begins teaching the value of education and citizenry in China; and the world's first democratic constitution is established in Athens.

- **559 B.C.** The Persian Empire is founded by Cyrus the Great, with Zoroastrianism as its main religion.

- **509 B.C.** The Romans conquer southern Italy and start a republic largely based on Athenian democracy. The Adena and Hopewell farming-based civilizations begin on the Ohio River in North America; they are known today for their pottery, elaborate burial rituals, dome-shaped mounds, and large-scale corn cultivation. Nok culture thrives in Nigeria, producing sculpture and iron works, and establishing an iconic style that remains evident in African art today. Europe's Iron Age begins.

- **469 B.C.** The philosopher Socrates is born in Athens.

- **440 B.C.** Greece is becoming an empire, with Athens as its capital. The reign of Emperor Pericles leads to a golden age of arts, culture, and government. The Celts, a tribe from northern Italy, dominate the British Isles.

- **400 B.C.** The site of London is first inhabited. Plato writes *The Republic*. Ice cream (usually credited to China) is invented.

Ellis Island processed 445,987 immigrants during its first year in service.

- **338 B.C.** Alexander the Great, king of Macedonia, conquers the Greek city-states and expands the Greek empire to Egypt, southern Europe, and northern India, spreading Greek culture and knowledge along the way. He builds the city of Alexandria on the Egyptian coast and commissions its library. The city will become the economic and cultural hub of Asia, Africa, and Europe, and will house the world's first university.

- **300 B.C.** The Greek mathematician Euclid writes *Elements*, considered one of the most important books on mathematics ever written.

- **260 B.C.** The first gladiator contests are held by the Romans, who now rule most of modern-day Italy. The Indian ruler Ashoka converts to Buddhism, spurring its spread through Asia. The first overland trade routes develop between China and India; they will soon become part of the Silk Road, connecting the goods, innovations, and philosophies of the Far East and Europe. Gunpowder is invented in China.

- **220 B.C.** Qin Shih Huang-di unites China for the first time and becomes emperor; work begins on the Great Wall of China (to keep out the Mongolians). Carthaginian commander Hannibal leads his army (and elephants) across the Mediterranean, Spain, and the Alps to attack the Romans. New technology: the Chinese invent the compass, leading to safer travel and improved mapmaking.

- **146 B.C.** Rome conquers Greece.

- **87 B.C.** Babylonians make the first record of Halley's Comet. Glassblowing is invented by the Phoenicians, greatly increasing the production and use of glassware.

- **54 B.C.** General Julius Caesar conquers Gaul (central and northern Europe) for the Romans. Upon returning to Rome, he declares himself dictator.

- **51 B.C.** Land trade routes are now firmly established between the Far East and West. Cleopatra becomes queen of Egypt. She will be the last pharaoh.

And then what happened? Turn to page 345.

THE TALENTED MISS AMERICA

The Miss America pageant added the talent portion to the contest in 1935. Most contestants sing or dance, but some display more unusual skills.

1943: Joan Hyldoft (Miss Ohio) planned an ice skating routine. They built a small rink for her but left it out in the sun and it melted before the pageant began. She had to perform the routine on a bare concrete floor.

1949: Carol Fraser (Miss Montana) rode a horse onto the stage to perform an equestrian routine. The horse stumbled and almost fell into the orchestra pit. Animal acts have been banned ever since.

1957: Marian McKnight's (Miss South Carolina) talent: an impersonation of Marilyn Monroe. (She won.)

1958: Mary Ann Mobley (Miss Mississippi) sang an aria, which turned into a burlesque routine, including a striptease. She only got down to shorts and a slip, but disrobing was banned from any future acts. (She won, too.)

1959: Lynda Mead (Miss Mississippi) became Miss America performing a dramatic recitation about schizophrenia.

1962: Mary Lee Jepsen (Miss Nebraska) accidentally threw a flaming baton into the judges' pit, leading to a ban on pyrotechnics. (She lost.)

1967: Jane Jayroe (Miss Oklahoma) won the crown by conducting the Miss America orchestra.

1995: Heather Whitestone (Miss Alabama) won after performing a ballet piece. What's unusual about that? She's deaf—she took her cues from the vibrations coming through the stage from the orchestra.

2000: Theresa Uchytil's (Miss Iowa) talent was a flashy baton twirling act. Lots of Miss Americas do baton-twirling. What made hers so impressive? Uchytil was born without a left hand.

Other actual "talents:"
- Properly packing a suitcase.
- Stomping on broken glass.
- Driving a tractor.
- Telling a fishing story with a Norwegian accent.

ANIMAL LIFE SPANS

Did you ever wonder how long a hippopotamus lives on average?
Or a butterfly? Or an ant? Well, neither did we...until BRI
member Phyllis Stein came up with this fascinating list.

Platypus: 10–15 years

Garter Snake: 8 years

Deer: 10–15 years

Dragonfly: 1 day

Coyote: 14 years

Irish Wolfhound: 6 years

Duck: 10 years

Cow (Farm raised): 5–7 years

Cow (Free range): 18–22 years

Manatee: 60 years

Hippopatumus: 30 years

Daddy-longlegs: 2–3 years

Groundhog: 4–9 years

Sheep: 12 years

**Monarch butterfly
(Summer bred):** 4–6 weeks

**Monarch butterfly
(Winter bred):** 7–8 months

Elephant (Wild): 50–60 years

Elephant (Zoo): 15–20 years

Horse: 20–25 years

Kangaroo: 4–6 years

Sturgeon: 80 years

Chihuahua: 16 years

Oyster: 6 years

Giant tortoise: 150 years

Guinea pig (Wild): 3 years

Guinea pig (Pet): 12 years

Cat: 11 years

Mouse: 2 years

Rabbit: 6–8 years

Honeybee: 30 days

Earthworm: 4–8 years

Squirrel: 8–9 years

Horseshoe bat: 17 years

Alligator: 35–50 years

Tarantula (Female): 25–30
years

Tarantula (Male): 5–7 years

Carpenter ant: 5–7 years

Black crocodile: 75 years

Caribou: 5–8 years

Bullfrog: 7–9 years

Polar bear: 25–30 years

Rattlesnake: 20–25 years

Pig: 10 years

Giant paa-aa-aa-ndas bleat like sheep.

THE ZOMBIE QUIZ

*Most people have seen so many vampire movies they'd know what to do
if attacked by a vampire: hold up a cross, pound a wooden stake into its
heart, yada yada yada. But what if you were attacked by a zombie?
Take this quiz...while there's still time. Answers are on page 516.*

1. What is a zombie?

a) Someone possessed by the devil.

b) Someone who's been given the evil eye by a gypsy.

c) A tropical drink containing lime, pineapple, and papaya juice,
and four kinds of rum.

d) A dead person come back to life, with an insatiable hunger for
human flesh.

2. How does a person become a zombie?

a) Have a few of those four-kinds-of-rum drinks, wander out into
traffic, and crash! You're a zombie.

b) Do you know how it feels to flip through 300 channels and still
find nothing on TV? Do it long enough and Zap! You're a zombie.

c) By getting bitten or killed by another zombie. (No word on
where the very first zombie, the "alpha zombie" came from.)

d) Ask your mother—it's not Uncle John's place to tell you about
the zombie birds and the zombie bees.

3. What do zombies drink?

a) Zombies.

b) Water.

c) Half decaf, half regular nonfat double lattes, easy on the foam.

d) Nothing—zombies don't drink.

4. How smart are zombies?

a) They'd be a lot smarter if they'd just lay off the zombies.

b) They have some intelligence but not much.

c) Except for shuffling around and eating humans, totally mindless.

d) Dumber than mindless. Typical zombie investment portfolio:
Enron, Beanie Babies, assorted dot-com stocks.

Wrinkles have three main causes...the sun, gravity, and facial expression.

5. What is the average "life span" of a zombie?
a) Until the next full moon, when they will die.
b) Two weeks at the most.
c) Three to five years.
d) With enough human flesh to eat, they can live forever.

6. How strong are zombies?
a) Weak—like one of those zombie cocktails if you left out the rum.
b) As strong as when they were alive, just stiffer and slower.
c) Double the strength of a human being.
d) Able to leap tall buildings in a single bound!

7. How do you kill a zombie?
a) Splash it with holy water.
b) Destroy its brain.
c) Feed it vegetarians—until it dies from malnutrition.
d) Tie it to a tree, then wait for the sun to come up and melt it.

8. What happens when you chop off a zombie's head?
a) It's dead. You win!
b) The head grows a new body; the body grows a new head. Nice going—now you've got two zombies to deal with.
c) The body is dead, but watch out for that head! It's still alive, and if it gets a chance it's going to bite you on the ankle.
d) Don't let it go to waste: Smear it with peanut butter, roll it in peanuts, and hang it from a tree. Your zombie-head birdfeeder will add a festive atmosphere to your yard as it feeds birds all winter.

9. What's the weapon of choice when trying to kill a zombie?
a) Hand grenade   b) Hatchet
c) Flamethrower   d) Rifle

10. How can you protect your pets from zombies?
a) Cats avoid zombies by instinct. As for the dog, add a new trick to its repertoire: 1) Sit! 2) Fetch! 3) Get away from that zombie!
b) Bathe your pets once a month with flea, tick, and zombie soap.
c) Dress them in little zombie costumes (zombies don't eat zombies).
d) Don't worry, zombies don't care about pets—they only eat humans.

Smile! The Mentawai tribe of Indonesia file their teeth into sharp points.

THE KING OF KUNG FU

Bruce Lee only finished four films in his lifetime, but many martial arts movie fans still consider them the best kung fu movies ever made. Here's a look at the man behind the myth.

FIGHT CLUB

In 1958 a bunch of Hong Kong teenagers who studied a style of martial art known as *choy li fut* challenged another group of teens, who studied a style known as *wing chun*, to a fight. Fights like this were fairly common in Hong Kong—the kids would go up on the roof of a local apartment building, pair off, and spar with each other until one fighter forced his opponent over a white line painted on the roof.

But this fight was different—it turned ugly when one of the choy li fut kids punched one of the wing chun kids, Lee Jun Fan, in the face and gave him a black eye. Lee Jun Fan (better known by his English name, Bruce Lee) flew into a rage and gave his opponent quite a beating, even knocking out a tooth or two. When the kid's parents saw what happened, they called the police. Bruce Lee's mom got hauled down to the station and had to sign a paper stating that she would assume full responsibility—and possibly even go to jail—if her son misbehaved again.

COMING TO AMERICA

Fortunately for Bruce's mom, her son had an option that most other Hong Kong teens didn't: He had American citizenship. He'd been born in San Francisco while his parents were touring the United States with a Hong Kong opera company, so he was free to return to America at any time. And as Mrs. Lee saw it, that was probably the best place for him.

Bruce wasn't much of a student—his bad grades and penchant for fighting had gotten him thrown out of more than one school—but even if he had been a good student, Hong Kong was still a British colony and nearly all the best job opportunities were set aside for the British kids. If Bruce stayed in Hong Kong, he'd likely end up on the streets, in jail, or dead. So, Mrs. Lee handed her 17-year-old son $100 and put him on a ship to San Francisco.

Bruce spent a short time there, then moved to Seattle, where he enrolled in high school and went to work as a waiter in a Chinese restaurant. Bruce was a champion cha cha dancer as well as a student of the martial arts, and he gave dancing and kung fu lessons on the side. In time he dropped the dance lessons and focused on martial arts full time.

BACK TO BASICS

By 1964 Lee was 24, married, and running two of his own martial arts studios, one in Seattle and a second in Oakland, California. Several months after the Oakland studio opened, a martial arts instructor named Wong Jack Man from nearby San Francisco demanded that Lee stop teaching martial arts to non-Chinese *gweilos* or "foreign devils." (In those days, many Chinese instructors were opposed to teaching anyone outside their own community.) If Lee refused, Wong Jack Man would challenge him to a fight, and if Lee lost he would either have to stop teaching martial arts to gweilos or close down his studio altogether.

Lee accepted, and then over the course of the next three minutes gave Wong Jack Man the beating of his life. Other fighters might have been content with such a victory, but Lee wasn't—he figured he should have been able to drop Wong after the first couple of blows. The experience caused Lee to question his entire approach to martial arts. Until then he had been a devotee of the wing chun school of kung fu (he spelled it *gung fu*), but now he began to study all forms of martial arts, including fencing, Western-style boxing, and Greco-Roman wrestling, incorporating anything he thought was useful and discarding everything else.

NO NONSENSE

Lee had little interest in classical fighting stances, black belts, breaking boards with his fists, and other kung fu clichés. He just wanted to win fights, as quickly and as skillfully as possible. Everything else was fluff—or as he once put it, "ninety percent of Oriental self-defense is baloney." Over the next two years, Lee developed his own stripped-down, back-to-basics style of fighting that he named *jeet kune do*, or "way of the intercepting fist."

Meanwhile, Lee was also beginning to find work in Hollywood. In August 1964, he gave a demonstration at a martial arts exhibi-

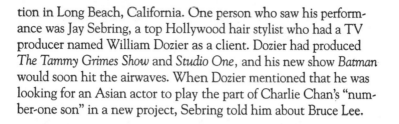

tion in Long Beach, California. One person who saw his performance was Jay Sebring, a top Hollywood hair stylist who had a TV producer named William Dozier as a client. Dozier had produced *The Tammy Grimes Show* and *Studio One*, and his new show *Batman* would soon hit the airwaves. When Dozier mentioned that he was looking for an Asian actor to play the part of Charlie Chan's "number-one son" in a new project, Sebring told him about Bruce Lee.

BECOMING AN ACTOR

The Charlie Chan project never materialized, but when *Batman* became a smash hit, Dozier decided to follow up with a similar show called *The Green Hornet*. Dozier cast Bruce Lee as the Hornet's Asian sidekick, Kato. Lee moved his family to Los Angeles, and in addition to working on the TV show, he began giving private martial arts lessons to celebrities such as James Coburn, Steve McQueen, and Kareem Abdul-Jabbar.

The Green Hornet aired for only one season: it premiered in September 1966 and went off the air in July 1967. Lee earned good reviews for his performance, but it was difficult for an Asian actor to land big parts. Three years passed and his career went nowhere. Lee's celebrity friends helped him land small roles in movies and TV shows, but they weren't the kinds of jobs that would advance his career. He helped develop the TV series *Kung Fu* only to learn in 1971 that he'd lost the lead role to David Carradine, a white guy who didn't know much about kung fu. *Kung Fu's* producers felt that Carradine was a better choice for the role because he had the calm personality that they were looking for in Caine, but Lee's chances were also hurt by the fear that if an Asian actor were cast in the lead, fewer people would watch the show.

ON THE OTHER SIDE OF THE WORLD

Lee didn't know it at the time, but while he was struggling in Hollywood, his star was beginning to rise in Hong Kong. By now *The Green Hornet* had been off the air in the United States for more than three years, but it was still playing in Hong Kong—where it had been renamed *The Kato Show*—and it was one of the most popular shows on the air. Viewers in Hong Kong were thrilled that one of their own had landed a major role in an American TV show.

When Lee took a quick trip back to Hong Kong to make arrangements for his mother to come to the United States, he was surprised to learn that he was famous there. Not only that, but two Hong Kong studios wanted to hire him to star in their movies. Lee was still determined to make it in Hollywood, but he decided that when he couldn't find work there, he'd turn to Hong Kong.

UP, UP, AND AWAY

In 1971 and 1972, Lee made three films for Hong Kong's Golden Harvest Studios: *The Big Boss* (U.S. title: *Fists of Fury*), *Fist of Fury* (U.S. title: *The Chinese Connection*), and *The Way of the Dragon* (U.S. title: *Return of the Dragon*), which Lee wrote and directed himself. They were all smash hits: *The Big Boss* made $3.5 million in Hong Kong in its first 19 days alone, making it the highest grossing film in Hong Kong history. *Fist of Fury* smashed that record by making $4 million in about the same amount of time, and *Return of the Dragon* made $5.4 million.

Now that Bruce Lee was Asia's biggest film star, Hollywood finally began to take notice. In late 1972, Warner Brothers agreed to co-produce *Enter the Dragon* with Golden Harvest Studios, the first time that a Hollywood studio had ever partnered with a Hong Kong studio to make a film.

TROUBLE

It took about 10 weeks to shoot *Enter the Dragon*. By May 1973, Lee was back in the Golden Harvest recording studio to dub the sound for the film. It was hot and humid at the studio on May 10—the air conditioners were turned off to keep the noise from interfering with the sound recording. Lee was exhausted from working nonstop on the film. At one point he excused himself and went to use the restroom. When 20 minutes passed and he didn't return, the recording crew went looking for him and found him passed out on the restroom floor. Lee regained consciousness, then passed out again and went into convulsions. The studio rushed him to the hospital, where doctors diagnosed cerebral edema (swelling of the brain). Lee made what was thought to be a full recovery, but in the weeks that followed he continued to complain of headaches.

EXIT THE DRAGON

Two months later, on July 20, 1973, Lee went to the apartment of an actress named Betty Ting Pei to go over some script changes in an upcoming film called *The Game of Death*. While there he got a headache, so Ting Pei gave him a tablet of Equagesic (a combination of aspirin and a tranquilizer called meprobamate). The 32-year-old Lee went into the bedroom to lay down and never regained consciousness.

That evening Ting Pei tried to wake him, and when she couldn't she called for an ambulance. Lee was dead by the time he arrived at the hospital. The cause of death was ruled to be cerebral edema, this time possibly brought on by an extreme allergic reaction to the Equagesic.

Four weeks later, *Enter the Dragon* premiered in Los Angeles. It was one of the highest-grossing films of 1973. Over the years it has gone on to earn more than $150 million, making it one of the most successful martial arts films in history.

So did Bruce Lee's story end when he passed away in July 1973? Not exactly—the rest of his strange tale begins on page 339.

the rest of his strange tale begins on page 339.

*   *   *

56 THINGS FROM BATMAN COMICS, MOVIES, AND TV SERIES WITH "BAT" IN THEIR NAME

Batalarm, Batanalyzer, Bat-a-rang, Bat-armor, Bat awake, Batbeam, Batbeam Firing Button, Bat Blowtorch, Batboat, Batcamera's Polarized Batfilter, Batcave, Batcentrifuge, Batcharge Launcher, Batclaws, Batcommunicator, Batcopter, Batcostume, Batcuffs, Batcycle, Batcycle Go-cart, Batantidote, Batparachute, Emergency tank of Batoxygen, Bat earplugs, Bat Gas, Batguage, Bathook, Batkey, Batknife, Batladder, Batlaser Gun, Batmagnet, Batmissile, Batmobile, Batmobile Antitheft Device, Batmobile Mobile Crime Computer, Batmobile's Superpower Afterburner, Bat-o-meter, Bat-o-stat Antifire Activator, Batphone, Batpole, Batram, Bat Ray Projector, Batresearch Shelf, Batrope, Batscanner Receiver, Batscope, Batshield, Batsleep, Batsignal, Bat Terror Control, Batzooka, Compressed Steam Batlift, Homing Battransmitter, Memory Bat Bank, Superblinding Batpellets

---

It takes Pluto 248.53 years to travel around the sun. It takes Mercury 88 days.

MYTH-LEADING

We might assume that the common names
we have for things are accurate descriptions
of them, but that's not always true.

BIRTHDAY PARTY. You can only have one birth day—the
day you were born. After that, every time you celebrate your
birthday you're really throwing an *anniversary* party.

WILD RICE. It's neither wild, nor rice. Officially known as
Zizania aquatica, this once-wild grass seed is now cultivated by
farmers worldwide.

KILLER WHALE. They're neither killers nor whales. They were
once thought to be man-eaters. The 1973 U.S. Navy diving manual even warns that killer whales "will attack human beings at every
opportunity." But they were wrong—there are very few documented cases of attacks on human. (Seals and penguins are a different
story.) And they're members of the dolphin, not the whale, family.

RADIATOR. Whether it's in your home or in your car, radiators
work by *convecting* heat—moving it via a liquid or gas, not by radi-
ating. The radiator in you home heats the air currents around it
until enough is heated to make the room feel warm. The one in
your car transfers heat from the engine to water, which passes it to
the atmosphere. The "radiators" radiate a little, but not much.

POISON IVY. It's not a poison, it's an allergen. Poisons are harmful to everybody; allergens only affect some people. Poison ivy can
cause severe itching and swelling, but many people aren't even
affected by it. It's not ivy, either—it's a member of the sumac family.

RINGWORM. This infection makes "ring-like" marks on skin—
but there's no worms involved. It's caused by a fungus.

HEAVY CREAM. When milk producers say "heavy," they actually
mean "full of fat," and the fat is the lightest part of the milk. That
means that "heavy cream," which contains as much as 30% milk fat,
is actually a lot lighter than skim milk, which contains only trace
amounts of fat.

False advertising? The Cape of Good Hope was originally named the Cape of Storms.

CLOSE, BUT NO CIGAR

Sometimes things that seem like good ideas at first don't live up to their expectations. Take these duds, for example:

THE RONSON VARAFLAME

Brilliant Idea: One of the problems of being in the butane lighter fuel business is that as soon as a smoker lights their cigarette, they stop using your product. In the late 1960s, the Ronson lighter fuel company formed a consumer products division to dream up new ways to for people to use butane. What'd they come up with? The Varaflame Butane Candle. The Varaflame offered many advantages over traditional wax candles: they weren't smoky, they didn't drip wax, and the size of the flame could be adjusted to suit the occasion: "Low for intimate dinners, medium for dinner parties, high for swinging soirees," as one ad put it. When full, a Varaflame could burn for hours—not bad if you're in the butane business.

Oops: Varaflame Butane Candles cost as much as $30; a lot of money in the late 1960s. Wax candles cost less than a buck and people liked them better. In 1981, after more than a decade of disappointing sales, Ronson extinguished its consumer goods division.

THE PONTIAC AZTEK

Brilliant Idea: Billed by Pontiac as a "party on wheels," the Pontiac Aztek looked great on paper when it was introduced in 2000. The minivan-based SUV had a fold-down tailgate specially designed to be comfortable to sit on, complete with built-in cup holders and rear stereo controls for tailgate parties. For camping, Pontiac offered an optional air mattress and a "tent extension" that wrapped around the open tailgate. There were four power outlets and the front seat center console even doubled as a removable ice chest.

Oops: The Aztek was also one of the goofiest looking cars ever made. It was met with stunned silence when it debuted at the Detroit Auto Show in 2000—one executive from a rival automaker called it the Pontiac "A** Crack," and when it arrived in showrooms things didn't get any better. "The back end of the Aztek is the ugliest thing I've ever seen in my life," Pontiac salesman Brad

Hernandez told the *Los Angeles Times*. "It looks like time was up and they stopped working on it. But we back it up against a wall and it looks great." Consumers didn't think so—first year sales were less than half what Pontiac had hoped for, and when the company redesigned the Aztek to make it less goofy-looking, sales dropped even further. Pontiac quietly phased out the Aztek in 2004.

POLAVISION

Brilliant Idea: In the mid-1970s, Polaroid spent $250 million researching and developing Polavision, the world's first instant motion picture system. It went on sale in 1978.

Oops: What did the company have to show for itself after spending all that money? Not much—the picture was grainy, the movies were only 2-1/2 minutes long, and they didn't have sound. The cameras cost $675—in 1978—and you also had to buy a special viewing screen because they couldn't be viewed on a TV. Competing Super 8 cameras sold for a fraction of the cost, made longer movies with a much better picture, and had sound. As if that wasn't competition enough, video cameras were just around the corner. Polavision never had a chance: By the time Polaroid scrapped the product in 1979 it had lost so much money—$68.5 million—that shareholders forced Edwin Land, the company founder and CEO, into retirement.

ZAPMAIL

Brilliant Idea: In 1984 Federal Express launched a new delivery service called Zapmail. Instead of physically shipping important documents across the country, the company would transmit them by satellite from one FedEx office to another, then deliver them by courier in two hours or less. Price: $35 for up to ten pages. Sure, the company would have to launch satellites and build its own network of ground stations, but since it was shipping fewer documents by plane it hoped to save a fortune on jumbo jets.

Oops: Federal Express failed to take one thing into consideration: the prices of fax machines—$3,500 or more in 1984—were already beginning to drop, and within just a few years they'd be so cheap that any business could afford them. Too late for Federal Express—by the time it pulled the plug on ZapMail in 1986, the company had zapped an estimated $500 million. (As soon as Federal Express announced it was ending the service, its stock price shot up 18%.)

COLOR-BLIND

We printed this article in black and white
(just in case you're color-blind).

EYE SEE THE LIGHT

Why are some people "color-blind," and what exactly does it mean? To answer that, we have to answer a bigger question: How do we see things in the first place? The simple answer is, we don't actually see *things*, we see the light that reflects off of them. That reflected light goes through a lens and hits the retina in the back of the eye. Special cells in the retina, called *photoreceptors*, convert that light into nerve signals that are sent to the brain's visual center. And the fact that seeing objects is actually seeing light explains how we see in color, because light *is* color. More precisely, light travels in wavelengths, and the different wavelengths are interpreted by our brains as different colors.

So back to the first question: Why are some people color-blind, and what exactly does that mean?

EYE SEE SOME OF THE LIGHT

There are two main types of photoreceptor cells in the retina: *rods* and *cones* (so called because of their shapes). Rods detect different amounts of light (bright to dark), and cones detect different wavelengths of light—meaning different colors.

Human cone cells come in three different types. One type contains a pigment that responds to short-wavelength light (the blue part of the spectrum), another to medium-wavelength light (the green part), and the third to long-wavelength light (the reds). Color-blindness is simply the condition of having defective or missing cone cells. Most commonly, people inherit the trait from their parents, but it can also be caused by injury, illness, and aging, and it comes in many different forms.

• **Protanopia:** Greens look like browns; reds look more like beiges and appear darker than they actually are. Violet and purple are seen as shades of blue because the red in them can't be seen.

• **Deuteranopia:** Deuteranopes lack medium-wavelength cones (the greens) and have red/green symptoms similar to protanopia.

When asked to name a color, 60% of any group of people will name the color "red."

This is the most common form of color-blindness.

- **Tritanopia:** An uncommon form of color-blindness—the lack of short-wavelength cones (the blues). Blues and greens are difficult to distinguish, and yellows can appear as shades of red.

- **Blue cone monochromacy:** Having only one type of functioning cones—the blues. Someone with blue cone monochromacy can see few colors, but otherwise has good vision in normal light.

- **Rod monochromacy:** A very rare condition and the only one for which the term "color-blindness" is actually accurate. Also known as *maskun*, this is the condition of having only rods—no functioning cones at all. A rod monochromat can't see any color at all. The world is black, white, and shades of gray.

COLOR-BLINDNESS FACTS

- About 8% of all men have some form of color deficiency; about half of 1% of all women do.

- Humans are all born color-blind. Cone cells don't begin functioning until a baby is about four months old.

- Color-blindness is also known as Daltonism, named after John Dalton, who wrote the first scientific paper about the condition (which he had) in 1794. In 1995, 150 years after his death, researchers determined that Dalton suffered from deuteranopia. How? They did a DNA analysis of his preserved eyeball.

- Complete color-blindness, or rod monochromacy, is extremely rare—except on the Pacific island of Pohnpei, where 8% of the population has it.

- Color-detecting cones work best in bright light. In very dim light only non-color-detecting rods are used, which is why everything seems to be in black and white in dim light.

- Rods are more numerous in the periphery of the retina. In dim light, use your peripheral vision—it sees better.

- Most mammals are dichromatic: they have two types of cone cells and can see fewer colors than we can. Honeybees, like humans, have three types. But honeybees can see colors in the ultraviolet range; humans can't.

- The mantis shrimp's eye has at least 12 different cone cell types for detecting different colors. Exactly how many colors they can see is still unknown.

THE LIMBURGER CHEESE WAR

From our "Dustbin of History" files, here's the pungent
tale of two midwest states whose pride and honor were
once challenged…by a slab of stinky cheese.

IT AIN'T EASY BEING CHEESEY

It began in the winter of 1935 when a doctor in Independence, Iowa, prescribed an odd medicine to an ailing farm wife: Limburger cheese. The doctor figured the heavily aromatic cheese would help clear the woman's clogged sinuses. (If you don't know what Limburger smells like, give it a whiff the next time you're at the supermarket.) So the order was put through to Monroe, Wisconsin, to send some Limburger cheese—post haste.

Why Monroe? Swiss cheesemakers first arrived there in 1845. At the time, Wisconsin was in the depths of an economic depression and cheese helped pull them out of it. By 1910, Wisconsin had become the cheese-making capital of the United States, producing more cheese than any other state. And Monroe was the Limburger capital of Wisconsin.

THE BATTLE LINES ARE DRAWN

Monroe's postmaster, John Burkhard, approved the delivery and sent it on its way. But the mail carrier in Independence, Iowa, who delivered the Limburger was so offended by the stench wafting through his roadster that he refused to deliver it. Citing a postal rule that said mail would only be delivered if it "did not smell objectionable," Independence's postmaster, Warren Miller, concurred without examining or even smelling the cheese. He had it sent back to Monroeon the grounds that it could "fell an ox at twenty paces."

Burkhard took it personally; to insult Limburger is to insult not just Monroe, but all of Wisconsin and its proud cheese heritage. So Burkhard rewrapped the package and sent it back to Iowa. Miller promptly returned it to Wisconsin. War was brewing.

THE BATTLE OF DUBUQUE

Burkhard took his gripe all the way to the United States Postmaster General in Washington, D.C. At first, he couldn't understand what all of the fuss was about. So Burkhard sent him some Limburger. The Postmaster General then decided that, yes, the cheese smelled bad, but no, it wasn't hazardous. And the war was over, right? Wrong.

By this time the press had sniffed out the story. At a time when the nation was mired in the Great Depression and Hitler was rising to power in Germany, a story about smelly cheese was a breath of fresh air. And unwilling to give in, postmaster Burkhard challenged postmaster Miller to a "cheese-sniffing duel"—if Miller could sit at a table and not wretch from the stench of freshly-cut Limburger, then he would never again raise a stink about Wisconsin or its cheese. Miller accepted. Dozens of people from each town—as well as a throng of reporters—showed up at the Julien Hotel in Dubuque, Iowa, on the cold afternoon of March 8, 1935, to witness the standoff.

A Duel to the Breath

The two men sat across from each other at a table. While flash-bulbs flickered and onlookers whispered, Burkhard placed a box on the table, unwrapped it, and produced a very strong sample of his state's pride and joy, praising not only its medicinal qualities, but boasting that nothing on Earth tasted better with beer. The tension was so thick that you could cut it with a knife. Famed *Milwaukee Journal* reporter Richard S. Davis sent out a dispatch calling it a "duel to the breath."

As Burkhard prepared to push the slab of cheese over to Miller, he offered Miller a clothespin and a gas mask. But Miller just shook his head and meekly surrendered. "I won't need that clothespin," he lamented, "I haven't any sense of smell."

The crowd gasped. The battle was over before it began. Burkhard was immediately declared the winner and Miller had to agree to allow any and all Wisconsin cheese safe passage throughout Iowa's postal routes. The next day newspapers in 30 states ran a picture of the olfactarily-challenged Miller looking bewildered next to a piece of steaming Limburger. And *now* the war was over, right? Wrong. The final battle was yet to come.

THE BATTLE OF BEAVER DAM

While Burkhard was basking in victory, something he'd said about Limburger at that table in Dubuque—that nothing tasted better with beer—was churning through Miller's head. Every good Iowan knew that the best food to eat with beer is smoked whitefish, not some stinky piece of cheese. Miller just couldn't let it go. So he challenged Burkhard with another contest: a fight for the title of "Best *Snack* in the World." Once again the press got whiff of the food feud, and they convened at the neutral site chosen for the contest: the American Legion hall in Beaver Dam, Wisconsin.

This confrontation was even more serious than the first—now there were judges. And with so much at stake, both sides used underhanded tactics: they bribed the judges with beer. The fish-heads bought a round, then the cheese-heads. And once all pallets were properly whetted, the showdown began.

Carnage

First came the sliced Limburger with beer. Then the Iowans gave the judges smoked whitefish…and more beer. The battle raged on: Limburger and beer, whitefish and beer. Limburger and beer, whitefish and beer. Finally, when the judges could eat or drink no more, they sent the least-inebriated member of their panel to the podium: "The judgeth have reached a dethision. It was unamus… unans…they all said the same darned thing! Cheese'n beer s'wunnerful. Fishes'n beer s'wunnerful too. But when you have Limburger cheese *and* smoked whitefish and beer, heck, it don't get no better'n that!"

Both sides were declared victorious, Burkhard and Miller retained their respective states' honor, and Limburger cheese had risen from being referred to as "hazardous material" to holding the co-title of "Best Snack in the World."

VICTORY PARADE

That October, Monroe, Wisconsin, held its annual Cheese Day parade. All of the press coverage from the Limburger cheese war made it the biggest Cheese Day ever. Fifty thousand people showed up to bask in the glory—including the farmer's wife (who had healed quite nicely). Warren Miller came all the way from Iowa and was given a place of honor in the parade—right next to his friend John Burkhard.

Last movie ever released on laserdisc: *Star Wars Episode 1: The Phantom Menace.*

OOPS!

More tales of outrageous blunders.

DON'T BEE STUPID

"In Gerbach, Germany, a roofing worker was attacked by a swarm of wasps. To protect himself, he used his blowtorch against the bees, setting one of the insects on fire. The wasp then flew back to its nest, which was located in the rafters, and set the house on fire."

—*Mail and Guardian* (UK)

NOW YOU SEE HIM...

"In a Miami courtroom, while the lawyer for defendant Raymond Jessi Snyder was vociferously protesting a prosecutor's demand that Snyder be locked up pending trial because he was a 'flight risk,' the sly defendant slowly eased from his seat and bolted out the door. (He didn't get far.)"

—*Miami Herald*

HOW TO MAKE A 17-WEEK WAIT SEEM SHORT

"A British hospital patient has been told he'll have to wait 192 years for a minor operation. Robert Smith, 48, has been sent a letter by Dewsbury District Hospital saying the waiting time is 9,999 weeks. The *Mirror* says bosses at the Mid-Yorkshire Hospital have apologized for the gaffe, blaming an administration error. A spokesman said: 'We are happy to confirm no one has ever had to wait 9,999 weeks.' Mr. Smith has now been told the waiting time for the operation to have a spot removed from beside his eye is actually 'only' 17 weeks."

—*Ananova*

RIDIN' THAT TRAIN

"It started out as a tranquil night watching the sun set and the stars rise. But for three Charleston, South Carolina, young people, it turned into a harrowing ride atop a speeding train. Jack Lowther, 22, his 18-year-old girlfriend Jacklyn 'Blair' Gary, and Mary Allison Morris, 21, were watching the sky from a bridge Tuesday evening when they decided to climb aboard a parked freight car for a better view. They soon discovered that was a bad idea. 'We were on top, and it started moving,' said Lowther. 'I tried to get everyone off the train, but it had already started to pick up speed.' They lay down on top of a box car as the train reached speeds of over 50 mph, slipping under bridges that were too low for comfort. Although the reception was poor, Morris finally managed to call 911 on her cell phone. By the time the train slowed, it was about 22 miles from where their journey began. Deputies charged the three with trespassing. 'I just want to tell everyone else not to try this,' Lowther said. 'It's not fun.'"

—**Associated Press**

MONNOPOLY
"Parker Brothers admitted that for the past sixty years it has misspelled Marven Gardens as 'Marvin' Gardens on its popular Monopoly board game. The company said correcting the error would be too costly."

—*More Dumb, Dumber, Dumbest*

TOP-NOTCH EDUCASHUN
"A chain of private California schools that taught immigrants was ordered to stop handing out diplomas, state Attorney General Bill Lockyer said. Authorities seized the assets of California Alternative High School and asked a judge to stop the company's 30 schools statewide from handing out 'high school diplomas.' The company, which charged its mainly Latino students $450 to $1,450 for a 10-week course, based its curriculum on a 54-page book that was riddled with errors. Among other things, students learned that: there are 53 United States; Congress has two houses—the Senate for Democrats and the House for Republicans; and that World War II occurred from 1938 to 1942.

"The company claims to have 78 locations nationwide and said it was actively expanding operations despite court orders blocking it from claiming the diplomas were 'official.'"

—**Reuters**

*　　*　　*

"Get your facts first, and then you may distort them as much as you please."

—**Mark Twain**

In 1977, American car makers recalled more vehicles than they produced.

BREAK A LEG!

Perhaps the oddest theatrical superstition is the practice of
wishing a performer a nasty injury as a way of saying
"good luck." What's so lucky about breaking a leg?

BACKGROUND
Telling someone to "break a leg" is such a well-known theatrical custom that most people think it dates back centuries. In fact, it has been commonly used only since the 1930s,
and its origins are unknown. Here are some possibilities:

• Actors traditionally thank an audience by bending into a bow.
The old military expression "take a knee," which means to bow,
may have been corrupted into "break a leg."

• The narrow curtains that cover the sides of the stage are sometimes called "legs." An actor who gives a great performance may be
summoned for several curtain calls, causing the mechanisms that
raise and lower the legs to be overused and eventually break. The
actor is wished a performance so good that it literally breaks a leg.

• John Wilkes Booth, President Abraham Lincoln's assassin, was
also one of the 19th century's most popular stage actors. After he
shot Lincoln, he leaped to the stage of Ford's Theatre. He escaped
but broke his leg in the process.

• In 1915 renowned French actress Sarah Bernhardt had a leg
amputated but returned to the stage later that year. Invoking the
spirit and memory of one of theater's most beloved actresses is said
to bring goodwill to a performer.

• The German phrase *Hals und Beinbruch* means "good luck," but
it literally translates as "neck and leg break." How did such a grue-
some expression come to mean good luck? *Hals und beinbruch* is
similar to the Hebrew expression *hatzlakha u-brakha*, which means
"success and blessing." The two expressions were probably linked
by German Jewish immigrants who came to the United States in
the early 20th century. The phrase may have come into theatrical
usage from the many second-generation immigrants who worked
in the entertainment industry, including the Marx Brothers, Jack
Benny, and George Burns.

COMPUTER VIRUSES

*Ever since computers first became affordable in the early 1980s,
viruses have been a threat. They have cost individuals, companies, and
governments billions in software, security, data replacement, and lost
productivity. Here are some of the most infamous viruses to date.*

ELK CLONER (1981)

Richard Skrenta, a 15-year-old high school freshman, gave his friends some disks of computer games. But there was a catch: the disks could only be used 49 times. On the 50th attempt, the screen went blank and this poem appeared:

It will get on all your disks. It will infiltrate your chips
Yes it's Cloner!
It will stick to you like glue. It will modify RAM too
Send in the Cloner!

What was intended as a prank turned out to be the first computer virus. Elk Cloner would hide in the computer's memory and then attach itself to the next disk inserted in the computer. Any other computer using *that* disk would then get infected in turn.

Hundreds of computers were damaged, and Elk Cloner hung around for years. But Skrenta was never punished—viruses were so new that they were not yet perceived as the crimes they are today.

MICHELANGELO (1992)

Technicians in New Zealand found this virus on a computer in late 1991, but there was no damage—the virus wasn't programmed to cause any destruction until the following March 6, the anniversary of Michelangelo's birthday. On that date it would make it look like the entire computer had been erased.

Only a handful of computers had the Michelangelo virus until January 1992, when a computer manufacturer accidentally shipped 500 infected PCs and another unwittingly distributed 900 infected floppy disks. Computer experts still didn't think it would spread very far, but then Reuters ran a story predicting that 25% of all American computers would be affected. Where'd they get that number? From anti-virus software manufacturers, who claimed Michelangelo would strike 20 million computers. When Doomsday

arrived, though, the virus damaged only about 10,000 computers.

Michelangelo is still floating in cyberspace, yet despite being programmed to attack computers every March 6, there have been no reports of it doing any harm since 1992. But because of the frenzy it created, anti-virus software is now a billion-dollar industry. And whoever unleashed the virus was never caught.

LOVE BUG (2000)

In 2000, computer users received e-mails with the subject line "ILOVEYOU." When the recipient downloaded the accompanying attachment, the virus attacked the computer and sent itself to every e-mail addresses stored in the computer, starting a volatile chain reaction. Love Bug was first spotted in Asia but quickly spread worldwide. It disabled computers at the White House, the Pentagon, British Parliament, and many European e-mail servers. The damage was estimated at $10 billion.

Who did it? Police tracked down the culprits: Onel de Guzman and Reomel Ramones of the Philippines. But the Philippines had no laws against cyber crime, so despite the damage they caused, Guzman and Ramones went free. (Guzman was actually offered several computer programming jobs after he was cleared.)

The virus is now gone, but its method of distribution still lives: dozens of viruses have spread through e-mail with deceptive subject lines such as "You gotta read this," "Important! Read carefully," and even "How to protect yourself from the ILOVEYOU bug."

CODE RED (2001)

Using Microsoft's Internet server software, Code Red sent itself to e-mail addresses stored in the computers it infected, then flooded the Web with billions of megabytes of gobbledygook. Result: Web sites had text replaced with the phrase "hacked by Chinese."

Code Red's real goal: To infiltrate, flood, and shut down the White House Web site. That didn't happen, but other major sites such as AT&T, Hotmail, and Federal Express all fell prey to it. At its peak, Code Red was infecting 2,000 computers a minute. Total cost of lost data and productivity: $1.2 billion. (It was rumored that the virus was the work of the Chinese government as part of a secret computer hacking war with the United States.) To date, nobody has been arrested for creating or spreading Code Red.

The term "hacker" was coined at MIT in 1961.

BLASTER (2003)

Also known as Lovsan, Blaster wasn't technically a virus, it was a *worm*. A virus damages whatever computer is unlucky enough to accidentally cross its path, but a worm seeks out vulnerable computers and then infects them.

Blaster initially caused more headaches than harm. Once on a computer, it didn't delete information, it messed with the operating system. A message appeared, counting down 60 seconds until the computer would shut down and restart. This on-and-off cycle would go on forever. And if you shut off the computer manually, all data could be lost. But Blaster actually had a second, more devious goal: to shut down Microsoft's Web site. Microsoft fought back, successfully blocking Blaster from its site. Yet despite Microsoft's efforts, 500,000 computers lost data. And despite the offer of a $500,000 reward for information leading to the parties responsible for Blaster, their identities remain a secret.

MORE VIRUSES

PC-Write Trojan (1986). Infected computers while pretending to be a popular word-processing program.

Christmas Worm (1987). Hit IBM mainframes and replicated at a rate of 500,000 times per hour.

AIDS Trojan (1989). Disguised as an AIDS information program, it crippled hard drives then demanded money for the decoder information.

Little Black Book (1990). Synchronized viruses designed to infect AT&T's long distance switching system.

Tequila (1991). Swiss in origin, it was the first virus that could change itself to avoid detection in infected computers.

Chernobyl (1999). Programmed to delete hard drives on April 26, 1999, the 13th anniversary of the Chernobyl nuclear accident.

Melissa (1999). Infected computers via a fake Microsoft Word document sent by e-mail. Caused more than $80 million in damage. Its creator, David Smith, went to jail for 26 months.

Trojan.Xombe (2004). Posing as an official Windows upgrade message, stole personal information stored in computers.

MyDoom (2004). Shut down search engines like Yahoo! and Google.

King George III survived two assassination attempts...in one day.

MMM...TRIVIA

Stuff you probably didn't know about The Simpsons.

Chief Wiggum is based on actor Edward G. Robinson.

The episode in which Homer loses his car at the World Trade Center was removed from circulation after 9/11.

Beatles reunion: Ringo Starr, George Harrison, and Paul McCartney have all made appearances on *The Simpsons*.

Michael Jackson secretly wrote the Bart Simpson novelty hit "Do the Bartman."

Among ham actor Troy McClure's many films: *Dial M for Murderousness, Meet Joe Blow, Leper in the Backfield, The Mediocre Journey,* and *Eenie, Meeni, Miney, Die.*

The incompetent Dr. Nick was inspired by George "Dr. Nick" Nichopoulos, the doctor who fueled Elvis Presley's prescription drug habit.

According to Guinness, *The Simpsons* holds the record for most celebrity guest stars.

In the opening credits when Maggie is scanned at a grocery store, she "costs" $847.63.

Thanks to Lisa, the number of female saxophone players in school bands has skyrocketed.

Homer has a tattoo reading "Starland Vocal Band forever."

Producers had to apologize for the 1992 episode in which Marge stars in a musical version of *A Streetcar Named Desire* and refers to New Orleans as "Stinking, rotten, vomiting, vile...Putrid, brackish, maggotty, foul."

The "J" in Homer J. Simpsons stands for "Jay."

Principal Skinner is named for behavioral expert B.F. Skinner.

The only thing in the world Ned Flanders hates are his beatnik parents.

Homer, Marge, Bart, Lisa and Maggie have traveled to every continent except Antarctica.

The Simpsons is the longest running animated series of all time. It passed *The Flintsones'* in 1997. By 2005, it will have surpassed *The Adventures of Ozzie and Harriet* as the longest running comedy in TV history.

The first insurance policy in what is now the United States was written in 1721.

IT'S A DOG'S LIFE

Canine news from around the world.

PUPTUALS
"Four-year-old Anju Karmakar was accident-prone. She broke her arm at the age of two, nearly drowned six months later, and burned herself in a kitchen fire in February this year. Anju's parents consulted an astrologer, who advised them to get her married off to a dog to break the jinx. A search for a suitable dog ended with a neighbor offering his six-year-old pet's paw to Subal Karmakar's daughter. The marriage, which was conducted according to Vedic rites, took place last Saturday night."

—Hindustan Times

RUFF-RUFF, BOW-WOW, BARK-BARK
"As many dog owners will attest, our furry friends are listening. Now there is scientific proof that they understand what they hear. German researchers have found a Border Collie named Rico who understands more than 200 words and can learn new ones as quickly as many children. Patti Strand, an American Kennel Club board member, called the report 'good news for those of us who talk to our dogs.' Rico knows the names of dozens of play toys and can find the one called for by his owner. That's about the same size vocabulary as trained apes, dolphins, and parrots, the researchers say."

—CNEWS

YOGA DOGS?
"At a new yoga class in California students are chanting 'arf' instead of 'ohm.' A gym instructor in Hollywood started offering free classes for dogs and their owners. Together, they work their way through all the yoga positions. Those who have tried it say these classes help calm neurotic pets. 'I really think all the benefits that humans get from yoga, dogs get most of them too. They get to stretch, and it relieves anxiety,' said Heather Stevens, yoga instructor. 'It's definitely kind of wacky,' said Martin Goodman, a yoga class member. "But it's a lot of fun.' "

—ABC News

President Gerald Ford once got locked out of the White House while walking his dog.

FROM A "PARENTING" COLUMN

"*Reader:* I can't keep my 20-month-old daughter out of the dog's food. I've tried scolding, distracting, time-out, but nothing works. *Reply:* From a strictly nutritional standpoint, most dog food is superior to the diets of many Americans. A pediatrician informs me that he has yet to see a child who suffered ill effects from eating dog food (except for chunk-type that might get stuck in the throat)."

—*Providence* (Rhode Island) *Journal*

POST POSTIES

"Dogs chomping on mail carrier-shaped treats is no laughing matter for Canada Post. The unamused Canadian postal service, whose carriers endure more than their share of real dog bites, convinced Pet Valu Inc. stores to stop carrying Bark Bars, dog biscuits that come shaped like cats and letter carriers. 'This is not in any way, shape, or form funny for us. I don't see that as humorous at all, not even in the least,' said John Caines, Canada Post's media relations manager, adding that in the first half of 2004 there were 160 dog attacks on mail carriers across Canada."

—Reuters

MAILDOG

"Toby arrives at the post office at 9:30 every morning, even though he's not allowed inside. The 12-year-old golden retriever has been delivering mail to his owner, Brad Sullivan, for the past two years. He makes the three-block trek to the post office with Gordon Lewis, Sullivan's neighbor, and waits outside until Lewis puts the mail in a green pouch around his neck. Sullivan was laid up from a vehicle accident a couple of years ago, so he started sending Toby. 'He's just crazy to get the mail,' Sullivan said. 'We put that pouch on him and he's a different dog. It's something important for him to do.'"

—*The Beaufort* (North Dakota) *Gazette*

HOW MUCH IS THAT DOGGY IN THE WHEELCHAIR?

"The Humane Society in Brookfield, Wisconsin, announced a 'scratch-and-dent sale' on disabled pets, offering half-off prices on animals such as a toothless cat and a blind dog."

—*News Is Stranger Than Fiction*

79% of boys and 89% of girls list acne as one of their biggest worries.

WHAT'D YOU McSAY?

*McDonald's has the healthiest and best-tasting food
in the world, and we support them in their effort to
protect their good name and their attractive logo.
(That's our story and we're sticking to it.)*

HE SAID: Edoardo Raspelli, one of Italy's leading culinary
critics, reviewed McDonald's for the newspaper *La Stampa*
in 2002. "The ambience was mechanical," he wrote, "the
potatoes were obscene and tasting of cardboard, and the bread
poor. I found it alienating and vulgar." The restaurant, he said,
"symbolized oppression of the palate."

McTROUBLE: In 2003 the McDonald's legal team heard about
the article and filed a $25 million lawsuit against the critic. The
unfavorable review, they said, amounted to defamation that "dent-
ed the company's image and profits."

McOUTCOME: Pending. But Raspelli won't back down. "I was
only saying what I thought of fast food." he said. "I find it repul-
sive."

THEY SAID: Steve Brown and Jenny Fraser wrote a play for a
children's theater in Glasgow, Scotland, in 1991. It was a satire of
the hamburger industry called *MacBurgers: Real Neat Scotch Fare*,
but it never mentioned the name "McDonald's."

McTROUBLE: On the day it was scheduled to open, McDonald's
reviewed the script and promptly threatened legal action. "The
play," they charged, "is riddled with anti-McDonald's propaganda."

McOUTCOME: The authors didn't have the money to fight
back, so they agreed to make script changes. They also had to
promise that the play would be performed only twice—and then
never again. (The original version of the play is still available
online.)

THEY SAID: In 1994 Vegan Action, an activist group in
Berkeley, California, decided to sell "McVegan" T-shirts to promote their cause. The shirts had the famous golden arches logo,
but instead of "Billions Served," it said "Billions *Saved*."

The average human body contains 10 to 20 billion miles of DNA.

McTROUBLE: McDonald's demanded that Vegan Action halt production of the shirts and send them the receipts of every one sold. They also demanded that the University of California, Berkeley student store, where most of the shirts were sold, immediately stop selling them (they did). But Vegan Action didn't give in so easily—they got pro-bono legal services and developed "a defense based on the First Amendment's protection of parody."

McOUTCOME: The press turned it into a David-and-Goliath battle. Two weeks later, McDonald's backed down.

HE SAID: In 1983 German filmmaker Peter Heller made a documentary called *Jungleburger*, examining the impact of fast food on Third World countries. In one interview, one of McDonald's Costa Rican suppliers implies that his beef comes from cattle farmed on ranches created by deforestation.

McTROUBLE: American McDonald's couldn't do much about a German documentary…until it was released in England, where the laws make it much easier to win a libel suit. When British TV aired the film in 1990, the McLawyers sprang into action, threatening the network with a lawsuit for showing the film.

McOUTCOME: The threat worked. Channel Four issued an apology for showing the film and promised never to air it again.

THEY SAID: The 2003 edition of *Merriam-Webster's Collegiate Dictionary* had some new words in it. One of them was *McJob*. Definition: "A low-paying job that requires little skill and provides little opportunity for advancement."

McTROUBLE: McDonald's CEO Jim Cantalupo wrote Merriam-Webster an open letter calling the definition a "slap in the face" of all restaurant employees. "A more appropriate definition of a 'McJob,'" he wrote, "might be 'teaches responsibility.'" Bottom line: "We are confident Merriam-Webster will eliminate its inaccurate definition of restaurant employment in the next edition."

McOUTCOME: No dice. Merriam-Webster refused to be cowed, and the word will appear in the next edition. "We stand by the accuracy and appropriateness of our definition," they said.

(Note: Editors of the *Oxford English Dictionary* had planned to include McJob in 1997 but changed their minds when lawyers, fearing legal action from McDonald's, advised them not to.)

LITTLE WILLIE

These morbid "Willie" poems were popular in the 1950s, although most were written in the 1890s. Either way, they're still funny (if you have a sick sense of humor...like you-know-who).

Little Willie hung his sister,
She was dead before
we missed her.
Willie's always up to tricks!
Ain't he cute? He's only six!

Willie poisoned Father's tea.
Father died in agony.
Mother was extremely vexed.
"Really, Will," she
said, "What next?"

Into the family drinking well
Willie pushed his sister Nell.
She's there yet
because it kilt her.
Now we have to buy a filter.

Little Willie, on the track,
Didn't hear the engine squeal.
Now the engine's
coming back,
Scraping Willie off the wheel.

The ice upon our
pond's so thin
That Little Willie's fallen in!
We cannot reach
him from the shore
Until the surface freezes more.
Ah me, my heart
grows weary waiting—
Besides, I want
to do some skating.

Willie saw some dynamite,
Couldn't understand it quite;
Curiosity never pays:
It rained Willie seven days.

Willie with a thirst for gore
Nailed his sister to the door.
Mother said with
humor quaint,
"Willie dear, don't
scratch the paint."

Little Willie fell down a drain;
Couldn't scramble out again.
Now he's floating in the sewer
The world is left
one Willie fewer.

Willie, in one of
his nice new sashes,
Fell in the fire and
was burnt to ashes.
Now, although the
room grows chilly,
We haven't the heart
to poke poor Willie.

Willie coming
home from school,
Spied a dollar near a mule.
Stooped to get it,
quiet as a mouse.
Funeral tomorrow
at Willie's house.

Dracula **author Bram Stoker also wrote children's stories. Critics called them "morbid."**

TREE-MENDOUS

*How big are the world's biggest trees? Imagine something
as wide as a house and as tall as a football field.*

STRATOSPHERE GIANT & GENERAL SHERMAN

One hundred forty million years ago, redwoods flourished
throughout the northern hemisphere. Today only three species
remain: the coast redwood, the giant redwood, and the dawn redwood. The coast redwood of Northern California and southern
Oregon grows to heights of over 300 feet, aided by heavy rainfall and
fog that condenses on the tree's tallest branches (so it doesn't have
to move water the full length of its trunk). The tallest, named
Stratosphere Giant, is located in Humboldt Redwoods State Park. It
stands 369 feet—five stories taller than the Statue of Liberty.

Another of the three remaining species, the giant redwood, is
found along the western side of the Sierra Nevada mountains. The
most famous of these giants is General Sherman, a mammoth tree
2,700 years old, 103 feet in circumference, and 274 feet tall. It
weighs an estimated 4 million pounds and comprises more than
50,000 cubic feet of wood, making it the largest tree on the planet.

EL ARBOR DEL TULE

Just outside the city of Oaxaca, Mexico, is an ancient piece of
Meso-American history known as El Tule. This Mexican cypress is
believed to be between 2,000 and 4,000 years old. Long before the
Spanish arrived in the 1500s, the Aztecs called the area surrounding the tree—now the village of Santa María del Tule—*Tollin* or
Tullin, meaning "aquatic plants." The cypress trees themselves were
called *ahuehuete*, meaning "ancients of the water" (it is believed
they once grew in the swamps of Mexico, which time has transformed into deserts).

Early Spanish settlers documented the native Zapotec people as
saying that, before it was struck by lightning in the 1400s, El Tule
was so large that it could provide shade for 1,000 people. The bolt
of lightning damaged the tree's branches and left a hollow so large
that there was "room inside for 12 horsemen." Fortunately El Tule
has since recovered and now has the second- or third-largest trunk
in the world, with a circumference of an amazing 176 feet.

IN THE NEWS: THE BIRDS & THE BEES

Some of the BRI staff bet Uncle John that he couldn't put together this collection of real news stories without mentioning "s–e–x." Uh-oh, he just lost!

CAREER COUNSELING. A German woman filed a complaint after a federal employment office sent her for a job interview—with an "adult" telephone service. They told her she'd be applying for "telemarketing consumer interface relations." But she got a surprise when the interviewer told her about the job: "He told me I had to answer the phone and moan a lot." A spokesman for the agency said it was an honest mistake.

HOLY...! A vicar in Lampoldshausen, Germany, distributed hundreds of videos about the life of Jesus to members of his congregation, only to find out there had been a mix-up at the factory: they were X-rated movies. The vicar, Father Frithjof, saw the bright side of the error: "God moves in mysterious ways," he said. "The people who ordered these movies now have our religious films about Jesus in their video recorders."

HOT-HOT-HOT? NOT-NOT-NOT! A 28-year-old Bulgarian woman sued her local heating company for refusing to turn her heat on—claiming that it was too cold for her and her husband to be intimate. The couple had paid all their bills, but the company had cut off heat to the entire building because so many of their neighbors hadn't paid theirs. The woman said that she and her husband were trying to have a second child, but the cold had frozen their attempts.

TALL TALE. The singer Sting admitted that he "stretched" the truth when he once bragged that he and his wife Trudi Styler could make love for eight hours at a time. "What I didn't say," he told Britain's *ITV*, "was that this included four hours of begging and then dinner and a movie."

When having a conversation, women make eye contact 15% more frequently than men.

FOUR-ALARM PHONE CALLS. Firefighters at the Jawahar Fire Control in India complained to the local *Mid-day* newspaper that the fire station was getting too hot: they were getting up to 70 amorous calls a day "from bored housewives or barmaids." The women were saying things like, "What kind of fires do you extinguish? How about dousing the fire in my heart?"

THIRSTY. In 2001 the water supply system in the Turkish village of Sirt broke down, forcing local woman to walk miles—and stand in line for hours—to get their water. When their pleas to fix the system went unheard, they decided to get serious: they told their husbands, "Get us a proper water supply or no more sex." And they meant it. A month later, after some serious pleading from the local men, government officials agreed to give the village five kilometers of piping. But the men had to lay all the pipe themselves—and the ban was still on. "They won't be able to get into our bedrooms until the water actually runs through the taps," a local woman told reporters. "The protest will continue."

FASHION POLICE. In Thailand more than 400 complaints a month came in from policemen. Why? Their new uniforms were too tight, which they claimed made them look "too sexy." The officers were getting lewd comments from people in the street.

HEY, IT WAS WORTH A TRY. A German man demanded a government grant to cover the cost of frequenting brothels and renting adult movies. The 35-year-old said that his wife had flown to Thailand and he was lonely. He wanted more than $2,000 a month, stating that, "I require the brothel visits for my physical and psychological well-being." A German court turned down the request.

NEWS OF THE OBVIOUS. In 2003 the European Psychoanalytic and Psychodynamic Society in Rome did a study with some not-so-surprising results. They tested the attention levels of 1,500 men as they watched a female newscaster that they found "attractive" deliver the news. Result: More than 1,100 of them couldn't remember a single thing said in the first 30 seconds of the newscast.

MORE "CREATIVE TEACHING" AWARDS

More stories to make you scratch your head.

SUBJECT: Fluid Mechanics

WINNER: Christopher Ogbe, head of the Business Studies Department at Bexley Heath School in Kent, England

CREATIVE APPROACH: Mr. Ogbe's trouble started in an airport bar in 2001, while he was getting ready to accompany 29 of his students on a flight to America. He had a few drinks too many, and then on the plane had a few more. Many pints of beer, glasses of wine, and nearly a quart of whiskey later, Ogbe was running wild all over the airplane, throwing food, pinching people on the butt, and flashing the flight attendants. He repeatedly groped a female colleague and referred to one Asian passenger as "Gandhi." Why'd he do it? Ogbe said he's claustrophobic and afraid of flying, and thought a drink or two might help calm his nerves.

REACTION: Ogbe's claustrophobia might be a bigger problem in his next assignment. He was convicted of assaulting his colleague and sentenced to one year...in a tiny jail cell.

SUBJECT: Police Procedures

WINNER: Pat Conroy, dean of students and assistant principal at South Haven High School in Michigan

CREATIVE APPROACH: In 2003 police brought in a drug-sniffing dog to search for drugs. None were found—not even in the locker of a student that Mr. Conroy strongly suspected of being a drug dealer. That came as a surprise, because as Conroy later admitted to the police, he had *planted* drugs in the locker himself, in the hope that they would be discovered during the search so that he could expel the student.

REACTION: Police raided Conroy's office and found drug paraphernalia and 10 bags of marijuana. He told officers he'd been collecting drugs seized from students to use as evidence during expulsion hearings. (According to the school board president, Conroy never brought drugs to any of the hearings the president had attended.) Charged with possession of marijuana, Conroy resigned. The student he suspected of drug dealing was not charged.

SUBJECT: Good Sportsmanship
WINNER: James Guillen, 24, a special ed teacher who also coaches basketball at Pleasantville Middle School in New Jersey
CREATIVE APPROACH: Coach Guillen invited a 13-year-old boy on the team to attend the team's annual banquet because he was getting a special award. The boy watched as other team members received certificates and trophies. Then the coach called him up...and presented him with a Crybaby Award—a trophy of a silver baby on a pedestal—because, the coach explained, the boy always "begged to get in the game, and all he did was whine."
REACTION: The boy—an honor student—was so humiliated that he stayed home the following Monday. Coach Guillen claimed he meant it as "a positive thing," but the board of education wasn't buying it—they banned him from ever coaching in the district again. Guillen also forfeited a $3,000 pay raise, was suspended for five days, and had to attend sensitivity training.

SUBJECT: Physics
WINNER: Randy Wilson, a high school science teacher in Colorado
CREATIVE APPROACH: Mr. Wilson let a 17-year-old junior build a bomb for the science fair. It wasn't a real bomb, just a test tube filled with a few ingredients that go into a live bomb, along with a list of other "key components" needed to finish the job.
REACTION: Wilson was suspended. Was the student punished? No—after all, he had his teacher's permission to build the bomb.

HONORABLE MENTION
SUBJECT: Music Appreciation
WINNER: Bruce "Blue Eyes" Janu, a social science teacher at Riverside-Brookfield High School in Illinois
CREATIVE APPROACH: When his students misbehave, Mr. Janu enrolls them in his Frank Sinatra Detention Club—he makes them stay after school and listen to his beloved Sinatra albums for half an hour. "You've got a Frank," he tells them.
REACTION: It works. "The kids hate it," he says. "This is the worst thing that has ever happened to them."

The Beta Israel temple in Los Angeles is home to the Shrine of Weeping Shirley Maclaine.

AMERICA'S FIRST PRIVATE EYE

If you're a fan of detective stories—which includes everything from
The Maltese Falcon *to* The Pink Panther *to* CSI—*then you
might be interested in this guy: he was the real thing.*

WHERE THERE'S SMOKE...

One day in June 1846, Allan Pinkerton, a 27-year-old barrel maker from Dundee, Illinois, climbed onto his raft and floated down the Fox River looking for trees that he could use for lumber. He found a lot more than that—when he went to chop down some trees on an island in the middle of the river, he discovered a smoldering fire pit hidden among them.

If someone found a fire pit in such a beautiful spot today, they probably wouldn't suspect anything unusual. But as Pinkerton explained in his memoirs, life was different in the 1840s: "There was no picnicking in those days; people had more serious matters to attend to and it required no great keenness to conclude that no honest men were in the habit of occupying the place."

GOTCHA!

Pinkerton went back to the island a few more times during daylight, but no one was ever there. So a few days later, he snuck back in the middle of the night and waited to see if anyone would show up. After about an hour he heard a rowboat approaching the island. He waited awhile and then crept close to the fire pit to see several shady-looking characters sitting around the campfire.

The next morning he went to the sheriff. After a few nights they went back to the island with a small posse and caught the men by surprise. Pinkerton's suspicions were correct—the men were a gang of counterfeiters, and the posse caught them red-handed with "a bag of bogus dimes and the tools used in their manufacture."

Counterfeiting was rampant in the 1840s: In those days each bank issued its own bills, and with so many different kinds of paper floating around, fakes were easy to make and difficult to detect. Less than a month after the dime bust, somebody passed fake $10

A guide dog's career lasts, on average, 8 to 10 years.

bills to two shopkeepers in Dundee. The shopkeepers were pretty sure that a farmer named John Craig had something to do with it, but they had no proof. Pinkerton had done a good job catching the last bunch of counterfeiters, so they asked him to look into it.

Pinkerton set up a sting: He met Craig, struck up a conversation, and convinced him that he was looking to make some dishonest money on the side. Craig sold him $500 worth of the fake bills, but rather than have the sheriff arrest him right there, Pinkerton decided to bide his time. He got Craig to reveal the location of his headquarters (a hotel in Chicago) then made an appointment to buy more counterfeit bills. A few days later, Pinkerton met Craig in the hotel bar. Then, just as Craig was passing him $4,000 worth of fake bills, two plainclothes police officers stepped out of the shadows and arrested him.

CAREER CHANGE

Had Pinkerton been left alone, he might have remained a barrel maker, but the Craig bust changed everything. "The affair was in everybody's mouth," Pinkerton later wrote, "and I suddenly found myself called upon from every quarter to undertake matters of detective skill." He quit making barrels and worked a number of different law-enforcement jobs over the next few years: deputy sheriff, Chicago police detective (the city's first), and finally as a U.S. Post Office investigator.

Then in 1850, he decided to go to work for himself—he and a lawyer named Edward Rucker formed what would become the Pinkerton National Detective Agency. Rucker dropped out after a year or two, but Pinkerton stayed with it for the rest of his life.

THE EYE HAS IT

For his company motto, Pinkerton chose "We Never Sleep." For his logo, he chose a large, unblinking eye. His agency wasn't the world's first private detective agency—a Frenchman named Eugène François Vidocq beat him by 17 years when he founded the Bureau des Renseignements (Office of Intelligence) in 1833. But it was Pinkerton who gave private detectives their famous nickname. Thanks to his choice of logo, they've been known as "private eyes" ever since.

Q: When do cannibals leave the dinner table? A: When everyone's eaten.

TRAIN OF THOUGHT

Pinkerton's timing was perfect. Railroads were beginning to transform the American way of life—in both good ways and bad. As rails began to link major American cities, people could travel greater distances in less time and at less cost than ever before. But criminals could, too: a bank robber could knock over a bank in one state, then hop a train and by the next morning be hundreds of miles away in another state.

Have you ever seen a movie where the sheriff chases a bad guy and has to stop at the county line? That really was the way things worked back then—law-enforcement agencies were organized locally, and a police officer's or sheriff's powers ended as soon as he crossed the city or the county line. There were few if any state police in those days, and no national police to speak of, either. The Bureau of Investigation, predecessor to the FBI, wouldn't come into existence until 1908. Pinkerton's *private* detectives had no formal police powers, but they were free to chase criminals across county and state lines and then work with local law enforcers to arrest criminals and bring them to justice.

With no one else to turn to protect their interests, the railroads went to Pinkerton. By 1854 the agency was earning $10,000 a year (about $200,000 today) on railroad company retainers alone.

UNDERCOVER

Pinkerton's agency achieved its greatest successes by sticking to the principle that Pinkerton himself had used to catch the counterfeiter John Craig back in 1846: The best way to catch a thief was by pretending to *be* a thief—a detective had to win the bad guy's confidence, then get him to spill the beans. The agents infiltrated organized gangs of all types: Confederate spy rings, unions, even the Mafia.

The Pinkerton agency was ahead of their time in many areas. They pioneered the use of the mug shot and by the 1870s had the largest collection in the world. Their centralized criminal filing system has since been emulated by the FBI and other law enforcement organizations worldwide. The agency hired a female detective, a 23-year-old widow named Kate Warne, in 1856; by comparison, the New York City Police Department did not hire its first female investigator until 1903.

After the Civil War, the Pinkerton Detective Agency helped bring the Wild West era to a close by sending manhunters into the field to hunt down infamous train and bank robbers: Jesse James, the Missouri Kid, the Reno brothers, and the Cole Younger gang. Why did Butch Cassidy and the Sundance Kid abandon their life of crime and flee to Argentina in 1901? Because Pinkerton detectives were hot on their trail. With the agency's "wanted" posters and mug shots circulating throughout the United States, there was no place in the country left for them to hide.

END OF AN ERA

After suffering a stroke in 1869, Pinkerton began turning more and more of his responsibilities over to his sons, Robert and William. But he never retired, and he was still working at the agency in June 1884 when he tripped and bit his tongue while taking a walk. In the days before antibiotics, such injuries were very serious—a few days later gangrene set in, followed by blood poisoning, and on July 1, Pinkerton died.

The world of law enforcement has changed a great deal since the Pinkerton National Detective Agency opened its doors in 1850, and if anything, the pace accelerated following Allan Pinkerton's death. The biggest change of all: in 1908 the Bureau of Investigation opened for business. The Pinkerton agency's detective services became increasingly redundant—why pay good money to hire private detectives when the FBI, backed by the resources of the federal government, would investigate crimes for free? As the crime detection side of the business dried up, the agency's security guard division, founded in 1858, came to assume a larger share. By the late 1930s, only a fraction of the company's revenue came from its original detective services. In 1965 Allan Pinkerton's great-grandson, Robert Allan Pinkerton II, acknowledged the inevitable by dropping the word "Detective" altogether and renamed the company Pinkerton's, Inc. He was the last Pinkerton to head the Pinkerton Agency.

So can you still hire a Pinkerton agent today, at least as a security guard? No—in 1999 an international security company headquartered in Sweden, Securitas A.B., bought the firm and stopped doing business under the Pinkerton name.

For some of Pinkerton's famous cases see page 499.

SAY GOODNIGHT, GRACIE

With her husband George Burns, Gracie Allen was a star of vaudeville, radio, movies, and television...and one of the funniest women of the 20th century. Here are some of her one-liners and comedy bits.

George: Gracie, let me ask you something. Did the nurse ever happen to drop you on your head when you were a baby?
Gracie: Oh, no, we couldn't afford a nurse, my mother had to do it.

George: Gracie, what day is it today?
Gracie: Well, I don't know.
George: You can find out if you look at that paper on your desk.
Gracie: Oh, George, that doesn't help. It's yesterday's paper.

"They laughed at Joan of Arc, but she went right ahead and built it."

George: This letter feels kind of heavy, I'd better put another three-cent stamp on it.
Gracie: What for? That'll only make it heavier.

Gracie: The baby my father brought home was a little French baby. So my mother took up French.
George: Why?
Gracie: So she would be able to understand the baby.

Gracie: On my way in here, a man stopped me at the stage door and said, "Hiya, cutie, how about a bite tonight after the show?"
George: And you said...?
Gracie: I said, "I'll be busy after the show but I'm not doing anything now," so I bit him.

Harry Von Zell: Gracie, isn't that boiling water you're putting in the refrigerator?
Gracie: Yes, I'm freezing it.
Harry: You're freezing it?
Gracie: Mmm-hmm, and then whenever I want boiling water, all I have to do is defrost it.

"This recipe is certainly silly. It says to separate two eggs, but it doesn't say how far to separate them."

Gracie: Don't give up, Blanche. Women don't do that. Look at Betsy Ross, Martha Washington— they didn't give up. Look at Nina Jones.
Blanche Morton: Nina Jones?
Gracie: I've never heard of her either, because she gave up.

LIMERICKS

Limericks have been around since the 1700s. Here are a few of the more "respectable" ones that our readers have sent in.

An accident really uncanny
Occurred to my elderly granny;
She sat down in a chair
While her false teeth lay there,
And bit herself right in the fanny.

"There's a train at 4:04," said Miss Jenny.
"Four tickets I'll take. Have you any?"
Said the man at the door,
"Not four for 4:04,
For four at 4:04 is too many."

A painter who came from Great Britain
Accosted two girls who were knittin'.
He said with a sigh,
"That park bench—well, I
Just painted it, right where you're sittin'."

A funny old bird is the pelican,
His beak holds more than his belican.
He can take in his beak
Enough food for a week.
I'm damned if I know how the helican!

There was a young lady who tried
A diet of apples, and died.
The unfortunate miss
Really perished of this:
Too much cider inside her inside.

There was an old skinflint named Green,
Who grew so abnormally lean
And flat and compressed,
That his back squeezed his chest,
And sideways he couldn't be seen.

There was an old man from Nantucket
Who kept all his cash in a bucket.
His daughter, named Nan,
Ran away with a man
And as for the bucket, Nantucket.

A daring young lady of Guam
Observed, "The Pacific's so calm
I'll swim out for a lark."
She met a large shark…
Let us now sing the 90th Psalm.

A man with the surname of Beebee
Wished to marry a lady named Phoebe,
But he said, "I must see
What the minister's fee be
Before Phoebe be Phoebe Beebee."

A bather whose clothing was strewed
By winds that had left her quite nude,
Saw a man come along…
And unless we are wrong,
You thought the next line would be lewd.

Among army ants, the "general" is always female.

THEY FELT THE PASSION

*In February 2004, Mel Gibson's much-anticipated and controversial
film* The Passion of the Christ *opened around the world.
Within weeks it had changed people's lives.*

JOHNNY OLSEN, OSLO, NORWAY: Olsen was known as a
neo-Nazi and one of Norway's most notorious criminals; he had
served 12 years for the murder of two youths in 1980. In March
he walked into the offices of the Norwegian newspaper *Dagbladet*
and made a confession: he was the person who had twice bombed
the Blitz House, an anti-racism center in Oslo, in 1994. "It was the
film that made him realize that he had to show his hand," said his
lawyer, Fridtjof Feydt. "It has been a long process, but the Jesus film
made the difference."

MELISSA AND SEAN DAVIDSON, GEORGIA: The
Davidsons, who had been married for 10 years, left a theater in
Bulloch County, Georgia, after seeing the movie. As they walked
home, they discussed whether "the Father" referred to in the film
was symbolic or human. By the time they got home, the discussion
had turned into an argument…and then into a fistfight. When
police arrived, Mrs. Davidson had bruises on her face and her husband had a stab wound on his hand from scissors. Both were arrested. "It was the dumbest thing we've ever done," Mr. Davidson said.
"We called the law on each other. It was one of those stupid things."

DAN R. LEACH, RICHMOND, TEXAS: Leach, 21, saw the
film, talked it over with a family friend, and then paid a visit to
the Fort Bend County Sheriff. The recent death of a 19-year-old
woman that had been ruled a suicide was actually a murder, he
told police, and he had done it. The young woman was carrying
his child, but he didn't want to raise the baby, he told officers.
So he killed her and carefully made the death look like a self-
strangulation. Then he saw the movie. "(It was) something the
friend said. Between that and the movie, he felt in order for him
to have redemption he would have to confess his sin and do his
time," Detective Mike Kubricht told reporters. Leach was arrested
the next day.

Heavy drinkers: Elephants love to drink alcohol.

JAMES ANDERSON, PALM BEACH, FLORIDA: The 53-year-old Anderson walked into a sheriff's office in Palm Beach and confessed to having robbed a bank in the city two years earlier. He had gotten away with $25,000, and police had no leads on the case at all. Anderson said he decided to come clean after seeing the movie (although police suspect he may have also wanted the free health care of prison—he had recently been diagnosed with prostate cancer).

A WOMAN IN NEW BRITAIN, CONNECTICUT: Someone called police to say they had seen a car drive into a creek in New Britain. When police arrived, the woman driver, whose name was not released, told them she had driven her Chevy Lumina into the water on purpose—to reenact a scene from *The Passion*. The woman wasn't hurt and no property was damaged, so no charges were filed. Police said they didn't know which scene it was that she was trying to reenact.

RONALD ANTHONY, WASHINGTON, D.C.: Anthony, a teacher at Malcolm X Elementary School, showed excerpts from Gibson's R-rated (and extremely violent) movie to his sixth-grade class. "I saw Jesus getting beaten," said upset 11-year-old Cutairra Ransom. "Needles were going in his arms." Children must have parental permission to see an R-rated film, yet no parents—or the principal—had been notified. Principal Vaughn Kimbrough suspended Anthony, saying, "You don't show the rated R, you don't show the religious." And if Anthony showed the film as a lesson in morality, he chose an ironic way to do it: it was a pirated copy.

TYLER WENDELL, EVANSVILLE, INDIANA: Wendell, 19, went to the Country Cinemas in Evansville specially dressed to see the movie—he wore a red devil costume. Angry audience members, many from local church organizations, threw food at the University of Southern Indiana student, and theater manager Brian Fitzgerald, who called Wendell "a misguided and deranged person," asked him to leave. Wendell later told reporters that he'd been trying to provoke a reaction. "If God really existed, he would have struck me down for dressing as the devil," he said. The cinema said they planned to write new admission rules: nobody dressed as "evil beings" would be allowed in the theater.

BATHROOM TIME KILLERS

This article was originally slated to go in Uncle John's Top Secret Bathroom Reader for Kids Only, *but then we thought, why should kids have all the fun?*

TOILET TENPIN

What You Need: Ten golf tees, or other objects that can serve as bowling pins, and a few rubber bands to serve as bowling balls. Set the golf tees up in a triangle like bowling pins as far from the toilet as you can while still having them within reach—that way you can set them up over and over again and bowl as long as you want.

How to Play: Have you ever shot a rubber band like a gun? Make your hand into a pistol—curl your pinkie around the rubber band, then stretch the rubber band around the back of your thumb and over the tip of your index finger. Hold the pistol square in the center of your chest, lean back as far as you can, and when you're ready to shoot, release your pinkie. Aim for the pins—try to knock them all down.

TRASH CAN FRISBEE

What You Need: A wastepaper basket and some paper plates. If the wastepaper basket isn't big enough to hold the paper plates, use a cardboard box or a paper shopping bag. Place the basket on the bathroom floor as far from the toilet as you can.

How to Play: Fling the paper plates like Frisbees—see if you can throw them into the wastepaper basket. For a bigger challenge, try to ricochet them off a wall into the basket.

BATHROOM DARTS

What You Need: A pie tin, a saucer, a small glass, and small objects you can throw. (Coins or caps from discarded toothpaste tubes work well.)

How to Play: Put the glass in the center of the saucer, and put the saucer in the center of the pie tin. Set them all down on the

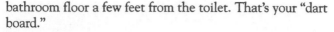

bathroom floor a few feet from the toilet. That's your "dart board."

Toss the coins ("darts") at your target—if they land in the glass, you get 10 points; if they land in the saucer, you get 5; if they land in the pie tin, you get 1. If you score too well, move the target farther away to make it more challenging.

BATHROOM BLOW GUN

What You Need: A soda straw, some wooden matches, and a hat

How to Play: Turn the hat upside down and place it on the bathroom floor a good distance away from the toilet. Put a match in the straw, hold the straw up to your mouth, and blow. Try to shoot all the matches into the hat.

FUN WITH A FUNNEL

What You Need: A rubber ball and a funnel. The funnel needs to be big enough to hold the ball.

How to Play: Hold the pointy end of the funnel. Bounce the ball off the wall opposite the toilet and try to catch it in the funnel on the rebound.

BATHROOM BOUNCY BALL

What You Need: An egg carton and some Ping-Pong balls.

How to Play: Write different point values in each of the 12 cups of the egg carton, then place it on the bathroom floor a few feet from the toilet.

Try to bounce the Ping-Pong balls into the egg carton. Start with one bounce, then, as your skills improve, move the carton farther away and bounce the balls twice before they go into the cups. Add up the values for your scores.

BATHROOM BROKEN NECK PREVENTER

What You Need: All the stuff you just spread out all over the bathroom floor to play all these games we just taught you.

How to Play: Pick all that stuff up off the bathroom floor— before somebody gets killed!

Don't wait up: The Milky Way takes about 200,000,000 years to make one revolution.

THE BESTSELLING BOOKS OF ALL TIME

When Gutenberg invented the printing press in 1451, he made it possible for books to be mass-produced. Five centuries later, it's almost impossible to come up with an accurate list of the top ten bestsellers...but here's what the experts think. (Check back in a decade—maybe the Bathroom Reader *will be on the list!)*

#1: The Bible (6 billion copies sold)
Background: The holy text for Christians, the Bible is believed to have been written over a 1,500-year span by at least 40 different people. First published in 1451 (the first book ever printed) it has been translated into more than 2,000 languages. The six billion sales figure includes numerous versions, interpretations, and translations by many different publishers all over the world. And of course it's just an estimate. Developing nations lack sales tracking technology, and many Bibles are distributed for free. Plus, exact sales figures prior to 1973 don't exist—the total could be much higher.

#2: *Quotations from Chairman Mao* (900 million sold)
Background: Known as the "Little Red Book" in the West, this book has been published by the Chinese government since 1966. Selling 900 million copies is no fluke—during the Cultural Revolution (1966–76), all Chinese citizens were required to own a copy. Failing to do so could result in anything from a beating by the military to years in a hard-labor camp. Made up of excerpts from Mao Zedong's speeches and writings, the book outlines the principles of Chinese socialism and, not coincidentally, glorifies Mao.

#3: *The American Spelling Book*, by Noah Webster (100 million sold)
Background: First published in 1783, this book actually sold more copies and had more influence than the one Webster is better known for: *The American Dictionary of the English Language. The American Spelling Book* was the standard grammar textbook and was used universally by 1840. It was also known as the Blue-Black Speller for its distinct two-tone cover. Webster's novel approach: he broke words down into syllables and emphasized them in stories and

fables, which made it easier for students to learn pronunciation and memorize spelling. Between his spelling book and his dictionary, Webster standardized the spellings of hundreds of words.

#4: *Guinness Book of World Records* (100 million sold)

Background: In 1951 the Guinness brewery hired a London fact-finding agency run by Norris and Ross McWhirter to settle an argument: what was the fastest game bird in Europe? (They said it was the spurwing goose.) They ended up compiling assorted facts, oddities, and achievements for what would become the *Guinness Book of Records*. First published in August 1955, it became a surprise bestseller by Christmas. Since then, many spin-offs have been released, but the original remains the most popular. It's the bestselling copyrighted book ever and has been translated into 37 languages.

#5: *The World Almanac and Book of Facts* (73.5 million sold)

Background: Published annually since 1868, this comprehensive reference book soberly presents page after page of records, lists, and facts on pretty much every subject, including geography, economics, sports, and entertainment. Fun fact: In 1923 Calvin Coolidge was sworn in as U.S. president by his father, a justice of the peace, who read the oath from a copy of *The World Almanac*.

#6: *McGuffey Readers*, by William H. McGuffey (60 million sold)

Background: First published in 1836, 80% percent of American schools used *McGuffey Readers* to teach reading. The publishers claimed that the series sold 120 million copies, but that wouldn't have mattered to William McGuffey—he earned just $1,000 for his efforts. The *McGuffey Readers*, along with *The American Spelling Book*, were the most common schoolbooks in the U.S. in the 19th century; neither is in print today.

#7: *The Common Sense Book of Baby and Child Care*, by Dr. Benjamin Spock (more than 50 million sold)

Background: Spock's child-rearing guide was first published in 1946 and became a necessity for generations of parents. It's the closest thing to a handbook for babies there is. The book was revolutionary: not only was Spock a man giving advice in what was considered a woman's domain, but he advocated a gentler approach to parenting and opposed spanking children. Despite the enduring popularity of this book and its many offshoots, by 1971 Spock came to feel that he "had gotten it wrong" when it came to giving parenting advice. (Still, not bad for a Vulcan.)

#8: *A Message to Garcia,* by Elbert Hubbard (40 million sold)
Background: It's barely a book; it's actually a 1,500-word essay about a Spanish-American War hero. A statement on labor relations, it was written to inspire workers to create a more efficient workplace. Coinciding with the Industrial Revolution in the U.S., *A Message to Garcia* fiercely extols the virtues of Big Business, which explains how it became a bestseller: companies bought copies by the truckload and gave them away free to employees.

#9: *In His Steps: What Would Jesus Do?,* by Rev. Charles Monroe Sheldon (More than 30 million sold)
Background: Sheldon wrote this guide in 1896, advice for Christians on how to apply Jesus' teachings to everyday decisions. The success of *In His Steps* led to two lucrative publishing phenomena that are with us to this day: self-help books and religious guidance books. Though still in print, the book isn't as popular today as it was a century ago, but "What Would Jesus Do?" bracelets, posters, T-shirts, bumper stickers, and keychains are.

#10: *Valley of the Dolls,* by Jacqueline Susann (30 million sold)
Background: A former Broadway starlet, Susann wrote this, her first book, in 1966. It's the bestselling novel of all time. The loosely autobiographical story follows three actresses desperate for fame in Hollywood as they get caught up in sex, pills, and booze. Susann's influence is widespread: later bestselling authors like Danielle Steel and Jackie Collins owe her a debt for developing the trashy sex and scandal-laden popular novel.

Some Bestsellers the Experts Might Have Missed:
- *Harry Potter and the Sorcerer's Stone,* by J. K. Rowling
- *To Kill A Mockingbird,* by Harper Lee
- *The Hobbit,* by J. R. R. Tolkien
- The Koran
- *Gone with the Wind,* by Margaret Mitchell
- *Catcher in the Rye,* by J. D. Salinger

Scales were invented in the Middle East as early as 4000 B.C.

KUNG FU WISDOM

Serious philosophy or TV gobbledygook? You be the judge. These quotes are from the only Buddhist Western in television history, Kung Fu.

"Man, like the animals, is meant to live in groups. But the meaning of belonging to a group is found in the comfort of silence and solitude."

—**Master Kan**

Master Po: Close your eyes. What do you hear?
Caine: I hear the water, I hear the birds.
Master Po: Do you hear the grasshopper that is at your feet?
Caine: Old man, how is it that you hear these things?
Master Po: Young man, how is it that you do not?

"No man can see through another's eyes or hear through his ears, or feel through his fingers."

—**Caine**

"Does not tomorrow begin now?"

—**Caine**

Caine: Do evil demons exist?
Master Kan: Do wars, famine, disease, and death exist? Do lust, greed, and hate exist? They are man's creations, brought into being by the dark side of his nature.

"Superstition is like a magnet. It pulls you in the direction of your belief."

—**Master Po**

"A man feels grief. One who does not fails in his capacity to be a man."

—**Caine**

"Learn first how to live. Learn second how not to kill. Learn third how to live with death. Learn fourth how to die."

—**Master Po**

Caine: Our bodies are prey to many needs. Hunger, thirst, the need for love. Shall we then seek to satisfy those needs?
Master Kan: Only acknowledge them, and satisfaction will follow. To suppress a truth is to give it force beyond endurance.

"Perfect wisdom is unplanned. Perfect living offers no guarantee of a peaceful death."

—**Master Po**

Caine: What is the greatest obligation that we have?
Master Po: To live, Grasshopper. To live!

IT'S ART TO SOMEONE

What is art? Almost anything, it seems. We at the BRI wonder: If we don't appreciate these high-concept "pieces," are we slobs? (B-u-u-u-u-urp!)

ARTIST: David Lynch

MEDIUM: Cutlery, fiberglass cow

IS IT ART? Lynch, well known as the director of the cult classic film *Blue Velvet* and the TV show *Twin Peaks*, was asked to contribute a sculpture for the 2004 Cow Parade in New York City. The parade is a traveling exhibit that gets local artists to decorate fake cows. Lynch's contribution: a large fiberglass cow with a bloody-looking stump where its head was supposed to be, the head rammed into its back, and forks and knives sticking out of its rump. Written on its side were the words "Eat My Fear." "They told me I could do anything I liked so long as it wasn't sexually explicit or X-rated," Lynch told *The Wolf Files*. The cow was supposed to be displayed on a city sidewalk, but when officials saw it, they banned it.

ARTISTS: *1157performancegroup*

MEDIUM: Corpse

IS IT ART? This experimental English theater group put out an unusual casting call in March 2004: they needed an actor to appear as a dead body—literally. The group hoped to find a terminally ill person who would consent to have their corpse "lie in state" on stage for the entire 24-night run of the show, entitled *DEAD...you will be.* Having an actual dead body, a spokeswoman said, "is important, we think, to help us to dispel the mysteries that surround death."

ARTIST: Karl Friedrich Lentze

MEDIUM: Corpse, fish

IS IT ART? The 56-year-old German artist wrote to several zoos around the country asking if he could be fed to piranhas when he died. Günther Nogge, director of the Cologne Zoo, liked the idea, saying that it might be very educational. "But," he added, "it would be better if you were fed to the piranhas alive—they're not keen on dead flesh." Lentze's counteroffer: Witnesses "could poke my body with sticks to get me moving and get the fish interested."

Ohio is the only U.S. state whose flag is not rectangular or square.

MORE ART: In 2002 Lentze wrote to Bonn city officials asking permission to be buried with an inflatable sex doll. (Request granted—as long as the doll was biodegradable.) And in 2003 he applied for a license to open a nightclub and brothel for dogs.

ARTIST: Andre Stitt

MEDIUM: Boots, litter

IS IT ART? In 2004 Stitt, an Irish performance artist, announced that his next act would be in Bedford, England. The act: He would walk out of a pub and kick an empty curry carton up and down the street while wearing silver-spangled platform boots. The work, entitled *White Trash Curry Kick*, is designed to "question the high spirits demonstrated by young people throughout the country on Saturday nights." The *real* kicker: He got the East of England Arts Society to give him a £12,200 grant (about $20,000) for the performance. Many people were outraged that he received public funds for kicking a carton down the street, but the Arts Council of England defended it, saying, "Art isn't only about paintings."

ARTIST: Orlan

MEDIUM: Her body

IS IT ART? From 1990 until 2000, the French performance artist worked on *The Reincarnation of Saint Orlan*, which consists of 10 videotaped plastic surgeries of her face. And the procedures weren't for the usual reasons: "I am against the ideas of normal beauty," the artist says. She had her chin done to resemble Botticelli's Venus; her lips to resemble Moreau's Europa, her eyes to look like Gérôme's Psyche, and had silicone implanted above her temples so she could have the forehead of Leonardo's Mona Lisa (sort of—it looks more like small horns). During the highly choreographed surgeries, Orlan, the surgeons, staff, and camera crew all dress in long robes. The artist, who takes only a local anesthetic so that she can remain conscious, reads poetry and philosophy during the operations. She completed the work by having doctors in Japan give her "the largest nose that her face is capable of supporting." Her videos and photographs—plus blood and fat from the operations—have been exhibited at major art galleries worldwide. "My body," she says, "is a place of public debate where crucial questions for our times can be asked."

NAME THAT TOWN

*If you had the opportunity to name a town, what would
you name it? Here's a look at how some towns
around the United States got their names.*

ALLIANCE, NEBRASKA

The town was originally named Grand Lake, but when the Chicago, Burlington, & Quincy Railroad came to town in 1888, the railroad's superintendent, G. W. Holdrege, wanted to change it. He thought a one-word name closer to the top of the alphabetical list of towns in Nebraska would be better for business. The U.S. Post Office gave him permission and he picked Alliance.

BANGOR, MAINE

When settlers in the area decided to incorporate and become a town in 1791, the Reverend Seth Noble talked them into calling the town Sunbury, then went to Boston to deliver the petition himself (Maine was part of Massachusetts then). He happened to be whistling a hymn titled "Bangor" when the court official asked him what he wanted to name the town. Thinking the official was asking about the hymn, he replied, "Bangor."

CALISTOGA, CALIFORNIA

In the early 1850s, Sam Brannan, publisher of San Francisco's *California Star* newspaper, learned of a natural hot spring in the Napa Valley north of San Francisco. He bought up more than 2,000 acres of the surrounding land and drew up plans for a resort town and a health spa fed by the spring. He wanted to model the town after Saratoga Springs, New York, and one night over dinner with friends (and after a few too many drinks), he gushed that the town would one day be "the Calistoga of Sarafornia!"

LESAGE, WEST VIRGINIA

Founded on the spot where Jules Lesage pulled ashore when his steamboat broke down. It took so long for the steamboat to be repaired that Lesage finally gave up and settled there instead.

Dolphins can produce notes 100 times higher than a human soprano.

CLEVELAND, OHIO

The town was surveyed in 1796 by a man named Moses Cleaveland and named in his honor by his employees. Cleaveland spelled his name with an "a," and that's how the town spelled its name until 1831, when the editor of the fledgling *Cleveland Advertiser* newspaper realized the town's name was too long to fit on the paper's masthead. He dropped the "a," and it's been spelled Cleveland ever since.

LOUISVILLE, OHIO

Settler Henry Lautzenheiser named the town after Lewis Lautzenheiser, one of his twenty-five children, in 1834. The name remained *Lewi*sville until 1837, when somebody noticed that there already was a town in Ohio named Lewisville. Rather than rename the town entirely, they changed the spelling to Louisville.

MONROE, LOUISIANA

The town, formerly named Fort Miro, got its new name when the first steamboat traveled up the Ouachita River in 1819. The townspeople were so thrilled at the sight of a boat travelling upriver under its own power that they renamed the town after the boat—the *James Monroe*.

PALM BEACH, FLORIDA

In 1878 the sailing ship *Providencia* shipwrecked on an island just off the coast of Florida. The ship's cargo—20,000 coconuts—washed up on the beach…and grew into the palm trees that give the island town its name.

PEKIN, ILLINOIS

Named in 1830 by one Mrs. Nathaniel Cromwell, who 1) wasn't much of a speller, and 2) was apparently convinced that Pekin was exactly on the opposite side of the globe from Peking, China. (She wasn't much of a geographer, either.)

SELMER, TENNESSEE

Named by one P. H. Thrasher, who wanted to name his town in honor of Selma, Alabama. (Apparently he was just as bad a speller as Mrs. Cromwell.)

"I WANT A BEER AS COLD AS MY EX-WIFE'S HEART"

You don't have to be a fan of country music to appreciate the toe-tappin' wit of these real-life country song titles.

"I Gave Her My Heart and a Diamond and She Clubbed Me with a Spade"

"You're a Hard Dog to Keep Under the Porch"

"Four on the Floor and a Fifth under the Seat"

"You Done Stomped on My Heart (and You Mashed That Sucker Flat)"

"I Went Back to My Fourth Wife for the Third Time and Gave Her a Second Chance to Make a First Class Fool Out of Me"

"You Can't Have Your Kate and Edith Too"

"I'd Rather Pass a Kidney Stone than Another Night with You"

"Feelin' Single and Drinkin' Doubles"

"If My Nose Was Full of Nickels, I'd Blow It All on You"

"I Bought the Shoes That Just Walked Out on Me"

"Jesus Loves Me but He Can't Stand You"

"I Fell in a Pile of You and Got Love All Over"

"One Day When You Swing That Skillet (My Face Ain't Gonna Be There)"

"I Gave Her the Ring, and She Gave Me the Finger"

"Thanks to the Cathouse, I'm in the Doghouse with You"

"You're the Ring Around My Bathtub, You're the Hangnail of My Life"

"I Want a Beer as Cold as My Ex-Wife's Heart"

"Did I Shave My Legs for This?"

"If You Can't Live without Me, Why Aren't You Dead?"

"I Wouldn't Take Her to a Dawg Fight, 'Cause I'm Afraid She'd Win"

"He's Got a Way with Women...and He Just Got Away with Mine"

Colgate was the first toothpaste to be sold in tubes rather than jars.

WHAT'S ON EBAY?

It's a game of virtual cat and mouse: smart alecks put crazy items up for auction on eBay, and eBay pulls them off the site. Here are a few of our favorites. (Winning bids are at the end.)

ITEM: My Toenail Clippings—31 inches long
DESCRIPTION: "These clippings were done by my teeth about an hour ago, off every single toe on both my feet. You can use them for absolutely nothing so buy them now!"
OPENING BID: $50.00

ITEM: Grandma—MUST SEE!!
DESCRIPTION: "We are so sure you will be happy with your grandma that we will throw in an extra pair of dentures. THAT'S NO TYPO! Warning: Grandma is known to spout profanity at times, and does get cranky if not given her medicine. (Medicine not included.)"
OPENING BID: $10.00

ITEM: The Meaning of Life
DESCRIPTION: "I have discovered the reason for our existence and will be happy to share this information with the highest bidder." (eBay note: "Contact the seller to resolve any questions before bidding.")
OPENING BID: $0.01

ITEM: 10 Fingers. Use them or eat them!
DESCRIPTION: "You might ask what it is you might do with 10 fingers. Just use your imagination, the possibilities are endless."
OPENING BID: $0.01

ITEM: Vial of Authentic *Melrose Place* TV Show Pool Water
DESCRIPTION: "Your favorite stars have swam and soaked in this pool for years. Now that the show is going to be gone forever you can still have a piece of history. 10 vials available."
OPENING BID: $7.99

ITEM: Fossilized Turtle Poop (called "coprolite")
DESCRIPTION: "I use coprolites just like this when I make fossil presentations at local grade schools and the kids love them. It seems everyone has a comment after holding one."
OPENING BID: $15.00

ITEM: One jar of air from Woodstock (the 1999 concert, not 1969)
DESCRIPTION: "I caught the air in the jar myself, it is real Woodstock air. So many came but how many thought to take some of the air with them? Get yours now."
OPENING BID: $9.99

ITEM: Two Weeks' Worth of Dog Hair!! L@@K!! No Reserve
DESCRIPTION: "This is prime shedding season with the dogs and I currently have more than I could ever possibly use. So why not let my windfall be your good fortune? Dog hair will be packaged in bubble wrap to avoid damage in shipping."
OPENING BID: $1.00

ITEM: One Package of 2 Krispy® Original Saltine Crackers
DESCRIPTION: "Seller reserves the right to eat this package of crackers at any time, and will replace said package with a suitable replacement. Buyer accepts all liability in case of irreversible product breakdown."
OPENING BID: $0.01

ITEM: Bob Eubanks, host of TV's *The Newlywed Game*
DESCRIPTION: "Buy Bob Eubanks and have him live with you. Is he the king of cool or what?!?!? How could you NOT bid on this item? Location: Beverly Hills, of course!!"
OPENING BID: $0.01

ITEM: $1.00—One dollar!
DESCRIPTION: "One dollar bill, slightly used, ready for you to use! Works in most vending machines!"
OPENING BID: $0.67 (Buyer pays 33¢ shipping & handling.)

30% of NBA players have tattoos.

ITEM: Justin Timberlake's French Toast
DESCRIPTION: "This is Justin's leftover french toast as eaten live on Z100 radio. You'll get his half-eaten french toast, the fork he used, and the plate...complete with extra syrup!! Any bids over $1,000 will be verified by Z100 by phone for authenticity."
OPENING BID: $1.00

ITEM: Fast Food Assistant Manager—Small Skill, Big Butt
DESCRIPTION: "Known by many names such as Ass. Man., Hamburger Pants, Hamburgler, this lumpy boytoy can mess up your store's paperwork, and be a useless, annoying, grunting womanizer too!!"
OPENING BID: $0.50

ITEM: My Dignity
DESCRIPTION: "Winning bidder will receive a piece of paper that says, 'My Dignity' on it, with my signature. Warning: I may become a sad man after relinquishing my dignity."
OPENING BID: $2.00

ITEM: Partially-Used Pack of Cigarettes
DESCRIPTION: "Hurry up and buy the remainder of my current pack of Parliament Lights. They're going fast—I'm smoking them right now. NO RESERVE!"
OPENING BID: $3.00

WINNING BIDS

Nail Clippings: Reserve not met
Grandma: $1,000,300
Meaning of Life: $3.26
10 Fingers: $0.01 (they turned out to be ladyfingers)
Melrose Place **Pool Water:** $7.99 (2 vials sold)
Turtle Poop: No bids
Woodstock Air: $9,999,999

Dog Hair: No bids
Crackers: $0.05
Bob Eubanks: No bids
One Dollar: $0.67
Justin's French Toast: $3,154
Assistant Manager: No bids
My Dignity: $10.50
Partially Used Pack of Cigarettes: $10,000,000

IRREGULAR NEWS

More proof that truth really is stranger than fiction.

PLEASE, MR. POSTMAN...

"A package marked 'Warning, bomb!', 'Now you'll have it!' and 'Look out!' was delivered without a problem by the Swedish postal services. Postal service spokesman Mattias Geijerstam said Wednesday the agency was embarrassed, but explained that the package was delivered because postal workers were convinced it was a hoax. The package was forwarded to a local shop to be picked up by the addressee. He said workers at the local store read the labels and called police. It was examined and declared bomb-free after it was found to hold a pair of shoes."

—*Manchester* (U.K.) *News*

KNOCK-KNOCK

"A pair of prisoners at a British low-security jail escaped—only to knock on the door of a more secure prison nearby and ask to be detained there instead. The two reformed drug users fled from Leyhill prison near Gloucester because they found narcotics too easily available there. Audie Carr, 29, and Benjamin Clarke, 23, were found to be missing at roll call last Sunday night, but by Monday lunchtime they had knocked on the doors of Gloucester Prison 32 kilometers (19 miles) away. 'They wanted to finish their sentences at Gloucester,' a prosecution lawyer told the court."

—ABC News

IT'S AN HONOR JUST TO BE NOMINATED

"*Awards World* magazine recently sponsored the 'Awards Awards' at London's Dorchester Hotel, handing out awards to members of the British awards-presentation industry for the year's best awards shows. *Awards World* editor Barbara Buchanan explained, 'Everybody likes to win an award, even the people who give out awards.' Buchanan (who staged about 1,000 major presentations in Britain last year) called this year's program a success, but said it is disqualified from receiving any awards at next year's Awards Awards."

—BBC News

Penicillin causes about 300 deaths per year in the United States.

NO LAUGHING MATTER

"Members of a 'laughter club' in Patna, India, described the decision to ban laughing at their local zoo as 'autocratic.' Chuckling was outlawed after Laloo Prasad Yadav, the president of Bihar state's ruling party, was angered by the group 'merrily laughing in chorus' when he walked past them in the Sanjay Gandhi Botanical Garden and Zoo. 'You are disturbing the peace of the flora and fauna of the zoo,' Laloo reportedly told the group, before issuing instructions to zoo officials to enforce an immediate ban. Laughter clubs, groups of people who gather to laugh loudly in public to relieve stress, are a phenomenon in parts of India."

—*The Economic Times*

BLOCKHEAD

"A U.K. driver was pulled over by police in Surrey when they noticed him driving with a box (with eyeholes) over his head. He told police the foil lining protected him from the car's electromagnetic emissions."

—*"The Edge," The Oregonian*

EGG HEAD

"When Briton Malcolm Eccles, 50, died of bowel cancer, his family turned him into a kitchen aid. In accordance with his wishes, they keep his ashes in a specially crafted glass egg timer. 'I can't boil a soft egg to save my life,' widow Brenda said, 'so he said I should turn some of his ashes into an egg-timer. Then he could help me and it would be a nice way of remembering him.'"

—*Wacky News*

DIDN'T SEE THAT COMING

"A Chinese pensioner who exercises by walking backwards around a lake had to be rescued after he lost concentration and fell in. *China Daily*, quoting the *Beijing Times*, says Yan, 72, believes his daily routine of walking backwards around Bayi Lake is good for his health. But he was apparently counting his steps instead of checking his surroundings, miscalculated, and fell backwards. Three other fitness enthusiasts saved him and took him to the hospital, where he received three stitches on his head."

—*Daily Times* (Pakistan)

National flower of the United States: the rose, adopted in 1986.

LOONEY LAWS

Believe it or not, these laws are real.

In Salem, West Virginia, it is illegal to leave home without knowing where you're going.

In Tempe, Arizona, you may drink alcohol in a city park, but only if the park is three acres or larger.

You can possess one bear gallbladder in California, but not two.

In Kentucky it is illegal for politicians to give away booze on Election Day.

Maine law states that you may not catch a lobster with your bare hands.

Funeral directors in Nevada can be arrested for cursing in the presence of a dead body.

In Washington, D.C., it's against the law to marry your mother-in-law.

Wearing high-heeled shoes is legal in Carmel, California… but you need a permit.

It's illegal to sleep naked in Minnesota.

Detroit law prohibits a man from scowling at his wife on a Sunday.

How many people in Victoria, Australia, does it take to change a lightbulb? Only one, but he has to be a licensed electrician.

In Jonesboro, Georgia, it's against the law to say, "Oh, boy."

In Mesquite, Texas, children are prohibited from having "unusual haircuts."

Exploding an atomic bomb in Chico, California, is punishable by a $500 fine.

In Arizona, donkeys may not, by law, sleep in bathtubs.

In Paulding, Ohio, it's legal for a police officer to bite a dog.

It's against the law in Chicago for "exceedingly ugly" people to appear in public.

In Huntsville, Alabama, you may not move your bed without a permit.

In Stockton, California, it's illegal to wiggle while you dance.

In Michigan, it's against the law to put a skunk in your boss's desk. (Darn!)

The average adult has about 46 miles of nerves.

SEGUE INTO SEGWAY

Inventor Dean Kamen holds over 150 patents for medical
technology and social welfare devices. But it's for his one
major failure he'll be remembered: the Segway.

EDISON REBORN?

Dean Kamen has been obsessed with the power of technology since he was a teenager. He never cared much for school, skipping homework to read complicated physics texts and create laser light shows. While still in high school, Kamen designed the audiovisual system at New York's Hayden Planetarium and the New Year's Eve Times Square ball drop. By 18, he was earning $60,000 a year, more than his father, an editor at *Mad* magazine.

He began inventing when his brother, a medical student, complained about how hard it was to administer intravenous drugs without having to keep patients constantly hospitalized. Solving his brother's dilemma consumed his life—he was even kicked out of college for spending too much time on it. But by 1976, at age 25, Kamen had patented the Auto-Syringe: a pocket-size infusion pump that delivers a steady stream of medication, freeing patients from hospital beds. (Today it's mostly used in insulin pumps for diabetics.) Kamen manufactured and marketed the device himself, and eventually sold his company for $5 million.

THE NEXT BIG THING

Barely 30 and a multimillionaire, Kamen took his money and created DEKA Research and Development. It was his dream job: companies would pay him to invent stuff. Under this arrangement, Kamen developed 150 devices, including a portable dialysis machine that freed patients with kidney diseases from constant visits to dialysis centers, and the IBOT, a robotic wheelchair that could climb stairs and raise its user to standing level. Following these successes, Kamen knew his next project would have to be nothing short of earth-shattering to meet expectations, especially his own.

For the better part of the decade, Kamen spoke very little about his next invention. The less he said, the more interest he generated in "It" (that was the codename). All Kamen would say was that It would revolutionize the world—and would "be to the car what the car was to the horse and buggy."

Science and technology magazines speculated wildly on what It might be: was It a personal hovercraft? A solar-powered engine? By 2000 no pictures or details had been released, although Kamen had been working on It (now being called "Ginger") for almost ten years and had raised $90 million from investors.

Kamen opened up a little in early 2001: he talked about the potential impact of Ginger, but not the invention itself. He promised it would end urban congestion, air pollution, and oil dependency. Kamen leased a giant factory in New Hampshire set to produce 10,000 units a week to meet what was sure to be an insatiable demand.

WOW, IT'S A...SCOOTER

What could possibly live up to such hype? Unfortunately, not Ginger. Kamen finally unveiled his top-secret invention to end all inventions on *Good Morning America* in December 2001. The device's real name was the Segway Human Transporter and it was...an electric scooter.

According to Segway Inc., the device was the "first self-balancing, electric-powered transportation device. With the ability to emulate human balance, the Segway HT uses the same space as a pedestrian, and can go wherever a person can walk." Resembling a podium on wheels, the Segway ran on synchronized gyroscopes that constantly balanced the rider at speeds of up to 13 mph.

By and large, the public didn't think a scooter had the capacity to alter world transport, nor was it worth the years of buildup or the $90 million investment. And there were all sorts of problems Kamen and his engineers didn't foresee. Segways were banned from the narrow sidewalks of older cities like New York and Boston. They were far too expensive ($5,000) to make people give up their cars. But perhaps most importantly of all—they looked silly.

HOW MANY DO YOU WANT?

In an attempt to build consumer confidence, Kamen went to trendsetting corporate clients first. Disney bought a few Segways for its theme parks, and Amazon.com and the U.S. Postal Service let workers test them out. Segways became available to the general public just before Christmas 2002. The general public didn't notice.

I'M A STAR

One segment of the country embraced the Segway: the media, but only as an oddity. A high-profile flop and a novelty, it was ripe for lampooning. The scooter showed up on the sitcoms *Frasier*, *Arrested Development*, *Father of the Pride*, and in the Ben Stiller movie *Envy*. All this coverage didn't help sell the Segway or improve its goofy image; it was still considered an extravagant toy for kooky millionaires. The Segway was recalled in 2003 after three riders were mildly injured falling off. At that point, only 6,000 had been sold.

The Segway has yet to catch on in the way Kamen predicted or anticipated, but he rides his virtually all day long through his office and around Manchester, New Hampshire. He hasn't lost hope, though. One day, Kamen insists, everyone will be riding Segways.

*   *   *

ROCK PAPER SCISSORS

• Did you know there's an international governing body for Rock Paper Scissors? The World Rock Paper Scissors Society sets rules, holds an annual worldwide tournament, and since the 1920s has published *Think Three*, an RPS strategy and lifestyle magazine.

• Names for Rock Paper Scissors around the world: Jenken (China), Jan Ken Pon (Japan), Roshambo (southern United States), Shnik Shnak Shnuk (Germany), Ching Chong Chow (South Africa), Farggling (parts of the United States).

• How does paper beat rock? Obviously, a rock crushes scissors and scissors cut paper. But why exactly does paper defeat rock? It's the question the World Rock Paper Scissors Society is most often asked. According to them, the answer lays in ancient China. Petitions were given to the emperor for approval. If he accepted it, the document was placed under a rock. If denied, it was draped over the rock. Paper covering rock came to be associated with defeat.

There is electricity in the clouds, in this book, and in you.

URBAN LEGENDS

Psst! Have you heard the one about the kid who ate the taco?
Remember the BRI rule of thumb: If a story sounds true, but
also seems too perfect to be true, it's probably an urban legend.

THE STORY: On a foggy November day, the California Highway Patrol finds the body of Stuart Bidasoe (called "Stu" by his friends) slumped over the wheel of his 1997 Saturn. He hit a fence post and the airbag deployed, but the accident was too minor to explain his death. So how did he die? Did he overdose on drugs? There aren't any drugs in the car—just a bag of Halloween candy on the passenger seat. The coroner solves the mystery when he pulls a lollipop out of Stu's throat. Apparently he was eating the lollipop when he drove off the road and hit the fence post. The impact activated the airbag, which shoved the lollipop down Stu's throat. Tragically, he choked to death before help arrived. Moral of the story: Don't eat while driving.

HOW IT SPREAD: By e-mail and then word of mouth, starting in 2002. Fear of technology—airbags—helped the story spread, as did the abundance of details in the original e-mail: Stu Bidasoe is identified by name, as is Officer Benson, who found him, the make and model of Stu's car, the county in which the accident happened, and the precise date.

THE TRUTH: Is this a true story or an urban legend? Say "Stu Bidasoe" five times fast and decide for yourself.

THE STORY: An adventurous young woman takes a trip to the rainforests in Guatemala. When she gets back home, she notices that a bug bite on her cheek isn't healing. Instead of going to a doctor she puts some ointment on it. It itches, but she tries to forget about it. A few days later her cheek is red, swollen and itching like crazy, so she finally gives in and scratches it. Pop! The skin bursts and hundreds of tiny spiders crawl out.

HOW IT SPREAD: Versions of this tale have been circulating since the 1960s. The location varies with each telling—sometimes it's Mexico, other times it's Spain, Central America, South America, or Africa. In some variations the young woman dies or goes insane, and sometimes the wound bursts open after a doctor tries to lance what he thinks is a boil. Fear of insects (especially spiders) is probably what keeps this story going.

THE TRUTH: Good news! According to experts, no species of spider is capable of laying eggs in your cheeks. So where does the story come from? One possibility: it's a modern incarnation of a 19th-century German fable in which a woman makes a deal with the devil, a deal that he seals by kissing her on the cheek. When she reneges, a black boil begins to grow on the spot where he kissed her. A few days later, it bursts open and hundreds of tiny spiders come out.

THE STORY: All military personnel wear ID tags known as "dog tags" around their necks to help identify human remains on the battlefield. Old-fashioned dog tags had little notches in them. The reason: If the person fighting alongside you dies in combat and you can't remove his remains from the battlefield right away, you're supposed to wedge the notch between his two front upper teeth and then give the jaw a swift kick to jam the dog tags into place. That way the tag is sure to stay with the remains.

HOW IT SPREAD: From one GI to another, helped along by the fact that there really *was* a notch in dog tags issued between 1941 and the 1970s.

THE TRUTH: According to the U.S. Military Department of Mortuary Affairs, "the only purpose of the notch was to hold the blank tag in place on the embossing machine. The machine used at this time doesn't require a notch to hold the blank in place, hence, today's tags are smooth on all sides."

THE STORY: Your local swimming pool contains a chemical that turns bright red if someone pees in the pool.

HOW IT SPREAD: By word of mouth from parents to kids, and then from one scared kid to another, since the late 1950s.

THE TRUTH: No such chemical exists. Urine is made up mostly of water with some acid. Swimming pools contain water…and some acid. So it's hard to come up with a chemical that can tell the difference between pee and pool water. Besides, even if such a chemical did exist, would anyone really want it? The temptation for pranksters would be too great—and we'd probably all end up swimming in pools full of red dye.

THE STORY: A mother puts waterproof sunscreen on her two-year-old son, Zack. She accidently gets some in his eyes, and the kid starts screaming. She tries to flush it out, but when that fails she calls poison control. They tell her to rush her son to the emergency room immediately, and that's where she learns the terrible news: waterproof sunscreen contains chemicals that cause blindness, and because the sunscreen is *waterproof*, once it gets in your eyes there's no way to wash it out. Zack goes blind for two days, but he only got a little bit of sunscreen in his eyes, so he recovers his sight. Other kids aren't so lucky—many go permanently blind each year.

HOW IT SPREAD: Via an e-mail that appeared in 1998 and then spread like wildfire from one suburban mom to another. Fear of huge corporations helped give it credibility—in the e-mail, the woman explains that when she called the manufacturer to complain, the company told her that they know their product causes many kids to go permanently blind each year, but since skin cancer is more serious than blindness, they're leaving the chemicals in.

THE TRUTH: When this e-mail hit, thousands of terrified parents flooded the switchboard of their poison control centers to see if the story was true. The New Jersey Poison Information and Education System received so many calls that it issued a press release denying the rumor. The truth: Yes, like a lot of things, waterproof sunscreen stings if it gets in your eyes, but relax—according to authorities, it won't make you go blind.

*　　*　　*

WHY ISN'T OUR KIDS MORE INTELLIGENTER?

The North Carolina State Board of Education recently asked a research firm to study how schools could combat illiteracy. Here was the research firm's response: "The conceptual framework for this evaluation posits a set of determinants of implementation which explains variations in the level of implementation of the comprehensive project."

JELLIED MOOSE NOSE

In 1967 the Canadian government published a collection of backwoods recipes from native and non-native peoples in the nation's far north. It's now out-of-print, but here are a few highlights. And if ever you find a copy of The Northern Cookbook, *grab it—it's a classic.*

MUSKRAT TAILS

"Cut off the tails and dip them into very hot water. Pull off the fur. Either cook them on top of the stove, turning them after a few minutes, or boil them. (This is the same method as for beaver tails. Both are very sticky to eat.)"

STUFFED MUSKRAT

"Clean the rats well and put them in a roaster with bread stuffing on top. Roast until the muskrats are soft."

BOILED PORCUPINE

"Make a fire outside and put the porcupine in it to burn off the quills. Wash and clean well. Cut up and boil until done."

GRIZZLY BEAR STEAKS

"Cut up meat as for frying and fry in deep grease in frying pan."

BEAR FAT PASTRY

"1-1/2 cups flour, 1/2 tsp. salt, 1/3 cup bear fat (from a little black bear that was eating berries). Makes rich white pastry."

MUKTUK (meat inside skin and fat of a whale)

"After taken from whale leave 2 days hanging up to dry. Cut into 6" x 6" pieces. Cook until tender. After cooked, keep in a cool place in a 45-gallon drum of oil, in order to have muktuk all year."

OVEN-ROASTED LYNX

"Wash and clean the hind legs of the lynx and roast it with lard and a little water."

BOILED LYNX

"Cut up the lynx and boil it until it is soft and well cooked. Good to eat with muktuk."

STEAMED MUSKRAT LEGS

"Cut off the muskrat's legs, dip in a bowl of flour with salt, pepper, and other strong seasoning. Put grease into a large frying pan. Put in the muskrat legs. Cover and cook for a long time as they take long to become tender. The strong seasoning takes away the actual taste of the muskrat."

During the Depression, 44% of all U.S. banks failed.

BOILED REINDEER HEAD

"Skin and wash the head well. Then chop it in quarters, splitting it between the eyes with an axe. Cover with cold water and boil until soft. One can also roast in an open pan in an oven very slowly."

BOILED REINDEER OR CARIBOU HOOFS

"Put hoofs (skin still on them) in a large pot. Cover and boil for a couple of hours. The skin will peel off easily. The muscles are soft and very good to eat. The toe nails also have some soft sweet meat inside them."

BOILED SMOKED BEAVER

"Smoke the beaver for a day or so. Cut up the meat and boil it with salted water until done."

FROZEN FISH EGGS

"Take fish eggs out and freeze them. They are good to eat like this."

BOILED BONE GREASE

"Boil whatever bones are left after all the meat has been cut off. Boil them all in a big pot for two hours. Then let the grease get cold in the pot. It is easy to pick the grease off. Keep the grease to eat with dry meat or add to pounded meat."

BOILED REINDEER TONGUES

"Boil tongues until thoroughly cooked. Potatoes and vegetables are good with this."

DRY FISH PUDDING

"Pound up 5 to 6 dry fish. Throw away skin. Add sugar, a little grease, and cranberries."

JELLIED MOOSE NOSE

"Cut the upper jaw bone of the moose just below the eyes. Boil in a large kettle for 45 minutes. Remove and chill. Pull out all the hairs (like plucking a duck) and wash until none remain. Place nose in a kettle and cover with fresh water. Add onion, garlic, spices, and vinegar. Bring to a boil, then reduce heat and simmer until meat is tender. Let cool overnight. When cool, discard the bones and cartilage. You will have white meat from the bulb of the nose and dark meat from the bones and jowls. Slice thinly and alternate layers of white and dark meat in a loaf pan. Let cool until jelly has set. Slice and serve cold."

BAKED SKUNK

"Clean, skin, wash. Bake in oven with salt and pepper. Tastes like rabbit (no smell)."

MR. POTTY MOUTH

On June 20, 2004, Vice President Dick Cheney made an off-color remark to Senator Patrick Leahy of Vermont and made history. We can't print exactly what he said, but neither could the news media. Here are a few of the creative ways they reported the story.

- **Washington Post:** "Cheney exploded in colorful profanity."

- **CBS News:** "Cheney Gives Leahy An 'F'."

- **Capital Times:** "Dick Cheney to Pat Leahy: Go f*$@! yourself."

- **Spokesmanreview.com:** "Cheney delivered a popular epithet (see *The Sopranos*)."

- **Boston Herald:** "Bleep the veep: Angry Cheney tells senator to **** OFF!"

- **Christian Science Monitor:** "The Vice President allegedly used a four-letter word to suggest Leahy engage in a procreative anatomical impossibility."

- **L.A. Times:** "Go…yourself."

- **Charleston Post Courier:** "Go [expletive deleted] yourself."

- **The Calgary Sun:** "Go (bleep) yourself."

- **Weekly World News:** "Cheney On F-Word Rampage!"

- **Herald Sun:** "Cheney swears an oath."

- **Springfield News Leader:** "Cheney dismissed Leahy with the offensive language."

- **CNN:** "Cheney replied "f— off" or "go f— yourself."

- **Japan Today:** "Cheney used a naughty word…"

- **USA TODAY:** "Tells Sen. Leahy to "go f*** yourself."

- **DNCNews:** "Cheney uses 'Big-time' swear word."

- **Canada Free Press:** "Oh, fudge!"

- **MSNBC:** "Cheney then used the "f" word."

- **Houston Chronicle:** "Cheney…vulgarly proposed that Sen. Leahy do something impossible to himself."

- **FOXNEWS:** "…one of George Carlin's seven deadly words."

- **Vice President Cheney:** "I felt better after I'd done it."

WORD ORIGINS

*Here are a few more interesting word
origins we've come across.*

LOLLAPALOOZA

Meaning: An extraordinary person or thing
Origin: "The French expression *allez-fusil*, 'Forward the musket!', became common in Ireland after French troops landed there in 1798. County Mayo residents pronounced it 'ally foozee' and coined a new word from it, meaning 'sturdy fellow,' from which comes *lollapalooza*." (From *Encyclopedia of Word and Phrase Origins*, by Robert Hendrickson)

BUCKAROO

Meaning: A working cowboy
Origin: "The term *buckaroo* is an anglicized pronunciation of the Spanish word *vaquero*, meaning cowboy. It was generalized in the 19th century to refer to ranch hands." (From *Western Lore and Language*, by Thomas L. Clark)

JUNK

Meaning: Something having no value or use; trash
Origin: "Even before the days of Columbus, *junk* was the name given to pieces of old rope found about a ship. Rather than being tossed overboard, *junk* was saved until another use could be found. It could be stuffed between leaky planks to seal the seams; long pieces were used to snug things down; and short chunks were used as wadding in guns during battle. Eventually the word made its way ashore and was used to refer to any discarded object for which another use might be found." (From *Scuttlebutt*, by Teri Degler)

DUD

Meaning: Anything that fails to live up to our expectations
Origin: "The original 15th century meaning was 'an article of clothing.' It eventually came to mean 'tattered clothes,' and by the 17th century, scarecrows attired in cast-off clothing were being called *dudmen*. Sometime in the 19th century we began to

---

Not so new-age: The term "aromatherapy" was coined in 1928.

use *dud* to mean anything ineffective or fraudulent, a usage that got a big boost during World War I, when unexploded artillery shells were called *duds*." (From *The Word Detective*, by Evan Morris)

RIGMAROLE

Meaning: Fast talk used to confuse the listener or hide the truth

Origin: "*Ragman* was a designation applied to certain feudal officials in England. When Edward I invaded Scotland in 1296, he forced all nobles and gentry to sign a 'ragman's roll' as a token of allegiance. He then sent couriers all over the country reading the names to commoners, hoping that announcing the submission of their leaders would bring resistance to an end. Edward's weary messengers reeled off the names so quickly that they were difficult to understand. Hence *any* jumble of words became a ragman's roll, and then, streamlined from frequent use, a *rigamarole*." (From *Why You Say It*, by Webb Garrison)

SLEUTH

Meaning: A detective or private eye

Origin: "In the 12th century, *sleuth* meant 'trail' or 'track.' But in the 15th century, *sleuth* came to be used as a shortening of 'sleuth-hound', that is, a species of bloodhound used for tracking game or trailing fugitives, especially in Scotland. The word was adopted in the 19th century for a detective, who carried out the duties of a 'sleuthhound' at a more sophisticated level." (From *Dunces, Gourmands and Petticoats*, by Adrian Room)

GOSSAMER

Meaning: Something delicate, light, or flimsy

Origin: "It originally meant 'fine cobwebs.' The theory: mid-autumn is a time when geese for the table are plentiful (November was once known as *gänsemonat*, 'geese-month' in German), so a warm period around then might have been termed *goose-summer* (we now call it *Indian summer*). Silken filaments of *gossamer* are most commonly observed floating in the air on such warm fall days, and so the spiders' webs were christened with the name of the season." (From *Dictionary of Word Origins*, by John Ayto)

UNCLE JOHN'S PUZZLERS

*Put on your thinking caps—some of these are
pretty tough. (Answers are on page 517.)*

1. Start with these letters:

ERGRO

If you place three letters in
front of them, and the same
three letters after them—in
the same order—you'll form a
common word. You may have
to dig deep for the answer.

2. These names may look
unfamiliar, but they're actually
anagrams of the names of
famous people. Can you figure
out who they are?
a. Charlie J. Damon
b. Dave Rio Larger
c. Ana Mond
d. Stella Big
e. Tina Borly
f. Uveka Serene
g. Joel Chunn

3. What should the 10th number in this series be? (We'd
like to give you a hint, but we
shouldn't have to spell it out
for you.)

3, 3, 5, 4, 4, 3, 5, 5, 4...

4. Divide 30 by 1/2 and add
10. What is the answer?

5. John's number is 47.
Thom's number is 56.
Brian's number is 44.
What's Jay's number?

6. What three letters can be
placed in front of each of these
words to form a new word?

TIME
SPORT
SAGE
SWORD
SABLE

7. The correct mathematical
signs have been removed from
this equation and replaced
with asterisks. Can you figure
out the correct signs?

$$18 * 8 * 2 * 2 = 71$$

8. The top row of a typewriter
keyboard has these letters:

QWERTYUIOP

What common 10-letter word
can you make using these letters? (You can repeat letters.)

9. There are four words in the
English language that begin
with the letters "dw." Name
them.

TTFN, SWEATER GIRL!

Supremo Uncle John thinks this whizzo page of expressions from the 1940s is unputdownable.

Beefburger: Another name for *hamburger*, which was considered misleading.

Steakburger: A high-class, high-priced beefburger.

Slimline: Sleek styling of consumer products such as radios and televisions, inspired by streamlined trains and planes.

TTFN: Good-bye (short for "Ta-ta for now!").

Mug: A violent robbery. From the boxing expression, "hit in the mug (face)."

Sweater girl: A movie starlet who wears tight sweaters to call attention to her bust.

Robomb: Short for *robot bomb*, the name given to German V-1 rockets before such weapons became known as *guided missiles*.

Toecover: A cheap, useless item given as a gift.

Oceanarium: An aquarium big enough to hold dolphins, whales, or other large creatures.

Peek-a-boo: A woman's hairstyle in which the hair falls over one eye, but not the other.

Unputdownable: Just what it sounds like: a book or magazine article that's so good you can't put it down.

Vacky: An evacuee. During World War II, British women and children moved from the cities to the safer countryside.

Shortie: A prefix for extra-short garments—shortie skirts, shortie pajamas, etc. It was eventually replaced by *mini*.

Tail-end Charlie: The person who mans the gun in the tail end of a World War II bomber.

Step out: To parachute from an airplane.

Whizzo: Wonderful.

Delhi belly: Intestinal disorder experienced by western visitors to India.

Atomize: Destroy something with a nuclear weapon.

Squillion: An unspecified, very large number, like zillion.

Supremo: The highest military officer in the land, kind of like *generalissimo*.

Nurembergs: Hemorrhoids.

Your capillaries are about 1/3000 of an inch in diameter...thinner than a hair.

THE CIA'S FIRST COUP, PART II

Here's the second installment of our history of the
1953 coup in Iran. (Part I is on page 155.)

TAKING OVER

When the *Majlis* (the Iranian legislature) required the government to renegotiate the Anglo-Iranian Oil Co. concession in 1947, Anglo-Iranian flatly refused. That prompted the Majlis to introduce the legislation revoking the concession. *That* got the company's attention. In 1949 they responded with a "supplemental agreement" that set the minimum annual payment at £4 million ($16 million), and promised to train more Iranians for administrative positions within the company. But Iranians would still play no decision-making roles and would still be banned from auditing company books.

Realizing that the Majlis was unlikely to accept the agreement, the shah stalled for nearly a year before submitting it for approval in June 1950. As expected, they rejected it. Then on March 15, 1951, the Majlis cast their historic vote to revoke Anglo-Iranian's concession and nationalize the oil industry. Six weeks later, Dr. Mohammed Mossadegh, the leader of the nationalization drive in the Majlis, was elected prime minister, and on May 1, 1951, fearing his throne and maybe even his life were on the line, the shah reluctantly signed the bill into law. A new company, the National Iranian Oil Company, took control.

SWITCHING GEARS

At this point, Great Britain was ready to invade Iran outright, but backed off when U.S. president Harry Truman refused to support the action. He wouldn't support a coup against Mossadegh, either, so when the British got themselves thrown out of Iran for plotting it, they were out of luck...for a while. But Truman's term of office was coming to an end, and in November 1952, Dwight D. Eisenhower was elected president. The British thought they might have better luck convincing Eisenhower to support a coup.

Eisenhower had run for president on an anti-Communist platform, so when the British sent a Secret Intelligence Service (SIS) agent named Christopher Montague Woodhouse to sell the Americans on having the CIA stage a coup, he abandoned the usual British argument—that Iran had stolen British property—and tried something different: the Communist threat.

THE IRON CURTAIN

Woodhouse had a lot to work with. In 1940 the Soviet Union had annexed Estonia, Latvia, and Lithuania, and after World War II, had set up Communist regimes in Bulgaria, Hungary, Poland, and Czechoslovakia, as well. The Soviet Union shared a border with Iran, and more ominously, they had recently recalled their ambassador to Iran and replaced him with the man who, as ambassador to Czechoslovakia, had helped organize the Communist coup there. "Only the naive could believe that the Russians were not organizing to gain political control of Iran through their agents in the [Iranian Communist] party," Daniel Yergin writes in *The Prize.* "The chicken was only waiting to be plucked."

Eisenhower approved the plot.

READY, SET, GO

Plans for the coup were well underway by the time Eisenhower gave his approval. A CIA agent named Kermit Roosevelt—grandson of Theodore Roosevelt—was already in Iran contacting a network of Iranian operatives set up by British intelligence.

The plan to overthrow Mossadegh, code name Operation Ajax, was fairly straightforward: The CIA would get the shah to sign papers dismissing him from office—even though under the Iranian constitution, he didn't have the power to dismiss prime ministers—and get him to appoint a retired pro-British general, Fazlollah Zahedi, in his place.

The trick was doing it without plunging the country into chaos in the process. Mossadegh was the most popular statesman in Iran—if he were dumped unceremoniously, the populace was likely to rise up in revolt. Before the CIA could overthrow Mossadegh they had to make him less popular.

SHUTTING OFF THE SPIGOT

Much of the work of undermining Mossadegh was already being done by Great Britain, which launched an international boycott of Iranian oil in June 1951. And because it withdrew British oil workers from Iran, there wasn't enough skilled labor left behind to operate the oil fields and run the refinery at Abadan. Iran tried to hire skilled oil industry workers from abroad, but Great Britain asked its allies to refuse exit visas to anyone with experience in oil. It added to the economic pressure by freezing Iranian assets in British banks.

Even though Anglo-Iranian paid Iran only a pittance for its oil, the Iranian economy was so underdeveloped that oil exports accounted for 70% of export income and half of all government revenues in 1950. Thanks to the boycott, by 1952 Iran's oil exports dropped to almost nothing. Inflation soared, the economy contracted sharply, and the Iranian government ran out of money. It was reduced to paying teachers, police, and other civil servants with IOUs. One by one, the various groups that had supported Mossadegh—merchants, the middle class, religious leaders, and the military—began to fall away. By the time that the coup plotters were ready for action in the late summer of 1953, Mossadegh's popularity was waning.

TURNING UP THE HEAT

The plotters added to the economic pressure by launching a psychological campaign that would split Mossadegh's coalition even further. The CIA bribed Muslim clerics to attack him from the mosques, and planted anti-Mossadegh articles and editorial cartoons in Iranian newspapers. Mobs were paid to stage marches against him. Iranian agents posing as Communists made threats against religious leaders, and on at least one occasion, the CIA bombed a prominent cleric's house to turn him against Mossadegh.

By the end of July 1953, Iran had been destabilized to the point that the plotters were ready to launch their coup. The only thing left was to get the shah to sign the decrees firing Mossadegh and replacing him with General Zahedi. The CIA considered Mohammed Reza Pahlavi "a creature of indecision, beset by formless doubts and fears," and when they went to him with the necessary papers, he stalled for more than two weeks before he finally

---

Sears stores originally refused to stock Barbie dolls. Why? They were "too sexy."

agreed to sign, and then only on the condition that he be allowed to leave Tehran as soon as he did.

The CIA agreed, but when they brought the papers, the shah had already fled to his hunting lodge on the Caspian Sea. So an Iranian colonel was dispatched to the lodge with the decrees and finally, on August 13, the shah signed the papers. The CIA scheduled the coup to begin on the evening of August 15.

TURNING THE TABLES

As simple as the plan was—deliver the decree to Mossadegh, arrest him, and have pro-shah troops and demonstrators in the streets before Mossadegh's supporters could organize—a lot went wrong. Mossadegh's people learned of the plot a few hours before it was scheduled to begin, and loyal army officers rallied to his side. When pro-shah soldiers arrived at his house to arrest him, they were taken into custody. Mossadegh then ordered his troops to take up defensive positions around the city.

When General Zahedi learned that the coup was failing, he went into hiding. So did the shah, who was still at his hunting lodge when Tehran radio announced the following morning that the coup had been put down. He and his wife fled the country, flying first to Baghdad and then to Rome.

Thinking that with the shah in exile, the coup was over and the danger had passed, Mossadegh relaxed his guard and recalled his troops that were stationed around the city.

But he may have been a little hasty.

For the final part of the story turn to page 464.

*   *   *

WHAT A GAS

What word was spelled out in the first neon sign? *Neon*. The small, bright red sign was created by Dr. Perley Nutting, a government scientist, and exhibited at the 1904 Louisiana Purchase Exposition in St. Louis, Missouri, 15 years before neon signs became widely used commercially.

Heads up! Rats have been known to survive falls from five stories high.

ANIMALS IN THE NEWS

Bad news got you down? Take a break from humanity.

HAIR CLUB FOR HEIFERS

Three Ohio livestock exhibitors were disqualified from the state fair for gluing hairpieces onto their prize-winning Holstein cows (to make their backs appear straighter). One judge got suspicious of the cows' appearance and ran his hand across their backs as they were leaving the show ring. When the hair came off in gluey clumps, officials disqualified Scott Long, Kreg Krebs, and Ken Krebs, and withheld the $335 prize. Using artificial enhancers is "unethical, and unfair to competitors who play by the rules," says Melanie Witt, an official with the Ohio Department of Agriculture.

ELECTRIC COILS

On May 19, 2004, the entire nation of Honduras was plunged into darkness when a generator at the country's biggest hydroelectric plant failed. What caused a whole country to go dark? A boa constrictor slithered into a sensitive area of the power plant. The unlucky snake was electrocuted, and the resulting short circuit caused the emergency systems to shut down the entire plant, which shut down the country's electricity for about 15 minutes.

BIRDIE DOG

Mike Wardrop, a bar manager at the Didsbury Golf Club in Manchester, England, liked to take his German Shepherd, Libby, for walks on the golf course, where Libby liked to pick up stray golf balls and bring them to Wardrop. When one day Libby lost her appetite and began coughing up blood, Wardrop never suspected that Libby might have swallowed some of the golf balls. But when Wardrop took Libby to the vet, "they didn't even have to do an X-ray; they could hear the balls rattling around," he says. "They were betting how many would be in there. I think the highest bet was 11, so they were shocked when 28 came out." $1,100 worth of veterinary and surgery bills later, Libby is back to normal and Wardrop is trying to break her golf ball habit. "I bought her two footballs," he says. "She can't swallow them."

REEL WISE

Some deep thoughts from the movies.

"Life is not a movie. Everyone lies, good guys lose, and love does not conquer all."
—**Kevin Spacey,** *Swimming with Sharks* **(1994)**

"There's a kind of freedom in being completely screwed— because you know things can't get any worse."
—**Matthew Broderick,** *The Freshman* **(1990)**

"Destiny is something we've invented because we can't stand the fact that everything that happens is accidental."
—**Meg Ryan,** *Sleepless in Seattle* **(1993)**

"Man is the only animal clever enough to build the Empire State Building and stupid enough to jump off it."
—**Rock Hudson,** *Come September* **(1961)**

"They say when you meet the love of your life, time stops, and that's true. What they don't tell you is that when it starts again, it moves extra fast to catch up."
—**Albert Finney,** *Big Fish* **(2003)**

"You know that point in your life when you realize the house you grew up in isn't really your home anymore? That idea of home is gone. Maybe that's all family really is: a group of people who miss the same imaginary place."
—**Zach Braff,** *Garden State* **(2004)**

"A good plan today is better than a perfect plan tomorrow."
—**Robert De Niro,** *Wag the Dog* **(1997)**

"Vice. Virtue. It's best not to be too moral. You cheat yourself out of too much. Aim above morality. If you apply that to life, then you're bound to live life fully."
—**Ruth Gordon,** *Harold and Maude* **(1971)**

"The greatest trick the devil ever pulled was convincing the world he didn't exist."
—**Kevin Spacey,** *The Usual Suspects* **(1995)**

"Death smiles at us all. All a man can do is smile back."
—**Russell Crowe,** *Gladiator* **(2000)**

James Dean made his first television appearance in a 1950 Pepsi commercial.

PLASTIC MONEY

The idea of buying on credit is as old as recorded history (the Sumerians did it 4,000 years ago), but the plastic in your wallet is a relatively new invention. Here are a few highlights from the history of the modern credit card.

- **1914:** Western Union issues charge plates—rectangular pieces of embossed metal (kind of like dog tags)—to its preferred customers. They allow the deferment of payment on their telegraph services (with no interest or added charges)…and the concept of a pocket "credit card" is born.

- **1924:** General Petroleum of California issues the world's first gas card. It's originally only for employees, but is later issued to the general public. Other gasoline companies soon follow suit.

- **1930:** AT&T offers the "Bell System Credit Card" which allows monthly payments on telephone services.

- **1946:** Flatbush National Bank in New York develops the "Charge-It" card, allowing customers to charge purchases at select local businesses. The bank collects payments from the customer and reimburses the merchants. It's the first bank-issued credit card.

- **1950:** The Diner's Club Card is established at 27 restaurants; by 1952 it can be used at thousands of stores (not just restaurants) in the United States, Canada, France, and Cuba. Customers pay a yearly fee for the cardboard card and can make monthly payments.

- **1951:** Post-war prosperity is making the concept of credit more acceptable—and banks begin to see new possibilities. The Franklin Bank of New York extends the normal 90-day pay-in-full period—and begins charging interest. The modern credit card is born.

- **Late 1950s:** Revolving credit begins: credit which remains available as long as regular payments are being made on the debt. From this point on, interest charges on credit cards will be a major source of profit for banks.

- **1958:** The American Express card is introduced. By the end of the year over 250,000 people have agreed to pay a $6 per-year fee to have one. The following year "plastic money" is born when they became the first company to issue plastic credit cards.

Who's on the $500 bill? William McKinley. The $1,000 bill? Grover Cleveland.

- **1959:** Bank of America introduces BankAmericard. In 1977 the card will change its name to VISA, and go on to become the world's largest credit card company.

- **1969:** 16% of American households regularly use credit cards.

- **1972:** BankAmericard introduces the world's first electronic card authorization system, BASE I, and credit cards with magnetic strips that hold simple account information. Authorization is now available 24 hours a day. Other cards will soon follow.

- **1977:** Fifty banks control more than 80% of the credit-card market. This will soon change.

- **1990:** The Consumer Federation of America estimates that 122 million Americans have at least one charge card.

- **2001:** Amount of Americans that use credit cards: 157 million. Average household credit card debt: $8,123. Revenue to credit card companies from late fees: $7,300,000,000 (Priceless?).

- **2004:** There are more than one billion credit cards in use—in the U.S. alone. The average American family pays between $1,000 and $1,500 in interest every year. Ten banks now control more than 80% of the credit card market.

THE FUTURE: Data storage devices get smaller and smaller. Examples: Keychain credit cards; credit cards with display screens built into them to view transactions, balances, or currency exchange rates; and cell phones that are also credit cards. Wave your phone over a wireless sensor and pay for your movie, gas, meal… (Futuristic? Not everywhere. They're already common in Korea and Japan.)

*　　*　　*

BE RIGHT BACK

"A pair of waiters in Shanghai, China, were arrested after taking a customer's credit card and using it to buy cell phones—while he sat in their restaurant. The diner, identified only as Mr. Zhu, had just finished lunch when his credit card company called. Had he just spent 25,000 yuan ($3,100) on new cell phones? Waiters Ling Hong and Wang Luole had told Zhu there was a problem with his card and asked him to wait for a few minutes, then took the card to a nearby electronics mart." (Associated Press)

Most frequently broken bone: the *clavicle* (collar bone).

LIVING A LIE

*Make-believe can be fun. But some people
don't know when to quit. Here are some
folks who took pretending a little too far.*

TRUST ME—I'M HIM

George Schira, head of Jimmy Carter's Presidential Center, was fired in 1987 for spending Carter Center funds on personal items (clothes and home furnishings). Impersonating Carter's voice, Schira called George Paraskevaides, a wealthy benefactor of the Carter Center, and asked him for $150,000. Paraskevaides sent the money, per "Carter's" request, to a London bank. A few weeks later, Schira called Paraskevaides again, this time posing as a Saudi prince acting on *behalf* of Carter, saying they desperately needed $500,000—immediately. Schira didn't even use a fake accent this time, but Paraskevaides again sent the money, which Schira promptly deposited in a personal Swiss bank account. Schira called one more time—as Carter—to thank Paraskevaides for his donations. A few months later Schira was indicted for 17 counts of fraud, but evaded capture for five years, at which point, facing 85 years in prison, he pleaded guilty and spent 28 months in jail.

TRUST ME—I'M A DOCTOR

Arthur Osborne Phillips wanted to study medicine, but when his family couldn't afford college, he enlisted in the army, working as an orderly in World War I. He was a fast learner and picked up some medical knowledge by shadowing his supervisor, Dr. James Phillips (no relation). After the war, he landed various low-level hospital jobs until his habit of writing bad checks landed him in prison.

Somehow Phillips convinced prison authorities that his hospital jobs had actually been medical positions, and they made him head of surgery. Released from prison in 1921, Phillips heard that his old boss, Dr. Phillips, had been committed to a mental institution, so he visited the doctor's family and stole his medical diploma right off the wall. Credentials now in hand, "Dr." Phillips worked for a while as a surgeon in West Virginia, but couldn't stay in one place for long. Later he made his living as a country doctor in small towns in the Southwest, where he also posed as a dentist and a vet-

---

Q: What was the original name of The Beach Boys? A: Carl and the Passions.

erinarian. Phillips was arrested for medical fraud a few times but was never convicted.

Then, while in Kansas in 1949, Phillips got in a car accident. He had gotten away with fraudulently practicing medicine for 24 years, but it was the fender bender that proved to be his undoing.

The other driver sued for $600 in damages, but rather than just pay up (and avoid going to court), Phillips countersued for $40,000. His claim: the broken arm he sustained in the accident prevented him from practicing medicine (apparently he forgot that he wasn't a real doctor). Attorneys for the other driver quickly discovered Phillips's true identity and criminal record. Not only did he lose the suit, he subsequently served 20 years in prison.

TRUST ME—IT'S SHAKESPEARE

Born in 1777, William Henry Ireland was a Shakespeare buff. Ireland's father, also a Shakespeare fan, collected Shakespeare memorabilia. The one item he dreamed of owning was a document bearing the Bard's signature, so Ireland decided to make his dad a gift.

While apprenticing as a lawyer in 1794, 17-year-old Ireland had access to old contracts and deeds, so he collected blank pieces of parchment from the early 1600s and, using specially treated ink, forged a promissory note "signed" by Shakespeare. Unaware that it was a fake, his father was elated. Ireland then forged love letters to Shakespeare's wife, a profession of his Protestant faith, and even portions of the original manuscripts of *Hamlet* and *King Lear*. Like the promissory note, the documents were certified to be real by handwriting experts.

Ireland became more ambitious. In 1795 he concocted a complete script of a "previously unknown" Shakespeare play: *Vortigern and Rowena*. It was the literary find of the century and was set to be performed at London's Drury Lane Theatre. But two days before the opening, scholar Edmond Malone published *An Inquiry into the Authenticity of Certain Miscellaneous Papers and Legal Instruments*, calling all of Ireland's Shakespeare documents phonies. When the play opened (to a packed house), it was so bad that everyone knew it couldn't have been written by Shakespeare. Ireland was forced to confess his fabrications. Over the next 30 years, he attempted to become a novelist and playwright (he even tried to revive *Vortigern and Rowena*) using his own name. He flopped.

JAIL FOOD FOLLIES

Are you sick of the cafeteria? Tired of the same old
fast food? Then maybe you'd like to sample the
cuisine at your local prison. Bon apétit!

PRISON: Rockwood Institution, Winnipeg, Canada
FOOD: Lobster and liquor
STORY: In August 2002, prison officials reported that a
"well-connected" inmate had managed to make prison a four-star
dining experience for his fellow inmates. They said that Ronald
Hickey, 48, who was serving a nine-year sentence for drug convictions, had somehow smuggled over a ton of gourmet seafood and
liquor into the prison. The officials couldn't prove it, though: the
accusations were based solely on tips from inmate informants—any
actual evidence is believed to have been eaten.

PRISON: Pozo Almonte jail in Santiago, Chile
FOOD: French bread sticks
STORY: Prison officials couldn't figure out why prisoners were
suddenly so fond of French baguettes, prompting a huge rise in
deliveries from certain local bakeries. But a November 2002 search
of one of the bakeries discovered the secret ingredient: the bread
sticks were being hollowed out and filled with marijuana.

PRISON: Caledonia County Work Camp, Vermont
FOOD: Beer and cigarettes
STORY: In December 2001, Mark Delude, a prisoner at this work
camp for nonviolent offenders, crawled under the fence surrounding the site, and took off. How far did he get? About a mile and a
half, to the nearest convenience store. Delude wasn't trying to
escape, he just wanted some beer and smokes. He bought a case of
beer and a carton of cigarettes, and had a few of both before trying
to sneak back into prison with the rest of his booty. Guards caught
the slightly inebriated Delude standing outside his tent...and
shipped him off to a more secure facility. "I don't remember ever
trying to catch people trying to break back in before," said State
Police Officer George Hacking. "But nothing surprises me."

WHERE THERE'S A WILL

*More proof that a little thing like death doesn't
have to stop you from being creative.*

The 1820 will of Colonel William H. Jackson made a bequest…to a white oak tree. "In consideration of the great love I bear this tree," Jackson wrote, "I give it entire possession of itself and of all land within 8 feet of the tree on all sides." The original "Tree that Owns Itself" died in 1942, but a second generation of the tree continues to own itself and the land around it.

• Sir Francis Drake (1540-1596) instructed that he be buried at sea, and that two of his favorite ships be burned and sunk at the same spot. (They were.)

• Martin van Butchell (1735–1812) was a British dentist. When his wife Mary died in 1775, he preserved her body, dressed it in a lace dress, put it in a glass-topped coffin—and displayed it in a window in his home. Why? A clause in his wife's will stipulated that he be provided income from her fortune after her death…as long as he kept her body above ground. The body eventually wound up in the Royal College of Surgeons in London, where it was destroyed in a German bombing raid in 1941.

• Tom Halley of Memphis, Tennessee, bequeathed $5,000 each to "the nurse who removed a pink monkey from the foot of my bed, and to the cook at the hospital who removed snakes from my soup."

• When Sandra West of San Antonio, Texas, died in 1977 she was buried, according to her will's instructions, "next to my husband, in my lace nightgown, in my Ferrari, with the seat slanted comfortably." It was a 1964 Ferrari 250 GTO Series II, and the grave was covered in concrete to stop grave-robbers from stealing it.

• When Ernest Digweed of Portsmouth, England, died in 1976, he left his entire estate, £26,000 (about $47,000)—to Jesus Christ, in the case that he arrived for his second coming. "If during the next 80 years," reads his will, "the Lord Jesus Christ shall come to reign on Earth, then the Public Trustee, upon obtaining proof which shall satisfy Him of His identity, shall pay to the Lord Jesus Christ all the property He holds on His behalf." (No takers so far.)

Vermont's Panache restaurant offers hippo, lion, and giraffe dishes on its menu.

HOW THE WEST WAS LOST

BRI stalwart Jeff Cheek—a proud Texan with a love of forgotten history—uncovered this fascinating nugget of Americana.

THE PLOT

In the spring of 1861, while politicians from the North and South were in Washington, D.C., debating about whether a state had the right to secede from the Union, clandestine meetings of a far less diplomatic nature were taking place in Richmond, Virginia. The Confederate government was plotting to conquer the Union-held territory of New Mexico—which included the future states of New Mexico and Arizona—then push on to southern California, all the way to the Pacific. Not only would they be creating an ocean-to-ocean slave empire, the Confederate State Department was certain that this bold gesture would also insure recognition of the Confederacy by France and England.

Although grandiose, the plan wasn't far-fetched. The Union had weakened their frontier garrisons by transferring troops east to guard Washington. The outposts were further weakened by the defection of Southern-born officers who resigned their commissions and joined the Confederate Army. And southern California, they reported, was a hotbed of Confederate sympathizers. The rebel army would be welcomed.

GO WEST, YOUNG MAN

Though supposedly waiting for a political solution, the southern government quickly put their plan in motion. Colonel John Baylor was ordered to deploy his 300-man cavalry unit to El Paso, on the extreme western edge of Confederate Texas. Three days after the first shots were fired at the Battle of Bull Run (the first major battle of the Civil War) in July 1861, Baylor and his 300 Texans invaded New Mexico, crossing the border near El Paso. They continued to advance north until they were blocked by a larger Yankee detachment commanded by Major Isaac Lynde. But being outnumbered didn't stop Baylor—he attacked. Lynde's troops tried to retreat to nearby Fort Stanton, but heat and exhaustion did them in before they made it, and they surrendered. Baylor marched on.

GAINING GROUND

Baylor now held only a tiny slice of southern New Mexico, but he claimed the entire territory as part of the Confederate States of America. When word of the victory got back to Confederate President Jefferson Davis, he promoted Baylor to military governor and gave Brigadier General Henry Sibley command of the Confederate Army of New Mexico. In late December, Sibley led his troops north from El Paso. His objective: take Fort Craig, a Union bastion in south-central New Mexico and headquarters of Colonel Edward Canby, the ranking Union officer in the territory.

On arriving at Fort Craig, Sibley changed his plan, deciding not to attack—the position was too well fortified. Instead he retreated south to Valverde, New Mexico, taking up a defensive position along the banks of the Rio Grande River. Canby left a token force to guard the fort and set out in pursuit with 3,700 men, outnumbering Sibley's troops by more than a thousand.

The two armies clashed on February 21, 1862, in what proved to be the bloodiest battle in the west. And despite being outnumbered, the rebels fought the better battle. After losing more than 200 men, Colonel Canby was forced to make a strategic retreat while waiting for reinforcements. A few weeks later, the Confederates took Albuquerque and then Santa Fe, the high-water mark of the Confederate Army of New Mexico.

SOUTHERN DISCOMFORT

By this time the Union army had been reinforced by several New Mexican militia units and 600 volunteers from Colorado, under the command of Major John Chivington, known as the "Fighting Parson." (He was a deacon in the Presbyterian Church, and fighting slavery, he preached to his troops, was "doing God's work.")

The two armies met at Glorieta Pass, 50 miles southeast of Santa Fe. Canby engaged the main rebel force, while Chivington outflanked them. When they located the rebel supply dump eight miles in the rear, the Fighting Parson launched an attack, killing or capturing the guards. The Confederates' supplies were

---

Alexander the Great enjoyed leading parades dressed as the goddess Artemis.

destroyed, every wagon burned, and all the mules driven off.

Casualties were relatively light (Confederates 189, Union 142), but the loss of the supplies guaranteed a Union victory. With no cannonballs for their artillery, no cartridges for their rifles, and no food other than what they could forage from the countryside, the Army of New Mexico disintegrated, and was forced to retreat to San Antonio. Of the original 2,700 rebel soldiers, only 1,500 made it back to Texas. The Confederate dream of a coast-to-coast empire was over.

*　　*　　*

HISTORICAL FOOTNOTE: THE DONKEY BOMB

The night before the Confederate victory at Valverde, a sneak attack that might have given the Yankees a victory failed. Captain "Paddy" Graydon, commanding a company of Union volunteers, came up with a novel idea. He asked for two old mules and a few boxes of howitzer shells and then rigged them up with fuses, turning them into "donkey bombs." The two armies were encamped on opposite sides of the Rio Grande, and the idea was that Graydon and a few volunteers would swim the river, infiltrate the enemy camp, and set the bomb-carrying mules free near the rebel corral. The Union mules would mix in with the Confederate mules, and the shells would explode, inflicting casualties, and destroying the enemy's supplies. Graydon's request was approved.

That night the raiders swam the river. They came within 150 yards of the enemy corral. They could smell the rebel mules. They lit the fuses on the howitzer shells, slapped the mules on the rump, and began their retreat. But they had forgotten one important detail: they hadn't briefed the mules on their part of the operation. Seeing their masters leaving, the mules turned and trotted toward them.

Paddy and his men took off, running barefoot through cactus and catclaw bushes. Naturally, the mules also sped up. The men were running, the fuses were burning, and the mules were gaining (one of nature's laws is that a four-legged mule can run faster than a two-legged man) when KABOOM!, a dozen 24-pound shells exploded, scattering mule parts over a large chunk of New Mexico and scaring the hell out of the soldiers in both camps. Paddy and his footsore Commandos limped back to camp at daybreak.

Salmon comes from the Latin word *salmo*, for "leaper."

THE NUMBER OF...

Just in case you're not inundated with enough numbers in your life.

- Times, on average, a person swallows during a meal: **295**

- Countries that joined the United Nations when it was formed in 1945: **51**

- Points scored by basketball legend Kareem Abdul-Jabbar over his entire career: **38,387**

- Bones in the human wrist: **8**

- Bones in a chimpanzee's wrist: **8**

- Yards a healthy slug can travel in a day: **50**

- Banana slugs that were eaten in a California slug-eating contest in 2002: **50**

- Chromosomes the average human has: **46** (the average cabbage has **18**)

- Pounds of fish a pelican can hold in its beak: **25**

- Pumpkins grown in Floydada, Texas, every year: **1,000,000**

- People booked for "offensive gestures" in Germany in 2003: **164,848**

- Steps to the top of the Empire State Building: **1,860**

- Industrial robots in Japan: **350,000**

- Islands in the Indonesian archipelago: **17,508**

- Species of penguin: **17**

- Pages the average bathroom reader reads at a "sitting": **2.7**

- Calories consumed during one hour of typing: **110**

- Calories consumed during one hour on the phone: **71**

- Pieces of paper the IRS sends to taxpayers every year: **8,000,000,000**

- Pounds that 8 billion pieces of paper weigh: **32,000,000**

- People in airplanes at any given time: **366,144**

- Students who streaked naked in Boulder, Colorado, on March 16, 1974: **1,200**

- People who die every minute: About **100**. (People who are born: **200**)

Mississippi's largest industry: catfish. 150,000 tons are produced each year.

GIMLI GLIDER, PART II

Here's the second installment of our story about the little jumbo jet that could. (Part I starts on page 125.)

LITTLE THINGS MEAN A LOT
To understand what happened aboard Flight 143, we need to revisit the math. It turns out that Captain Pearson made a slight error in his calculations. When you multiply liters by 1.77, you convert them into *pounds*, not kilograms (to convert a liter to a kilogram, you multiply by 0.8). Flight 143 had 20,302 *pounds* of fuel in its tanks when it left Montreal, not 20,302 kilograms. And since 1 pound weighs less than half of 1 kilogram, Flight 143 had less than half the fuel it needed to get where it was going.

Normally Captain Pearson and First Officer Quintal would have known long in advance that they were running low on fuel—the gauges would have triggered a little red warning light. But not in this case. Since Pearson and Quintal's original estimate was so far off, the low-fuel light never came on. The estimated fuel gauge showed plenty of fuel left…even as the last drops were being sucked from the tanks.

BEEP! BEEP! BEEP! BEEP!

The first hint of trouble came just minutes before the engines quit, about two hours into the flight. Four quick audible beeps sounded in the cockpit and a warning light came on, indicating that one of the two fuel pumps in the left wing was reporting low pressure. That's not unheard of, and at first Captain Pearson assumed that there was something wrong with the fuel pump. But moments later four more beeps sounded and the *second* fuel pump in the left wing reported low pressure. What are the odds that two pumps would fail at the same time? Captain Pearson concluded it couldn't be the pumps. It had to be the fuel.

He decided to divert Flight 143 to Winnipeg, the nearest major airport. Whatever the problem was with the left fuel tank, he wanted it fixed before they flew any farther. He took the plane down from 41,000 feet to 28,000 feet, and made plans to land with only one engine, if it came to that.

More people on the West Coast prefer chunky peanut butter; East Coasters, creamy.

TANKS FOR NOTHING

About five minutes after the first alarm sounded, four *more* beeps sounded and two *more* lights came on. Then *another* four beeps and *another* four lights. Now the two fuel pumps in the right wing tank, as well as the two fuel pumps in the center tank, were reporting low pressure. (The pumps themselves were fine—they were reporting low pressure because the fuel tanks were empty and pumping nothing but air.)

Nine minutes after the first beeps, a loud *bong!* sounded in the cockpit. The left engine, completely starved of gas, sputtered out. Pearson and Quintal, still trying to figure out what was going on, prepared to land the 767 at Winnipeg with only one engine. It was an emergency situation, but it was something the plane was designed to do and something they had been trained to handle.

Then, three minutes later, the right engine ran out of fuel and quit. Pearson and Quintal hadn't been trained to land a 767 with both engines out. Nobody had—jumbo jets aren't supposed to run out of gas.

FROM BAD TO WORSE

In a normal aircraft with conventional mechanical instruments, the instruments keep working even if all the engines quit. But as Captain Pearson quickly realized, glass cockpits are different. They get their power from electrical generators powered by the jet engines. When both engines fail, the generators quit producing electricity...and all the computer screens go dark.

In an instant, Pearson lost the digital instruments that displayed the plane's airspeed, altitude, and heading. He lost his transponder, which gives the plane's location, speed, and altitude to air traffic controllers, and he lost his vertical speed indicator, which told him how fast the plane was losing altitude. He didn't even have a clock.

There was more. The hydraulic system, which controls the landing gear and rudders, is also powered by the engine. So as the engines were quitting and the cockpit was going dark, Pearson felt his control yoke (similar to a steering wheel) and his rudder pedals stiffen and become unresponsive.

He had no fuel, he had almost no instruments, and he was quickly losing his ability to control the aircraft.

FOR EMERGENCY USE ONLY

Airplanes are designed with many redundancies built in, so that if a piece of equipment fails, there's usually a backup and the plane can fly and land safely. Quintal flipped the switch to activate the auxiliary power unit (APU), which is designed to provide backup electricity and hydraulics. There was just one problem: like the generators, the APU was powered by jet fuel. The hydraulic system and the glass cockpit flickered to life for a moment, then went dark again when the APU sputtered out.

That was it for the digital instruments—there was no other source of power for them. But there *was* one more backup system to power the hydraulics.

SECOND WIND

Did you ever stick a pinwheel out the window of a moving car when you were a kid? The Boeing 767 has a device called a ram air turbine (RAT), located near the right wheel well. It's a propeller on a long arm and in an emergency it can be manually extended out into the airstream, just like a kid's pinwheel. When the RAT hits the airstream, the propeller spins, generating just enough hydraulic pressure in the process to power basic flight controls.

As Captain Pearson wrestled with the controls, Quintal engaged the RAT. Then he grabbed the 767's emergency procedures manual and started looking for the section that told them what to do when both engines failed. There was no such section. So many redundancies had been built into the 767 that its designers never bothered to plan for the ultimate failure—no fuel in the tanks. They figured that all of the other redundancies and alarms would prevent such a thing from ever happening. The planes weren't supposed to run out of fuel—not in the air, not on the ground, not ever.

And because the 767 had never been flight tested with both engines off, nobody knew how the jet would perform as a "glider," or what amount of altitude it would lose for every mile traveled. Pearson knew that the plane was at about 28,000 feet when the second engine failed. But how far could it glide before it hit the ground? Were nearby airports close enough for the plane to glide to, or would it crash before they got there? He just didn't know.

CHANGE OF PLANS

Thankfully, Flight 143's radios had a backup battery, so *they* still worked. With help from Winnipeg Air Traffic Control, Quintal was able to estimate that the plane was losing about 5,000 feet of altitude for every 10 miles traveled. That wasn't good news. By now they were only about 35 miles away from Winnipeg, but according to Quintal's calculations, if they stayed the course they would crash about 12 miles short of the runway. They had to find a closer place to land.

The air traffic controllers suggested the old Canadian Air Force base in Gimli, Manitoba, about 50 miles north of Winnipeg. The base had been closed since 1971, but one of the two parallel landing strips was still used by civilian aircraft. Each one was more than twice as long as the one at Winnipeg, and long runways are a nice thing to have when you're trying to land a 300,000-pound aircraft without any power. More importantly, Quintal was already familiar with the airport, because he had trained there when he was in the Air Force.

Flight 143 was going to Gimli.

For Part III, turn to page 483.

*   *   *

FORECAST: CHANCE OF TOAD-CHOKER

Arizonans have their own slang when it comes to rain. A few samples.

Dust-Settler: A teaser. Enough rain to do just that—settle the dust.

Turd-floater: This happens when it rains so much that the ground and everything on it gets completely saturated, lifted from its place of deposit, and transported to a lower elevation.

Tank-filler: This is the next best kind of rain—enough to fill the livestock water tanks, saving the ranchers from having to haul it in. Tank fillers are usually heavy rains that come after a "turd floater."

Toad-choker (or "frog strangler"): Lots of rain in a short time. Result: drowned amphibians on the open range.

Gully-washer: This type of rain can be deadly. It happens when rain falls faster than it can be absorbed into the ground, turning gullies and just about any other low spot into a temporarily raging river.

The whistling swan has the most feathers of any bird, about 25,000.

SPEAK OF THE DEVIL

You can blame your problems on bad luck or boneheaded mistakes. But is it possible, at least once in a while, that they're the devil's fault?

RAGE AGAINST THE MACHINE

Microsoft users experienced problems in 2002 due to a network administration program known as Security Administrator Tool for Analyzing Networks (SATAN). According to news reports, computers "possessed" by SATAN performed slowly and caused numerous unrelated programs to malfunction.

UNLUCKY NUMBER

The British Driver and Vehicle Licensing Agency announced in 1990 that license plates with the number "666" would no longer be issued. Reason: The office had received numerous complaints from previous 666-plate holders that their lives and cars were cursed. One man reported that a week after receiving a 666 plate, his home was burglarized, his water became contaminated, and his car was run over by a truck.

AN OFF-HANDED GESTURE

Thomas Passmore of Virginia chopped off his own hand with a power saw because he believed it was possessed by the devil. He was rushed to a hospital, but refused to let doctors reattach the hand. Passmore later sued the hospital, saying that the doctors should have ignored his refusal and realized his pleas of being possessed by the devil were signs he was psychotic. (He lost the case, too.)

IN OTHER NEWS: YOU'RE THE DEVIL!

The usually sedate Croatian newspaper *Vecernji* caused a panic in 2001 when it ran an article that estimated 100,000 citizens of the Croatian capital city Zagreb were possessed by the devil. As proof, *Vecernji* noted that victims were suffering the telltale symptoms of satanic possession: nausea and fatigue (which also happen to be symptoms of the flu, food poisoning, and numerous other medical conditions). The mass possession, the article said, was part of a plot by an international league of satanists who were planning their annual convention in Zagreb and had invited the devil.

'70s fans, rejoice: Corduroy literally means "the cord of kings."

BAD KITTY

In preparation for a trip to the Hague in 2001, newly appointed Attorney General John Ashcroft sent an advance security team to the American embassy. According to one report, they found cats in the residence and were concerned that some might be calicos. Ashcroft reportedly dislikes being around calico cats because he believes they are minions of the devil.

DEVIL MUSIC

A "voodoo priest" calling himself Doktor Snake used eBay to offer struggling musicians a unique opportunity: achieve success by signing a contract with the devil. Snake says he got the idea from the legend that blues musician Robert Johnson traded his soul to the devil in exchange for guitar brilliance. Doktor Snake's deal includes a guided tour through the Crossroads (where many such satanic pacts are made) and a genuine contract. Snake's work is guaranteed (musical success or your money back), and he has references! He says many of today's major rock stars are clients.

WWW.SATAN.COM

While scoring the film *The Passion of the Christ*, composer John Debney told an interviewer for Assist News Service that the face of the devil frequently appeared on his computer screen to interrupt his work or crash the machine. "The first time it happened, it scared me," he said. But after the ninth crash, Debney got frustrated and started screaming at the devil to meet him in the parking lot for a fistfight. Did Satan show up? "He didn't manifest himself," Debney admits. "But I wished that he would have."

*   *   *

A WORD ORIGIN: THUG

Meaning: A violent person or criminal

Origin: "From the Hindustani *thag*, which means 'thief.' But these Indian thugs were not ordinary thieves. They were members of a religious society that waylaid wealthy travelers, then strangled and buried them, supposedly committing these heinous crimes in the name of the goddess Kali (after whom Calcutta is named)."

—From *The Story Behind the Word*, by Morton Freeman

Pope John XXIII installed a bowling alley in the Vatican.

STRANGE LAWSUITS

It seems that people will sue each other over practically anything.
Here are some real-life examples of unusual legal battles.

THE PLAINTIFF: Barbara Hewson
THE DEFENDANT: Virgin Atlantic Airways
THE LAWSUIT: After an 11-hour flight from Wales,
Hewson arrived in Los Angeles with torn leg muscles, a hematoma
in her chest, and a permanent case of sciatica. Cause of injury:
Hewson claimed to have been crushed by the obese woman seated
next to her. The woman was so large that she couldn't fit into her
seat without removing the armrest, effectively sitting on top of her
neighbor. When Hewson complained, attendants told her to "ask if
another passenger would exchange seats." She should have asked
the woman's husband—he was sitting in the row behind them and
apparently knew better than to book a seat next to his wife.
THE VERDICT: Initially Virgin Atlantic sent Hewson a £15
($22) gift basket of canned goods. Eventually it was upped to
£13,000 (about $19,500), plus all of her medical and legal fees.

THE PLAINTIFF: Lee Williams
THE DEFENDANT: Eternal Tattoos
THE LAWSUIT: Williams got the word "VILLAIN" tattooed on
his right forearm in 1996. Years later a friend noticed the word was
misspelled: it said "VILLIAN." It turns out that when Williams
went in to get the tattoo he wasn't sure how to spell the word. But
rather than look it up in a dictionary, he decided on what turned
out to be the incorrect spelling. Knowing that it was his own mistake didn't stop Williams from seeking $25,000 in damages from
the tattoo parlor.
THE VERDICT: Unknown (but he got the tattoo removed).

THE PLAINTIFF: Troy Bowron
THE DEFENDANTS: The Jannali Inn, and Ross Lucock,
a customer
THE LAWSUIT: Bowron sued for "future loss of earnings" (he's

an upholsterer) due to the nasty spill he took in the Sydney, Australia, pub. Lucock had been refused service at the bar because he wasn't wearing shoes. Extremely drunk (but very creative), he attached two pork chops to his feet with masking tape and, incredibly, was permitted back in the bar. Bowron slipped on Lucock's greasy trail of disintegrated meat and broke his left arm.

THE VERDICT: A judge awarded Bowron $42,000 at the expense of the Jannali Inn, but ruled that Lucock wasn't liable for Bowron's legal bills. Why? Lucock "was so drunk that he didn't even remember putting the pork chops on his feet."

THE PLAINTIFF: Suzanne Vasquez
THE DEFENDANT: Wal-Mart
THE LAWSUIT: Vasquez claimed to have developed epilepsy after a 13-pound ham came crashing down on her head as she reached up to check its label. She said the accident, which occurred in 1997, had caused her to "hear cement grinding in her head" and sued for $500,000. Wal-Mart attorneys said it was Vasquez's fault—the ham hung on a peg out of customers' reach, and was "accessible only to Wal-Mart employees…by ladder."
THE VERDICT: Wal-Mart won.

THE PLAINTIFFS: Gregory Roach and Gordon Falkner
THE DEFENDANT: Para-Chem Co.
THE LAWSUIT: In 1998 the two plaintiffs, carpet installers for Callahan Carpet House, decided to use an all-weather outdoor adhesive inside a client's home, ignoring the warning on the label: "Do not use indoors because of flammability." Only when a hot water tank clicked on did they realize the severity of their goof. The fumes from the adhesive ignited, then the entire three and a half gallon container exploded, leaving Roach and Falkner burned over most of their bodies. Roach sued the adhesive manufacturer, Para-Chem, for $20 million; Falkner sought $15 million.
THE VERDICT: Initially five of the eight jurors sided with Para-Chem. But the judge ordered deliberations to continue until at least six jurors agreed on the verdict. When the jury returned, to Para-Chem's shock, the tally was 6–2 in favor of Roach and Falkner. They got $5 million and $3 million, respectively.

The official Boy Scout handshake is done with the left hand.

LUCKY CRITTERS

Why is Uncle John's dog, Porter, so lucky? Because he gets to spend his days at the BRI. Here are some other fortunate animals.

CAT ON A...

Adria Bryan couldn't figure out why people were flashing their lights at her as she was driving to work in Rhyl, Wales. "I thought I may have left my handbag on the roof but it was on the seat next to me so I carried on." Finally one driver pulled up close and pointed to her roof. Turns out her 14-year-old cat, Joc, was up there. "I must have been doing 60," she said, "but Joe clung on for dear life." She said the cat had fallen asleep on top of the car, adding, "He's a very heavy sleeper."

Lucky Again: Just days later a Bull Terrier attacked Joe. He suffered three cracked ribs and a punctured lung—but survived that, too. "It's unbelievable he's got through the week," said a thankful Bryan.

FISH STORY

Leicestershire, England, police officers arrived at the scene of an auto accident and immediately noticed that the inside of the car was soaking wet. The driver, 23-year-old Sophia Underhill, told officers, "I think I've killed my fish." (She had been transporting her pet goldfish, Bercy, from her family home in London.) Sergeant Mark Watling frantically searched the car for the pet, to no avail. A short time later, officers clearing glass from the road found the fish—15 feet from the car. They rushed the fish to paramedics, who were able to revive it in a cardboard box of water. "Thankfully," Sergeant Watling told reporters, "this incident ended happily."

NO TANKS

Somebody tossed the contents of a fish tank into a street drain in Newcastle upon Tyne, England. A passerby saw the plants and pebbles, along with some dead fish...but one small goldfish still seemed to be alive. A crowd gathered as local residents tried to remove the drain grate—but they couldn't do it. So they called the RSPCA, but they couldn't get it off, either. So *they* called the city's council, and after a three-hour, 11-person rescue attempt,

---

Nothing to envy: A dog can recognize its own urine markings a year after making them.

William—the name they gave the goldfish—was saved. RSPCA inspector Sue Craig was displeased with whoever dumped William. "Goldfish may not be as cute as cats or dogs," she said, "but they still deserve our respect."

NO QUIERO TACO BELL

In August 2003, a Chihuahua in a New York City park was attacked by a domesticated hawk, part of a program to keep the park pigeon- and rat-free. Bystanders rushed over to aid the dog, which was later treated for puncture wounds. Falconer Thomas Cullen, in charge of the park's four hawks, defended his bird's actions, saying, "I'm absolutely certain my bird mistook it for a rat." The program has been grounded until further notice.

LEMME OUT!

In 2004 an Austrian man was involved in a car crash on an icy highway. When he got out he heard a hissing noise, so he opened the hood, expecting to see a leaky radiator. But what he saw was an angry cat stuck in the engine compartment. It had been there for the entire 40-mile car trip and the crash that ended it. Mechanics had to remove part of the engine to free the cat, but it survived the accident unharmed and was reunited with its surprised owner, the driver's next-door neighbor.

THE HOSE KNOWS

In November 2003, 12-year-old Menelaos Fischer of Manitowoc, Wisconsin, lost his pet hamster, Jinny. He'd only had it for a month when it escaped from its cage. Then one day about six weeks later, his father heard a scratching sound in his shop vacuum. The hamster? Yes! Jinny must have crawled up the vacuum hose—which is similar to the hamster's "tube" cage—and made itself at home. The animal probably foraged for food at night and brought it back to the shop vac. "My best Christmas present," Menelaos wrote to the local paper, "is something money can't buy."

*   *   *

A Groaner: What kind of coffee was served on the *Titanic*? Sanka.

LOST IN TRANSLATION

On page 56 we told you about a British company's poll of the world's most difficult-to-translate words. Here's their list of the 10 English words voted most difficult to translate:

A **ND THE WINNERS ARE:**
10. Kitsch. "An item, usually of poor quality, that appeals to common or lowbrow tastes." (Need examples? Stop by Uncle John's house.)

9. Chuffed. A British word. Comes from *chuff* ("puffed with fat") and means "proud, satisfied, or pleased."

8. Bumf. More Brit-speak. A shortened version of *bumfodder*, it once meant "toilet paper," but now refers to paperwork in general.

7. Whimsy. "A quaint or fanciful quality."

6. Spam. The luncheon meat, not the junk e-mail.

5. Googly. A term from cricket, a sport played in England and its former colonies. Means "an off-breaking ball with an apparent leg-break action on the part of the bowler." To explain the meaning of googly, you first have to explain the game of cricket—that's what makes this word so difficult to translate. "I am from Lithuania," says translator Jurga Zilinskiene. "We simply do not have googlies in Lithuania."

4. Poppycock. "Nonsense; empty writing or talk." From the Dutch word *pappekak*, which translates literally as "soft dung."

3. Serendipity. Finding valuable, useful, or pleasant things that you haven't been searching for; happy accidents.

2. Gobbledygook. Wordy, unintelligible nonsense.

...and the most difficult-to-translate word in English is:

1. Plenipotentiary. "A special ambassador or envoy, invested with full powers to negotiate or transact business."

In an average year, 13 Americans are killed by vending machines that fall on them.

ROCKS ON THE GO

They say that the desert can play tricks on you. If that's the case,
then California's Death Valley is the trickiest of them all.

MOVE ON OVER
While traveling through the hot California desert in
1915, a mining prospector named Joseph Crook made a
startling discovery: the rocks had trails behind them—as if they
had slid across the desert floor all by themselves. That portion of
desert is now known as Racetrack Playa in northwestern Death
Valley National Park, and curious people travel from great distances to witness one of nature's most puzzling mysteries: the
moving rocks of Death Valley.

Happy Trails

These otherwise ordinary rocks are somehow transported across a
flat desert plain, leaving erratic trails in the hard mud behind
them. The stones come in every size and shape, from pebbles to
half-ton boulders. The tracks they leave also vary. Some rocks
travel only a few feet; others go for hundreds of yards, although
they may have started right next to each other. The trails go every
which way, crossing and looping, even doubling back on themselves. Many rocks carve zigzag paths along the *playa* (Spanish for
"beach"), and some have even made complete circles. But nowhere
is there a trace of what propelled the rocks—no footprints or tire
tracks, nothing to reveal what force pushed the hundreds of
pounds of rock.

Weird Science

Although geologists have yet to prove their method of movement,
they've offered quite a few theories—most of them having to do
with wind, rain, and in some cases, ice. (Some people contend that
aliens are to blame.) Even recent GPS studies of the rocks fail to
give a concrete explanation. The fact of the matter is that Death
Valley is the deepest hole in the Western Hemisphere and one of
the warmest places on Earth—a veritable "hotbed" of strange
phenomena. All scientists know for sure is that yes, the rocks
move—a lot. But to this day, no one has ever seen one in motion.

(BAT) BOMBS AWAY!

Here's a batty bit of World War II history
you may not have heard before.

BAT MAN

In the days and weeks following the bombing of Pearl Harbor on December 7, 1941, a lot of people wrote letters to President Roosevelt. Some wrote to express their sympathy with the victims or their outrage at the attack; others made suggestions about how to fight back against Japan.

One man, a dentist from Irwin, Pennsylvania, wanted to talk about bats. His name was Lytle S. Adams, and he had recently been to the Carlsbad Caverns in New Mexico, home to one of the largest bat colonies in North America. When Adams learned of the attack on Pearl Harbor, his thoughts returned to the bats he'd seen—could they be useful to the war effort? He was convinced they could.

COM-BAT

In his letter to the president, Adams explained that bats are capable of carrying more than their own weight in flight. In many species, for example, the mother bat carries two or even three of her young as she searches for food. If bats could carry their children, Adams reasoned, why couldn't they carry tiny bombs?

The dentist's plan went further: Bats hate sunlight, so if bats carrying time-delayed incendiary devices could be released over a Japanese city shortly before dawn, as the sun rose, the bats would seek refuge from the light. Many would roost in the eaves and attics of buildings—a great number of which were made of flammable materials like wood, bamboo, and paper soaked in fish oil. When the firebombs detonated, thousands of tiny fires would start in buildings all over the city.

Not only that, bats typically hide out of sight in hard-to-reach places, and that would make the fires difficult to detect. By the time they were discovered, the fires would be well established but still small enough at first (each bat would weigh less than half an ounce, so the bombs would have to be small, too) that people would have a fighting chance to escape. Casualties would be lower than with conventional firebombs, which weighed hundreds of pounds and engulfed entire buildings on impact, giving occupants no warning and no chance to escape. For all their destructive power, Adams believed that "bat bombs" could be a more humane weapon of war than regular firebombs.

How many fires could be started with bats? "Approximately 200,000 bats could be transported in one airplane," Adams wrote, "and still allow one-half the payload capacity to permit free air circulation and increased gasoline load. Ten such planes would carry two million fire starters."

ASSAULT AND BAT-TERY

Perhaps the most impressive feature of bat bombs was not their destructive power, but the psychological impact they could have on the Japanese. The bats would be dropped by planes before dawn, and by the time the bombs went off, the planes would be long gone. Entire cities would ignite spontaneously and burn to the ground...with no warning and no explanation.

"The effect of the destruction from such a mysterious source would be a shock to the morale of the Japanese people as no amount of ordinary bombing could accomplish," Adams wrote to Roosevelt. "It would render the Japanese people homeless and their industries useless, yet the innocent could escape with their lives."

How flammable were Japanese cities? When a woman living in Osaka, Japan, knocked over her hibatchi-type cookstove in 1911, 11,000 homes burned to the ground. And it was *raining*.

TO THE BAT CAVE!

President Roosevelt forwarded Adams's letter to Colonel William J. Donovan, who would soon head the Office of Strategic Services, forerunner of the CIA. "It sounds like a perfectly wild idea but is worth looking into," FDR wrote. "This man is *not* a nut."

Dr. Adams got the go-ahead to assemble a 20-person staff and begin working out the details on how such a weapon might be built. What species of bats would be best? What kind of firebomb would be used? How would the device be attached to the bat? How would the bats be dropped over cities? There was a lot to fig-ure out. Here's what they came up with:

The Bats

The researchers decided early on that they would use a species called the Mexican free-tailed bat. They weighed about half an ounce but were capable of carrying a load of as much as three-quarters of an ounce. Tens of millions of them made their summer homes in caves in Texas and other southwestern states. Just as important, these bats hibernated in the winter. That meant they could be put into artificial hibernation so that the bombs could be attached, then kept in cold storage until they were ready to be released over Japan.

The Incendiary Bombs

One of the researchers assigned to the project was an incendiary bomb specialist—a chemist named Louis Fieser. He devised a tiny bomb that weighed a little over half an ounce and consisted of a timer and a thin plastic capsule measuring three-quarters of an inch in diameter by two inches long, filled with a jellied gasoline he'd invented, napalm.

Initially the designers planned to attach a bomb to each bat's chest with a piece of string and a surgical clip that mimicked the way baby bats latched onto their mother's fur with their claws. But that turned out to be too complicated, so they switched to a simple adhesive and just glued the bombs to the bats.

The "Bombshell"

If you just threw a bunch of hibernating bats out of an airplane, their fragile wings would break the moment they hit the airstream at 150 mph or else they would fall all the way to the ground—and die on impact—before they could emerge from hibernation. So the researchers designed a protective bomb-shaped canister to put the bats into. The "bombshell" was cigar-shaped and had fins, just like a regular bomb—except that it was filled with bats and was poked full of holes so they could breathe.

Inside the canister, the hibernating bats were packed into cardboard trays similar to eggshell cartons, and these cartons were stacked one on top of the other. Each bombshell held 26 cardboard trays, each of which held 40 bats. That meant each bomb would contain 1,040 bats.

HOW IT WORKED

• The bombshell was designed so that when it was dropped from a plane, it would free-fall to an altitude of 4,000 feet, at which point a parachute would deploy, slowing its descent.

• When the parachute opened, the bomb's outer shell would pop off and fall away. The stacked cardboard trays, which were tied to one another with short lengths of string, would then drop down and hang from the parachute about three inches apart, like rungs on a rope ladder.

• As the cardboard trays dropped into position, a tiny wire would be pulled from the incendiary device attached to each bat. Just like pulling a pin from a hand grenade, when the string was pulled, the firebombs would be armed and set to go off in 30 minutes, 60 minutes, or whatever interval the bombers chose.

• The bats, now exposed to the warm air and floating slowly to earth, would have enough time to warm up, emerge from their hibernating state, climb out of their individual egg-carton compartments, and fly away to seek shelter.

• When time ran out, the incendiary device glued to their chest would explode into flames, incinerating them instantly and setting fire to whatever structure they had taken refuge in.

BAT-TLE GROUND

A bombshell filled with bats and tiny firebombs sounded clever, but would it really work? Dr. Adams's team built a prototype, loaded it with 1,040 bats fitted with dummy bombs, and dropped it from a plane in a remote region outside Carlsbad Air Force Base in New Mexico. The test went off nearly without a hitch: the parachute deployed, the trays dropped open, and the bats awakened from hibernation and flew off in search of shelter from the sun.

The only snafu was that the researchers misjudged how far winds would carry the bat trays. Instead of landing in the middle of nowhere (the project was top secret, after all), the bats ended up flying to a ranch and roosting in the barn and ranch house. The researchers caught up with the creatures half an hour later and collected them as the mystified rancher looked on (he never did learn what the bats were carrying or what they were for).

BAT REVENGE

But the real proof of the power of bat bombs came later that day when Louis Fieser, the incendiary specialist, wanted some film footage of a bat armed with a live incendiary bomb actually exploding into flames. He took six hibernating bats out of cold storage and set their bombs to detonate in 15 minutes, figuring that in such a short time, the bats would still be hibernating and wouldn't fly away.

What Fieser failed to take into consideration was that on a hot New Mexico afternoon, the bats would come out of hibernation quickly. All six bats woke up within 10 minutes, escaped, and roosted in the rafters of various buildings of the airfield where the test was being conducted. Five minutes later the bombs went off, and every building on the airfield—the control tower, barracks, offices, and hangars—burned to the ground.

BAT TO THE DRAWING BOARD

Believe it or not, bat bombs were found to be *more* effective than conventional firebombs. One study concluded that a planeload of conventional firebombs would start between 167 and 400 fires, whereas a planeload of bat bombs would start between 3,625 and 4,748 fires.

So how many bats died in combat during World War II? Not even one. After spending 27 months and $2 million looking into the feasibility of bat bombs, the Pentagon canceled the program in March 1944. The military claimed that the bats were too unpredictable to be useful, but Jack Couffer, a research scientist who worked on the project, has a different theory. Couffer speculates in his memoirs that the government knew the Manhattan Project was making steady progress toward the world's first atomic bomb, and the military decided to focus on that instead.

Which explanation is true? Only the U.S. government knows for sure. Sixty years later, the reasons for the cancellation of the program, like the blueprints to the incendiary device itself, are still classified.

*   *   *

"A weapon is an enemy even to its owner."
—**Turkish proverb**

Mel Gibson turned down the role of James Bond.

AMAZING LUCK

There's no way to explain dumb luck—some folks just have it. Here are a few examples of people who lucked out... in midair.

HEADIN' DOWN THE HIGHWAY

Howard Hamer had only just begun his ascent from the Chiloquin airport in Oregon when his plane inexplicably lost power. Hamer searched for a place to set down his homemade Lancer 235 aircraft and decided that an emergency landing on the northbound lane of U.S. 97 was his best option. But as he was watching for oncoming traffic while attempting to keep the plane's nose pointed up, Hamer didn't see the truck right beneath him. Apparently the truck driver didn't see him, either. When they crashed, the propeller got caught on the truck's sleeper cabin, and the tail of the plane landed on the truck's flatbed. Amazingly, both the driver and the pilot walked away unharmed.

THAT'S USING YOUR HEAD

Al Wilson, a barnstorming plane-changer in the 1920s, was flying over southern California when he accidentally fell off the plane's wing—and he wasn't wearing a parachute. Lucky for Wilson, Frank Clarke was flying a Jenny biplane just below him. Clarke happened to catch a glimpse of the impending accident and accelerated his plane toward the falling Wilson. Wilson landed on Clarke's plane headfirst and got stuck in the upper wing, which immobilized him while Clarke landed the plane and saved them both.

ANT SHE LUCKY?

In 1999 amateur skydiver Joan Murray jumped from a plane at 14,500 feet. Her main parachute failed to open. At 700 feet her reserve chute opened briefly but then deflated. Murray hit the ground hard, landing directly on top of a fire ant hill. The ants attacked, stinging Murray again and again. Murray went into a coma, but miraculously, the ants' relentless assault helped keep her heart beating until she was rescued. (She came out of the coma a few weeks later; she returned to skydiving two years later.)

HAVE FUN WITH...

As a kid, Uncle John played a game where he'd substitute new nouns, verbs, and other parts of speech for the ones in a given written passage. The old ones made sense—the new ones made him laugh. If you're having trouble getting through your daily newspaper, give it a try.

THE GREENSPAN EFFECT

Trying to understand the blathering babble of a government technocrat can be frustrating. And Federal Reserve Chairman Alan Greenspan is a prime example. A newspaper article that starts, "Alan Greenspan said today..." may generate the numbing sensation of your brain being dropped into a bucket of custard.

But wait! Don't despair! The BRI has come up with a way for any ordinary person to actually enjoy quotes from Mr. Greenspan.

DIRECTIONS

1. Take any quote of Mr. Greenspan's, like this one:
"Spreading globalization has fostered a degree of international flexibility that has raised the possibility of a benign resolution to the U.S. current account imbalance."

2. Make a list of the nouns in the quote:

- globalization
- degree
- flexibility
- possibility
- resolution
- account imbalance

3. Replace them with some more interesting nouns:

- globalization—poodles
- degree—trousers
- flexibility—funkiness
- possibility—exoskeleton
- resolution—Keith Richards
- account imbalance—banana cream pie

4. Now, fixing the grammar as necessary, the quote becomes:

Q: What chemical is the most utilized by humans? A: Salt. It has over 14,000 uses.

"Spreading poodles have fostered trousers of international funkiness that have raised the exoskeleton of a benign Keith Richards to the current U.S. banana cream pie." Isn't that better?

5. But wait—you can keep going. Make a list of the verbs in the quote and replace them with your own:
- spread—yodel
- foster—mutate
- raise—ooze

6. Now you have:
"Yodeling poodles have mutated trousers of international funkiness that have oozed the exoskeleton of a benign Keith Richards to the current U.S. banana cream pie."

7. Now, the adjectives:
- international—yellow
- benign—moldy
- current—charbroiled
- U.S.—aboriginal

8. And we get:
"Yodeling poodles have mutated trousers of yellow funkiness that have oozed the exoskeleton of a moldy Keith Richards to the charbroiled aboriginal banana cream pie."

Fascinating, and it works with any quote! Try another quote, insert your own words, and have fun with...

> George W. Bush...Bill Gates...Madeline Albright...
> John Ashcroft...Jimmy Carter...Henry Kissinger...
> Condoleeza Rice...Uncle John

*   *   *

COULD YOU REPOOT THAT?
According to researchers at the University of British Columbia, herring communicate with each other through high-pitched "raspberry" sounds emitted from their rear ends.

Worldwide, cell phone users spent $232.5 million on musical ring tones in 2003.

THE CREEPIEST MOVIE EVER MADE

Can a dead person star in a movie? Well, if a star unexpectedly dies before film production is complete, what's the studio supposed to do—pass up a great opportunity for free publicity? Not a chance.

BIG TIME

In 1970 a filmmaker named Raymond Chow quit his job at Shaw Brothers Studios, Hong Kong's largest film studio at the time, and formed Golden Harvest Studios. Not long afterward he signed an up-and-coming young martial artist to play the lead in his first movie. The actor was Bruce Lee and the movie, *The Big Boss*, was his first feature-length kung fu film.

The Big Boss shattered Hong Kong box-office records when it premiered in 1971. Lee's follow-up film, *Fist of Fury,* was even more successful. His third film, *The Way of the Dragon,* did better still when it was released in 1972.

These three blockbusters put Golden Harvest on the map and helped introduce the Hong Kong film industry to the international market. In 1973 Golden Harvest became the first Hong Kong studio to partner with a major Hollywood studio when it collaborated with Warner Bros. on Lee's fourth and "final" film, *Enter the Dragon*. Today Golden Harvest is Hong Kong's largest and most successful movie studio. They owe much of their success to Bruce Lee.

THE CLONE WARS

When Lee died suddenly in July 1973, only four weeks before *Enter the Dragon* debuted on the silver screen, how did the studio honor him? By cashing in on the publicity surrounding his death, of course. And they weren't the only ones: Hong Kong studios flooded the market with Bruce Lee knock-off films as fast as they could make them—movies with titles like *New Fist of Fury, Bruce Lee Fights Back from the Grave, Exit the Dragon, Re-Enter the Dragon, Enter Another Dragon,* and *Enter the Fat Dragon,* starring kung fu copycats like Bruce Le, Bruce Li, Bruce Liang, and Dragon Lee.

UNFINISHED BUSINESS

But by far the strangest of these films was *Game of Death*, which Lee started but did not live to finish. The only parts that he completed were the fight scenes, including one with pro basketball player Kareem Abdul-Jabbar. There was no plot line in any of the finished scenes, but Golden Harvest plowed ahead anyway, taking just 11 minutes of the original fight footage and creating an entirely new movie around it, using a double to play Bruce Lee's character Billy Lo, a movie star who refuses to submit to gangsters who control the Hong Kong film industry.

PROBLEM SOLVING

How do you make a movie using a dead actor? Golden Harvest tackled the problem in a number of different ways:

• Lee's double was filmed in wide angle shots, from behind, or in the dark whenever possible.

• Reaction shots of the real Bruce Lee, recycled from his earlier films, were spliced into the scenes with Lee's double.

• In one scene they literally cut out a still photograph of Bruce Lee's head and pasted it on the screen over the double's head.

• In scenes where the double does show his face, he wears a large pair of dark sunglasses and sometimes even a fake moustache and beard. In other scenes he wears a motorcycle helmet with the darkened visor pulled down.

• The plot was written to explain the character's changed appearance: Early in the film a gangster tries to kill Billy Lo by shooting him in the face. Lo survives, but undergoes plastic surgery to repair the damage, and emerges from the hospital literally a new man.

SOME THANKS

Had Golden Harvest simply left it at that, *Game of Death* would hardly be worth anyone's while. But they didn't. When Billy Lo gets shot and is rushed to the hospital, he decides to fake his death and even arranges his funeral, so that his assailants won't know he's still alive and coming after them. Golden Harvest added this element to the plot to give them an excuse to incorporate footage of Bruce Lee's *actual funeral*, including close-up shots of the open casket as mourners file past. For a brief moment the camera even peeks inside the coffin, showing Lee's embalmed face—probably the only time in history that a movie star's cadaver appears in his own feature film.

TRAGIC COINCIDENCE

When the gangsters shoot Bruce Lee's character Billy Lo, they do it by sneaking onto the movie set where he's filming a gun battle and fill the gun with real bullets instead of blanks. Moments later, Billy is "accidentally" shot while filming the scene.

Fifteen years after *Game of Death* premiered, in March 1993, Bruce Lee's only son, 28-year-old Brandon Lee, died on the set of the movie *The Crow*. While filming a scene in which his character is shot and killed, the prop gun, supposed to be loaded only with blanks, was loaded with a real .44-caliber slug.

Police concluded it was an accident resulting from the film crew's negligence: Sometimes "dummy" bullets—real bullets with the gunpowder and primer removed—are used to make it look like a gun contains real bullets. On this occasion one of the dummy bullets apparently came apart inside the gun, and a slug remained lodged in the barrel. Nobody bothered to make sure the barrel was clear before blanks were loaded into the gun. When the gun was fired at Lee, the slug shot out and struck him in the lower abdomen. He died in surgery 12 hours later.

LESSON LEARNED

Game of Death was unfinished when Bruce Lee died and was later finished without him. Similarly, *The Crow* was unfinished when Brandon Lee died and was later finished without him, using computer-generated special effects. This time the Lee family approved, believing that Brandon would have wanted the film to be completed.

The footage of him being shot was left out. In fact, mindful of the way Bruce Lee's death had been exploited in *Game of Death*, the family had the footage destroyed. As a family spokesperson put it, "they didn't want it to fall into the wrong hands."

*   *   *

"If you love life, don't waste time—for time is what life is made of."

—Bruce Lee

TAKING THE LOW ROAD

*Political pundits say that anything can
happen in an election. Here's proof.*

C ANDIDATE: Mike Rucker
OFFICE: County Commissioner in Tallahassee, Florida
(2002)
CAMPAIGN: Rucker was putting up "Vote for Rucker!" lawn
signs one morning when he noticed that someone had removed a
sign put up just minutes earlier. He installed a new one (he had
permission from the homeowners) and continued on his way. A
few minutes later he drove by the house again—the new sign had
disappeared. Miffed, he rang the doorbell but got no answer. So he
went into the backyard...and found the missing signs. About that
time, coincidentally, he felt the call of nature, so he relieved himself—right in the backyard. Unluckily for him, the owners saw him
and told the papers about it, and his "pee of revenge" ended up in
the national news.
OUTCOME: His campaign petered out...and he lost the election.

CANDIDATE: Arnold Schwarzenegger
OFFICE: Governor of California (2003)
CAMPAIGN: During the 2003 campaign to recall California governor Gray Davis, several women accused Schwarzenegger of
touching them inappropriately during his acting career. One of
them—Rhonda Miller, a stunt double in *Terminator 2*—made the
claim just one day before the election. Within hours,
Schwarzenegger's press secretary, Sean Walsh, sent an e-mail press
release to reporters and editors pointing to the L.A. Superior Court
Web site. There, he said, anyone who typed in the name "Rhonda
Miller," would find that Miller had a long rap sheet, including four
convictions for prostitution, three for drug possession, and one for
forgery. Conservative talk shows and Internet sites jumped all over
the story, bringing Miller's credibility into serious question.
OUTCOME: Schwarzenegger won the election, but the next day
an interesting fact emerged: the Rhonda Miller on the court Web
site was not the Miller who had made the accusations. A simple

background check would have shown that the two women had different birthdays. But the damage had been done—Miller the stunt double had to endure being labeled a drug addict and prostitute. "When I turned on the TV set," she said, "oh my God. I was in shock. What they were saying about me was horrible. I just stood there and cried."

Radio stations and Web sites issued retractions, but the press secretary claimed he had nothing to apologize for. "We did not make any allegations," Walsh said. "I wrote that memo myself. I wrote it very, very carefully."

CANDIDATE: Howard Metzenbaum
OFFICE: Senator of Ohio (reelection, 1974)
CAMPAIGN: During the Ohio Democratic primary race, Senator Metzenbaum was running against famed astronaut John Glenn. Metzenbaum accused Glenn of being a lifetime "government employee" and "never holding a real job." What was Glenn's government job? He served for 23 years in the Marine Corps, fought in two wars (WWII and Korea), and went on to become the first American to orbit Earth. Glenn responded to the insult by giving the "Gold Star Mother" speech. He asked Metzenbaum to look any "Gold Star Mother"—a mother who had lost a son in combat—in the eye and tell her that her son had not held a "real job."
OUTCOME: The speech made national news and Metzenbaum looked like a buffoon. Glenn won the primary by more than 100,000 votes and then went on to win the November election and become senator.

CANDIDATE: Ernie Eves
OFFICE: Premier of Ontario (reelection, 2003)
CAMPAIGN: During the campaign, a staffer for Conservative premier Eves sent an e-mail to media representatives about their opponent, Liberal candidate Dalton McGuinty. The e-mail ended with the statement, "Dalton McGuinty. He's an evil reptilian kitten-eater from another planet." When asked by reporters if he really ate baby cats and was a space alien, McGuinty smiled and said, "I love kittens, and I like puppies too." Eves, the incumbent, refused to apologize and blamed the release on a staffer who "had too much coffee."
OUTCOME: The kitten-eater won.

Ronald Reagan once appeared in a *GE Theater* production of "A Turkey For President."

TICK-TOCK…

It's about time.

"Time is very important on television. We buy it, we fill it, we start on it, we must finish on it. And appropriately enough, we occasionally kill it."
—**Alfred Hitchcock**

"Tobacco, coffee, alcohol, hashish, strychnine, are weak dilutions; the surest poison is time."
—**Ralph Waldo Emerson**

"At my back I often hear Time's winged chariot changing gear."
—**Eric Linklater**

"Time is a river of passing events, and strong is its current; no sooner is a thing brought to sight than it is swept by and another takes its place, and this too will be swept away."
—**Marcus Aurelius**

"The future is something which everyone reaches at the rate of 60 minutes an hour, whatever he does, whoever he is."
—**C. S. Lewis**

"I have noticed that the people who are late are often so much jollier than the people who have to wait for them."
—**E. V. Lucas**

"Time is the coin of your life. It is the only coin you have, and only you can determine how it will be spent. Be careful lest you let other people spend it for you."
—**Carl Sandburg**

"Time is the only critic without ambition."
—**John Steinbeck**

"You have been warned against letting the golden hours slip by; but some of them are golden only because we let them slip by."
—**James M. Barrie**

"You may delay, but time will not."
—**Benjamin Franklin**

"I wasted time, and now doth time waste me."
—**William Shakespeare**

"The bad news is time flies. The good news is you're the pilot."
—**Michael Althsuler**

"Time is a great teacher, but unfortunately it kills all its pupils."
—**Hector Berlioz**

AND THEN
WHAT HAPPENED?

Our next installment in the history of (nearly) everything that ever happened.

PART III: FROM CAESAR TO CHARLEMAGNE

• **47 B.C.** Roman troops destroy Egypt's Alexandria library, the classical world's largest archive of knowledge. As many as 100,000 ancient Greek and Roman texts are lost forever.

• **27 B.C.** Octavius, successor to Julius Caesar, declares himself Augustus, the first Roman Emperor. Rome conquers Egypt, which they will rule for almost 700 years.

• **4 B.C.** Jesus is born in Judaea (Israel).

• **33 A.D.** Chinese silks reach Rome for the first time. Pontius Pilate, Roman governor of Judaea, orders the execution of Jesus.

• **43** Christianity begins its spread: the apostle Paul takes it to Turkey, Greece, and Syria. Thomas takes it to India. Romans invade England for the third time and will conquer it in 77 A.D.

• **64** The city of Rome is destroyed by fire. Emperor Nero falsely blames the Christians, spurring their first persecution.

• **70** Jewish citizens in Judaea rebel against the Romans after the temple is desecrated. Most of the city—including the temple—is destroyed as the Romans crush the uprising.

• **117** The Roman Empire is at its peak. It now extends from the Persian Gulf to Egypt to Turkey to North Africa to most of Europe and Britain. It has more than five million inhabitants.

• **250** The classic Mayan period begins in Central America and Mexico. It will last until 900 A.D., marked by the building of temples, pyramids, and large city-states, such as Palenque, Chichén Itzá, and Tikal. It is also the beginning of the Axum Empire in Ethiopia, which will have prosperous cities along the major trade route of the Red Sea.

Before 1950, Americans bathed about once a week. Now it's almost once a day.

- **300** The weakening Roman Empire is divided into two halves, eastern and western, with two emperors. The Hohokam people found "Snaketown" on the Gila River in Arizona, employing organized labor to build an elaborate irrigation network. New technology: stirrups are invented in China; warriors can now use swords and spears more effectively on horseback.

- **312** Constantine, emperor of the western half of the Roman Empire, converts to Christianity. This is known as the beginning of the Roman Catholic Church and is the impetus for the Christian domination of the Western world. The first church is built on the site of what will become the center of the Catholic Church—the Vatican. Within 20 years, Constantine will conquer the east and become emperor of a reunited empire. He moves the capital from Rome to Byzantium and changes the name to Constantinople (present-day Istanbul in Turkey).

- **330** Buddhism continues its spread through Asia and is now practiced in China and Mongolia.

- **410** Teotihuacán (in central Mexico) is a highly developed city—and the largest in the world, with a population of about 200,000. The Visigoths, a Germanic tribe, attack and plunder Rome. New technology: Greeks invent the catapult, the first artillery weapon.

- **450** Under the leadership of Attila, the Huns, a nomadic equestrian tribe from central Asia, invade northern Europe and the eastern Roman Empire. Attila's palace is built in Hungary.

- **476** Rome falls, marking the end of the western Roman Empire and the start of the European Dark Ages. The eastern Roman (or Byzantine) Empire will last another 1,000 years.

- **486** Although he is little more than a tribal chieftain, Clovis expels Roman rulers from Gaul and becomes the first king of France.

- **541** The Justinian Plague, named after the Byzantine emperor, affects the Mediterranean region. By 544 it will kill 25% to 50% of the population. Buddhism reaches Japan.

- **570** Mohammed is born in Mecca.

- **600** Beginning of extensive slave trade from sub-Saharan Africa to the Mediterranean. New technology: Yokes and collars that allow animals to pull heavier plows, and new methods of crop rotation increase production and population. Mayans make paper from bark.

- **610** According to Islamic belief, Mohammed is visited by the angel Gabriel near Mecca and given the word of God, written as the Koran. Mohammed's flight from Mecca in 622 marks the start of the Islamic calendar and the beginning of the Islamic Era. In 630 his army takes Mecca, and by the time of his death in 632, he will have converted most of the Arabian Peninsula to Islam.

- **640** Caliph Omar conquers Egypt (*caliph* was the title for the religious and political successor to Mohammed). Islam begins to spread through North Africa.

- **656** Ali, son-in-law of Mohammed, becomes caliph. Bloody civil wars lead to a major split of Islam: the majority Sunnis, who will take control, and the Shiites, who followed Ali. The split endures today.

- **670** Only decades from its inception, the Islamic Empire now extends from India through the Middle East and North Africa, soon to expand to Spain and southern Europe. This includes Jerusalem, a holy city to Jews, Christians, and Muslims, who will build the Dome of the Rock mosque on the Temple Mount in 692.

- **756** Pépin III of France defends Rome against invaders. Pope Stephen II crowns him king of France; Pépin gives territories to the pope. This establishes a papal state, sets a precedent for Church-appointed rulers in Europe, and gives the Roman Church actual political power.

- **800** French king Charlemagne (Charles the Great) conquers almost all of Europe. He is crowned emperor by Pope Leo III, marking the start of the Holy Roman Empire in Europe. The first castles are built in western Europe.

And then what happened? Turn to page 472.

Living up to the name: Buffalo Bill Cody killed 4,280 buffalo in one year alone.

THE FOUR DRAGONS

In China, dragons are revered as wise friends, not reviled as enemies.
More serpentine than Western dinosaur-like dragons, they have been
at the center of Chinese culture for thousands of years, and still are
(just visit any Chinese restaurant and count the dragons). Here's
an old myth about four dragons who would rather help the people
than listen to the gods—for which they paid the ultimate price.

DRAGON PLAY

Once upon a time, there were no rivers or lakes on Earth. The people had to rely on rain to bring water to their crops. The only water on the Earth was far off in the Eastern Sea. Four giant dragons lived there: the Long Dragon, who was the leader, the Yellow Dragon, the Black Dragon, and the Pearl Dragon.

One day the Four Dragons decided to leave the sea for a little while to play in the sky. They soared and dove, playing hide-and-seek in the clouds. They played for so long that they ventured far from the sea. And it was then that the Pearl Dragon saw something that upset him. "Come here quickly!" he said.

"What is it?" asked the other three. The Pearl Dragon pointed down to the earth. There they saw thousands of people in great torment. Their crops were withering, the grass was yellow, and the fields cracked under the scorching sun. But even though the people were starving, some were laying out offerings of fruits and cakes. Others were praying. An old white-haired woman kneeled to the ground with a thin boy on her back and looked to the sky. "Please send rain quickly, God of Heaven, to give our children some rice to eat. Our food is nearly gone, yet we leave you these gifts so you might find it in your kind heart to bring life to our dying villages."

A CALL TO ARMS

The old woman's prayers went unanswered, for the Jade Emperor, whose job it was to oversee all of the happenings on the earth and in the sea, didn't bother to listen to the lowly people. But the four dragons heard the prayers, and they could not ignore them. "How poor those people are!" said the Yellow Dragon. "They will all die if it doesn't rain soon."

"You are right," said the Long Dragon. "Let us go ourselves and beg the Jade Emperor for rain. Perhaps he will listen to us." So saying, he leaped higher into the sky. The others followed closely and flew up to the Heavenly Palace.

EMPTY PROMISES

The Jade Emperor was displeased to see the dragons enter his great hall. "Why do you come here to bother me? Your job is to stay in the sea, not to meddle in the affairs of the gods."

The Long Dragon came forward and said, "Please forgive us, Your Majesty. We were merely playing in the sky when we noticed the plight of the starving humans. Their crops are withering and dying. We humbly beg you to send rain down quickly."

The four dragons bowed and awaited an answer. Finally, the Jade Emperor told them to go back to the sea. "I will send some rain down tomorrow, but you must promise from now on not to bother with humans or annoy the gods. You are dragons of the sea and there you must stay."

"We will. Oh thank you,

Your Majesty." The four dragons bowed and returned to the sea. But still they looked to the sky and to the land far off where all of the farmlands lay dry. And no rain came the next day. Nor the day after that or the day after that. The people were starving, forced into eating tree bark and dried grass roots. When they ran out of those, they ate white clay. Now ten days had passed since the Jade Emperor's promise, and still no rain came. The four dragons could see that the Jade Emperor cared only about his own pleasure; yes—it would have to be up them to relieve the miseries of the people. But how?

THE DRAGON BRIGADE

The Long Dragon had an idea. "Look," he told the others. "Is there not plenty of water here in the sea where we live? More than we or the fish will ever need. We could scoop it up and spray it toward the sky. The water will then fall like raindrops and save the people and their crops."

The others agreed, but then the Long Dragon realized the flaw in the plan. "If we do this and the Jade Emperor learns of what we have done," he said, "we may be blamed—

and perhaps punished."

The Yellow Dragon replied, "Speaking for myself, I will do anything in my power to save these starving people." The Black Dragon and Pearl Dragon nodded their heads in agreement.

"So be it," said the Long Dragon. "We shall save the people and hope we do not come to regret it."

The four dragons then filled their giant mouths and flew into the sky, releasing the water down to the scorched lands below. They flew back and forth, back and forth, making the sky dark all over the countryside as the water formed rain clouds. The people cried and leaped with joy. "It's raining! It's raining! Our crops will be saved!" The wheat stalks raised their heads and the sorghum stalks straightened up. The old woman gave the starving boy a life-giving cup of water.

EMPEROR'S WRATH

While the four dragons were bringing water to the people, the god of the sea was watching them. He promptly went to the Jade Emperor and reported what was happening. The Jade Emperor became very angry. "How dare the four dragons bring rain to those undeserving creatures without my permission!" He called for his generals to gather their armies and prepare to attack. The four dragons' celebration ended abruptly when they saw thousands of soldiers from the heavens flying toward them. Being far outnumbered, they surrendered peacefully and were taken to the heavenly palace.

The Jade Emperor scolded them: "I told you to return to the sea, but you disobeyed me. Now you shall be banished from both the sea *and* the sky forever! You are very large and powerful dragons, so your cages must be much larger and even more powerful. Therefore I have commanded the Mountain God to get four mountains so that I might lay one upon each of you—mountains so massive that you will never be able to escape!" The Mountain God used his power to make four mountains fly there, whistling in the wind from afar, and the Jade Emperor pressed the mountains down upon the prisoners.

THE FOUR RIVERS

The four dragons did not even struggle to escape—the mountains were too big. Nor did they ever come to regret defying the Jade Emperor's orders. Instead, the four dragons vowed to do whatever good they could for the helpless people. And they needed to do something fast, for the rain had already stopped and soon the crops would start to wither again.

So the four dragons mustered up what little power they had left and turned their scaly backs into riverbeds that wrapped around the mountains. Their insides became water, which flowed down these riverbeds, meandering through the valleys and flowing all the way to the sea. And that is how the four dragons became China's four great rivers—the Heilongjiang (Black Dragon River) in the far north, the Huang (Yellow River) in central China, the Chang (Yangtze, or Long River) farther south, and the Zhu (Pearl River) in the very far south.

And as long as the kind spirits of the four dragons remain under the mountains, the water will flow forever.

A pair of nylons is made from a single filament four miles long, knitted into 3 million loops.

UNCLE JOHN'S STALL OF FAME

Here's another in-stall-ment of a Bathroom Reader *favorite.*

Honoree: Leila LeTourneau, a nurse in Longview, Texas
Notable Achievement: Striking oil...in the water closet
True Story: When LeTourneau left her house for work one Monday in February 2004, everything seemed normal...but when she returned home at the end of her shift, "there was this black ooze coming out from my house," she told the *Longview News-Journal*.

The black ooze turned out to be crude oil bubbling up through her toilet, her bathtub, her shower, even her kitchen sink. By the time she got home her entire house was inundated with the stuff. So is she rich now? No—just a victim of bad plumbing. It turns out that instead of being connected to a sewer line, LeTourneau's house was accidentally hooked up to the drainpipe of a nearby oil field. When that pipe backed up, oil flooded her house. At last report she was living in a rental home, waiting for the mess to be cleaned up. "I was always proud to have an oil derrick in my backyard," she says. "Now, I don't know."

Honoree: Dilubhai Rajput, a diamond merchant in Gujarat, India
Notable Achievement: Creating the world's most valuable cow manure
True Story: Gujarat state is known for its diamond cutting and dairy industries. Rajput worked in both, and that's what got him into trouble. In January 2004, he hid a bag of 1,722 small diamonds (estimated value: $900) in a haystack outside of his house. A hungry cow came along...and Rajput spent the next three days following the cow around until it "gave" the diamonds back. He got only 300 at first, but at last report was still confident the others were on the way. "I am sure within a week I will retrieve the rest," he told the *Economic Times*.

Honoree: An unnamed man in Jinjiang, China (Xinhua, China's government-run news agency, did not release his name)

Notable Achievement: Going above and beyond the call of duty to serve the bathroom needs of his community

True Story: Apparently, there is a restroom shortage in Jinjiang. In March 2004, an unnamed man offered to convert his own ground-floor apartment into a public bathroom. "There are not enough public toilets in this area, and I often see people relieve themselves stealthily in the far corners of the community," the man told Xinhua. (At last report his neighbors—worried about the stink—were fighting his plan.)

Honoree: Paul Stafford, director of Foundation Studies in Art and Design at Kingston University in southwestern London

Notable Achievement: Teaching an old restroom new tricks

True Story: In early 2003, Stafford asked the local Kingston upon Thames council to let him convert an abandoned 1950s-era ladies' room into an art gallery. With their approval, he and a group of volunteers cleaned and painted the restroom. But rather than rip out all of the fixtures, Stafford integrated as many as he could into the gallery's design: all of the toilet stalls were retained, and the sinks were mounted on the ceiling and converted into light fixtures.

Ironic note: The only toilet they kept, they turned into a decorative fountain. So when the (toilet paper) ribbon was cut and the Toilet Gallery opened to the public in October 2003, any of the 80 people attending had to go down the street to Starbucks if they needed to use the bathroom.

*　　*　　*

DO EARS OF CORN LISTEN?

In 1960 botanist George Smith planted two sets of corn seeds in flats in his greenhouses. Both sets were treated identically, with the exception that one set "listened" to George Gershwin's "Rhapsody in Blue" 24 hours a day. Result: The Gershwin plants sprouted earlier and were healthier. The next year, Smith continuously broadcast music to a small plot of corn. The plot yielded 137 bushels an acre, versus 117 for an identical plot kept in silence.

WHEN CELEBRITIES ATTACK

Famous people are just like everyone else—they act erratically, they make fools of themselves in public, they even start fights. The main difference: there's always a reporter around to record their actions.

CELEBRITY: Richard Simmons
INCIDENT: In March 2004, Simmons, the famous fitness guru, was waiting in Phoenix's Sky Harbor International Airport for a flight to Los Angeles when another waiting passenger recognized him. Christopher Farney, a 6'2", 250-pound ultimate cage fighter and martial arts expert, pointed out Simmons to the rest of the passengers and yelled, "Hey everybody, it's Richard Simmons. Let's drop our bags and rock to the '50s." In response, the 55-year-old fitness pro approached Farney and said, "It's not nice to make fun of people with issues," and then smacked him across the face. Although unharmed, Farney called the cops. The charges were later dropped, but Simmons insisted that Farney deserved the slap.

CELEBRITY: Courtney Love
INCIDENT: After giving an unannounced performance at a Manhattan nightclub, Love was arrested and charged with reckless endangerment. In the early hours of Thursday morning on March 18, 2004, she was performing in front of about 400 people when she decided to toss a microphone stand into the audience. Despite the fact that it struck a 24-year-old man in the head and he had to be taken to the hospital in an ambulance, Love did a few more songs and finished her set before being placed under arrest. A spokesperson later explained, "She didn't know she hurt someone, and felt terrible about it, but she didn't feel she was guilty of a crime, either."

CELEBRITY: Naomi Campbell
INCIDENT: On her way to the Toronto movie set of *Prisoner of Love* in 1998, the supermodel was delayed by Canadian customs

officials. Finally arriving at her hotel, the diva blamed her assistant Georgina Galanis for the wait, grabbed her by the throat, and slammed her against a wall. Still furious, Campbell reached for a telephone and hit Galanis twice in the head with the handset, then threatened to throw her from a moving car on a busy highway. A Toronto criminal court ordered Campbell to take anger-management classes. Did she learn anything in class? Apparently not—according to news reports, the supermodel attacked another assistant in 2001.

CELEBRITY: Marilyn Manson
INCIDENT: The gender-bending rock star made headlines in September 2003 when a Minnesota jury found him not guilty of battery or any of the other charges against him (causing emotional distress, mental anguish, and humiliation). The charges were the result of a stunt during a 2000 concert. Security guard David Diaz was working the front of the stage when Manson suddenly grabbed him and began rubbing his pelvis against Diaz's head. In July 2001, while performing in Michigan, Manson pulled the same stunt on security guard Joshua Keasler. That time he had to pay a $4,000 fine.

CELEBRITY: Russell Crowe
INCIDENT: In 1999, while spending some time on his 560-acre ranch in Australia, Crowe and his brother Terry went out for a drink and wound up in a brawl. Crowe spied radio DJ Andrew White at a local bar, approached him, and said, "I've listened to your program, and it's crap." White quickly replied, "So are most of your movies," prompting Crowe to turn to the DJ's wife and exclaim, "I'm going to belt the crap out of your husband!" The gladiator then went after White and several other bar-goers. Security cameras captured him in three separate fights kicking, punching, and biting like a wild man; during the melee Crowe even took a swing at his brother before biting a bouncer in the neck and fleeing the bar.
NOTE: Crowe once attacked the director of the British Academy of Film and Television Arts awards show for editing a four-line poem out of Crowe's Best Actor acceptance speech. Witnesses said Crowe's own security had to remove him, kicking and cursing.

BIRTH ANNOUNCEMENT

Science seems to have all the answers. We know certain
things absolutely, definitely, and positively...until
something happens that science can't explain.

WHAT'S NEW AT THE ZOO?

In January 2002, a bonnethead shark at the Henry Doorly Zoo in Omaha, Nebraska, had a baby. What's so unusual about that? The shark lived only with other females and hadn't had contact with males since she was a baby herself. The story of the "virgin birth" quickly appeared in newspapers around the world. Zoo officials and shark experts were perplexed—no one could explain it.

One person who read the stories was Doug Sweet, a curator at the Belle Isle Aquarium in Detroit. Sweet had a tank with two female bamboo sharks living in it, and one of them had recently laid some eggs (bamboo sharks don't give birth to live young like bonnetheads do—they lay eggs). That shark hadn't had any contact with males, either, and in such cases the eggs are thought to be sterile and are thrown away. But Sweet had read about the shark in Omaha, so he saved the eggs and put them in an incubator. Fifteen weeks later, the eggs began to hatch.

LONE SHARK

Until then scientists had always believed that sharks could only reproduce when a male fertilized a female, but the experiences of these two sharks forced them to think again. One possibility: Some species of sharks may have both male and female reproductive organs and can fertilize their own eggs. Another possibility: The eggs are able to develop into embryos *without* being fertilized, in a process known as parthenogenesis. Many species of reptiles and even one species of turkey can reproduce through parthenogenesis, but nobody thought that sharks could do it.

One thing is for certain: Sweet isn't throwing his shark's eggs away anymore. "We're definitely holding them now and incubating them," he told *National Geographic* magazine. "If you have one parthenogenetic shark, you may as well have a whole tank of them."

GRANDMA CELIA, CARD SHARK

Never play poker with Grandma Celia—you'll lose your shirt. But if she offers to show you some card tricks, prepare to be entertained. Here are a few of her favorites.

SPLIT PERSONALITY

"While I'm shuffling the cards, see if you can answer this one question," Grandma Celia told me. "Dave had some cards and dealt them to his three brothers.

- "To the oldest brother, he gave half the cards plus half a card.

- "Then he gave half the cards he had left, plus half a card, to the middle brother.

- "Then he gave half the cards he had left, plus half a card, to his youngest brother.

"After that he had no cards left. And he did all of this without cutting or tearing up any cards. How many cards did Dave start out with, and how many cards did he give to each brother?"

BY THE NUMBERS

Grandma Celia handed me the deck. "For this trick," she explained, "you get to pick 1 numbered card (no jacks, queens, or kings), and I get to pick 1. Aces count as ones. Don't show me yours, and I won't show you mine." I picked the 8 of clubs and set it face down on the table. She picked her card and put it face down next to mine. Next, Grandma handed me a pencil and a piece of paper.

- "Multiply your card's number by 2," Grandma Celia said. I multiplied 8 by 2 to get 16.

- "Now add 2 to the total." I added 2 and got 18.

- "Multiply that number by 5, then subtract 7 to get your final number." 18 times 5 is 90. 90 minus 7 is 83. "What did you get?" she asked.

"Eighty-three," I said.

"Now turn over both of our cards," Grandma Celia said. I turned over my 8 of clubs…and her 3 of diamonds.

"An 8 and a 3," she said. "83."

"How did you do that?!"

TURNING 30

Grandma Celia dealt 30 cards onto the table. "Pick up at least 1 card, but don't pick up any more than 6," she said. "Then I'll do the same thing, and we'll take turns picking them up until all the cards are gone. Whoever picks up the last card wins."

We played the game seven times. Sometimes I got to go first, and sometimes Grandma Celia did. Not that it mattered—Grandma Celia won every time. How did she do that?

"It's easier than you think," she said.

ELEVENSES

Grandma Celia selected 3 cards from the deck—the 3 of spades, the 7 of hearts, and the 4 of spades—and slapped them down on the table like lightning.

"Three-seven-four. Three hundred seventy-four. That's evenly divisible by 11," she said quickly. "Check it and see for yourself." I did the math: 374 divided by 11 equals 34. No remainder, just like she said.

"How'd you do tha…"

Grandma Celia slapped 3 more cards on the table: the 5 of diamonds, the 8 of spades, and the 3 of hearts. "Five-eight-three. Five hundred eighty-three," she said. "That's divisible by 11, too. No remainder," she said. Before I could say anything, she slapped down the 2 of diamonds, the 8 of clubs, and the 6 of clubs. "Two-eight-six. Two hundred eighty-six. Divisible by 11," she said.

She was right. 583 divided by 11 equals 53; 286 divided by 11 equals 26. No remainders. Grandma Celia *hates* math—it was her worst subject in school. So how'd she do it?

For the solutions to these tricky puzzles, turn to page 515.

*   *   *

Actual Bathroom Graffiti: "Beauty is only a light switch away."

A Boy Scout must earn 21 badges before he is eligible to become an Eagle Scout.

A SPY? NOT I!

A story of intrigue, from our "Famous for 15 Minutes" file.

SETTING: The bar in the Hotel Meurice in Paris

CHARACTERS: 1) Felix Bloch, a senior U.S. diplomat living in Washington, D.C., in the late 1980s. **2)** A **Russian spy** for the KGB, real name unknown—most of the time he posed as a Finnish businessman named Reino Gikman, but Bloch says he knew him as Pierre Bart, and thought he was French.

PROLOGUE

On April 27, 1989, the U.S. National Security Agency intercepted a transatlantic phone call between Gikman and Bloch. The two men were making plans to meet in Paris while Bloch was there on government business. U.S. State Department officials aren't supposed to meet with KGB agents, so when NSA agents heard that, they figured they had stumbled onto something big. They passed the information on to the CIA, which gave it to the FBI, which immediately launched a classified investigation. They asked French counterintelligence to observe and videotape the Paris meeting, hoping to catch a spy.

CLOAK AND DAGGER (AND BAG)

On the evening of May 14, Bloch met Gikman at the Hotel Meurice. They had a drink at the bar, then went down to the restaurant and had dinner. To the untrained eye, nothing about the meeting seemed out of the ordinary. To the eyes of the French intelligence agents posing as diners at a nearby table, however, something was definitely up: Bloch entered the restaurant carrying a black shoulder bag, and placed it under the table. When dinner was over, he left without it. Gikman, who left a few minutes later, took the bag.

By the time Bloch returned to Washington, the investigation into his activities was well underway. His phone line was tapped, his house was bugged, and so was his car. Three teams of FBI agents were watching him in shifts 24 hours a day.

Why go to the trouble, when the government already knew

that Bloch had given something to a KGB agent? Because they didn't know what that "something" was—only Bloch and Gikman knew what was in the bag. Espionage charges are hard to prove: to win a conviction, you have to be able to prove the spy handed over classified information, and the only way to do that, other than getting them to confess, is to catch them in the act. The FBI wasn't about to pin its hopes on Bloch confessing, so it made plans to follow him constantly until the next rendezvous.

BEST-MADE PLANS

Everything went according to plan for about a month—the FBI felt it was only a matter of time until they could close in. Then on June 11, Gikman suddenly returned to Moscow and disappeared. Eleven days later, Bloch received a strange early-morning phone call from a man who identified himself as "Ferdinand Paul," who said he was calling on behalf of "Pierre Bart" (Gikman).

Pierre "cannot see you in the near future," Paul said, because "he is sick," and that "a contagious disease is expected." Paul then added, "I am worried about you. You have to take care of yourself." There was no mystery about what the caller was really saying: somehow the KGB had figured out that Gikman had been compromised, and now they were calling to tell Bloch he might be under investigation, too.

DEAD END

Once Bloch had been alerted, there was no point in keeping the investigation secret. That same day, FBI agents went to the State Department and confronted Bloch directly, but he denied everything—he wasn't a spy, he insisted, and he was shocked to learn that "Pierre Bart" was a KGB agent. When the agents showed Bloch still photographs of the meeting in the Paris restaurant and asked about the shoulder bag, he shrugged it off. He and Gikman were both stamp collectors, Bloch explained. The shoulder bag contained stamp albums.

State Department officials trading stamps with KGB agents? The FBI agents didn't believe a word of it. But since they couldn't prove anything, they were stuck. One of the agents tried to bluff Bloch by pointing to a stack of documents and claiming that they were recovered from Bloch's shoulder bag. It didn't work—Bloch

---

The indentation on the bottom of an apple is called the *calyx basin*.

flatly denied it, and the FBI was left with nothing.

The next day the FBI interviewed Bloch again and then searched his apartment, carting away several boxes filled with financial documents, address books, and other personal items. Again, nothing. "Bloch denied he had engaged in espionage," the FBI later wrote, "and ultimately declined to answer any further questions." But they kept the pressure on, subjecting Bloch to round-the-clock "obvious surveillance."

THE SPY AND HIS ENTOURAGE

That's when Bloch, the highest State Department official accused of spying since the 1940s, became an international media star. It started on July 21, 1989, when ABC News broke the story that he was under investigation. From that moment on, whenever Bloch walked his dog, took his clothes to the cleaners, or did his grocery shopping, he was followed by as many as seven cars filled with FBI agents, who were, in turn, followed by hordes of reporters and TV camera crews. When Block visited relatives in New York, his unofficial motorcade tailed him up the interstate. When he went on a 22-mile hike in the Maryland countryside, scores of out-of-shape reporters and FBI agents huffed and puffed to keep up with him. Bloch made the evening news night after night after night.

Usually when someone is accused of criminal activity, they keep quiet and try to stay out of sight. Bloch was just the opposite: He wouldn't talk about the government's suspicions against him, but he was happy to talk about anything else, and reporters followed him around for weeks, hoping he'd eventually crack and start talking about the case. But he never did. Over time the media's interest in him waned, and soon it was just him and the FBI again.

Then in early December on a trip to visit relatives in New York, Bloch looked around and suddenly realized that for the first time in nearly six months nobody was following him. The FBI had called off its surveillance. The case was still open, but the investigation had ended without Bloch ever being formally accused of anything.

ALL OVER NOW

Whether or not he was guilty of spying, Bloch's diplomatic career was over. In November 1990, the State Department fired him on the grounds of making "deliberate false statements or misrepresentations to the FBI in the course of a national security investigation." In August 1993, it stripped him of his pension.

Bloch's fall was swift: In 1989 he had been one step away from becoming an ambassador; a year later he was bagging groceries and driving a city bus in Chapel Hill, North Carolina. In 1993 he was arrested for stealing $100 worth of groceries from the store where he worked and was fired from his job. In 1994 he was arrested again, this time for stealing $21 worth of merchandise from another store. Bloch has never been charged with spying, but he has paid $160 in fines and spent a night in jail...for shoplifting.

That might have been the end of the story, had the feds not arrested an FBI agent named Robert Hanssen in February 2001. The charge: spying for the Soviet Union. How the FBI caught him was unique—it paid $7 million to a retired KGB agent who had stolen Hanssen's entire file from the Russian archives—including a tape of a telephone conversation between Hanssen and his handlers.

The Hanssen file shed new light on the Felix Bloch affair: It was Hanssen who alerted the KGB that both Gikman and Bloch were being watched. The KGB warned Gikman, who returned to Moscow on June 11. Eleven days later, Bloch got his mysterious phone call. Hanssen even mentions Bloch in a letter. "Bloch was such a shnook," he wrote, "I hated protecting him, but he was your friend, and there was your illegal [Gikman] I wanted to protect."

UPDATE
So was Felix Bloch a spy for the KGB? No one knows for sure... except Bloch and the KGB. More than 15 years have passed since the FBI launched its investigation, and after all that time the agency still hasn't been able to put together a strong enough case to formally accuse him or bring him up on charges. Bloch is still a free man, and at last report was still a bus driver in North Carolina. If he was a spy for the KGB in the 1980s, the Russians probably still have a file on him. Maybe someday it will find its way into the hands of the United States, as Hanssen's did. Maybe not.

In any event, the case will probably remain open until it is solved or Bloch dies...and that may be a while. "Longevity runs in my family," Bloch said. "This could go on another 35 years."

IT'S THE WRONG SONG

National anthems played at sporting events are a sign of respect by the host country and a source of pride for competitors. But when the wrong anthem is played it provides a great source of bathroom reading.

COUNTRY HONORED: Ethiopia
SPORTING EVENT: 1964 Olympics in Tokyo
WRONG SONG: Ethiopian Abebe Bikila had won the gold medal for the 26-mile marathon in 1960, becoming the first black African to win a gold medal in any event. But his chances didn't look very good for the 1964 games: he'd had an emergency appendectomy just 40 days before the race. He ran anyway and captured the world's attention when 75,000 screaming fans greeted him as he entered into Tokyo's Olympic Stadium—four minutes ahead of the second-place runner. He set a world record time and became the first person ever to win two marathon golds. As he stood for the medals ceremony, expecting to sing along with his country's song, Bikila got a surprise: the Japanese orchestra didn't know the Ethiopian national anthem (no one ever dreamed Bikila would win)—so it played Japan's anthem instead.

COUNTRY HONORED: Spain
SPORTING EVENT: 2003 Davis Cup (tennis) in Melbourne
WRONG SONG: Before the finals match between Spain and Australia, trumpeter James Morrison was called upon to play the Spanish national anthem. As soon as Morrison started playing, though, the Spaniards reacted with outrage. Why? He was playing "Himno de Riego," the long-defunct anthem of a regime that had deposed King Alfonso XIII in 1931. (One version of the song has a verse about a man wiping his bottom on the king.) And Alfonso was the grandfather of Spain's current monarch, the hugely popular King Juan Carlos I. When the team threatened to pull out of the competition, the organizer quickly apologized.

COUNTRY HONORED: Philippines
SPORTING EVENT: 2003 Southeast Asian Games in Ho Chi Minh City

WRONG SONG: After the Philippine judo team won two gold medals, the winners were confused during the awards ceremony to hear an anthem they didn't recognize. "We didn't know which one it was, but it wasn't ours," said Bong Pedralvez of the Philippine consulate. Response: The entire delegation ignored the music and sang the correct anthem a cappella.

BONUS BLUNDER: That wasn't the only slip-up. During the volleyball competition, the Philippine team noticed that their flag was upside down. The red stripe was on top and the blue was on the bottom. The error had more meaning than most knew: "If we put red on top," Pedralvez explained, "that means we're at war."

COUNTRY HONORED: Italy

SPORTING EVENT: 2002 World Cup in Japan

WRONG SONG: During the 2002 soccer season the Italian national team was criticized because their players didn't sing along when their national anthem was played. The coach took the criticism to heart and insisted his players learn the song, "Fratelli d'Italia" ("Hymn of Mameli"), and practice singing it. But the players were insulted by the criticism and announced that they would protest at the World Cup...by not singing the anthem. And they didn't. (In reporting the incident, European newspapers pointed out that many Italians admitted to disliking the song, which ends with the words "We are ready for death!")

*   *   *

HALF-WITS AT HALFTIME

During the halftime of a high school football game in Dallas, the marching band from Paris, Texas, put on a show entitled "Visions of World War II." Part of the performance featured a student displaying a large flag with a gigantic swastika on it. At the same time the band broke into "Das Deutschland Lied," better known as "Deutschland Uber Alles" ("Germany Above All"), the national anthem of Nazi Germany during WWII. It could not have been worse timing: it was Rosh Hashanah, the first day of the Jewish New Year. The stunned crowd booed, yelled, and even threw things at the performers. Band director Charles Grissom apologized for the incident, saying that he was just trying to be historically accurate. But the performance was, he conceded, "an error in judgment."

WORD ORIGINS

More interesting origins of everyday words.

MASCARA

Meaning: A cosmetic applied to darken the eyelashes
Origin: "Anyone applying this substance to eyelashes to thicken them for an evening may not enjoy the etymology that, through Spanish *mascara* and Italian *maschera*, for 'mask,' returns them to Arabic *maskharah*, for 'buffoon' or 'clown.'" (From *The Secret Lives of Words*, by Paul West)

UMPIRE

Meaning: Person appointed to rule on plays, especially in baseball
Origin: "From the French *noumpere*, which meant the same: 'one who decides disputes between parties.' Around the 15th century, people began to transfer the *n* in the word to the article: '*a noumpere*,' becoming '*an oumpere*,' and finally '*an umpire*.' (It's the same way 'a *napron*' became 'an *apron*,' and 'an *ewt*' became 'a *newt*')." (From *Grand Slams, Hat Tricks & Alley-oops*, by Robert Hendrickson)

SHERIFF

Meaning: An elected official responsible for keeping the peace
Origin: "In Anglo-Saxon England, the sheriff was the king's chief representative in each county. The Old English form was *scirgerefa*, a compound of *scir* ("shire") and *gerefa*, ("officer," ancestor of the word *reeve*). Like many ancient titles, the meaning has changed. Today an English sheriff has chiefly ceremonial duties, such as presiding over elections; a Scottish sheriff is a judge; and an American sheriff is a law enforcement officer." (From *Word Mysteries & Histories*, by *The American Heritage Dictionary*)

LIEUTENANT

Meaning: A military rank
Origin: "From two French words, *lieu*, (meaning 'place') and *tenant*, (meaning 'holding')—an officer of lower grade who takes the place of a captain. The English pronunciation of lieutenant as 'leftenant' is due to an early printing confusion of 'u' with 'v' which later became an 'f.'" (From *More About Words*, by Margaret S. Ernst)

The United Parcel Service (UPS) was started by two teenagers.

SOY YA LATER

Soy you thought soybeans were for just for health food nuts....

SACRED GRAIN

Soybeans were first cultivated 5,000 years ago in Asia. The ancient Chinese considered them one of the five sacred grains needed to sustain life (rice, wheat, barley, and millet are the others).

In 1765 a sailor named Samuel Bowen came back from China with a sack of soybean seeds. He gave them to Henry Yonge, the surveyor-general of Georgia, who planted them with phenomenal success, reaping three crops in a single growing season. Bowen harvested the beans and invented a process for making soy noodles. King George III awarded Bowen a patent and a medal from the Society of Arts, Manufacturers, and Commerce. Alas, when Bowen died in 1777, most Western interest in the soybean died with him.

A SACK OF SEEDS

Then, in 1851 a Japanese junk foundered off the coast of Japan, and a ship called the *Auckland*, bound for San Francisco, rescued the stranded sailors. But California port authorities wouldn't allow the Japanese sailors off the ship for fear they would spread disease. By coincidence, Dr. Benjamin Edwards was in the area waiting for a ship to take him back to his home in Illinois. He examined the Japanese sailors and pronounced them healthy, and they gave him a thank-you gift: a package of soybeans. Edwards took the beans to Illinois and gave them to a local horticulturist named John Lea, who planted them. They grew so well that Lea began passing seeds to other people, who in turn grew them and passed the seeds along to others.

It wasn't long before American ranchers learned the value of soybeans. Livestock thrived on nearly all parts of the soybean plant. And by the late 1890s, Western scientists began to make new discoveries. They found that soybean plants actually improve the quality of the soil they grow in by taking nitrogen from the atmosphere and converting it into a form that enriches dirt. All plants need nitrogen to grow, but few plants can get it from the air.

Researchers for automobile giant Henry Ford found ways to turn the soybean into paint, plastics, and fabric. Ford also had his chef, Jan Willemse, use them in as many dishes as possible, and many of Willemse's recipes were showcased at the 1934 World's Fair. Health guru John Kellogg promoted the use of soybeans at his spa in Battle Creek, Michigan. People began to think of soybeans as more than just livestock feed.

By 1938 the United States was exporting soy meal to other countries. When World War II began, production soared; soybeans fed millions of starving refugees. Soybean oil replaced imported fats and oils needed to make glycerin, which was used as a solvent and lubricant. Soybean meal increased animal production and soy protein was used as a meat extender.

THE ORIGIN OF SOY SAUCE

Centuries ago in Japan, people salted meat and fish to preserve it. Any liquid that seeped out of the fish and collected in the bottom of the barrel was used in soups and seasonings. Molds often covered this aging food, and when the liquid lay in the bottom of the barrel all winter, it fermented.

This fermented fish sauce became very popular in ancient Asia. When Buddhism became widespread, however, vegetarianism became the norm and fermented fish sauce was forbidden. In 1254 A.D., a Zen monk discovered how to make a similar sauce out of fermented soybeans, and it remains one of the world's most popular condiments.

SOYBEANS TODAY

• In 1924 the United States produced five million bushels of soybeans. Today it's up to 2.6 billion per year, making soybeans the nation's third biggest crop (following corn and wheat).

• Soybeans are now grown on more than 73 million acres—an area about the size of Arizona.

• The United States grows more soybeans than any other nation —half the world's supply. Soybeans are the nation's single biggest source of vegetable oil.

• Soybeans contain 40% protein, compared to only 18% protein in beef. Two pounds of soy flour contains about the same amount of protein as five pounds of meat.

Shellfish lover: An oyster may change its gender multiple times in its life.

- Soybeans contain seven of the eight amino acids essential for human health, but soybean oil has the lowest levels of saturated fats of any vegetable oil.
- According to the FDA, "25 grams of soy protein a day, as part of a diet low in saturated fat and cholesterol, may reduce the risk of heart disease."
- In addition to being used to make foods such as tofu, soy milk, and soy-based ice cream, soy beans are also used to make hundreds of consumer and industrial products, including car wax, chain oil, cleaning solvents, fuel additives, hydraulic oils, grease, motor oil, paint strippers, spray foam insulation, dust suppressants, ink, crayons, odor reducers, nail polish remover, hand lotion, hand cleaners, lawn fertilizer, candles, graffiti remover, fire extinguishers, bug sprays, disinfectants, soap, varnish, explosives, and more.
- Economically speaking, it's the most important bean in the world. U.S. Treasury Secretary George Shultz once joked that America might have to switch from the gold standard to the soybean standard.

*   *   *

VIRTUAL FOLDING

Conventional wisdom says that it's physically impossible to fold a piece of paper in half more than seven times. However, according to *The Economist* magazine, if you *were* able to keep folding it (and doubling its thickness), math principles theorize that the concentrated piece of paper would grow to astronomic heights:

- 10 folds   Width of a hand
- 12 folds   Height of a stool
- 14 folds   Average adult height
- 20 folds   Quarter of the Sears Tower
- 25 folds   Height of the Matterhorn
- 30 folds   Outer atmosphere of Earth
- 50 folds   Distance to sun
- 70 folds   11 light years from Earth
- 100 folds   Radius of the known universe

According to one study, a toilet has 49 germs per square inch. A desktop has 20,961.

PUNDITSPEAK

Pundits are an odd breed. They're part journalist, part politician, and part town crier. And they're paid very well to spout their opinions.

"The American political system is like fast food: mushy, insipid, made out of disgusting parts of things—and everybody wants some."
—**P. J. O'Rourke**

"Anybody who wants the presidency so much that he'll spend two years organizing and campaigning for it is not to be trusted with the office."
—**David Broder**

"America is the only country in the world that's still in the business of making bombs that can end the world and TV shows that make it seem like a good idea."
—**Bill Maher**

"Instead of just being dazzled by these corporate mega-mergers, there should be a nagging voice in all of us asking: Is democracy going to be bought up too?"
—**Thomas Friedman**

"If Thomas Jefferson thought taxation without representation was bad, he should see how it is with representation."
—**Rush Limbaugh**

"Having the right to do something does not mean that doing it is right."
—**William Safire**

"Any nation that can survive what we have lately in the way of government is on the high road to permanent glory."
—**Molly Ivins**

"A liberal is someone who feels a great debt to his fellow man, which debt he proposes to pay off with your money."
—**G. Gordon Liddy**

"The harder you try to suppress the truth, the more inevitable it is that it will find a way to come out."
—**Arianna Huffington**

"Creative semantics is the key to contemporary government; it consists of talking in strange tongues lest the public learn the inevitable inconveniently early."
—**George Will**

"Put a federal agency in charge of the Sahara Desert and it would run out of sand."
—**Peggy Noonan**

The only reptile capable of making loud vocalizations is the alligator.

THE COST OF WAR (MOVIES)

In his book Operation Hollywood, *David Robb writes about dozens of films and TV shows that have been through the government screening process. Here's a behind-the-scenes peek at how the Pentagon shapes Hollywood.*

SEAL OF APPROVAL

If you're trying to make a military-themed movie on a budget, you'll probably want to enlist the aid of the military, which can supply ships, planes, tanks, and even soldiers for little or no cost. But Pentagon support comes with strings attached. The U.S. military actually has a "film liaison office" that reads scripts and decides whether or not they want to participate. Often, support is conditional—they'll support the film if the script is changed to put the military in a positive light. Filmmakers are highly motivated to cooperate: they can save tens of millions of dollars if they do. Here are a few examples of movies that did—or didn't—go along with the Pentagon.

***Tomorrow Never Dies* (1997),** starring Pierce Brosnan
Story Line: James Bond battles a media mogul who wants to drive up ratings by starting World War III.
Status: Cooperation approved—but only after producers agreed to remove a line from a scene where Brosnan is about to parachute into the waters off the coast of Vietnam: A CIA agent (played by Joe Don Baker) warns Bond not to get caught: "You know what will happen. It'll be war, and maybe this time we'll win."

***Crimson Tide* (1995),** starring Gene Hackman and Denzel Washington
Story Line: When rebels take over a Russian nuclear missile installation, the submarine commanded by Hackman receives an order to launch a nuclear missile against them before the rebels can launch one against the United States. As the submarine is preparing to launch, it's attacked by a Russian submarine, which

prevents the sub from receiving a second message that may (or may not) rescind the launch order. Hackman decides to launch anyway, prompting Washington's character to lead the mutiny.

Status: Cooperation denied. The Navy objected to both the mutiny and the idea that a submarine could launch a missile in error (even though it actually can).

Black Hawk Down (2001), starring Ewan McGregor

Story Line: A Black Hawk helicopter is shot down over Mogadishu, Somalia, and the crew has to fight to survive.

Status: Cooperation approved. But the Pentagon did insist on one important change: the name of McGregor's character, a real-life Army Ranger named John Stebbins, couldn't be used in the film. Stebbins *was* one of the heroes of the battle of Mogadishu and won a Silver Star, but by the time the script was submitted for approval, he had been court-martialed for molesting a 12-year-old boy. The military didn't want anything to do with him, so McGregor's character was renamed Danny Grimes.

Stripes (1981), starring Bill Murray and Harold Ramis

Story Line: Two screwballs join the army and eventually become heroes.

Status: Cooperation approved. Believe it or not, the military thought *Stripes* would make a good recruiting film. They did, however insist that all references to drug use, sexism, and jokes about "raping and pillaging" be removed. The misfit platoon's drill sergeant had to be "toned down" to make him less sadistic, too. The producers complied, and in return received permission to film at Fort Knox, Kentucky. And just as the Pentagon predicted, Army recruiting went up after *Stripes* hit theaters.

Star Trek IV: The Voyage Home (1986), starring William Shatner and Leonard Nimoy

Story Line: Captain Kirk and company travel back in time to the 1980s to capture a pair of humpback whales and bring them to the future so that they can save the world. But their spaceship is severely weakened by traveling through time. So Uhura (Nichelle Nichols) and Chekov (Walter Koenig) have to sneak onto the USS *Enterprise*, a nuclear aircraft carrier, to "siphon" off some nuclear power that they can use to recharge the spaceship.

Status: Cooperation approved, but the USS *Enterprise* scene had to be changed. In the original script, the spaceship is so drained of energy that the transporters don't work, and Uhura and Chekov must sneak past military security to board the ship. The Navy objected to the idea that intruders could outwit military security, so producers rewrote it: the transporters have enough power to beam the two *onto* the carrier, but not enough to get them off again.

Broken Arrow **(1996),** starring John Travolta and Christian Slater

Story Line: An Air Force pilot (Travolta) steals a nuclear weapon, and another pilot (Slater) has to stop him.

Status: Cooperation denied. The military rejected the idea that one of its officers would or could steal a nuclear bomb, or that they could detonate one if they did steal it. Still, the military did manage to wrest one concession from filmmakers: Travolta, the villain, removes his military flight suit after he steals the bomb, visually lessening his ties to the military. Slater, the hero, leaves his on.

Mars Attacks **(1996),** starring Jack Nicholson

Story Line: Earth is invaded by aliens from Mars. The invasion fails when a grandmother and her grandson discover that the Martians' heads explode when they listen to a recording of the Slim Whitman song "Indian Love Call."

Status: Cooperation denied. According to David Robb, the Pentagon didn't like the idea that the military was "less effective at combating alien invaders than Slim Whitman."

The Perfect Storm **(2000),** starring George Clooney

Story Line: A fishing boat gets caught in one of the biggest storms ever to hit the North Atlantic. The film is based on a true story.

Status: Cooperation denied at first, then approved. In the script, as in real life, the Coast Guard is the branch of the service that rescues fishing boats. But the Coast Guard declined to participate because they thought the script was inaccurate. When the Air Force agreed to help, producers rewrote the scene so that the Air National Guard, not the Coast Guard, attempts the rescue.

In the original draft of *Star Trek,* the *Enterprise* was called the U.S.S. *Yorktown.*

I CAN'T TAKE IT ANYMORE!!!

Uncle John presents these true stories of extreme overreactions to serve as a reminder: Always keep your cool.

THE ANNOYED: George Furedi

SITUATION: A local church's public address system was keeping Furedi awake at night.

FREAK-OUT: Furedi drove his SUV to the church and slammed into the front of it. He was arrested a short time later for malicious mischief, driving while intoxicated, and numerous hit-and-run charges (he rammed into several cars on his way to greet parishioners). How did the cops find Furedi? They ran a check on his license plate. (He left his truck wedged in the church doors.)

THE ANNOYED: Chris Baugh

SITUATION: Someone vandalized the building Baugh was renovating. He was convinced that local skateboarders were responsible.

FREAK-OUT: There was a community skate park not far from Baugh's building site. Seeking retribution, Baugh drove a bulldozer to the park and demolished ramps, rails and fences. Police charged Baugh with second-degree criminal mischief. (No charges were ever filed against the skateboarders—Baugh didn't have any proof that they were responsible for vandalizing his building.)

THE ANNOYED: Charles Booher

SITUATION: An Internet company swamped Booher's computer with e-mails and Internet pop-up ads for male enhancement.

FREAK-OUT: Booher, who'd battled testicular cancer, contacted Doug Mackay, one of the people whose name appeared on one of the ads, and asked him to stop sending them. When they continued to arrive, Booher barraged Mackay's company with e-mails and phone calls for the next three months, threatening to torture and kill him and his employees. Mackay called the FBI; they placed Booher under arrest. He faces five years in prison and a $250,000 fine. "I blew my cool," he says.

The Masai people of Africa spit on their newborns to ensure good luck.

THE ANNOYED: A 45-year-old German man

SITUATION: In the apartment next door, the man heard the tell-tale signs of redecorating: furniture being moved across the floor and pictures being nailed to the walls.

FREAK-OUT: After an hour or so, the man went to the apartment and found two teenage boys fixing up the place. He threatened them at gunpoint: "Stop this racket or you'll be sorry." It worked...kind of. He didn't hear any more noise because the police came and took him to jail.

THE ANNOYED: Ashley Carpenter, a bicyclist from Dorset, England

SITUATION: Carpenter always tried to share the road with cars, but often felt that motorists ignored him.

FREAK-OUT: When a car splashed him with water in December 2003, the 37-year-old Carpenter snapped and started a vigilante campaign to rid the road of rude drivers. His method: slashing tires. In all, Carpenter slashed more than 2,000 tires on 548 cars, causing more than £250,000 ($447,000) worth of damage. He was nabbed by police after being caught in the act by surveillance cameras.

THE ANNOYED: A 30-year-old Norwegian man

SITUATION: His girlfriend liked to drink alcohol. He didn't. So he spent night after night after night as her designated driver.

FREAK-OUT: Apparently not knowing how to say no, he decided his only way out was to lose his driver's license. So on the way home one night, he passed a police car at 85 mph in a 50 mph zone. It worked: He was banned from driving for a year. (He also got a two-week vacation from his girlfriend—in jail.)

*　　*　　*

OTHER FREAK-OUTS

• After a neighbor's dog pooped on his lawn, Walter Travis, 68, shot the neighbor several times (but not the dog).

• Danny Ginn stole a garbage truck at gunpoint because the truck's driver kept using his driveway to turn around.

• Kevin French, 45, shot his neighbor in the head with an air rifle because he "mowed his lawn too often." (The neighbor recovered.)

BY THE TIME WE GOT TO WOODSTOCK, PART I

The Woodstock Music and Arts Festival was an event like no other in the 20th century. Nearly half a million young people gathered in upstate New York on a hot, rainy weekend in 1969 to watch one of the most impressive musical lineups in history. But what they got was much more than a concert—Woodstock was both a cultural milestone and the end of an era.

TENSE TIMES

In the late 1960s, the United States was a divided nation. The war in Vietnam had essentially put people on one of two sides: pro-war or anti-war. And both sides were vehement in their beliefs—the violent confrontation between police and protesters at the 1968 Democratic Convention in Chicago had proved that. By 1969, as the anti-war movement felt more and more marginalized by the media, the only way left to spread the message of peace was through music.

San Francisco was the West Coast headquarters of the hippie movement; on the East Coast, it was New York City. But after a while, the hustle and bustle of the cities became too much for musicians to deal with—especially for recording music—so a lot of them started moving to the country.

About 100 miles north of Manhattan, the rural town of Woodstock, New York, had been a pastoral retreat for artists and musicians for nearly a century. Bob Dylan, Janis Joplin, and Van Morrison, to name a few, decided to build homes and record there. Young people liked Woodstock for its back-to-nature appeal, but the local farmers weren't too thrilled to see long-haired hippies rolling into town. Because there were only a few at first, the locals just shrugged it off. They had no idea what was about to hit them.

THE FANTASTIC FOUR

There was one thing Woodstock lacked: a state-of-the-art recording studio. In the spring of 1969, four entrepreneurs—all young men in their 20s—decided to build one.

Your eyesight is sharpest in the middle of the day.

- Michael Lang, the oldest of the four at 26, was a stereotypical longhair, described by his friends as a "cosmic pixie." A year earlier, he had produced Florida's largest-ever rock concert—the two-day Miami Pop Festival, which drew 40,000 people.

- Artie Kornfeld was a vice president of Capitol Records and an accomplished songwriter with 30 hit singles to his credit, including Jan and Dean's "Dead Man's Curve."

- John Roberts was the one with money. He was heir to a toothpaste fortune and had served in the Army. The only concert he'd ever been to was a Beach Boys show.

- Joel Rosenman was a Yale Law School graduate, but he cared more about playing guitar in a lounge band than practicing law.

LET'S PUT ON A SHOW

Kornfeld and Lang were friends who shared a New York City apartment and a love for progressive music. One of their dreams was to put on a huge music festival. When they heard of the exodus up to Woodstock, they wanted to be a part of it, and building a studio would be their in. They thought a rock concert might be a good way to raise money and generate publicity for the studio—but first they needed money to put on the concert.

Meanwhile, in another New York City apartment, Roberts and Rosenman were busy thinking up new and inventive business ideas. They had some money between them, but true to the times, they wanted to use it for some unconventional, cutting-edge business venture. But what? They decided to write and produce a television sitcom about two oddball businessmen who got into a different wacky business venture every week. For plot ideas, they put an ad in the *New York Times* in March 1968:

Young Men with Unlimited Capital looking for interesting, legitimate investment opportunities and business propositions.

MEETING OF THE MINDS

The show never made it off the drawing board. The ad, however, caught the eye of Lang and Kornfeld's lawyer, who knew his clients were looking for business partners to put on their concert. A meeting was arranged in February 1969. Although they came from different backgrounds—Roberts and Rosenman were button-down college graduates; Kornfeld and Lang were tie-dyed flower children—they all agreed that the summer of 1969 in Woodstock, New York, would be the time and place for an unprecedented festival, what they called "three days of peace and music." They expected between 40,000 and 50,000 people to show up.

FINDING A FIELD, PART I

The four men formed Woodstock Ventures. In the spring of 1969, they scouted around upstate New York for a concert site in or near Woodstock. In Wallkill they found an abandoned industrial park. It was the right size (300 acres), was in a good location (right off the highway), and had all the utilities in place. Roberts shelled out $10,000 to rent the park, and the town of Wallkill welcomed them with open arms...at first.

Although the industrial park had all the amenities the four were looking for, the "vibe" didn't feel right. Lang, for one, hated it: the industrial feeling of the park was a far cry from the back-to-nature theme he'd envisioned for the concert. The people of Wallkill were wary of the prospect of 50,000 hippies converging on them, but Rosenman assured town supervisor Jack Schlosser that it would be a low-key folk festival—they'd get 50,000 people if they were lucky. Schlosser reluctantly agreed, and so did Lang. Roberts tried to ease the tensions between hippies and townsfolk by hiring a minister to take care of local relations and a former assistant at the justice department named Wes Pomeroy to head security. Even though the site wasn't perfect, it was the only one they had.

FINDING THE ACTS

As spring turned to summer, the four promoters went to work trying to book the biggest folk and rock acts of the day. But performers were understandably hesitant—Woodstock Ventures had never put on a concert before, and now they were trying to put on the largest one of the year. "To get the contracts," remembered Rosenman, "we had to have the credibility, and to get the credibility, we had to have the contracts." They got the contracts the only way they could think of: they promised incredible sums of money to performers. One of the most popular groups of the time, Jefferson Airplane, agreed to play for $12,000, twice their usual fee. Then Creedence Clearwater Revival and The Who signed for similar fees.

Ancient Egyptians slept on stone pillows.

Those groups gave the show the credibility it needed. Other acts soon began to follow: the Grateful Dead and the headliner, Jimi Hendrix. (The musician they wanted most, Bob Dylan, couldn't make the show—he had already signed on to play the Isle of Wight Festival in England on the same weekend.)

With all the wheels in motion, an army of longhaired hippies descended upon Wallkill to begin setting up the site and start construction on the largest sound system ever created. The influx proved to be too much for the already suspicious locals. "I don't care if it's a convention of 50,000 ministers," Schlosser told Woodstock Ventures. "I don't want that many people in my town." So on July 15, 1969—a month before the concert was scheduled to begin—the Wallkill council ran Woodstock Ventures out of town.

FINDING A FIELD, PART II

Losing the site was a huge blow. The people at Woodstock Ventures were disconsolate; some were even packing up their stuff to go home. But then something unexpected happened: the press found out about what happened in Wallkill and ran with it. While the promotion for Woodstock was limited mostly to radio stations and independent newspapers, the story of the town that reneged on its concert deal made headlines everywhere. Suddenly, Woodstock was a part of the national conversation. And that may have been the best thing to happen to the festival. Many think that if the concert had gone on in Wallkill, it would have turned out badly—tensions there were already high, and some Wallkill citizens had threatened to "shoot the first hippie that walks into town."

But the fact remained that Woodstock still had no venue. Then, sometime during the week of July 20, when most of the people of the world were focused on the first moon landing, Lang heard about Max Yasgur, an eccentric old pipe-smoking dairy farmer from the town of White Lake. He owned a 600-acre farm and might be willing to rent it. Lang went to the field and fell in love with it. "It was magic," he said. "The sloping bowl, a little rise for the stage. A lake in the background. The deal was sealed right there in the field."

THE BUSINESS OF PEACE

Woodstock Ventures may have started out with the best of inten-

---

The human body creates and kills 15 million red blood cells every second.

tions for the festival, but it was evident early on that they would have to utilize some tough business tactics to make it happen.

• Rosenman had maintained that maybe 50,000 people at most would show up. That's what he told Wallkill and that's what he told the people of White Lake, even though he knew it wasn't true. He expected five times that amount. At that point they would have told anyone anything to make the show happen. But Max Yasgur was wise to the ways of Woodstock Ventures. He tallied up his expenses for lost crops and destruction of his land and charged $75,000 for his field—in advance—and got it.

• The bands were misled, too. There was supposed to be a $15,000 cap on artists' fees, but word leaked out that Jimi Hendrix had been promised $32,000. Rosenman explained that it was because Hendrix was the headliner and was slated to do two sets. But in the end it didn't matter, because many of the acts were never paid in full, anyway.

HERE IT COMES

A week before the start of the festival, the citizens of White Lake and Bethel realized the full magnitude of what was about to happen. There were at least 1,000 people on the site building the stage, the sound towers, the clinics, tent cities, and two huge ticket booths. That was on the inside. On the outside, tens of thousands of people were driving up Route 17B, inundating the small town of Bethel.

In an attempt to pacify the locals, Woodstock Ventures invited them to attend a pre-festival event in order to prove that the Woodstock performers were harmless and wholesome. They hired an avant-garde acting troupe called Earthlight Theater to perform a play. Bad idea: The play was called *Sex. Y'all Come*, and the script involved having the actors strip naked, pantomime an orgy, and shout obscenities at the crowd. The townsfolk were not amused. White Lake pulled the permits with just a few days left before the event. But by this point, it was too late. The "Stop Work" signs were ripped down almost as soon as they were put up. Like it or not, Woodstock was going to happen.

Don't freak out, man. Part II of the story is on page 503.

WEIGHTS AND MEASURES

You're used to pounds, meters, and minutes, but how about parsecs or fathoms? Here are a few weights and measures you might find a little unfamiliar.

BTU: A measure of heat energy, one BTU (British thermal unit) is the amount of energy needed to raise one pound of pure water by 1°F.

Fathom: Originally equal to the distance between the tips of the left and right middle fingers with the arms outstretched. Today one fathom is equal to six feet.

Stone: A British measure of weight equal to 14 pounds.

Light-year: The distance a pulse of light travels in one year (about 5.88 trillion miles).

Parsec: 3.26 light-years.

Acre: Originally described the amount of land that could be plowed by oxen in a single day. Today it is 4,840 square yards. There are 640 acres in a square mile.

Acre foot: Amount of water needed to submerge one acre of land under one foot of water.

Skein: A measure for yarn or thread. A skein is 360 feet long.

Dobson unit: A measure of the concentration of ozone in the atmosphere.

Apgar score: A number score between 1 and 10 given to newborn babies as a measure of health. The healthiest babies score a 10.

Barrel (petroleum): 42 gallons.

Section: The U.S. term for one square mile of land (one mile wide by one mile long).

Furlong: A measure of distance, used mainly in horse races. One furlong is equal to one-eighth of a mile.

Cord: Measures quantities of chopped wood—the amount in a pile four feet high, four feet wide, and eight feet long.

Shake: A measure of time. One shake is equal to one hundred-millionth of one second.

Work triangle: An imaginary triangle connecting the kitchen sink, refrigerator, and stove. The ideal perimeter of such a triangle is no less than 12 feet; no more than 22 feet.

A Boeing 747 holds 57,285 gallons of fuel.

DON'T EAT THAT!

*Some of the creepiest rumors and urban legends are
the ones concerning the stuff we eat and drink.
Are any of them true? Read on to find out.*

RUMOR: The skins of bananas from Costa Rica are infected with the bacteria that causes *necrotizing fasciitis*—flesh-eating diseases.

BACKGROUND: In January 2000, an e-mail from the "Mannheim Research Institute" began making its way around the Internet. It claimed that the flesh-eating infection had recently decimated the Costa Rican monkey population, and that the bacteria were passed from one monkey to another via banana peels. The U.S. Food and Drug Administration, it claimed, estimated that 15,000 people would be maimed or killed by exposure to infected bananas...but that this was an "acceptable number," so the FDA was holding off on issuing an alert because it didn't want to start a panic. "Please forward this to as many of the people you care about as possible," the e-mail pleads. "We do not feel 15,000 is an acceptable number."

THE TRUTH: Go ahead and eat your banana—the e-mail was a hoax. The monkeys are fine, and there is no "Mannheim Research Institute," but this was one of the hottest food rumors of 2000. The FDA and the Centers for Disease Control received so many e-mails that they issued a public statement debunking the story and set up a special banana hotline.

RUMOR: Red Bull gives you wings...and brain tumors.

BACKGROUND: The Austrian energy drink first found its way to the United States in 1997. By 2000 e-mails were circulating about it, claiming that one of the drink's ingredients, the ominous sounding *glucuronolactone*, is "an artificially manufactured stimulant developed in the early 1960s by the American Government." It was first used "in the Vietnam conflict to boost morale amongst GIs who were suffering from stress and fatigue, but was banned after a few years following several deaths and hundreds of cases involving anything from severe migraines to brain tumors."

The traditional American "log cabin" style home originated in Sweden.

Another rumor claimed that Red Bull gets its "energy" from the private parts of bulls.

THE TRUTH: Glucuronolactone is a naturally occurring carbohydrate, not an artificial stimulant. Every other claim in the e-mail is false, too. Red Bull is threatening to sue the person who started the rumor…if they ever track him down. And no, Red Bull does not contain the private parts of bulls. But is Red Bull fighting *that* rumor? Not a chance. It's "one of our favorite rumors," says company spokesperson Emmy Cortes. "It's kind of fun."

RUMOR: Evian is *naive* spelled backward—it's a backhanded slap at people who waste money on bottled water.
BACKGROUND: Well…Evian really *is* naive spelled backward, isn't it?
THE TRUTH: It's just a coincidence. Evian is bottled at a spring in the town of Evian-les-Bains in the French Alps near Lake Geneva. And it's nothing new, either—Evian's waters have been bottled and sold since 1826.

RUMOR: French wine contains ox blood.
BACKGROUND: When France opposed the U.S. invasion of Iraq in early 2003, some U.S. politicians started looking for ways to retaliate. House Speaker Dennis Hastert proposed putting "bright orange warning labels" on French wine bottles to warn consumers that they might contain ox blood. "People should know how the French make their wine," his spokesperson told reporters.
THE TRUTH: The claim is false but does contain a kernel of truth. Powdered ox blood was once used in France (and other countries, including the United States) to clarify cloudy wine. So were egg whites. The substances were introduced into the wine while it was still fermenting in barrels. Proteins floating in the wine, which caused much of the cloudiness, would then stick to the blood or egg whites, forming clumps that settled to the bottom of the barrel and could be easily removed from the wine. But the European Economic Union formally outlawed the practice of using dried ox blood in 1998. Modern wineries use clay filters to accomplish the same task.

Food tip: To make ketchup pour more quickly, shake the closed bottle vigorously.

ALABAMA KLEENEX

Does your city, state, or province have some cool slang term named after it? If so, send it to us for next year's Bathroom Reader.

Kansas sheep dip. Whiskey

Michigan bankroll. A big wad of small-denomination bills with a large bill on the outside

Chicago violin. A Thompson submachine gun

Vermont charity. Sympathy, but little else

Cincinnati oysters. Pickled pigs' feet

California banknote. A cowhide

Bronx cheer. Sound made by sticking out one's tongue and blowing to express disapproval

Arkansas wedding cake. Cornbread

Albany beef. Sturgeon. The fish was so plentiful in the Hudson River during the 19th century that it got this nickname

Boston strawberries. Baked beans

West Virginia coleslaw. Chewing tobacco

Missouri featherbed. A straw mattress

Cape Cod turkey. Codfish

Tennessee toothpick. A raccoon bone

Arizona nightingale. A burro

California collar. Hangman's noose

Mississippi marbles. Dice (for craps)

Full Cleveland. A '70s-style leisure outfit: loud pants and shirt, white belt, white loafers

Texas turkey. An armadillo

Missouri hummingbird. A mule

Tucson bed. Sleeping on the ground without cover

Colorado Kool-Aid. Coors beer

Arizona paint job. No paint at all

Arkansas fire extinguisher. A chamber pot

Alabama Kleenex. Toilet paper

Oklahoma rain. A sandstorm

Kentucky breakfast. Steak and bourbon (and a dog to eat the steak)

First non-royal to be portrayed on a British stamp? William Shakespeare (in 1964).

THE WORLD'S WORST NOVELIST

Could there actually be a world's worst novelist? According to the Oxford Companion to English Literature, *it's Amanda McKittrick Ros. We were skeptical, so we read some of her work. They were right.*

PEN OF PERSUASION

If you spent all your spare time reading romance novels and then decided to try writing one yourself, how good would it be? That's what an Irish schoolteacher named Amanda McKittrick Ros wanted to find out: in 1895 she wrote *Irene Iddesleigh*. Two years later, her husband paid to have it published as a gift for their 10th wedding anniversary.

The novels that inspired Ros weren't very good to begin with, and when she tried to imitate them she did even worse. Her prose is wordy and alliterative ("frivolous, frittery fraternity of fragiles flitting round and about" reads one passage), her grammar is quirky, and she embellishes insignificant details for no particular purpose. Her characters don't cry—instead, tears "fall from their sorrow-laden orbs." They don't sweat, they "shed globules of liquid lava." And they don't go crazy, either—they become "berthed in the boat of insanity." It isn't enough for the character Lady Gifford to simply clear her throat, she has to clear it "of any little mucus that perchance would serve to obstruct the tone of her resolute explanation," while Lord Gifford's body shakes "as if electrically tampered with."

INFLICTING PAIN

Ros's work would probably have gone unnoticed and be completely forgotten today had a satirist named Barry Pain not read a copy of *Irene Iddesleigh*. He found the bad writing so funny that he wrote a mocking review in *Black in White*, a popular literary magazine. *Irene Iddesleigh* is "the book of the century," he raved. "*Irene* is enormous. It makes the Eiffel Tower look short...never has there been anything like it. I tremble."

Overnight, Pain's review turned Ros into the talk of London literary society. People snapped up copies of *Irene Iddesleigh* by the thousands, formed Amanda Ros clubs, and threw Amanda Ros dinners and parties at which they took turns reading the worst passages aloud. People wrote fawning letters to the Great Lady in the hope that she might write back in her own hand, and many admirers made the trek to Larne in Northern Ireland to meet her in person. Even Mark Twain read *Irene Iddesleigh*; he pronounced it one of the great works of "Hogwash Literature."

DISTURBING THE BOWELS

As flattered as Ros may have been by the attention, she was deeply hurt by the bad reviews and lashed out at critics for the rest of her life. Ros never doubted her own abilities. The negative reviews only steeled her determination to continue writing, or as she put it, "disturbing the bowels of millions" with her work.

• In 1898 she published her second novel, *Delina Delaney*—twice as long as *Irene Iddesleigh* and every bit as bad.

• A decade later, Ros published her third work, a book of verse called *Poems of Puncture*. By then she'd spent more than five years in court fighting over an inheritance. She wrote *Poems of Puncture* to lash out at her enemies (first critics, now lawyers), and then used the proceeds from book sales to pay her legal bills.

END OF THE ROAD

After *Poems of Puncture*, Ros began work on a third novel, *Helen Huddleson*. Inexplicably, she named many of the characters in the book after fruit—Madam Pear, the Earl of Grape, Sir Christopher Currant, Sir Peter Plum, Lord Raspberry, and his sister Cherry Raspberry among them. (Years later, biographer Jack Loudan asked her why she gave Lord Raspberry that name. "What else would I call him?" she snapped back.) The cast of characters is rounded out by a servant named after a flower and a legume, Lily Lentil.

Helen Huddleson promised to be a doozy, but Ros was not able to finish it. Getting on in years, she had terrible arthritis in her hands, which prevented her from writing the last chapter. She did, however, manage to complete a final book of poems, titled *Fumes of Formation*. Published in 1933, it would be the last of her works published in her lifetime.

Sherlock Holmes author Sir Arthur Conan Doyle was an ophthalmologist.

In 1939 Ros fractured her hip in a fall and died a few days later. After her death, relatives sorting through her personal effects were preparing to burn all of her papers but were stopped at the last minute by William Yeates, a neighbor and admirer who managed to fill a potato sack full of memorabilia, including the unfinished manuscript for *Helen Huddleson*. It remained unpublished for 30 years, until Ros's biographer Jack Loudan edited the manuscript, added a final chapter, and had the book published in 1969.

A ROS SAMPLER

Is Amanda McKittrick Ros the worst novelist in literary history? Here are some excerpts from her work—you be the judge.

Opening line of the book:
"Have you ever visited that portion of Erin's plot that offers its sympathetic soil for the minute survey and scrutinous examination of those in political power, whose decision has wisely been the means before now of converting the stern and prejudiced, and reaching the hand of slight aid to share its strength in augmenting its agricultural richness?"
—*Delina Delaney*
(If you can tell us what it means, let us know.)

Attacking a lawyer named Michael McBlear:
"Readers, did you ever hear
Of Mickey Monkeyface McBlear?
His snout is long with a flattish top
Lined inside with a slimy crop:
His mouth like a slit in a
    money box
Portrays his kindred to a fox."
—*Poems of Puncture*

On an Atlantic Ocean crossing:
"They reached Canada after a very pleasant trip across the useful pond that stimulates the backbone of commerce more than any other known element since Noah, captain of the flood, kicked the bucket."
—**Helen Huddleson**

"Her superbly-formed eyes of grey-blue, with lightly-arched eyebrows and long lashes of that brownish tint, which only the lightly-tinted skin of an Arctic seal exhibits, looked divine."
—*Delina Delaney*

"Leave me now deceptive demon of deluded mockery: lurk no more around the vale of vanity, like a vindictive viper: strike the lyre of living deception to the strains of dull deadness, despair and doubt..."
—*Irene Iddesleigh*

During the Middle Ages, murdering a traveling musician was not thought a serious crime.

GOBBLED UP

Where does the money go when you buy "health food" products?
To some New Age hippies who live in rustic communes and give
the profits to charity, right? Well, they might have started
out like that, but in some cases you'd be surprised.

BOCA BURGERS

Humble Origin: This soy-based, vegetarian product was invented by a natural food restaurateur in 1993 and touted as a healthy alternative to Americans' favorite meal.

Gobbled Up By: Kraft Foods, makers of Oscar Mayer bologna, Jell-O, Cool Whip, and Cheez Whiz, in 2000. (Kraft is owned by Altria, also known as Philip Morris, the cigarette maker.)

POWERBAR ENERGY AND NUTRITION BARS

Humble Origin: Started in a Berkeley, California, kitchen in 1986.

Gobbled Up By: Swiss mega-corporation Nestlé. They bought the brand in 2000 for a reported $375 million and said it "demonstrates Nestlé's commitment to health and nutrition." Some of Nestlé's other "health" foods: Butterfinger candy bars and Nesquik instant chocolate drink.

CASCADIAN FARM ORGANIC FOODS

Humble Origin: Cascadian was a small organic farm when they started in 1972. They were "committed to sustainable agriculture for the environment—and delicious food for you!"

Gobbled Up By: General Mills, the third largest food company in North America, and makers of Betty Crocker cake mixes, Lucky Charms, and Hamburger Helper. They bought Cascadian in 1999.

BEN & JERRY'S ICE CREAM

Humble Origin: Started in a Vermont gas station in 1978 by two guys with a commitment to high-quality foods and social justice. If ice cream can be a health food, this is the brand.

Gobbled Up By: Dutch multinational corporation Unilever. They bought Ben & Jerry's in 2000 for $326 million. (They also own the company that makes Slim-Fast.)

A single toad will eat about 10,000 insects over the course of a summer.

ODWALLA NATURAL JUICES

Humble Origin: Started by three musicians in Santa Cruz, California, to fund school music programs.

Gobbled Up By: Coca-Cola, which bought Odwalla in 2001 for $181 million.

SILK SOY MILK

Humble Origin: Created by White Wave, makers of soy products since 1977 under the credo "business without guilt." It was marketed as a healthier alternative to cow's milk.

Gobbled Up By: Dean Foods, which also make powdered creamers and Gracias Nacho Cheese Sauces, in 2002. Another of Dean Foods' products: cow's milk. They claim to produce more than two billion gallons a year.

KASHI ORGANIC PROMISE CEREALS

Humble Origin: "Kashi Company was founded in 1984 on the belief that everyone has the power to make healthful changes!"

Gobbled Up By: The Kellogg Company, makers of Cocoa Krispies, Eggo waffles, Cheez-Its, and Pop-Tarts. They bought Kashi in 2000 for an estimated $40 million.

SUPRO SOY PROTEIN POWDER

Not So Humble Origin: Supro Soy Protein is made "for Fitness and Health" by Protein Technologies International—a subsidiary of DuPont. In 1999 they successfully petitioned the FDA to permit claims that soy protein reduces the risk of heart disease. Some of DuPont's other products: Over their long history, DuPont has made lead paint, insecticides, gunpowder, explosives, plutonium, and Agent Orange.

*   *   *

INCENTIVE TO WIN?

At the end of every New York Yankees home game, the P.A. system plays the song "New York, New York": the Frank Sinatra version if they win…and the Liza Minelli version if they lose.

DOG GIVES BIRTH TO KITTENS!

...and other great tabloid headlines.

ALIENS PASSING
GAS CAUSED HOLE IN
OZONE LAYER!
—Weekly World News

**KEY TO
HAPPINESS...YOUR
GRANNY'S ARMPITS!**
—New York Post

**I FOUND JESUS
UNDER MY WALLPAPER**
—The Sun

*NUDIST WELFARE MAN'S
MODEL WIFE FELL FOR CHI-
NESE HYPNOTIST FROM THE
CO-OP BACON FACTORY*
—News of the World

**HOTCAKES NO LONGER
SELLING WELL**
—Weekly World News

OATMEAL PLANT BLOWS
UP; OMAHA BURIED IN ICKY
GOO
—National News Extra

*MOST UFOs LOOK LIKE
REGULAR PLANES!*
—Weekly World News

*GIRL SCALPED BY BERSERK
TORTILLA-MAKING MACHINE*
—National News Extra

I THOUGHT MY WIFE WAS
CHEATING WITH KEVIN
COSTNER...BUT I FOUND HER
WITH PRINCE ANDREW!
—The Star

*FOUNTAIN OF YOUTH
FOUND IN NYC SUBWAY
TOILET*
—Weekly World News

**HUBBY SUES EX: "GIVE
ME BACK MY KIDNEY!"**
—The Sun

DA VINCI'S ROBOT COMES TO
LIFE AFTER 500 YEARS
—Weekly World News

ELVIS IS DEAD!
—National Enquirer (2003)

Tough guy: An adult male gorilla can bench press about 4,000 pounds.

SAGAN SAYS

*Carl Sagan (1934–1996) was an outspoken
astronomer and author whose life's mission
was to explain the unexplainable.*

"In order to make an apple pie from scratch, you must first create the universe."

"The fact that some geniuses were laughed at does not imply that all who are laughed at are geniuses. They laughed at Columbus, they laughed at Fulton, they laughed at the Wright brothers. But they also laughed at Bozo the Clown."

"It is of interest to note that while some dolphins are reported to have learned English—up to 50 words used in correct context—no human being has been reported to have learned dolphinese."

"The universe is neither benign nor hostile—merely indifferent."

"We live in a society exquisitely dependent on science and technology, in which hardly anyone knows anything about science and technology."

"We are like butterflies who flutter for a day and think it's forever."

"Who are we? We find that we live on an insignificant planet of a humdrum star lost in a galaxy tucked away in some forgotten corner of a universe in which there are far more galaxies than people."

"If we long to believe that the stars rise and set for us, that we are the reason there is a universe, does science do us a disservice in deflating our conceits?"

"All of the books in the world contain no more information than is broadcast as video in a single large American city in a single year. Not all bits have equal value."

"In science it often happens that scientists say, 'You know, that's a really good argument; my position is mistaken,' and then they actually change their minds and you never hear that old view from them again. It happens every day, but I cannot recall the last time something like that happened in politics or religion."

NOT WHO THEY SEEMED TO BE

Have you ever lied about your age to get into a movie or stood on your tiptoes to be tall enough to get on a carnival ride? Here are some people who took "faking it" to extremes.

SUBJECT: Willie James Young, Jr., of Miami

POSING AS: Assistant principal of North Miami Middle School

NOT WHO HE SEEMED TO BE: Young had been working for the school district for 22 years, but according to police, his true career was dealing narcotics. Young, it turns out, was a distributor for the Luis Cano international drug ring, accused of selling more than $100 million worth of cocaine on American streets. The assistant principal gig? Just a cover.

CAUGHT! In 1998 Young was arrested by undercover Drug Enforcement Agency agents when he tried to buy 66 pounds of cocaine…just two blocks from his school. He later claimed that he only bought the drugs in order to get them off the street before dealers could sell them to kids. "I was going to take the stuff down to the North Miami Police Department," he explained.

But the DEA had been building their case against Young for months, and had even negotiated drug deals with him in his office at school. "Someone called in the middle of one meeting, and he told them he was in a parent conference," DEA spokesperson Pamela Brown told reporters. "Then he laughed about it [to me], saying it was a pretty good cover." Young was convicted and sentenced to 30 years in prison.

SUBJECT: Raul Cruz of Houston

POSING AS: Rita Fry

NOT WHO HE SEEMED TO BE: Rita Fry, a housewife, was actually Raul Cruz, a special education teacher at Woodson Middle School in Houston. Students at the school knew Cruz as a man, but neighbors had no inkling that Rita was anything but a woman.

And nobody (except for the cops, that is) knew that Cruz and the man he lived with were drug dealers.

CAUGHT! Police had Rita and her "husband," Jeffrey, under surveillance for more than two months before arresting them in September 1986 on charges of delivering cocaine to undercover police officers. "This bit about her being a man is absolutely incredible," next-door neighbor Eloise Saylor told the *Houston Chronicle*. "I just can't imagine her being a man. She will always be a she to me."

SUBJECT: Baldrick the cat, owned by Julie Coulthart, an English barmaid

POSING AS: Scruffy the cat

NOT WHO HE SEEMED TO BE: One morning in July 1991, Coulthart put the cat out and went off to work. But when she got home, Baldrick wasn't there to greet her. He didn't come home the following day, either, and after a couple of days, Coulthart assumed that he had run away or died. Not quite. Three weeks later, Baldrick turned up again, with a plaster cast on his leg. Where had he been? And who gave him the cast?

Coulthart assumed that some kind stranger must have taken Baldrick to the vet after he'd broken his leg, so she started going door to door, canvassing the neighborhood to see if she could find the Good Samaritan who had taken her cat to the vet.

CAUGHT! Three doors down she found her woman, Frances Orgee, and thanked her for taking care of her pet. "She said, 'That's *my* cat.' It turned out we had been sharing him for three years without either of us knowing," Coulthart reports. Baldrick— a.k.a. Scruffy—had been having breakfast at Orgee's at 6:00 a.m., then (after a nap on Orgee's bed) having lunch at Coulthart's, and then returning to Orgee's for another snack at 3:00 p.m.

"He had it all worked out," Coulthart says.

*   *   *

PURR-FECT GRAMMAR

What's the difference between a cat and a comma? One has the paws before the claws, and the other has the pause before the clause.

YOUR #1 NEWS SOURCE

From the news stream...

CAUGHT YELLOW-HANDED

"It wasn't tracks in the snow that helped police in Nevada break the case. It was the yellow snow. According to officers in Elko, a burglar relieved himself from the roof of a restaurant that he robbed, and the yellow snow yielded enough DNA to link Roger Gray to the scene. Investigators are now looking at his possible involvement in burglaries at a pizza place and a JC Penney."

—*azcentral.com*

PEE (FOR PESTICIDE)

"The *Times of India* newspaper reported in June 2003 that India is planning to export compost and pesticides made from the urine and dung of cows to the United States. The scheme, says the *Times*, is the brainchild of the Municipal Commission of Delhi, which has been trying to round up the 35,000 or so stray cattle on the streets of the Indian capital. According to authorities, the strays can produce enough urine and dung to yield 160,000 tons of vermicompost and 70,000 litres of biopesticide each day."

—**Agence France Presse English**

CHEERS!

"Cameroon health minister Urbain Olanguena Awono says people should forget about using urine for therapeutic purposes even though reports say it can cure 64 diseases. And Awono warns that people caught ingesting urine—which can be toxic—will be prosecuted. Supporters of urine therapy say it can cure hemorrhoids, ulcers, infertility and snakebites, among other things. Emile, who uses it for hemorrhoids, told *Le Messager* newspaper: 'Everyone uses it in secret. But you need to be brave—not everyone has the necessary courage.'"

—**United Press International**

I FOUND SOME GATORADE, MA!

"It's not a pretty sight, but plastic jugs filled with urine are becoming a common sight along highways, particularly at freeway inter-

---

There are 7,000 varieties of apple in the United States alone.

changes. 'You wonder what's happening in our society,' said Karen Cagle, who supervises highway cleanup crews in Eastern Washington. In 2002 one Adams County highway cleanup crew picked up 2,666 jugs of urine. That prompted Adams County Waste Reduction & Recycling to take out a full-page newspaper ad that features a photo of a plastic milk jug filled with urine, prefaced with a message: 'Okay, one last time: This is not a urinal.'"

—*The Tri-City Herald*

STRAIGHT FROM THE COW TO YOUR HOME

"Robert J. Wall and his Department of Agriculture team are the first researchers to genetically engineer animals that concentrate a pharmaceutical product in their urine. They have developed mice that produce human growth hormone in their bladders. Although the mice produce only a tiny amount, Wall says they show that urine farming techniques work. But collecting urine from farm animals may also prove challenging, researchers warn. Drug farmers may have to keep their herds attached to catheters."

—*Sciencenews.org*

URINE CANDID CAMERA

"Mystified by the recurring stench behind their garage, Wes and Heather Skakun used video surveillance equipment to catch their neighbor in the act of splashing a jug full of urine on the garage door. Robert Kukura, 60, pleaded guilty to mischief in provincial court and was ordered to pay $1,732 restitution. The Saskatoon couple thinks Kukura kept the urine in his sun-heated garage for many days between applications. 'He was saving it and letting it steep in the sun,' Skakun said."

—*National Post* (Ottawa)

THE LIVING MOP!

"Accountant Danny Miller considers his two Cockapoos his children. That's why he was particularly horrified when he watched a PETsMART groomer use his dog, Mocha, as a mop, wiping up a puddle of urine she had created. 'I was speechless,' he says. The store says the groomer was using a form of 'aversive training,' but was not acting in accordance with the store's philosophy of animal training. Miller received a refund on his $36 grooming charge for Mocha."

—*Phoenix* (Arizona) *New Times*

Internal revenue: In the 4th century, Rome levied a tax on urine and excrement.

BONEHEADS

What's the difference between horns and antlers?
Which animals have which? And why do they
have them? Inquiring minds want to know.

R ACK 'EM UP
Many different mammals in many parts of the world have
what is known as *headgear*—horns or antlers. All the
species that have them have unique varieties which grow in their
own special way: Some are straight as an arrow, some spiral like
vines, some are only inches long, and some weigh more than 40
pounds each. Nearly all headgear comes in the form of *true horns*
and *antlers*, but there are some rare exceptions: *keratin horns* and
pronghorns.

• **Horns** are found only on *bovids* such as cattle, sheep, goats and
antelopes. They are made of compressed *keratin*—the same thing
that human hair and fingernails are made of. True horns grow in a
single tine—they have no branches—and are permanent fixtures
that keep growing throughout the animal's life. In most species
they appear on both the male and the female.

• **Antlers** are found only on *cervids*, members of the deer family.
They are made of solid bone and always branch out to form several
tines or "points" (as in a five-point buck). While antlers are still
growing they're covered by a layer of soft, very sensitive skin,
known as *velvet*. The velvet contains veins and nerves that actually "grow" the antlers. They're the fastest growing bone on any animal—up to an inch a day on some species—and only the males
have them (the caribou is the one exception).

Antlers are *deciduous*. Just before mating season the velvet dries
up and the antlers stop growing. The animal scrapes off the dry
velvet on trees or bushes, and the antlers become hard and sharp.
After mating season the antlers fall off, and within a few months
they start growing again. Each year (on healthy animals) they will
grow a little larger.

• **Keratin horns** only appear on some species of rhinoceros. Just
like horns, they are permanent and appear on both sexes. They
don't grow in pairs—they jut out from the midline of the snout.

Whales don't have hips or legs, but they do have hip bones and leg bones.

• **Pronghorns** are only found on…the *pronghorn* (often called the *pronghorn antelope*, although it is not a true antelope) found in western North America. Their headgear is a unique mix of both horns and antlers. They have the bone core and the keratin sheath of a horn, but they're not permanent—the keratin falls off each year like antlers do, leaving only the bone core.

SO THAT'S WHY THEY CALL IT "HORNY"

The most important role of headgear: sex. It's no coincidence that antlers grow to prominence just in time for mating season and then fall off when the work is done. Males of nearly all species with headgear use it to fight off rivals for mates. It's usually done in harmless, ritualistic ways, but can sometimes get brutal and bloody. And sometimes the bull with the mightiest headgear doesn't even have to fight—his display alone can ward off contenders and impress the females.

Bambi Bites Back

All animals with headgear are *herbivores*, or plant-eaters; they are prey, not predators, which means they lack the sharp claws or teeth of carnivores. Their headgear is their weapon—nature's way of providing them with "teeth." Take the bull elk for example: his first instinct is to flee, but if necessary he will stand down a 150-pound mountain lion, with dagger-sharp antlers up to five feet across. (And not just lions: The elk at yellowstone National Park have been known to gore careless visitors. A few have even attacked automobiles, poking holes right through car doors with their antlers.)

Headgear can also be used for marking trees, digging in the ground for food, or scratching a hard-to-reach itch.

HEADGEAR STANDOUTS

• **The Moose** is the largest member of the deer family, often reaching seven feet at the shoulder. Every year the male grows a set of *palmate* antlers. They spread out like the palm of a hand with large flattened areas and tines sticking out of the flats. His anlters can span more than six feet, have as many as thirty spikes, and can weigh 40 pounds each.

• **Elk's** antlers grow to five feet, with six to ten spikes on each side. During mating season their battles get fairly violent: some stab wounds can kill outright or cause so much damage that the loser cannot escape from danger. Worst-case scenario: two bulls interlock their antlers and are unable to get them apart. Both animals will eventually die of starvation or be killed by predators.

• The **Indian Water Buffalo** has the longest horns of all. In 1955 a bull's horns were measured from tip to tip around their long, sweeping curve. Length: 13 feet, 11 inches.

• **Big Horn Sheep** have thick, stout horns that curve back around, beneath their ears, and then forward again. And the horns can weigh more than all the other bones in their bodies put together. Each mating season the males fight for social dominance, running into each other and bashing the thick bases of their horns together—at speeds of over 20 mph with a force of 2,000 pounds per square inch. Their battles can be heard up to a mile away.

• The **Chousinga** is a member of the true-horned bovid family, but instead of two horns, it has four. Also known as the four-horned antelope, this small creature lives in India and Nepal and grows an extra set of horns on its forehead, just above its eyes.

• **Giraffes** are unique: Their horns aren't covered with keratin—they're covered with skin.

GET TO THE POINT

• The Asian Musk Deer is one of the few members of the deer family that have no antlers. What do they have instead? Tusks—long, fang-like teeth that grow down over their lower jaw.

• Imagine seeing a tusked animal only 20 inches long that looks like a cross between a deer, antelope, and a pig. That's the mouse deer from Malaysia.

• The Irish Elk is the name given to an extinct species of deer. Their antlers measured over 13 feet across, and weighed up to one hundred pounds—each.

• Not only are all of the animals with headgear herbivores. They also share one other characteristic: they all have hooves.

• Animals with headgear are native to every continent except Antarctica and Australia. No native Australian mammals have antlers, horns, or hooves.

HUNTING FOR DVD EASTER EGGS

*Uncle John finally bought a DVD player, and now he's got
a new hobby: finding "Easter eggs"—deleted scenes,
alternate endings, bloopers, etc.—that are hidden
on many discs. Here are a few he's found.*

CITIZEN KANE (1941)

Easter Egg: From the main menu, choose "Special Features." Then click the right arrow on your remote control. When the *Rosebud* sled appears onscreen, press Enter.

What You Get: A five-minute interview with actress Ruth Warrick, who starred as Emily Kane

Bonus: Click on "Production Notes," then "In the Beginning," and then "Still Galleries." If you click on the sleds, you'll get two more bonus features: an interview with editor Robert Wise, and one with film critic Roger Ebert.

THE SIXTH SENSE (1999)

Easter Egg: From the main menu, choose "Bonus Materials," then click all the way down and choose "More." At the bottom of this page is a jewelry box. Click down to it—the lid will open, and you'll see an image of a videotape that says "Night's First Horror Film."

What You'll Get: A 1-1/2 minute horror film that director M. Night Shyamalan made when he was 11 years old

THE SIMPSONS: SEASON 1 BOX SET (1989)

Easter Egg: Insert the third disc. From the main menu, choose "Extra Features" and go to the second page. Click on "'Some Enchanted Evening' Script," press the left arrow key, then press Enter.

What You Get: Remember how controversial *The Simpsons* was when it first went on the air? This genuine 1990 TV news report will refresh your memory.

AUSTIN POWERS: THE SPY WHO SHAGGED ME (1999)

Easter Egg: From the main menu, choose "Special Features." Wait about 30 seconds until Dr. Evil's spaceship appears at the bottom of the screen and flies up to the top, leaving a big E in its wake. Click over to the E, and when it turns red, press Enter.

What You Get: A page called "Dr. Evil's Special Features" lets you view four hidden features, including a mock documentary called "The Dr. Evil Story"

THE GODFATHER (1972)—DVD COLLECTION

Easter Egg: Insert the fourth disc, the one labeled "Bonus Materials." From the main menu, choose "Setup," then press the right arrow. When the globe appears, press Enter.

What You Get: A few classic scenes dubbed into foreign languages

Bonus: Ever wondered what prompted author Mario Puzo to write the novel *The Godfather?* From the main menu, select "Filmmakers," and then select "Mario Puzo." Press the left arrow button twice—a dollar sign will appear, and when it does, press Enter. Puzo will answer the question while shooting a game of pool with Francis Ford Coppola.

PLANET OF THE APES (2001)

Easter Egg: Insert the first disc. From the main menu, choose "Special Features," and then click on "Commentaries." Press the down arrow two times, then press Enter.

What You Get: A film commentary—in ape language

CAST AWAY (2000)

Easter Egg: Pop in the second disc. From the main menu, choose "Video and Stills Galleries" and click down to "Raft Escape." *Don't* press Enter—instead, press the left arrow button. That will cause yellow and blue wings to appear on the left of the screen. Press Enter.

What You Get: Did you ever wonder what was in the FedEx package that Tom Hanks's character has with him the entire film? Press Play, and director Robert Zemeckis will give you the answer.

Bye-bye VHS: Since 1997, more than 2 billion DVDs have been sold in the U.S. alone.

MORE NICE CROOKS

We love dumb crooks, but lately we've
discovered another variety: nice ones.

THE SINGING DETECTIVE

In May 2004, an off-duty police detective named Dave Wishnowsky noticed Willie Mitford sitting in a karaoke bar in Palmerston North, New Zealand. Wishnowsky had worked a case that resulted in theft charges against Mitford, and Mitford had already beaten one of the charges. The detective went over to Mitford, and the two started chatting over a few beers. Before long, Mitford made a surprise offer: "You get up there and sing a song, and if you're good, I will go guilty." So Wishnowsky, who—unbeknownst to Mitford—was a former singer in a pub band, got up and started belting out "Better Man" by Robbie Williams. "I had only sung two lines," he said later, "and he came over to me and said 'I'm guilty.'" Mitford lived up to his word and changed his plea to guilty later that month because, he said, the singing cop was so good.

DON'T FORGET TO SAY "THANK YOU"

In January 2004, a man went into a Wells Fargo branch in Phoenix, Arizona, waited his turn in line, and walked up to the counter. "This is a robbery," he told the teller. "I need $1,500 in fifties, please." He made no threats and had no weapon. The teller gave him what she had and he strolled out the door. "It was like Emily Post does a bank robbery," said Officer Rick Tamburo.

CHECKING OUT

Nazareno Rodriguez and Sebastian Gallardo, two prisoners in Argentina who had been accused of robbery, were able to unscrew their jail cell door and make a middle-of-the-night escape. Police were surprised when they later found a note in the empty cell. "We love our freedom and can't live locked in," it read. "We're sorry for any inconvenience we might have caused you." "They were so cheeky," a police officer said. "We couldn't believe they left a note. But we'll find them!"

BAG MAN

A thief stole more than $207,000 from a London ATM machine …and seven days later returned $187,000 of it. Barclays bank employees found it in a garbage bag just inside their door. A bank spokesperson told *The Sun*, "We do offer cashback facilities but we didn't expect anything quite like this."

U R 2 NICE

Lee Alaban's car was stolen from outside her workplace in Port Macquarie, New South Wales, Australia. Later that night she realized that her son's cell phone was in the car, so she called the thief. He answered, but then quickly hung up. So she text-messaged him. She explained that the car was a gift from her now-deceased father, and that gifts for her 13-year-old son's birthday (which was the next day) were in the trunk. "Next thing I get this text saying he'll return the car," Alaban told news reporters. "I raced around to the carpark where he said he'd left it, and couldn't believe my eyes." The thief had returned her car (but kept the phone) and then text-messaged an apology. "I'm so sorry I was very desperate I didn't want 2 cause damage or pain in any way," he wrote. Alaban sent the man a final message: "Thanks 4 your apology. If I ever lock myself out of my car I'll send you a message. Ha ha ha."

AN ANNIVERSARY PRESENT

In May 2004, Lonnie and Tammy Crawford had just left a restaurant in Crestview, Florida, where they celebrated their 20th wedding anniversary, when an armed man appeared and demanded their money. They gave him the $8 they had on them and their cell phone, then noticed that the man seemed uneasy with the crime. "I could tell just by looking at him that he was having second thoughts," said Lonnie Crawford. The thief told them he had never robbed anybody before, he was just broke and wanted to get to his home in Georgia. Before long he had put the gun away, apologized, and given them back the phone and the money, but the couple refused to take the cash. They said he needed it more than they did. Restaurant employees called police, but they couldn't persuade the victims to press charges. "You could tell he was a nice person that had just made a mistake," they said.

Burrito is Spanish for "little donkey."

YOUNGEST & OLDEST

More examples of some folks who prove that age doesn't matter.

BASEBALL PLAYER
Youngest: Joe Nuxhall played one game for the Cincinnati Reds in 1944, just shy of his 16th birthday.
Oldest: Satchel Paige pitched for the Kansas City Athletics in 1965 at age 59.

MOTHER
Youngest: Lina Medina of Peru bore a child in 1939 at age 5.
Oldest: Satyabhama Mahapatra of India gave birth to a son in 2003 at the age of 65.

PERSON TO CLIMB MOUNT EVEREST
Youngest: Temba Tsheri of Nepal did it in 2001 at age 15.
Oldest: Yuichiro Miura of Japan did it in 2003 at age 70.

SCREENWRITER
Youngest: Nikki Reed co-wrote *thirteen* when she was 15.
Oldest: Arthur Miller wrote *The Crucible* at age 80.

OLYMPIAN
Youngest: Marjorie Gestring, a diver in the 1936 Olympics, was 13. (She won a gold medal.)
Oldest: Oscar Swahn, a shooter in the 1912 Olympics, was age 64. (He won one, too.)

COLLEGE GRADUATE
Youngest: Michael Kearney earned a degree from the University of South Alabama at the age of 10 years, 4 months.
Oldest: Ocie Tune King graduated from West Virginia University at 94.

WINNER OF THE NOBEL PRIZE FOR LITERATURE
Youngest: Rudyard Kipling won it in 1907 at the age of 42.
Oldest: Christian Matthias Theodor Mommsen became a laureate in 1902 at age 84.

BRITISH MONARCH
Youngest: King Henry VI was crowned in 1422, when he was 8 months old.
Oldest: Queen Victoria died in 1901 at the age of 81.

EMMY WINNING ACTOR
Youngest: Michael J. Fox won Best Lead Actor in a Comedy (*Family Ties*) in 1986 at age 25.
Oldest: Ruth Gordon won Best Lead Actress in a Comedy (*Taxi*) in 1979 at age 82.

U.S. PRESIDENT
Youngest: John F. Kennedy was just 43 when he took office.
Oldest: Ronald Reagan was 69.

Largest rodent in North America: the beaver. The porcupine is second.

WOMEN IN SPACE, PART II

Here's the second installment of our story on the 13 American women with "the right stuff" to become astronauts in the early 1960s. (Part I is on page 179.)

FLAT BROKE

By communicating its lack of interest in women astronauts, NASA effectively scuttled the FLAT program in 1962, at least for the time being. The official explanation was that the space agency would only consider military test pilots with extensive experience flying jet aircraft. And since women were excluded from flying jets in the military (not to mention the airlines), they couldn't qualify. Experience, not gender, was the determining factor, NASA claimed.

In truth, however, NASA's ban on women was motivated by a fear that the space program would be irreparably harmed if a woman died in space. "Had we lost a woman back then because we decided to fly a woman rather than a man, we would have been castrated," Mercury Program flight director Chris Kraft admitted years later.

REFUSING TO QUIT

All of the Mercury 13 women had made tremendous sacrifices to get this far—Sarah Gorelick and Gene Nora Stumbough had quit their jobs, and Jerrie Sloan's husband divorced her when she refused to drop out of the program. After all the trouble they'd been through, they didn't want to take no for an answer.

Janey Hart, married to Senator Philip Hart of Michigan, decided that she could no longer keep her promise to Dr. Lovelace to remain silent. She started working her connections in Washington, D.C., writing letters to each member of the congressional space committees. She released a copy of the letter to the press and, with Jerrie Cobb, began giving interviews to reporters. Hart also managed to arrange a meeting with Vice President Lyndon Johnson, who was head of the President's Space Council and the White

---

Early guns took so long to load and fire that a bow and arrow was 12 times more efficient.

House's liaison with NASA. Johnson listened politely to Hart and Cobb, and then brushed them off by telling them that while he wanted to help, it was NASA's responsibility to decide who became an astronaut, not his. With that, he ended the meeting and had the two women shown out of his office. After they left, Johnson scrawled a note to his staff: "Let's Stop This Now!"

LAST CHANCE

The meeting with LBJ had gone nowhere, but Hart and Cobb kept pushing. Result: In June 1962, the House of Representatives Committee on Science and Astronautics announced that it would hold three days of subcommittee hearings to investigate whether NASA discriminated against women. A total of six witnesses would be called—three representing the Mercury 13 and three representing NASA.

But that wasn't quite how it worked out. Hart and Cobb were selected to be two of the witnesses for the Mercury 13. The third witness was an aviator named Jacqueline "Jackie" Cochran.

WITNESS FOR THE PROSECUTION

You've probably never heard of Jackie Cochran, but in the early 1960s, she was the most famous female pilot in the world. She'd broken more speed, distance, and altitude records than any female pilot alive, and was the first woman to break the sound barrier. Yet she opposed the continued testing of the Mercury 13.

Cochran had initially supported the FLAT project and even financed the first phase of testing at the Lovelace clinic. Since then, however, she had turned against the program. Why? One theory: She could never be an astronaut herself. Cochran was in her mid-50s and had tested poorly during her physical at the Lovelace clinic. That ruled her out as a potential candidate, and that's when she began to oppose the Mercury 13. Perhaps the most famous female aviator since Amelia Earhart did not want to be overshadowed by the first women in space.

HAVING THEIR SAY

On the first day of the hearings, Cobb and Hart testified in favor of testing the women. Then it was Cochran's turn. And just as Cobb and Hart had feared, Cochran told the committee that there was "no shortage of well-trained and long-experienced male pilots to serve as astronauts," and that adding women to the mix would "slow down our [space] program and waste a great deal of money."

On the second day of testimony, the committee questioned George Low, NASA's director of spacecraft and flight missions, and then questioned astronauts John Glenn and Scott Carpenter. None of the men were receptive to the idea of allowing women into their ranks. Like Cochran, Glenn argued that testing women for the space program was a waste of money, since NASA had already spent millions of dollars training men for the job and had all the astronauts it needed. "The men go off and fight the wars and fly the airplanes and come back and help design and build and test them," Glenn said. "The fact that women are not in this field is a fact of our social order."

THE END

The hearings were scheduled to last for three days, but shortly before noon on the second day, Congressman Victor Anfuso of New York, who chaired the hearings, banged his gavel and called the proceedings to a close. He had collected enough information to write his report, he explained, so no further testimony was necessary.

"NASA's program of selection is basically sound," the final report stated, acknowledging that at "some time in the future" NASA should revisit the possibility of conducting "research to determine the advantages to be gained by utilizing women as astronauts."

The Mercury 13 program was over, this time for good.

WE'RE (NOT) #1

Less than a year later, on June 16, 1963, Soviet cosmonaut Valentina Tereshkova, a mill worker and parachuting hobbyist, became the first woman in space. How much longer would it take an *American* woman to make the same trip? Twenty years.

In 1983 physicist Sally Ride became the first when she made a six-day flight on the space shuttle *Challenger*. But Ride was a flight engineer, and did not pilot the shuttle. The first woman to command a space shuttle mission was Lieutenant Colonel Eileen

Collins, who piloted the *Columbia* into orbit in 1999—nearly 40 years after the first Mercury space mission.

UPDATE

Where are the Mercury 13 now? Some have passed away, others are still flying, and two of them—Jerrie Cobb and Wally Funk—still hope to fly in space.

When 77-year-old John Glenn returned to space aboard the space shuttle in October 1998 as part of a scientific study on the effects of aging, Cobb's supporters launched a campaign to get her included on a future mission. At the time, NASA officials said they still have no plans to send Cobb into space, and the grounding of the entire space shuttle program following the *Columbia* disaster in 2003 makes her chances even more remote.

Wally Funk, now 64, isn't waiting for NASA to come around. Over the years, she has completed her astronaut testing at her own expense, even traveling to Russia in 2000 to train with Russian cosmonauts. She is currently working as a test pilot for Interorbital Systems, a California-based company that plans to launch privately owned, privately funded spacecraft. "I'm still pedaling! I never lost the faith," she told the *Los Angeles Times* in January 2004. "Whether we make it with Interorbital or not, I'm going to make it. I don't know how, but I know it's going to happen."

* * *

UNCLE JOHN'S PUZZLER

Using only one straight line, make this equation true.

5 + 5 + 5 = 550

(One possible answer is to add a line through the equal sign so it becomes a "does not equal" sign, but there is a much more clever solution than that.)

Answer:

Add a line to the first plus sign so it becomes a 4. 545 + 5 = 550

Do they hold their nose? Elephants fart more than any other animal.

NUDES & PRUDES

*Once again, we bare all to bring you
all the news that's fit to print.*

NUDE...In February 2004, a Madison, Maine, business-man named Normand St. Michel announced he was having second thoughts about opening a topless coffee shop, even after the planning board approved his business application. Why the change of heart? St. Michel started to worry about "the potential danger of semi-nude waitresses serving hot coffee."

PRUDE... The Indonesian parliament introduced an amendment to the country's anti-pornography bill that would make kissing in public punishable by a $29,000 fine and up to five years in jail. "I think there must be some restrictions on such acts," said Aisyah Hamid Baidlowi, head of the committee that introduced the bill. "They are against our traditions of decency."

NUDE... In April 2004, the Yamato Wind Village restaurant in Kunming, China, announced a promotion in which it planned to serve sushi on the bodies of naked women, but health officials banned the event before it could take place. "Some residents were indignant, claiming that it is humiliating to women," the *China Daily* newspaper reported, "but others were curious and tempted to have a try."

PRUDE... In 1999 school officials in two Georgia school districts spent two entire weeks applying touch-up paint to a picture of the famous painting "Washington Crossing the Delaware" in more than 2,300 fifth-grade social studies textbooks. Why? They feared that kids would mistake the ornamental orbs of Washington's pocket watch, which lay across his right thigh in the painting, for his family jewels. "I know what it is and I know what it is supposed to be," said Muscogee County Schools Superintendent Guy Sims. "But I also know fifth-grade students and how they might react to it."

NUDE... In May 2004, 60 partiers on Austin's Lake Travis capsized their double-decker party barge, known as Club Fred. The cause of the accident is still under investigation. One theory: According to onlookers, the boat started to tip over when everyone aboard crowded over to one side to gawk at the sunbathers at Hippie Hollow, the only nude beach in Texas.

PRUDE... In May 2004, Louisiana state representative Derrick Shepherd introduced legislation to criminalize the wearing of low-slung pants or any other clothing "that intentionally exposes undergarments or any portion of the pubic hair, cleft of buttocks, or genitals." While reading the bill, Representative Shepherd was repeatedly interrupted by laughter, catcalls, and by Representative Tommy Wright's chants of "No more crack! No more crack!"

NUDE... Indianapolis police arrested Erica Meredith, 25, as she was picking up her eight-year-old daughter at school in January 2004. The charge: "Disseminating matter harmful to minors," a felony punishable by up to three years in prison and a $10,000 fine. The crime: She was driving her boyfriend's car, which had a three-by-five-foot painting of a naked woman airbrushed on the hood. The prosecutor dropped the charges after the boyfriend agreed to airbrush a bikini onto the painting.

BONUS: PRUDISH NUDISTS!

• Desert Shadows Inn Resort and Villas, a nude resort in Palm Springs, California, has installed a $500,000, 110-foot-long bridge over a busy street that separates nudist condominiums from the rest of the resort. Now nudists can cross the street without being gawked at by passing cars.

• Nudists at Wreck Beach in Vancouver, Canada, are up in arms over a plan by the University of British Columbia to build two 20-story dorms on the cliffs above the beach. Nudists worry that privacy will vanish when college students are able to spy on them with binoculars and Web cams. University vice president Dennis Pavlich says they don't need to worry—the university's board members have to sign off on the dorm plans, and they aren't about to sign off on housing that provides a view of the beach. "All that's been approved so far is the concept," he says.

Q & A:
ASK THE EXPERTS

*Here are more answers to life's important questions
from the people who know—trivia experts.*

SPILT MILK

Q: *Why does milk turn sour?*
A: "Because bacteria grow in it. If you were to boil milk and put it in a sterile container, it *couldn't* turn sour, because the boiling and sterilization would have killed the bacteria. In America, most milk is *pasteurized*—heated to 145 degrees Fahrenheit for a period of 30 minutes. This process kills those bacteria known to be harmful to humans. Some bacteria survive the heat, but these aren't harmful to humans. Still, if you don't keep your milk in a cool place, it is these bacteria which will turn it sour. Most people don't like the taste, but fresh clean milk which has gone sour is not harmful." (From *A Book of Curiosities*, by Roberta Kramer)

YOU'RE THE TOP

Q: *Why do chefs wear those funny-looking hats?*
A: "A chef's hat is tall and balloons at the top so as to counteract the intense heat in the kitchen; the unique shape allows air to circulate around the scalp, keeping the head cool." (From *Who Knew?*, by David Hoffman)

SHATTERED

Q: *Can you really break a wineglass by singing?*
A: "Yes, it really can happen. Sound does special things to objects as it bumps into them. Depending on how fast the sound vibrates, it can even make them move. When an object is pushed by sound and continues to be pushed so that it exaggerates its natural rhythm, resonance occurs. All hard substances have what is called *resonant frequency*. Glass has a high frequency, which means that only a very high sound can break it. No musical instrument or human voice can produce a pure note, but female singers' top notes are claimed to be higher than the resonant frequency of glass, and in the right combi-

nation are strong enough to break certain kinds, particularly delicate wineglasses." (From *Why?*, by Eric Laithwaite)

FLAKING IT

Q: *How do they know that no two snowflakes are alike?*

A: "There are sound scientific reasons why this is so. Every snowflake starts out looking pretty much the same: a simple hexagonal crystal that forms on a particle of dust. But as it falls through a cloud, it grows and changes form dramatically. Depending on how cold and moist it is inside the cloud, a snowflake can assume many different shapes. And then as it descends, it tends to grow one way, then another, building on itself in an endlessly complex pattern. Says John Hallett of the Desert Research Institute in Reno, 'Two snowflakes would look alike if they followed the exact same trajectory as they fell through the sky—but they don't.'" (From *Why Moths Hate Thomas Edison*, edited by Hampton Sides)

VACUUM-WHACKED

Q: *In the movies, people explode when they're sucked out into the vacuum of space. Would this really happen?*

A: "Here on Earth, at sea level, the air is squeezing our bodies at a pressure of about one kilogram per square centimeter. The higher you go, the less pressure there is squeezing your body. If you go out into space, there is no pressure at all. You become, basically, a bag of skin containing the fluids and gases that are inside. In the movies, they exaggerate the effect, but as the pressure of the air is released, all of the gases that are dissolved in your blood are going to bubble out. While your body wouldn't explode, the fluids would start to form bubbles in your blood vessels and this would cause damage. You'd have a fatal case of the bends, and you'd be done for." (From *Quirks and Quarks Question Book*, released by CBC Radio One)

*　　　*　　　*

RIDDLE ME THIS

Q: What singular English word becomes plural when you add an "s", but singular again when you add another "s"?

A: Prince. (Prince + s = princes. Princes + s = princess.)

Small comfort: Short people typically outlive tall people.

MADE IN CANADA

A few random origins, eh?

BOB AND DOUG MCKENZIE

SCTV was a popular Canadian comedy show similar to *Saturday Night Live*. In 1975 the show's producer told writers Rick Moranis and Dave Thomas to come up with a two-minute skit with "identifiable Canadian content." They thought that was a ridiculous idea, so as a spoof, they created a fictional talk show, *The Great White North*, featuring the fictional McKenzie Brothers, two beer-drinking tuque-wearing losers, as hosts. They put in every Canadian stereotype they could think of, and it was an immediate hit. *The Great White North* made Moranis and Thomas international stars. As Bob and Doug, they recorded a million-selling album, starred in a spin-off movie, and were made members of the Order of Canada for their "contributions to Canadian culture."

CANADA'S NATIONAL COLORS

During the Crusades (1095–1291), European soldiers wore cloth crosses as badges. French soldiers wore red crosses; the English wore white. When Canada created its coat of arms in 1921, it was made red and white to reflect both its English and French heritage. The red-and-white maple leaf flag was adopted in 1965.

TIM HORTONS

Tim Horton was the Toronto Maple Leafs' star defenseman for 17 years and helped the team win four Stanley Cups. In 1964 he invested in a small doughnut shop in Hamilton, Ontario. He continued to play hockey while his business partner Ron Joyce gradually expanded the shop into a large chain. In 1974 Horton died in a car accident, and soon after Joyce bought out the Horton family's stake in the chain. But Joyce kept the name: by then it was a household word. Today, there are approximately 2,400 Tim Hortons doughnut shops in Canada—one shop for every 12,500 people. That's more per capita than there are outlets of Starbucks, Krispy Kreme, Dunkin Donuts, and McDonald's in the United States *combined.*

The brain continues to send electrical wave signals up to 37 hours after death.

CLOSE THE LID

When Uncle John was a kid, Mama John used to tell him to lower the toilet lid before he flushed. "Why?" he'd ask. "Because I said so," she'd answer. Here's an even better reason—the "aerosol effect."

THE FOUNTAIN

Every time you flush the toilet with the lid open, hundreds of tiny water droplets spray out of the bowl, traveling as far as eight feet in an invisible cloud, carrying with them millions of viruses and bacteria. Scientists refer to it as the "aerosol effect."

Everything in the bathroom is affected: the toilet (lid, seat, and handle), toilet paper, floor, walls, and ceiling—often neglected during cleaning, which allows bacteria to thrive for months, even years—and anything else within range, including your toothbrush. Even if you wash your hands immediately, germs can land on you and stay there until your next shower. You also run the risk of inhaling the airborne particles (which can stay in the air for more than two hours) and having them settle in your lungs.

University of Arizona biologist Charles Gerba has spent 20 years studying the aerosol effect. He analyzes dishrags and sponges from homes, washcloths from hotels, and towels from swimming pools. Some germs that can be spread with an open-lid flush: E.coli and shigella bacteria, streptococcus, staphylococcus, hepatitis A, and the common cold, to name a few. You're most likely to find them under the toilet seat or in the sink, where it's moist.

TRY THIS AT HOME

According to Gerba, you can test the aerosol effect on your toilet at home. Put a colorful yet harmless substance (such as mouthwash or food coloring) in your toilet bowl. Flush the toilet, holding a piece of white paper over the bowl at different levels and angles to see exactly where and how far your toilet water travels.

The best way to avoid the aerosol effect: put the lid down like your mother told you, says Gerba. What about in public restrooms where there are no lids? Relax—it's a toilet, not a landmine. Wash your hands with soap and water and you'll be fine. (But it might not hurt to hold your breath while you're in there, too.)

First time the sound of a flushing toilet was heard on the big screen: *Psycho* (1960).

THE GREAT SEATTLE WINDSHIELD EPIDEMIC

One of Uncle John's favorite movies is the 1956 classic Invasion of the Body Snatchers. *So imagine his horror (and delight) when he found this article by Alan J. Stein about an incident that occurred in Washington in 1954. Stein's acccount, which appeared in Seattle's* History Ink, *is remarkably similar to the movie plot. The only difference: this one really happened.*

IT BEGINS

The strange phenomenon started in late March, 1954, when tiny pits in automobile windshields were first reported to police in the northwestern Washington community of Bellingham. The small size of the pits led police officers to believe that the damage had been the work of vandals using buckshot or BBs. Then, within a week, a few residents in Sedro Woolley and Mount Vernon, 25 miles south of Bellingham, also began noticing damage to their windshields. By the second week of April, the "vandals" had attacked farther south in the town of Anacortes on Fidalgo Island. Losing no time, all available law enforcement officers in the area sped to town in the hope of apprehending the culprits. Roadblocks were set up south of town, and all cars leaving or entering the city were given a detailed once-over, as were their drivers and passengers.

To no avail.

THEY'RE GETTING CLOSER!

Farther south, cars at the Whidbey Island Naval Air Station in Oak Harbor were discovered to have the same mysterious dings. Nearly 75 Marines made an intensive five-hour search of the station looking for evidence—anything that might lead to the source of the mystery. They came up empty, yet by the end of the day, more than 2,000 cars from Bellingham to Oak Harbor were reported as having been damaged.

Two things became abundantly clear: This could not be the work of roving hooligans; and whatever was causing windshield pits and dings was rapidly approaching Seattle.

SEATTLE UNDER SIEGE

On the morning of April 14, Seattle newspapers ran front-page reports of the events that had transpired to the north. The afternoon papers carried similar stories. At 6 p.m. a report came in to Seattle police that three cars had been damaged in a lot at 6th Avenue and John Street. At 9 p.m. a motorist reported that his windshield had been hit at North 82nd Street. Then the floodgates opened.

Motorists began stopping police cars on the street to report windshield damage. Parking lots and auto sales lots were hit. Even police cars parked in front of precinct stations suffered damage. Extra clerks were brought into the stations to answer the flurry of calls from angry and perplexed car owners. By the next morning, windshield pitting had reached epidemic levels.

GLASS MENAGERIE

The sheer number of the damaged windshields ruled out hoodlums, and experts couldn't explain these strange pits and holes appearing out of nowhere. On Whidbey Island, Sheriff Tom Clark postulated that radioactivity released by recent H-bomb tests in the South Pacific was peppering windshields. Geiger counters were run over windshield glass, but all were free of radioactivity. Still, the sheriff held firm that "no human agency" could have created the scars on the glass. Other theories abounded:

• Some thought that the Navy's new million-watt radio transmitter at Jim Creek near Arlington was converting electronic oscillations to physical oscillations in the glass. Navy Commander George Warren called this theory "completely absurd."

• Cosmic rays bombarding the Earth from the sun were considered, but since so little was known about cosmic rays, this theory could be neither proved nor refuted.

• A mysterious atmospheric event was theorized (although no one could explain exactly what kind that would be).

•A few people reported seeing the glass bubble right before their eyes, leading some to postulate that sand-flea eggs had somehow been laid in the glass and were now hatching.

• Alternative suggestions: supersonic sound waves, non-radioactive coral debris from nuclear bomb tests, or a shift in the Earth's magnetic field. Other folks simply blamed the event on gremlins.

A *gamomaniac* is someone obsessed with proposing marriage. Now will you marry me?

SAVE US, IKE!

By April 15, 1954, police were swamped with calls. Close to 3,000 windshields had been reported as being pitted, and no one knew what to do. Desperate, Seattle Mayor Allan Pomeroy first wired Washington Governor Langlie, and then President Eisenhower.

> What appeared to be a localized outbreak of vandalism in damaged auto windshields and windows in northern Washington State has now spread throughout the Puget Sound area. Chemical analysis of mysterious powder adhering to damaged windshields and windows indicates the material may simply be spread by wind and not a police matter at all. Urge appropriate agencies be instructed to cooperate with local authorities on emergency basis.

Governor Langlie contacted the University of Washington asking a committee of scientists to investigate the phenomenon. The experts (from the environmental research laboratory, the applied physics laboratory, and the chemistry, physics, and meteorology departments) did a quick survey of 84 cars on the campus. They found the damage to be "overly emphasized," and most likely "the result of normal driving conditions in which small objects strike the windshields of cars." The fact that most cars were pitted in the front and not the back lent credence to their theory.

"Tommyrot!" remarked Dr. D. M. Ritter, a U. of W. chemist, after inspecting windshields and residue found on some of the cars. "There isn't anything I know of that could be causing any unusual breaks in windshields. These people must be dreaming."

PITFALLS

King County Sheriff Harlan Callahan disagreed. His deputies examined 15,000 cars throughout the county, and found damage to more than 3,000 of them. The sheriff and his deputies felt that this level of damage could not be explained by ordinary road use. They also claimed they'd found odd little pellets near some of the cars, and that the pellets reacted "violently" when a lead pencil was placed next to them. (Nobody knew what this meant, though.)

But further investigation by the Seattle Police Department disproved the deputies' claims. The police determined that most of the dings pitted the windshields of older cars. In cases where auto lots were involved, brand-new cars were unpitted; used cars were.

The Dead Sea contains about 11,600,000,000 tons of salt.

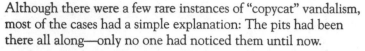

Although there were a few rare instances of "copycat" vandalism, most of the cases had a simple explanation: The pits had been there all along—only no one had noticed them until now.

The same reasoning applied to particulate matter found on windshield glass and near cars. It wasn't radioactive debris, it was coal dust. These tiny particles had been drifting through Seattle's air for years, only no one had ever looked closely at them before. And although the coal dust particles had nothing to do with the pitting, the populace at large finally noticed them—just as they noticed the window dings—for the very first time. Sergeant Max Allison of the Seattle Police crime laboratory declared that all the damage reports were "5 per cent hoodlum-ism, and 95 per cent public hysteria." Puget Sound residents had become participants in a collective delusion.

And by April 17, 1954, pitting incidents abruptly ceased.

ONE FOR THE BOOKS

The Seattle Windshield Pitting Epidemic of 1954 became a textbook example of collective delusion, sometimes referred to as "mass hysteria." To this day, sociologists and psychologists refer to the incident in their courses and writings alongside similar events, such as Orson Welles's *War of the Worlds* Martian invasion panic of 1938, and sightings of the "Jersey Devil" in 1909.

The Seattle pitting incident has all the key factors, including ambiguity, the spread of rumors and false but plausible beliefs, mass media influence, recent geopolitical events, and the reinforcement of false beliefs by authority figures (in this case, the police, military, and political figures). This combination of factors—added to the simple fact that for the first time people actually looked *at* their windshields instead of *through* them—caused the hubbub. No vandals. No atomic fallout. No sand fleas. No cosmic rays. No electronic oscillations. Just a bunch of window dings that were there from the start.

You probably have them on your car right now...but please don't alert the media or your local police.

WINSTON CHURCHILL'S DIRTY BIRD

This tweet little tale combines some of Uncle John's favorite themes:
historical figures, gullible reporters, and talking animals.

POTTY-MOUTH

Sir Winston Churchill, Great Britain's prime minister during World War II, died in 1965 at the age of 90. So it was big news in January 2004 when his parrot, Charlie, a 104-year-old blue and gold macaw, was discovered alive and well living in a garden store in Reigate, a town south of London. The foul-mouthed fowl was still cursing "@#$& Hitler!" and "@#$& the Nazis," just as Churchill had taught it to do so many years ago. Even in the darkest days of the war, the bird could always be counted on to shock important visitors and bring a smile to Churchill's face with its obscene tirades against the Führer.

That was the story the nursery's owner, Peter Oram, told reporters, anyway.

IT'S TRUE...I SWEAR

Oram claims that his father-in-law sold Churchill the parrot in 1937, and then took it back when Churchill passed away. For a time the bird lived in Oram's pet store, but he had to take it home after it kept swearing at children. The story attracted the attention of Churchill historians, who immediately went to work looking for more information on Charlie.

What did they find? Nothing. No documentation, no photographs, and not even one person who remembers an opinionated talking macaw.

"My father never owned a macaw or anything remotely resembling it," Churchill's 81-year-old daughter, Mary Soames, told the press. "The idea that he spent time in the war teaching it to swear is too tiresome for words." But despite all proof to the contrary, Oram still insists that Charlie—who he also claims is the oldest bird in England—was once Churchill's. At last report Charlie was still alive and well...and still swearing at Hitler.

ROLE MODELS

When you were growing up, did anyone ever tell you, "Do as I say, not as I do"? For these folks, it's a code they live by.

Role Model: Drug Enforcement Administration agent
Setting an Example: The agent—whose name was not released—gave a gun safety demonstration to a group of 50 adults and children in Orlando, Florida. He removed the magazine from the gun, pulled back the slide, and asked an audience member to look inside to be sure the gun wasn't loaded. Then the agent accidentally released the slide and—BANG!—shot himself in the thigh. The good news: The demonstration had the desired effect. "The kids screamed and started to cry," says Vivian Farmer, who brought her 13-year-old nephew to the demonstration. "After seeing that, my nephew doesn't want to have anything to do with guns."

Role Model: Dr. Paul Agutter, lecturer on medical ethics at England's Manchester University
Setting an Example: The university fired Dr. Agutter after learning that he had served seven years in prison for attempting to murder his wife. In 1994 Agutter spiked his wife's gin and tonic with the drug atropine, then tried to cover his tracks by poisoning several bottles of tonic and putting them on the shelves of the local supermarket. Agutter's wife survived because her drink tasted funny and she stopped drinking after just a few sips. Her husband was caught when security camera tapes showed him placing the poisoned bottles on store shelves. "The university has decided not to offer Dr. Agutter a further contract of employment," a school official told reporters.

Role Model: Dennis O'Neil, a priest in southern California
Setting an Example: A Los Angeles jury awarded more than $950,000 to Maria Vega, a Sunday school teacher who accused Father Dennis of punching her in the head because he disapproved of the way she was teaching catechism. "Mrs. Vega is Catholic and shouldn't be punched by a priest, particularly in front of her students," Vega's attorney told reporters.

Roll of a lifetime: Vivien Leigh used her Oscar as a toilet paper holder.

Role Model: Pastor Jerry Hayes, 53, a Pentecostal minister in Hartford, Maine

Setting an Example: Pastor Hayes was sentenced to six and a half years in prison after pleading guilty to robbing five banks during a three-month crime spree. (Total haul: $13,309.) Prosecutors say he laundered the money through church bank accounts, then spent it on things like a camper, a car, and the .38-caliber revolver used in some of the heists. Pastor Hayes was literally caught red-handed during the fifth robbery, when an anti-theft dye pack exploded in his bag of money as he was fleeing the scene.

Role Model: Bob Bateman, a councilman in Weston-super-Mare, England

Setting an Example: Bateman racked up the equivalent of $460 in traffic fines in a single day in early 2004 after traffic cameras photographed him breaking the speed limit four times in two hours on the same stretch of road. Bateman blames the cameras, which he says serve no public safety purpose. "If these cameras are used in areas where there's a history of accidents, that's fine, but otherwise they are just there to create revenue," he says. Incidentally, Bateman sits on the council that decides where the traffic cameras should be placed.

Role Models: Bishop William Ellis of the Apostolic Pentecostal Church of Morgan Park, Illinois; and Father Arthur LaPore of St. Anthony's Catholic Church in Joliet, Illinois

Setting an Example: Federal prosecutors charged Bishop Ellis with skimming $1,000 a week from Sunday offerings, as well as using church credit cards and bank accounts for personal reasons. Total haul: Hundreds of thousands of dollars over a four-year period. Prosecutors say he blew the money on trips, clothes, and a second Mercedes to go with the one his church had already bought him.

That same month, they charged Father LaPore with misappropriating $24,860 of church funds, *plus* skimming an additional $100 a week from collection plates and $2,700 from parish spaghetti dinner fundraisers. Father LaPore used the money to buy a $537,000 house. When suspicious parishioners couldn't figure out how he could afford such an expensive home on his priestly salary, they called the police. Prosecutors say the two cases are unrelated.

Loud noise, aspirin, caffeine, and quinine can all cause tinnitus (ringing in the ears).

A DAY IN PALINDROMIA

Our readers seem to love palindromes, words or phrases that are spelled the same forward and backward. So, on a recent trip to the BRI archives, we pulled out some of our favorite palindromes and used them to create this silly story. There are 52 hidden here (not including doubles). Can you find them all? (Answers are on page 518.) Good luck!

OTTO
One day a zoologist named Otto paddled his kayak to Los Angeles, eating a banana sandwich. He had heard there was something amiss with the animals there and wanted to help. When Otto reached the shore, a familiar voice called out, "Yo, Banana Boy, what's happening?" Otto looked up and saw his old friend Ed, a general, a renegade who had left the military. General Ed was standing next to his new race car—a Toyota with attitude.

"Wow!" said Otto. "Nice wheels!"

"Yeah, but if I had a hi-fi stereo with a DVD player, it would be perfect," replied Ed. "Hey, want a ride?"

"Sure," said Otto, and the two friends headed downtown.

"Pull up, pull up!" yelled Otto as they passed a newsstand. Ed got out and bought the afternoon edition. The headline read "L.A. Ocelots Stole Coal." Otto read aloud: "Authorities believe the ocelots are being controlled by a giant mutant rat who calls himself King Ognik. Injected with a 'pure evil' gene, Ognik had grown to the size of a yak and escaped the lab. Whereabouts: unknown."

GNU DUNG

The two men were pondering the story when Ed caught something out of the corner of his eye. "Was it a rat I saw?" he asked. Sure enough, there was a yak-sized rat waddling into the L.A. Zoo. "You're on your own, Otto," said Ed. "I'm outta here."

Even though Ed is on no side, thought Otto, his military experience could help. "You have to stay. We must capture that oozy rat in a sanitary zoo and stop him before he infects the other animals!"

Ed paused, then remembered his duty. "I will help you, but we need a battle cry." So Otto made Ed a motto: "Now, sir, a war is won." The two warriors then followed the giant rat into the zoo.

When they were near the entrance, Otto warned, "Make very sure that you step on no pets." Too late—General Ed walked into a pile of irradiated gnu dung. It started creeping up his leg. Ed screamed but could not move.

"Can't go on," Ed said, frothing at the mouth and babbling incoherently. "I am lonely. Tylenol won't help me now."

KING OGNIK

Otto, not knowing what else to do, left his friend and entered the zoo. It was the strangest place he'd ever been. Completely devoid of humans, the animals had free reign. To Otto's right, there was a pride of senile felines fighting over a bird rib. One of the crazy cats looked at him and then ran away. To his left, he saw a llama mall complete with llama stores and llama customers. And down a dark pathway, Otto spotted King Ognik. It looked like some sort of laminated E.T. animal as it ran into a building marked "DNA Land." Otto followed Ognik into a large room, where the rat sat regally on a throne made of stack cats. Behind Ognik were lots of ocelots holding stolen coal, fueling a cauldron.

"Aha!" said King Ognik, "I knew there would be at least one human brave—and stupid—enough to confront me. I have infected these animals to do my evil bidding. Now you are all that I need to enslave the human race!"

"You dirty rat," said Otto. "You'll never get away with it!"

"Oh yes I will. Meet my sergeant at arms, Sara Sim." Out walked an armor-clad ewe with one giant eye. She was pointing a gun at Otto. "Now," the king continued, "You will take this bar crab to the llama mall and go to a store called Strapgod's Dog Parts. Then swap for I, a pair of paws. You either borrow or rob it, I don't care. You see, after the dog paws touch human DNA, they will mix in with this lion oil, thus completing the creation of my vile virus, which will end your insignificant reign on this planet! Miss Sim will accompany you while I prepare a huge party to celebrate the end of humanity. Now go!"

STRAPGOD'S DOG PARTS

They left DNA Land just as all of the animals were gathering for the party. "Don't make a peep," ordered Miss Sim. Otto was led into the llama mall, past a store called the Tangy Gnat, and then

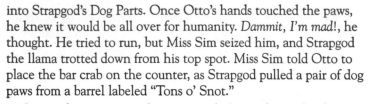

into Strapgod's Dog Parts. Once Otto's hands touched the paws, he knew it would be all over for humanity. *Dammit, I'm mad!*, he thought. He tried to run, but Miss Sim seized him, and Strapgod the llama trotted down from his top spot. Miss Sim told Otto to place the bar crab on the counter, as Strapgod pulled a pair of dog paws from a barrel labeled "Tons o' Snot."

Just as the paws were about to touch Otto's skin, a familiar voice shouted in from the store's entrance: "Yo, Banana Boy, need some help?" Otto and Miss Sim spun around. It was General Ed, and he had a huge shopping cart full of TNT! It was not a ton of dynamite, but more than enough to blow the zoo sky high. "Let him go, you ewe. If you refuse, I'll light this fuse right now!"

MAPS, DNA, AND SPAM

Miss Sim released Otto and ran toward the exit to warn the rat king, but General Ed captured her and tied her to the cart. Then Otto stepped up and said to her, "Go deliver a dare, vile dog. Tell your deified demigod that his diseased days of diabolical destruction are done! Not even a rat can live forever of evil."

Otto lit the fuse on the TNT, and General Ed pushed the party booby-trap into DNA Land as the two heroes ran out of the zoo. Just as they reached safety, a huge explosion rang out, ending the evil reign of King Ognik and his insane animal army.

"Wow! Thanks a lot, Ed!" said Otto. "But how? I thought you were finished when you stepped in that evil poop."

"Yes, my palindromic friend, it seemed I was done for, but then this senile cat came out of the zoo and gave me a strange gift: a shopping cart full of dynamite, maps, DNA, and Spam."

"He did, eh?"

"Yes. So I ate the Spam to give me strength, injected the DNA to counter the effects of the gnu dung, used the maps to find you in the llama mall, and you know what I did with the TNT."

Otto was so relieved. He could name no one man as brave as General Ed. Thanks to them, the world was safe again for both humans and animals. And so, their civic duty done, Otto and General Ed turned to more urgent matters—they were famished. With a hankering for banana sandwiches, they hopped into Ed's Toyota and drove off to the Yreka Bakery.

NEWS OF THE WILD

Tired of reading about politics? Has the international news got you down? Take a break from humanity...and have a look at some animals that have been in the news lately.

BAD CHOICE

Thieves broke into the Australian Reptile Park north of Sydney. They had to climb over two barbed-wire fences to get in but they made off with a four-foot-long alligator, worth nearly $5,000 on the black market. The crooks had six alligators to choose from, so which one did they steal? The one named Mr. Cranky Pants. A few days later, the alligator was recovered unharmed from a nearby creek, where he'd apparently been abandoned by the thieves. "They messed with the wrong alligator. Mr. Cranky Pants *is* a cranky pants," says Al Mucci, who works at the park. "He gets moody. That's probably why they dumped him."

DO NOT ADJUST YOUR SET

In February 2004, Sheba and Inuka, two polar bears at the Singapore Zoo, suddenly turned bright green. Why? Because polar bear fur has hollow hair shafts. The white you see in their fur is actually sunlight reflecting off the shafts. But these shafts can fill with algae, and when they do, the polar bears can turn green. "The harmless algae is the result of Singapore's warm and humid tropical conditions," said, a spokesperson for the zoo. The bears got a bleach job a few weeks later, and now they're back to normal.

NUMBER, PLEASE

Someone at the Oslo, Norway, home of Aleksander Elden dialed 113 (the Norwegian equivalent of 911) at 1:00 a.m. on May 9, 2004. Emergency operators couldn't make sense of the distressed caller's whimpering, but they were afraid someone needed help so they called in the police. Elden was the only person home, but he was sleeping and couldn't have made the call. When they searched the house, they found Raia, Elden's four-month-old Norwegian Elkhound puppy, lying on the floor next to a telephone covered in saliva and chew marks. "It could only have been her that called," Elden said. "She was the only one there."

Pig in a blanket: The blonde Mangalitza pig has thick fleece like a sheep.

REGISTERED DE-MOO-CRATS

Brenda Gould of Newmarket, England, has run afoul of the law by registering her cows to vote. Gould and her husband cooked up the stunt after the town council sent a registration form addressed to the occupants of their barn, and then refused to believe that nobody lived there. "We ignored it until someone came around to ask why we hadn't filled it in. My husband said, 'If they want to know who's living in the barn, we'll tell them.'" Soon "Henry and Sophie Bull" were registered to vote. The council was not amused and fined the Goulds £100 (about $189). "We never thought it would come to this," Brenda says. "I don't suppose we'll be doing it again."

HE STOLE HER HEART...AND HER FROOT LOOPS

"Bandit," listed in the *Guinness Book of World Records* as the world's fattest pet raccoon, passed away at age 10 in May 2004. Most adult raccoons weigh about 20 pounds; some males grow as large as 40 pounds—Bandit weighed nearly 75. His owner, Deborah Klitsch of Palmerton, Pennsylvania, attributes his girth to: 1) a bad thyroid gland, and 2) Bandit's penchant for breaking into the kitchen cabinets in the middle of the night to feast on potato chips, Froot Loops, cheese curls, cookies, and other treats. In the last year of his life, Bandit developed cancer, and in the end Klitsch decided to have him euthanized. "I could see he was suffering, because he stopped eating," she says. "In the entire world, he was my best friend."

MAN'S BEST FRIEND

A Bristol, Pennsylvania, man named Ed Crossan passed away at the age of 73. He'd always been close to his daughter's dog, Polo, but family members never realized just *how* close until after his death. A few days after Ed died, his daughter, Donna, let the dog out, and he disappeared. Donna didn't see Polo again until she went to the Wade Funeral Home to finalize the funeral arrangements...and there was Polo, pacing back and forth in front of the building. "It was just a dog looking for his pal," says veterinarian Dr. Eric Meihofer. "It's an amazing story. It shows that the dog was very loyal and loving."

Route 46 in North Dakota is America's longest straight stretch of highway (110 miles).

USED-LESS INVENTIONS

These real inventions might inspire two other inventions: a Stupefied Head-Scratcher and a Mocking-Laugh Suppressor.

"HIGH FIVE" SIMULATOR
Patent Number: 5,356,330
Invented in: 1994
Description: Essentially a spring-loaded arm mounted on a wall, the "High Five" Simulator is always ready for a good slap. A fake hand attached to a forearm piece is connected to a lower arm section with an elbow joint for pivoting. When the hand is struck, the raised arm bends backward briefly before returning to the ready position. This invention is perfect for the lonely and excessive high-fiver.

GRAVITY-POWERED SHOE AIR CONDITIONER
Patent Number: 5,375,430
Invented in: 1994
Description: The air-conditioned shoe can either cool your foot or warm it up, depending on your preference. Hidden inside the shoe's heel are expanding and compressing chambers powered by the natural pressures that occur while walking. With each step, networks of heat exchange coils work with the chambers to alter the temperature of the air surrounding your foot. End result: A sweat-free (but bulky and cumbersome) shoe.

GREENHOUSE HELMET
Patent Number: 4,605,000
Invented in: 1986
Description: Why go to the country for fresh air when you can get it at home? Like a cross between a space suit and an indoor garden, the greenhouse helmet fits securely over a person's head and houses at least one plant. The transparent dome contains the carbon dioxide exhaled by its user while the plants convert the waste into oxygen. (Note: If you make one of these for yourself, be sure to poke some holes in it so you can breathe!)

Over 125 women are known to have fought in the Civil War...dressed as men.

BIRD TRAP AND CAT FEEDER
Patent Number: 4,150,505
Invented in: 1979
Description: For the crippled cat or the sparrow hater, this invention promises to "continuously supply neighborhood cats with plenty to eat." The trap lures birds with what appears to be an appealing perch and house, but once the feathered creature climbs through the entrance, it's caught in a pivoting plastic tube. The tube then lowers, dumping the bird into a wire mesh cage. Specifically designed for sparrows, the mesh is just big enough for the bird's head to poke through, which draws the cat's attention. A feeding frenzy presumably follows.

ANTI-EATING FACE MASK
Patent Number: 4,344,424
Invented in: 1982
Description: The anti-eating device fits to the shape of a person's head with a series of flexible straps, rods, and hoops, while a grate-like mask covers the user's mouth from chin to nose, completely preventing the intake of food—except in liquid form. It's also fitted with a small padlock for insurance. Instead of locking the whole family out of fridge, dieters can lock up their own mouths.

THE INITIATIOR
Patent Number: 819,814
Invented in: 1906
Description: Before fraternities relied heavily on alcohol to enhance the initiation process, this electric shock treatment helped spark the fun. The apparatus, described as "entirely harmless in its action and results," was specifically "designed for use in lodges and secret societies." Two metal rails about an inch wide are laid down as tracks and hooked up to a battery or generator. The victim—pledge or inductee—then walks down the track wearing a pair of shoes with metallic soles, heels, and interior contact plates. Every time the subject takes a step, the electric circuit is opened and closed, continuously shocking whoever dons the metal slippers.

OFFENDERS OF
THE FAITH

Religion is a cornerstone of civilization.
So when people take pot shots at it, it's just
bad taste...but sometimes kind of funny.

O FFENDED FAITH: Hinduism
INSULT: In 2000 Hindu groups were outraged by Sittin'
Pretty, a Seattle company that makes toilet seats—with
images of Hindu gods on them. The brightly colored seats featured
Lord Ganesh and the goddess Kali beneath the lids. "They should
stop doing this at once," said Vijay Pallod, a spokesman for the
Hindu Anti-Defamation Coalition. "It's absolutely the wrong place
to put our gods."
WHAT HAPPENED: The company apologized and ceased sell-
ing the seats.

OFFENDED FAITH: Baptists
INSULT: Landover Baptist Church has a Web site. But the
church isn't really Baptist; it's not even a church—it's a parody of
Christian fundamentalism started by two former students of Jerry
Falwell's Liberty University (they were expelled). Landover gets
volumes of hate mail every month, testimonials to its ability to
offend even people who know it's a parody. The site's "news stories" feature such headlines as *Demon-Possessed Baby Bites Off
Pastor's Thumb in Baptismal Pool, St. Patrick's Day: Another Excuse
for Catholics to Get Drunk,* and *Can Star Trek Help Us Understand
Muslims?*
WHAT HAPPENED: Nothing—the Web site is still up and
running.

OFFENDED FAITH: Sikhism
INSULT: One level of the 2002 video game *Hitman 2: Silent
Assassin* takes players inside a temple to shoot turban-wearing "ter-
rorists." What group wears turbans? Sikhs. And the temple in the

game closely resembles the Golden Temple in India, the holiest shrine of Sikhism. Human rights advocates slammed the game's maker, Eidos, accusing them of inciting violence against Sikhs. "What would the Christian, Muslim, or Jewish people say," one critic asked, "if their holiest site was depicted as a terrorist hideout?"

WHAT HAPPENED: Eidos changed the game. "No offense was intended," they said, "but we apologize to the Sikh community for any offense taken."

OFFENDED FAITH: The Church of Jesus Christ of Latter-Day Saints (the Mormons)

INSULT: In 2001 the Wasatch Brewery of Salt Lake City came out with a beer called Polygamy Porter. The slogan, "Why have just one?" and a billboard ad featuring a man surrounded by scantily clad women with the words "Take some home for the wives" were not-too-subtle digs at the Mormon Church, which permitted polygamy until 1890.

WHAT HAPPENED: When the billboard company refused to put up the ad, brewery owner Greg Schirf blamed it on pressure from the church, but canceled the ad campaign anyway. "So many polygamists marry underage women," Schirf said. "We didn't want to be at risk for targeting minors."

OFFENDED FAITH: Buddhism

INSULT: In May 2004, a Japanese candymaker introduced a new treat called Snot from the Nose of the Great Buddha, also known as Buddha Boogers. Offended priests from the Todaiji Temple, one of Japan's most famous Buddhist temples, went to court to try to block the sale of the sweets (they failed). The package features a drawing of the Buddha picking his nose.

WHAT HAPPENED: At last report, the candy is still being sold.

*   *   *

"The world is my country, all mankind are my brethren, and to do good is my religion."
— **Thomas Paine**

After humans, cats thrive in more places on Earth than any other mammal species.

THE NIGERIAN SCAM

*When Uncle John checked his e-mail this morning, he found one
from someone claiming to need help moving millions of dollars out
of their country. Sound familiar? Here's some background info
on one of the most popular Internet scams of all time.*

YOU'VE GOT MAIL

To: TRUSTWORTHY AMERICAN
From: MIRIAM_ABACHA@NIGERIA.GOV
Subject: URGENT BUSINESS PROPOSAL

DEAR SIR, SINCE MY HUSBAND THE FORMER PRESI-
DENT DIED THE NIGERIAN GOVERNMENT HAS
FROZEN OUR FAMILY BANK ACCOUNT IN SWITZER-
LAND (US$22,000,000).

PLEASE HELP US TRANSFER THIS MONEY INTO
YOUR COUNTRY. IF YOU ALLOW US TO DEPOSIT THE
FUNDS IN YOUR BANK ACCOUNT TEMPORARILY, WE
WILL GIVE YOU 20%, OR $4,400,000.

THIS TRANSACTION IS 100% SAFE. THIS MATTER IS
STRICTLY CONFIDENTIAL. THANK YOU.

MRS. MIRIAM ABACHA

If you're online, there's a very good chance that an e-mail similar
to this one may be sitting in your in-box right now. Requests for
help moving large sums of money out of third world countries are
believed to be the second-most common type of spam (after sales
pitches for male virility drugs). And as you've probably already
guessed, the offer *is* too good to be true—it's a classic scam.

OUT OF AFRICA

Cons like these are called "Nigerian scams," because when they
first started circulating in the 1970s, many came from the west
African nation of Nigeria. They're also known as "419 scams,"
after the section of the Nigerian criminal code that deals with
e-mail crime. Today they can originate from any number of countries. Since the fall of Saddam Hussein, they've even come from
people claiming to have connections to the former dictator or his

dead sons, Uday and Qusay. But Nigeria is still considered to be the capital of these scams, so the nickname has stuck.

THE BASIC SCAM

• Collecting $4.4 million for doing almost nothing is a pretty attractive come-on and, for many, too powerful to resist. If you do reply, the scammer will promise the money again—but this time, he'll also ask you to send a small sum up front, $1,000 or more, to help in transferring the funds out of Nigeria and into your bank account. Maybe they'll claim they need it to bribe an official, or to pay a fee or tax that's holding up the millions that will soon be yours. But sending $1,000 or even $5,000 to secure a payoff of $4.4 million seems like a bargain, doesn't it?

• What happens if you wire the $1,000 to Nigeria? One thing is certain: You won't get $4.4 million. The scammer will invent new obstacles to explain why the money is being held up and will ask you for more money to clear up the red tape. No matter how many times you send more money, some new problem will always arise, requiring still more money to help sort it out.

ADVANCED SCAMS

Bank Account Clean Out: Why settle for stealing your money in installments? The e-mailer may ask you for your bank account number(s), as well as your business cards and blank sheets of letterhead. If you send them the numbers and the materials, they'll use them to empty all your bank accounts in one fell swoop.

The Travel Plan: Some scammers even invite victims to travel to Nigeria, where they pose as bank or government officials, meeting in borrowed offices in a bank or government building. While there, you'll be asked for even more money. If you don't have it, or refuse to hand it over, you can be beaten, held for ransom, or even killed. The U.S. State Department estimates that at least 15 people have been murdered after being lured to Nigeria as part of a 419 scam.

Foreign Lottery: Have you ever received an e-mail telling you that you've won millions in a foreign lottery? Or that you've inherited a fortune from a relative you've never heard of? Any time you're promised a fortune but are asked to pay money up front, it's a version of a 419 scam.

eBay Car Purchase: There's even a version of the scam that targets people selling cars on eBay. The scammer will buy your car and ask you to ship it to Nigeria, but will explain that a friend in the United States who owes them money will pay for it. If the car sells for $5,000, the friend will send you a cashier's check for $10,000—the amount they supposedly owe to the buyer—and arrange for you to wire the difference to the buyer. By the time the issuing bank notifies you that the cashier's check is a fake, you've already sent your $5,000 (and perhaps even your car) to Nigeria.

HISTORY

The Nigerian scam started in the 1970s. In those days, scammers sent airmail letters to names and addresses pulled out of old phone books and business directories. Sending letters was expensive, so the scammers usually targeted businesses instead of individuals, since businesses were likely to have more money.

And the volume of mail sent was miniscule by today's electronic standards: At the peak of the snail mail phase in the early 1980s, it's estimated that 250,000 Nigerian scam letters were sent to the United States every year. When fax machines caught on, the scam became cheaper than ever. But what really revolutionized it was, of course, the Internet. Who needs stamps or long-distance fax charges? Computers made it possible to send thousands or even millions of scam e-mails with a single keystroke. Costs dropped so low that scammers could afford to target individuals instead of businesses, and they set their sights on pulling lots of little scams instead of a few big ones.

A lot of people have gotten rich off the scams, and in addition to buying mansions and luxury cars, many of Nigeria's newest millionaires invested their ill-gotten gains in Internet cafés—from which even more Nigerian scam e-mails could be sent.

SCAM FACTS

• No one knows for sure just how much money Nigerian scammers fleece from their victims each year because many victims are too embarrassed to come forward. The U.S. Secret Service estimates that Americans lose as much as $100 million a year.

• For years the Nigerian government ignored the problem, but now they're taking steps to fight it—taking out ads in major

American newspapers, allowing the U.S. Secret Service to open offices in Nigeria, and even warning westerners as they arrive at Murtala Mohammed International Airport in Lagos. But nothing seems to stem the flow of victims.

BIG FISH

The National Consumers League calculates that the average loss to 419 scams in 2001 was $5,957. Have *you* been conned? Take heart—some of the largest losses have been racked up by people working in law, banking, or finance—people who should have known better. Take these folks, for example:

Graeme Kenneth Rutherford. Rutherford, a star money manager and former Citibank executive in New Zealand, was taken in by scammers who told him they wanted to pay him $300,000 a year to manage $30 million for a Nigerian oil company...but first he had to help them transfer the money out of Nigeria. Rutherford poured $600,000 of his own money into the scam, borrowed more from his father, then talked wealthy friends and business associates out of $7 million more, telling them he was investing their money in safe European investments with "locked-in profits" of at least 70%. He sank every penny into the scam and lost it all.

In July 2000, Rutherford was convicted on 23 counts of forgery and fraud and sentenced to six and a half years in prison. He blames his poor judgment on painkillers he was taking for his sore back. "My resolve was hardened by my absolute conviction that the Nigerian scheme was genuine," he says.

Nelson Sakaguchi. Sakaguchi, a Brazilian, was a director of the Banco Noereste Brazil in the mid-1990s, when scammers claiming to control the Central Bank of Nigeria "awarded" him a million-dollar contract to finance the construction of a new international airport in Nigeria. The airport didn't exist, of course, but that didn't stop Sakaguchi from transferring $250 million of the bank's money to Africa without notifying any of his superiors, making this by far the largest 419 scam to come to light so far.

Why'd he do it? The scammers promised Sakaguchi that they'd give him a $40 million kickback as his share of the deal, which, of course, he never got. Banco Noroeste collapsed in 2001. As of April 2004, Sakaguchi was jailed in Switzerland awaiting trial on embezzlement and bank fraud.

The average American six-year-old watches two hours of TV a day.

ON THE WART PATH

Warts are caused by a virus called human papillomavirus (HPV).
You can only catch it from someone who has warts or carries the virus.
The virus attacks skin cells, causing them to reproduce at a faster rate
than normal tissue, which results in an overgrowth—the nuisances we
know as warts. If you're out of Compound W, here are some folk
remedies to hold you over until you can get to the drug store:

Rub the wart with a rooster comb. Bury the comb in your backyard and wait two weeks for the wart to disappear.

Sit in a cemetery for three consecutive nights. Place flowers on a fresh grave while wishing for your wart to disappear. Two weeks later, your wish should come true.

Rub the wart with a piece of wild turnip (or fresh potato peel) once a day for 15 days.

Boil a bone (any kind) and let dry. Rub the bone vigorously over the wart, throw it over your shoulder.

Cut a pinto bean in half. Rub both halves on the wart and plant the bean during a full moon.

Poke the wart so it bleeds. Drip one drop of the blood onto seven grains of corn. Feed the corn to an old black hen. Wait 10 days for the wart to vanish.

Dig up the roots of a pokeweed plant. Fry them in lard and apply the grease to the wart.

Drip a drop of milkweed juice on the wart twice a day until it disappears.

Rub the wart several times a day with your mother's gold wedding band.

Tie a human hair around the wart. Hammer a nail into a green tree and immediately remove the nail. Put the hair in the nail hole. Drive the same nail back into the hole. When the hair rots, the wart should be gone.

Mix equal amounts of brown soap and spit. Apply the paste to the wart. Wait 24 hours, then wash the paste off—the wart should come off with it.

Chew on some tobacco leaves. Spit out the leaves and squeeze the juice onto the wart. Repeat until the wart is gone.

An adult human head weighs about 12 pounds—as much as an average bowling ball.

SIN BINS & BUCKET BAGS

Hey you in the drainpipes with the Tony Curtis! How many of these expressions from the 1950s have you heard before?

Drainpipes: Tight pants with straight legs.

Silver Jeff: A nickel (it has Thomas Jefferson on it).

Sudsable: Washable with soap and water, as opposed to requiring dry-cleaning

Wock: A bowl-shaped Chinese frying pan. By the 1970s they were known as *woks*.

Tony Curtis: A haircut that mimics the one worn by the actor: combed back on the sides, forward in front.

Megadeath: A unit of measure: one million deaths. Used to estimate the destructive power of megaton bombs.

Bottle: Guts. A person who "loses their bottle" loses their nerve.

Beatnik: A member of the artistic "beat" generation.

Neatnik: Someone who's obsessively neat.

Intoximeter: What *Breath-alysers* were called before that term was invented in 1960.

Flaptabs: Ears.

Hi si: High society.

Smaze: A combination of smoke and haze; similar to *smog*, a combination of smoke and fog.

Sack dress: A short dress that doesn't gather at the waist: it looks like a sack.

Rabbit: To talk continuously; babble.

Sin bin: Another name for the penalty box that hockey players have to sit in when they break the rules.

Peepie-creepie: A portable TV camera used to film in the field (derived from walkie-talkie).

Bucket bag: A purse that's shaped like a bucket.

Tatt: Garbage; junk.

Skijamas: Pajamas that look like a ski suit.

Coca-Colonization: Refers to the inroads that American commercial products—such as Coca-Cola—made around the world in the 1950s.

Cube: A nerd; someone who's squarer than a square.

Occupational hazard: About 25,000 workers died building the Panama Canal.

(NOT) COMING TO A THEATER NEAR YOU

You'd be surprised by how many films in Hollywood are started...without ever being finished. Here's a look at a few that will probably never make it onto the big screen.

AVATAR (1999)

Great Idea: After *Titanic* made $1 billion and won 11 Academy Awards, director James Cameron could make any movie he wanted—and this was the one he wanted to make. Set in the year 2040, *Avatar* follows a paralyzed war veteran named Josh on a mining expedition to the distant planet Pandora, where, through a computerized psychic link, he inhabits the body of a purple-skinned, nine-foot-tall, ammonia-breathing Pandoran.

Kiss of Doom: Cameron wanted to use a cast of ultra-lifelike computer-created actors. Plus, most of the special effects needed to render Pandora would have had to be invented. *Avatar*'s budget: a staggering $400 million. No studio would fund it, so the movie was scrapped.

DIETER (2001)

Great Idea: This was an adaptation of the "Sprockets" skit from *Saturday Night Live*, written by and starring Mike Myers. The plot: Dieter, a German talk-show host, travels to America to kidnap David Hasselhoff (playing himself), who is a huge star in Germany. The script was reportedly hilarious, and Myers assembled a dream cast, including Jack Black and Will Ferrell. Universal Studios thought they'd have another *Austin Powers*-size movie franchise.

Kiss of Doom: Filming began in July 2000, but Myers hated his script, panicked, and asked Universal to delay the film. They refused, so Myers quit. Universal then sued him for breach of contract. It took months to settle the suit, but by that time the cast had lost interest or moved on to other projects. Plus, Myers and Universal execs weren't eager to work together after fighting in court. *Dieter* died. (But Myers says he still wants to do it someday.)

THE MAN WHO KILLED DON QUIXOTE (2001)

Great Idea: Even after filming surreal fantasy epics like *Brazil*, *The Adventures of Baron Munchausen*, and *Time Bandits*, director Terry Gilliam still hadn't made his dream movie: an adaptation of the classic novel *Don Quixote*. No one in Hollywood would finance it because of Gilliam's chaotic sets and his tendency to go way over budget. After trying to develop the film for ten years, Gilliam finally got the production money from European investors and began filming in the Spanish countryside in 2000.

Kiss of Doom: A few days into shooting, Jean Rochefort (starring as Don Quixote) developed an infection that left him unable to ride a horse, leaving the movie without its lead actor. Entire days were lost due to flash flooding. Other scenes were ruined by deafening noise from a nearby Spanish military base. And when Gilliam tried to shoot indoors, the soundstage he'd rented had such poor acoustics that the dialogue was unintelligible. Ultimately, the movie was cancelled. The production's insurance company lost so much money on the project that it took all rights to Gilliam's script and to the movie itself as compensation. (The fiasco was captured in the documentary film *Lost in La Mancha*.)

THE ROAD TO TOMORROW (1978)

Great Idea: Between 1940 and 1962, Bing Crosby and Bob Hope made seven "Road" pictures (*The Road to Morroco*, *The Road to Hong Kong*, etc.). Both were enjoying a comeback with younger audiences in the late 1970s—Hope was the subject of a Woody Allen documentary and Crosby recorded a duet with David Bowie (a surreal version of "The Little Drummer Boy"). So the time seemed right for one final "Road" movie: a reprise of their classic roles that would be both a tribute and a farewell to the series. This one would be a family film with Hope and Crosby as grandparents who accidentally get caught up in comic intrigue.

Kiss of Doom: Filming was to start after Crosby's summer concert tour, but he died in Spain of a heart attack while golfing. Crosby's death didn't kill the project, though—George Burns agreed to replace Crosby. But Hope and screenwriter Ben Starr got into a public spat over U.S. involvement in the Vietnam War, refused to speak to each other...and the movie died.

MORE IRREGULAR NEWS

Just when you think you've heard everything...

LET'S NAME HIM BUTTOCKS!

"Japan's system of writing, which evolved from ancient Chinese script, was simplified after World War II when the government abolished thousands of characters. In recent years, however, authorities in Tokyo have been under pressure to reinstate obscure and archaic characters so that more interesting and original children's names can be created, says the *Daily Telegraph*. As a result, the justice ministry proposed an additional 578 characters for names, but included dozens that most parents might view as in poor taste, such as 'Piles,' 'Buttocks,' and 'Prostitute.'"

—*Ananova*

BAD OWNER!

"A police patrol in Nuremberg, Germany, noticed a woman, identified only as Gerda M., walking her dog Leonie in the city centre. The large mixed-breed dog only weighed 12 kg (32 pounds). It was taken to a pet shelter, where one worker told reporters, 'I have seen many miserable things, but never something this cruel. This dog should weigh at least 25 kilos (66 pounds).' He said the owner told him she was trying to get the dog down to 5 kg (13 pounds) so she could take it on a plane as part of her carry-on luggage."

—Pakistan *Daily Times*

ANYTHING TO DECLARE?

"In this age of airport security, screeners are under stringent orders to carefully check all baggage. Yesterday at Boston's Logan Airport they discovered one for the books: the severed head of a harbor seal. They discovered it in a small cooler and immediately notified authorities. The head was apparently checked in by a Colorado man who told investigators that he is a biology professor and had found a dead seal on Revere Beach. He then cut off its head so he could take it home 'for educational purposes.' After more than an hour of questioning, investigators allowed the man to board a plane—without the seal's head."

—*Boston Globe*

Thirsty? Each day, the U.S. uses 134,000,000,000 gallons of water to irrigate crops.

LOST AND FOUND

"The family of Maryland resident Joynal Abedin worried for more than two weeks after he failed to return home from work the week before Christmas. Then, on Jan. 5, Abedin's wife received a $17,000 bill from Washington Hospital Center in the mail. Her husband had been killed in a hit-and-run accident in Prince George's County. Although he was carrying ID, some of it contained an old address and police had been unable to locate his family, officials said. Abedin's family is now asking why police couldn't find the family when the hospital could—to send them a bill."

—*Washington Post*

DO AS I SAY...

"The owner of one of the largest fashion empires in North America is fighting a child support claim for $68,000 per month plus $5.5 million in back payments because he doesn't want his 16-year-old son to suffer from 'affluenza.' A lawyer for multi-millionaire clothier Peter Nygard told Madam Justice Ruth Mesbar he would be calling an expert to testify 'too much money is bad for children.'"

—*Toronto Star*

SERIOUSLY WHACKED

"A boardwalk game called 'Whack the Iraq,' is causing controversy at the Jersey shore. It's located at the end of Morey's Pier in Wildwood. Players shoot paint balls at live human targets dressed as Iraqis. Figures of Saddam Hussein and Osama bin Laden adorn the arcade. The operator of 'Whack the Iraq' said the game is just seaside fun and is not meant to offend anyone. A sign at the game states that 'Whack the Iraq' is intended to insult only one person, Saddam Hussein."

—NBC

BACK TO NATURE

"Officials in Botswana have issued a plea to people who want to commit suicide: use trees, not trains. 'I am sick of these people who throw themselves in front of the trains,' Minister of Transport Tebelo Seretse told a newspaper. 'The drivers are people—why turn them into murderers?'"

—*Deutsche Presse-Agentur*

More than 90% of the actions performed by the nervous system are reflex actions.

HOW *NOT* TO GET STRUCK BY LIGHTNING

On page 215 we told you about some people who were struck by lightning and lived to tell the tale. But don't tempt Mother Nature. Here are some tips on how to avoid getting the shock of a lifetime.

THE 30-30 RULE
How do you know when you're close enough to a thunderstorm to be at risk? Experts say that if you can hear thunder, you're near enough to the storm to be struck by lightning. A more precise rule of thumb is the "30-30 rule."

30 Seconds: When you see a flash of lightning, count off the seconds until you hear the accompanying thunderclap. If you count 30 seconds or less, you're close enough to be at risk of being struck by lightning. Seek shelter indoors.

30 Minutes: Remain indoors until 30 minutes after the last flash of lightning. After that it's safe to go back outside.

The 30-30 rule applies even if it hasn't started raining, or if the storm clouds are far away. Lightning can travel horizontally as far as 10 miles before striking the ground, so even if the sky overhead is blue, you can still be in danger.

STAYING LOW
Because air is a poor conductor of electricity, lightning takes the shortest path to the ground. It does this by striking high ground, tall trees, or other prominent features on the landscape. So one way to avoid lightning is to make sure *you* aren't the tallest object around and that you aren't standing next to—or under—the tallest object, either.

• Avoid trees and hilltops. Open fields aren't much better—if you're standing in the middle of one, you're probably the tallest thing around. Head for a gully or whatever low point is nearby.

• If you're in a forest and avoiding trees isn't possible, stay away from the taller ones. Take cover under shrubs or a grove of low trees.

• If you're high up on a mountain, go back down below the tree line and seek shelter underneath a grove of small trees.

A mouse's heart is smaller than an M&M.

• Lightning is also attracted to water, so stay out of swimming pools, lakes, rivers, and other bodies of water.

THE LIGHTNING SAFETY POSITION

• If you're stuck out in the open, assume the "lightning safety position." Squat to lower your profile and touch your heels together, so that if lightning does strike nearby, it will—hopefully—pass through your legs without going through your heart and other major organs. Cover your ears to protect against the sound of thunder.

• Some victims say they were able to tell that they were about to be struck by lightning—the hair on their arms or their head stood up just before the strike. If you ever experience this during a thunderstorm, head for shelter immediately. If none is available, crouch down and assume the lightning safety position.

GIMME SHELTER

Not all storm shelters are equal. The best shelters are the ones that provide lightning with an easy path to the ground.

• The very best, of course, is a building with a lightning rod—a metal rod on the roof of the building that's connected by a wire to another metal rod buried in the ground.

• Next best is a building with plumbing, electric wiring, cable TV, or telephone lines. Even rain gutters with downspouts can provide a path for lightning to reach the ground.

• Shelters with no plumbing or wiring, such as bleachers and garden sheds, offer little or no protection from lightning.

• Cars do offer protection. Just roll up the windows and be careful not to touch any metal surfaces. Bicycles, motorcycles, and other open vehicles can actually attract lightning, so get away from them.

• Once indoors, stay away from windows and open doors and avoid touching plumbing fixtures, electrical wires, and phone lines. Stay away from electrical appliances: unplug them if you can, and do it before the storm arrives to avoid possible electric shock.

• Talking on a corded phone during a thunderstorm is the number one cause of indoor lightning injuries in the U.S., so hang up.

• Concrete walls and floors may look safe, but they're likely to contain metal mesh and reinforcing bars—which conduct electricity—so avoid contact with them.

NEPHEW OF A DICTATOR

*Imagine being related to someone so universally despised that
you couldn't even use your own last name. We recently came
upon David Gardner's book,* The Last of the Hitlers, *and pieced together this forgotten bit of history.*

THE NAME RINGS A BELL

On August 21, 1942, a young Englishman walked into the local draft board so he could enlist in the U.S. military to fight in World War II. The board looked over his enlistment forms and then turned him down on the spot, just as he'd been turned down by Canada, and just as he'd been turned down when he tried to enlist in the British armed forces back home.

What was it that caused the armed forces of three different countries to reject his application out of hand? On the part of the form where enlistees have to identify living relatives who have served in the armed forces of either the Allied or Axis powers, he had entered the following:

> 1. Thomas Dowling. Uncle. England. 1923–1926. Royal Air Force.
>
> 2. Adolf Hitler. Uncle. Germany. 1914–1918. Corporal.

The young man's full name was William Patrick Hitler. He was the son of Adolf Hitler's older half-brother Alois, and Alois's first wife, an Irishwoman named Bridget Dowling.

FAMILY TIES

For both William and his mother, the association with the Hitler side of the family was troubled from the start. Bridget was only 17 when she met Alois at the 1909 Dublin Horse Show. Alois dressed sharply and told her he was in the "hotel business," but as Bridget's suspicious father soon discovered, he was actually a penniless waiter with few prospects. He ordered his daughter to break off the

---

Get outta town! In Fairbanks, Alaska, moose are banned from mating within city limits.

relationship, but she and Alois eloped to England instead. Nine months and nine days later, Bridget gave birth to William Patrick.

Marital bliss did not last long. Alois beat his infant son and sank what little money the family had in one get-rich-quick scheme after another. He finally abandoned his family in 1914 and skipped off to Germany, never to return. Bridget claimed in her memoirs, *My Brother-in-law Adolf,* that Alois even had a friend write to her during World War I saying her husband had died in battle, just so she'd never try to track him down for alimony.

UNCLE ADOLF

For nearly a decade both Bridget and William believed Alois was dead. It wasn't until Adolf Hitler staged his Beer Hall Putsch in Munich in 1923 that they learned the truth. The event made headlines in English newspapers, and when 14-year-old William Patrick read them he realized that Adolf was his uncle. He thought "Uncle Adolf" might be able to tell him more about his father's death and where he was buried, so he wrote him a letter in care of the mayor of Munich.

Adolf Hitler never wrote back—but *Alois* Hitler did. He announced to his son that he not only was still alive, but that he had remarried (without ever bothering to divorce Bridget) and fathered another son, named Heinz. And thanks to William's letter to the mayor of Munich, he was now facing trial for bigamy. Alois needed Bridget's help to beat the bigamy rap. He pled poverty as usual, but he promised that if Bridget helped him out of the mess he was in, he'd soon be wealthy with the help of his brother's growing influence and would be able to repay her for all the years she'd raised their son alone.

Bridget agreed, and with her help Alois got off with the minimum fine and no jail time. Not surprisingly, he never did send Bridget any money.

IN THE NEWS

William had to wait six more years before he was finally reunited with his father, during a two-week visit to Germany in 1929. He met his Uncle Adolf during a second trip to Germany the following year. That meeting went well, but relations between the dictator and his nephew soon soured.

By 1931 Hitler's international profile had risen to the point that the British press began taking an active interest in his career and was interviewing his relatives. The very thought of this sent Adolf into fits of rage. He was afraid that if his brother's bigamy became public knowledge, it might cost him the support he needed to get to the top. So he summoned his nephew to Berlin and screamed at him uncontrollably for the better part of an afternoon. That got William to stop talking to the press...for a while.

BLACK SHEEP

By this time, England was in an economic depression. Finding and keeping a job wasn't easy, even if your last name wasn't Hitler, but for William, it was impossible. Both he and his mother were fired from their jobs for being related to Adolf Hitler.

After more than a year and a half without a job, in October 1933, William Patrick was finally offered a job as a department store clerk in Berlin. Hitler was now chancellor of Germany, and didn't like the idea of one of his relatives working in a department store, so he forbade William from taking the job. Hitler controlled the economy, so William couldn't get any job without his uncle's approval. And because Hitler refused to advance his career, William bounced from one low-paying job to another. But he never gave up his British citizenship, and never became a Nazi.

Finally, after about five years, nephew and uncle decided they'd had enough of each other. Adolf summoned William to his offices, screamed at him again, and told him either to become a German citizen or get out. William left Germany in February 1939.

FRESH START

By this time, Hitler had already invaded Czechoslovakia and Austria, and was seven months away from invading Poland, the start of World War II.

William had no future in Germany, and things didn't look bright in England either, not for him and especially not for his mother. Though she'd been born in Ireland, then a part of the British Empire, when Bridget married Alois Hitler she became a citizen of Austria. When Hitler absorbed Austria into the Third Reich, she became a citizen of Nazi Germany. Now she wasn't just a Hitler trying to find a job in wartime England, she was a *German*

Liberace owned a retracting toilet. It sank into the bathroom floor at the flip of a switch.

Hitler looking for work.

She and William decided to try their luck in America. William found that he could make enough money to support them by writing newspaper and magazine articles with titles like "To Hell with Hitler" and "Why I Hate My Uncle," and by touring the country making speeches against the Führer.

William then set his sights on joining the U.S. military. Upon being rejected, he wrote a letter to President Franklin Roosevelt. Roosevelt forwarded it to FBI director J. Edgar Hoover, who launched an investigation into William's background. A month later, Hoover wrote back to the president that "no information was developed to indicate that [Hitler] was engaged in any activities of a subversive nature."

Finally, after waiting over two years, William was inducted into the U.S. Navy in March 1944. Very little is known about his time in the military, other than that he served in the medical corps and received a shrapnel wound to his leg, apparently while in action.

INTO HIDING

Adolf Hitler committed suicide on April 30, 1945, and Germany surrendered a few days later. His nephew remained in the Navy until March 1946. After his discharge, he moved to New York and became a U.S. citizen. Then he and his mother changed their last names and disappeared from public view.

William lived in complete anonymity for nearly 30 years, until Pulitzer Prize–winning historian and Hitler biographer John Toland made a trip to Hamburg, Germany, in the early 1970s to interview Hitler's distant relatives. One relative showed him a picture of William holding his infant son. Using information the family members gave him, Toland tracked William down to the New York City area. William did not want to talk, and Toland agreed not to disclose his new last name or place of residence.

William apparently retained some form of admiration for his uncle—or at least a perverse form of pride in being related to such a major, albeit notorious, historical figure. The photograph of William and his infant son was the first sign to anyone outside the Hitler family that William might actually be proud of his family tree. The child's name was written on the back: Adolf.

FOUND

The story stopped there until 1995, when British journalist David Gardner tried to track William Patrick Hitler down for an article on the 50th anniversary of Adolf Hitler's suicide. The anniversary came and went without Gardner being able to find Hitler's nephew, but he kept digging. Finally, after three years of sifting through Social Security records and chasing down every possible lead, Gardner located Bridget Hitler's grave in a cemetery in a small town on Long Island, New York. She had died in 1969. There on the same tombstone was the name of William, who had died in July 1987. By the time Gardner found his man, he'd been dead 11 years.

Once he'd found the grave, finding out where William's widow lived wasn't difficult. Not surprisingly, she didn't want to talk, although she did confirm that she was his widow and that he was indeed Hitler's nephew. She and William had four sons: Adolf (who now goes by the name Alex), born in 1949; Louis, born in 1951; Howard, born in 1957; and Brian, born in 1965.

Howard, the only son who ever married, died in a car accident in 1989. He had no children. At last report Alex, Louis, and Brian were all still alive, still living under the assumed name that their father chose when he went underground after World War II.

In his book, Gardner does not reveal the name. But, providing further insight into William's seemingly ambivalent attitude toward his uncle, Gardner describes the name as a "double-barreled alias derived from an English author whose racist texts helped mold Hitler's Nazi doctrines."

DESCENDANTS

Today Alex counsels Vietnam veterans, and Louis and Brian are partners in a landscaping business. Gardner reports that the three surviving sons of William Patrick Hitler have made a pact never to marry or father children, in order to ensure that the male line of the Hitler family dies out when they are gone.

When Gardner asked William's widow and sons to sit for formal interviews for his book, they all declined. But Alex did make one request: "Just make sure you say good things about [Dad] because he was a good guy," Gardner quotes him as saying. "He came to the United States, he served in the U.S. Navy, he had four kids and he had a pretty good life."

Ernest Hemingway appeared in magazine ads for Parker Pens and Ballantine Ale.

CODE BROWN

More colorful language from our friends
in the healthcare profession. Stat!

TMB: Too Many Birthdays (suffering from old age)

FORD: Found On Road Dead

House Red: Blood

TRO: Time Ran Out

Frequent Flier: Someone who is regularly taken to the hospital in an ambulance, even though they aren't sick (because it's free and something to do)

Code Zero: Another name for a "Frequent Flyer." The real radio codes range from Code 1 (not serious) to Code 4 (emergency)

Code Yellow: A patient who has wet the bed

Code Brown: (You can guess this one yourself)

FOOSH: Fell Onto Outstretched Hand (a broken wrist)

T&T Sign: Tattoos-and-teeth. (Strange but true: Patients with a lot of tattoos and missing teeth are more likely to survive major injuries)

DFO: Done Fell Out (of bed)

MGM Syndrome: A "patient" who is faking illness and putting on a really good show

WNL: Will Not Listen

SYB: Save Your Breath, as in, "SYB, he WNL"

Insurance Pain: An inordinate amount of neck pain following a minor auto collision with a wealthy driver

ALP: Acute Lead Poisoning —a gunshot wound

ALP (A/C): Acute Lead Poisoning (Air Conditioning) —multiple gunshot wounds

Flower Sign: Lots of flowers at a patient's bedside (may indicate the patient is a good candidate for early discharge, since they have friends and family who can care for them)

ART: Assuming Room Temperature (deceased)

Bagged and Tagged: A body that is ready to be taken to the hospital morgue (it's in a body bag and has a toe tag)

AMF Yo Yo: Adios, Motherf@#*!, You're On Your Own

MADE IN CHINA

Have you ever noticed that it seems like everything is made in China? Well, almost everything is made in China. Here's why. (And if you want to know what's not made in China, see page 450.)

IN THE RED

Prior to World War II, China was a major economic force, exporting huge amounts of raw goods (such as tea and rice) all over the world. When Mao Tse-Tung's Communist government assumed control of China in 1949, it took over all of the country's businesses. Not content with only exporting agricultural goods, Chairman Mao wanted China to become a major industrial power. So he implemented China's first "Five Year Plan" for economic development. Money, resources, and labor were all allocated by the government, which also set wages and prices. Even consumption of food and goods would be controlled through strict rationing.

Result: industry grew rapidly, but agricultural production suffered. The next Five Year Plan (1958) aimed to revive the agricultural sector to such heights that China could be completely self-sufficient. Farming output increased as planned, but the government neglected to update food storage and transportation technology. A huge grain crop went to waste and, coupled with huge floods from failed irrigation experiments, 30 million people in China starved to death between 1958 and 1961—the worst famine in recorded history.

After China publicly criticized the USSR for bowing to American pressure and removing missiles from Cuba during the Cuban Missile Crisis, the Soviet Union withdrew economic assistance in 1962. The rest of the world turned its back on China after it invaded India twice (1959 and 1962), suppressed a rebellion in Tibet (1959), and aided Vietnam in the Vietnam War. By 1970, China was almost completely alone. Self-sufficiency was the goal—but isolation was the result.

NIXON GOES TO CHINA

Conditions would begin to improve after President Richard Nixon's 1971 visit to Beijing. China agreed to re-establish ties with the

---

Money well spent: It cost $1,505,675 to build the Eiffel Tower in 1887.

United States on the condition that American troops would leave Taiwan. (They had been stationed in the Chinese province since the Communist takeover.) Nixon agreed; tensions eased between China and the U.S.

OUT WITH THE OLD...

Chairman Mao died in 1976 and was replaced by the moderate Deng Xiaoping. Rejecting Mao's failed plans for self-sufficiency, Deng opened China to the world in 1980. To hasten modernization, the government encouraged foreign investment and invited western companies to bring their technology to China in the form of entire state-of-the-art Western factories. State-owned businesses remained the standard, but private ownership of companies became legal. Most revolutionary of all, the government took a capitalist approach to taxing businesses: it took a cut of the business' profits and allowed the remainder to be reinvested into the companies. The result of Deng's policies: China's industry grew at an annual rate of 11 percent in the 1980s and 17 percent in the 1990s, the fastest rate in the world at the time.

But here's what motivated American companies to open factories in China: cheap labor and lots of it. (As of 2002, the Chinese workforce was 762 million people.) China's large population creates huge demand (and competition) for jobs. This drives down wages, and they're made even lower by the government, which keeps pay rates low to control business costs. A worker in China earns about five percent of what a worker doing the same job in the United States would earn. Plus in China, there are no benefits, sick leave, or worker's compensation. China's labor laws are very relaxed: shifts can be 12 hours a day and most factories operate like sweatshops. One of the highest costs of doing business is labor, so low wages means products manufactured in China are unbeatably inexpensive, both to make and to buy.

WORLD DOMINATION

Today Western companies in almost every industry have factories in China. Even with the expense of moving overseas and constantly having to ship materials and goods to Chinese factories, the low wage rates (and lower taxes) still make it highly profitable. Economists estimate that as much as 90 percent of retail goods available in the United States were made in China.

- Some of the products: Apple computers, Avon cosmetics, Boeing airplanes, Clorox bleach, John Deere tractors, Dow chemicals, General Motors car parts, Hewlett-Packard printers, Johnson & Johnson first aid products, Mattel toys, Motorola cell phones, Toshiba televisions, Black & Decker drills, Intel microprocessors, Maytag appliances, Dell computers, Outboard Marine boats, Head & Shoulders shampoo, Rand McNally maps, Sony Play Stations, Serta mattresses, Sherwin-Williams paint, and Xerox copiers.

- Other companies use Chinese facilities to manufacture satellites, ships, trains, mining machinery, oil drilling equipment, power generators, plastics, pharmaceuticals, bicycles, sewing machines, metal knick-knacks, cement, coffee makers, shoes, and dishes.

- China produces more clothes than any other country. Its industry includes cotton, wool, linen, silk, and chemical fibers, as well as printing, dyeing, knitting, and automatic manufacture.

- China is the largest producer of steel in the world. From stainless steel to sheet metal to pipes, China passed Britain as the world's largest steel producer in the 1960s. The Chinese government increased industrial production so quickly by reassigning millions of farmers to crude backyard furnaces where they made steel from low-grade ore, scrap metal, and even household items.

- The world's six largest producers of American flags are all based in China. Most religious merchandise (like Virgin Mary statues, rosaries, and Buddha figurines) sold in the United States are made in China...a country with little religious freedom.

*　　*　　*

IRONIC DEATH

In 1958 Tyrone Power made a promotional film for the American Heart Association: "For all of us, the most precious element we have is time. But time runs out all too soon for millions of us because of an enemy that takes more lives than all other diseases combined: the heart." It was the last film he ever completed. A few months later, while filming a scene in *Solomon and Sheeba*, Power keeled over and died. The cause: heart attack.

The *Palustris hefner* species of rabbit is named for Playboy mogul Hugh Hefner.

(NOT) MADE IN CHINA

*Economists estimate that as much as 90% of all retail goods
available in the United States are made overseas, particularly in
China. These products include stereos, plastic toys, cups, belts,
TVs, shoes, T-shirts, backpacks, telephones, coffee makers,
toasters, and even religious memorabilia, just to name a few.
Even though so many things are made in China, the things
you might assume come from China probably don't.*

• **Fine china.** Most fine china plates are bone china, a high-quality porcelain. The majority of the world's china is made not in China, but in England, Italy, and the United States.

• **Tea.** The phrase "not for all the tea in China" is misleading—India is the world's largest grower of black tea, accounting for a third of the world's supply. China, where tea originated, produces 10%.

• **Opium.** Ever seen an old movie with a scene of Chinese men relaxing in an opium den? Opium isn't Chinese. The British smuggled it into China from India.

• **Rice.** Rice is closely associated with Chinese food. But China isn't the world's largest exporter. Not even close. Thailand shipped 7.5 million tons of rice in 2002. China exported only 2 million.

• **Chinese restaurants.** There are 73 Chinese food restaurants in China's capital city, Beijing. In New York City, there are more than 300.

• **China dolls.** They were *never* made in China. Germany, France, and Denmark began making these porcelain dolls in the 1840s.

• **Fortune cookies.** They were invented in 1914 at San Francisco's Japanese Tea Garden. While there are now fortune cookie factories in China, most are made by the Wonton Food Company in New York—they churn out 2.5 million cookies daily.

• **Chinese checkers.** Based on Halma, an earlier game played on a square board. Pressman Brothers created a star-shaped game board in 1928 and called it Chinese Checkers to capitalize on the popularity of mah-jongg.

According to the experts, 75% of people wash their stomach first when showering.

OOPS!

More tales of outrageous blunders.

NEXT TIME, BRING A MAP

"A $200,000 diamond on the front of Christian Klien's Formula One car is missing after he crashed during the Monaco Grand Prix yesterday. The button-sized diamond was part of a promotion for the forthcoming film, *Ocean's 12*, starring George Clooney. The diamond disappeared between Klien crashing his car on the opening lap, and the car reaching the Jaguar garage more than two hours later. Klien said: 'That will be the most expensive drive I'll ever take around Monte Carlo.'"

—*Ananova*

IT'S ALL COMING BACK TO ME NOW

"A report in the *Rochester Democrat and Chronicle* described a local patient's remarkable recovery from botulism paralysis. After the toxin struck her in June 2000, the woman lay in her hospital bed, able to hear everything around her but unable to communicate in any way. Someone erroneously said she was a big fan of singer Celine Dion and after that, in an effort to aid the woman's recovery, the hospital staff played the singer's music in her room around the clock for weeks. When the paralysis left the woman, one of the first joys she experienced, she said, was stopping the music because she actually never cared for Dion."

—*Albany* (New York) *Times-Union*

DON'T SLEEP WITH YOUR MOUTH OPEN

"A sleeping Indian street worker had to be rushed to the hospital when he woke to find a mouse had climbed into his mouth and lodged in his windpipe. 'It was a terrible experience,' said the man. 'The mouse has ruined my appetite.' (The mouse didn't survive.)"

—**Universal Press Syndicate**

SOMETHING'S FISHY

"Firefighters in London believe a goldfish bowl may have acted as a magnifying glass which concentrated the sun's rays and set fire to a rat-catcher's poisonous chemicals. The sun's rays entered a shed where the goldfish were kept and then passed through to another where tablets of aluminum phosphide were stored. The chemicals gave off noxious fumes when firemen tried to dampen them down. Eighteen firefighters, four paramedics, and four neighbors were taken to the hospital suffering from vomiting, nausea and burning chest sensations. The goldfish did not survive the conflagration."

—**Reuters**

SURPRISE!

"A lovesick couple passed each other mid-flight when they both tried to surprise their partner with a round-the-world visit. Ian Johnstone, a bricklayer in Australia, took a flight back to the Yorkshire home he shared with his girlfriend Amy Dolby with the intention of proposing to her. At the same time, Dolby was on her way to Sydney to surprise him. The couple even both had stopovers in Singapore at the same time. He arrived at their flat with champagne, flowers, and an engagement ring only to find it empty. He was woken that night by a phone call from Dolby, who was 11,000 miles away, wondering where he was. 'It was as though someone was playing a cruel joke,' she told the *Daily Telegraph*. The couple ended up spending two weeks apart, and will not see each other again for six months."

—**BBC News**

TROPHY CHILD

"An 11-month-old baby became stuck in the European Cup after his father put him in it for a photo. The Barcelona fan was at the club's museum when he put the baby in the replica of the original. It took police and firemen more than 20 minutes to get the baby out. The baby was unharmed."

—*Ananova*

ADULT EDUCATION

"The Derry School District in Derry, New Hampshire, has removed the link to the 'Save Our Schools' committee from its Web site. Reason: When a town official clicked on the link, it took him to a porn site, instead. It turns out that someone at the 'Save Our Schools' committee let their domain name expire, and it was purchased by the porn site. 'It's embarrassing,' district superintendent John Moody told reporters, 'but inadvertent.'"

—*Parker's Compendium*

Ani-mail: Cows, camels, reindeer, and cats have all been used to deliver mail.

A DUMMARY OF WORDS

Here's a fun game from the Washington Post: *pick a word and add, subtract, or alter a single letter to give it a new meaning.*

Philaunderer. He may hop from bed to bed, but he always washes the sheets.

Palindromeo. Casanova von Asac, a legendary 18th-century seducer, later revealed to have gone both ways.

The Fundead. Corpses who walk around at night with lampshades on their heads.

Apocalypso. Day-o, me-day-day-day-ay-o. Doomsday come, and me want to go home.

Guiltar. A musical instrument whose strings are pulled by your mother.

Sitcoma. Typical TV fare.

Frognostication. The science of predicting the exact day and month that France will surrender.

Errorist. A member of a radical cult who blows himself up in a mannequin factory.

Siddhmartha. A young Indian mystic who discovers the true meaning of life as a ferryman serving only the finest in freshly caught, hickory-grilled, and lightly lemon-seasoned fillets.

Wisenheifer. A calf who sneaks up and tips over sleeping cows.

Idiotarod. An annual Alaskan race in which morons pull huskies sitting on sleds.

Nimby-pamby. Not being able to decide what to keep out of one's backyard.

Dummary. An unnecessary explanation of a patently obvious concept (e.g.: "Dummary: an unnecessary explanation of a patently obvious concept").

Eficient. Extremely efficient.

Urinpal. A guy who uses the one next to you even though all the others are unoccupied.

Whorde. Group of prostitutes.

Hippopotamush. Love letters from Marlon Brando to Roseanne.

Rescute. Saving the attractive women, children, and puppies first.

Tskmaster. An ineffective slave driver.

Platyplus. A mammal with webbed feet, a duck bill and opposable thumbs.

First wildflower of the year: the skunk cabbage, which starts blooming in February.

BATHROOM STATISTICS

You'd be surprised how many corporations and other organizations finance surveys of bathroom-related opinions and behaviors...just to see what you're doing in there. Some recent findings:

AT HOME
- 30% of people suffer from *nocturia*—they have to get up at least once a night to pee.
- 74% of people read in the bathroom (Go team!); 47% talk on the phone; 11% eat in there.
- Top five pet peeves of sharing a bathroom:
   1) Not replacing the toilet paper when it runs out.
   2) Leaving the seat up (according to women).
      Too many cosmetics on the counter (according to men).
   3) Leaving toothpaste globs in the sink.
   4) Leaving spots on the mirror.
   5) Leaving dirty clothes on the floor.
- When watching the Super Bowl, 38% of viewers go to the bathroom during the commercials, so they won't miss the game; 23% go during the game, so they won't miss the commercials.

AWAY FROM HOME
- 74% perform some type of "maintenance" task—wiping the seat, flushing, putting down a seat cover—before using a public toilet. Nearly a third say they bring their own materials—Kleenex, sanitizing wipes, etc.—to perform the task.
- 7% suffer from *paruresis*—shy bladder syndrome.
- 40% flush restroom toilets with their feet instead of their hands.
- 38% of people say they've peeked into someone else's medicine cabinet. (4% of these snoops say they were caught in the act.)

PAPER TRAIL
- Most valued quality in toilet paper: softness (absorbency is #2).
- Survey respondents are almost equally divided on how they use toilet paper: 51% "crumple or wad" it; 49% "fold" it.
- 60% are annoyed by scratchy toilet paper in public restrooms.

Jack Nicholson has a rattlesnake embedded in his toilet seat.

ABBEY-NORMAL

Holy cow! Strange news from the church!

DELIVER US FROM CLOTHING

St. Martin's Church in Gloucestershire, England, published a fund-raising calendar in 2004—an all-nude calendar featuring 13 of the church's female parishioners posing in the buff. They hope to raise $75,000 to aid women's groups in Rwanda.

CHRISTIAN SCIENTIST?

A 22-year-old man broke into Bethel Moravian Church in North Dakota and set up a methamphetamine lab in the kitchen. He was caught and arrested just as he had all the supplies and paraphernalia set up and ready to go. "A church almost makes sense," said Sheriff Lieutenant Rick Majerus. "If nobody is using the church during the week, it doesn't take a rocket scientist to see the possibilities." Pastor Dave Sobek took a slightly more cynical view, noting, "I'd prefer that our kitchen be used for bake sales."

SPECIAL DISPENSATION

In 2004 the Croatian Church officially requested that priests be exempt from certain laws—drunk-driving laws. At the time, the Croatian government was considering lowering drivers' legal blood-alcohol limit from 0.05% to zero. Church officials protested that many priests had to drive home or to parishioners' homes directly after drinking small amounts of wine while giving mass. "If this law goes ahead," said one incredulous official, "a huge number of priests will soon be behind bars."

AN INSULT TO GOD (AND MY ACCOUNTANT)

Guests at a June 2004 wedding in North Yorkshire, Australia, were surprised to see a sign next to the collection plate, reading: "Paper Money Only." The Reverend Mark Sowerby explained that anything less than $10 would be an "insult to God." But it was the bride who was insulted. "It was my big day," said 20-year-old Anne-Marie Whitton. "It cost a lot of money, took a lot of organizing, and the vicar ruined it." The reverend disagreed: "Christians

---

A single snowflake is made of up to 200 separate snow crystals.

worship a God who is to be praised and glorified, not tipped with less than the price of a pint."

HERE COMES PETER COTTONTAIL—WHACK!

Several parents complained after the Glassport Assembly of God church in Pennsylvania put on an Easter show in 2004. It featured performers breaking Easter eggs and whipping the Easter Bunny. Melissa Salzmann, who took her four-year-old to the show, said the boy was traumatized. "He was crying and asking why the bunny was being whipped," she said. Minister Patty Bickerton defended the performance, saying it was meant to be educational. "We wanted to convey that Easter is not just about the Easter Bunny, it is about Jesus Christ." Said Salzmann, "It was a nightmare."

DOGMA?

Every year thousands of tourists come to the 155-year-old Phe Chaung Buddhist monastery in a desolate part of Myanmar (formerly Burma). But they don't travel all that way to see the six monks who live there—they go to see the jumping cats. The monks recently took in some stray cats and, out of boredom, decided to teach them to jump through hoops. Videos of the cats—named Madonna, Marilyn Monroe, Leonardo DiCaprio, and Diana—have been shown on TV and have made them famous around the world. "Nobody ever asks about Buddhism," complained one of the monks. "They just want to see the cats."

MIXED MESSAGE

The 12th century Spanish Monastery in North Miami Beach, Florida (it was disassembled and moved to the U.S. in 1925), is known for its stark gothic architecture and is often rented out for commercials, music videos, and films (parts of Ace Ventura: Pet Detective were shot there). But in 1998 the monastery's staff accidentally allowed filmmaker Ron Atkins to shoot parts of Dark Night of the Soul there. What's wrong with that? The film contains scenes of opium-smoking zombies in bizarre sex scenes spouting anti-religious dialogue—with the monastery in the background. After the movie came out, the staff announced that its filmmaking rules would be reviewed. "We probably missed that one," said spokeswoman Tonya Witten.

WHO WAS DEEP THROAT?

Thirty years after Watergate, Washington's best-kept secret is still a secret. Only four people know the answer—and they aren't telling. (Hint: It wasn't Uncle John...or was it?)

BACKGROUND

BThe Crime: In the early morning of June 17, 1972, a team of five burglars were arrested in the act of breaking into the Democratic Party's National Committee offices in the Watergate Hotel in downtown Washington, D.C.

The Burglars: The break-in, it turned out, was not a random burglary—it was led by the security director for President Richard Nixon's reelection committee, a former CIA agent named James McCord. McCord and the other four burglars, one a soldier of fortune and the other three Miami Cubans, had all been CIA operatives in the failed 1961 Bay of Pigs invasion of Cuba.

The Masterminds: The people behind what Nixon press secretary Ron Ziegler later called a "third-rate burglary" were former FBI agent G. Gordon Liddy and former CIA agent E. Howard Hunt (another Bay of Pigs veteran). They were part of a group known as the "Plumbers," a secret White House team assembled to stop "leaks" after defense analyst Daniel Ellsberg revealed classified documents to the press in 1971.

The Reason: Exactly what the burglars were after remains a mystery. One possibility: They were trying to photograph financial documents or plant listening devices in hopes of obtaining information damaging to the Democrats. But G. Gordon Liddy has claimed publicly that the burglars were sent by White House counsel John Dean on a very specific counterintelligence mission: to retrieve a photo of Dean's fiancée that was in a package of information about call girls the Democratic committee used to entertain guests. (Dean dismisses Liddy, who is now a talk-show host, as a man who "earns his living making a jackass of himself.")

The Aftermath: As bad as the bungled break-in was, the White

Grass guzzler: In 1986 Ben Garcia rode his lawnmower from Maine to California.

House compounded the problem by trying to cover it up. What followed were two years of FBI investigations and Senate hearings, which led to more than 40 criminal convictions and culminated with the resignation of President Richard Nixon.

The Reporters: None of it would have come to light if it hadn't been for a fledgling *Washington Post* reporter on the night shift. Bob Woodward had been assigned to cover the break-in, which looked like a routine burglary. But at the arraignment, Woodward heard one of the men arrested admit that he worked for the CIA and realized that the bungled burglary might not be so routine after all. Over the next two years, Woodward and his partner Carl Bernstein wrote some 400 Watergate-related stories that implicated many in the Nixon administration, including the president himself, in a wide-ranging attempt to cover up not only the Watergate break-in, but numerous other politically motivated dirty tricks as well. That work made Woodward and Bernstein famous, and changed the political landscape of America.

The Source: The pair interviewed hundreds of sources and sorted through conflicting and often misleading information. But they had help: Woodward claims he was guided by a mysterious inform- ant, dubbed "Deep Throat" by *Washington Post* managing editor Howard Simons (a reference to an X-rated movie of that name).

As Deep Throat put it, the Watergate burglary was "just the tip of the iceberg."

MAN OF MYSTERY

Deep Throat demanded anonymity, so Woodward promised his identity would remain a secret as long as he was alive or until he released Woodward from his promise. But Woodward did tell two other people: his partner, Carl Bernstein, and *Washington Post* executive editor Ben Bradlee. After Nixon's resignation, Bradlee insisted that Woodward tell him Deep Throat's identity, and Woodward did. Ever since, those four—Woodward, Bernstein, Bradlee, and Deep Throat—have kept the secret safe, which has led to intense speculation about Deep Throat's identity.

In June 2002, the 30th anniversary of the Watergate break-in, brought a renewed flurry of speculation as to the identity of Deep Throat. A journalism class at the University of Illinois, led by for- mer Pulitzer Prize-winning investigative journalist William

Gaines, narrowed the field to seven likely candidates after extensive research.

Former White House counsel John Dean published an e-book at Salon.com that revealed his best guess after 25 years of research —a list of five. (But Dean has publicly named Deep Throat twice before and admits he was wrong both times.)

In two books about Watergate and in numerous public appearances, Woodward has dropped some intriguing clues. The University of Illinois journalism class, Dean, and others have used these clues, as well as travel records, personality profiles, and speculation as to who knew what when, to try to solve the 30-year mystery. But first, the questions:

• **Was Deep Throat someone who worked in the White House?** Because of the extensive and accurate inside information Deep Throat gave Woodward about Nixon's White House, some think he must have worked for the president. John Dean insists that only someone on the inside could have known all the information Deep Throat gave to Woodward. The university journalism class agrees.

• **Was Deep Throat in the CIA?** The clandestine nature of the relationship between Woodward and Deep Throat seems to suggest a skill at what the spy community calls "tradecraft"—tricks of the trade taught to CIA agents. According to Woodward, he and Deep Throat would meet in an underground parking garage. Woodward would put a flower pot with a red flag in it on the balcony of his apartment when he wanted Deep Throat to contact him. Deep Throat contacted Woodward by marking the copy of the morning *New York Times* delivered to Woodward's door.

• **Was a disgruntled FBI officer getting revenge on Nixon by passing classified info to Woodward?** Much of Woodward and Bernstein's coverage seemed to parallel the FBI's findings, and the Bureau's discoveries found their way into *Washington Post* stories with remarkable speed. FBI director J. Edgar Hoover died just seven weeks before the Watergate break-in, and it shocked many within the Bureau when Nixon appointed an outsider, Assistant Attorney General L. Patrick Gray, to become the FBI's acting director. What about Gray? Did Nixon misjudge his loyalty?

THE BEST GUESSES
The White House? The FBI? The CIA?

✗ **Patrick Buchanan, Nixon speechwriter.** Voted "most likely" by the University of Illinois journalism class and one of the five named by John Dean, Buchanan was in a position to know all of the information Deep Throat passed on to Woodward. Though he was perceived as a Nixon loyalist, the staunch right-winger was upset with Nixon for recognizing Communist China.

✗ **Ron Ziegler, Nixon press secretary.** Another person suspected by John Dean, Ziegler was privy to what was going on inside the Nixon White House. Ziegler was in Washington on all the dates Woodward says he met with Deep Throat.

✗ **Henry Kissinger, Nixon's secretary of state.** Paradoxically, Kissinger was perhaps Nixon's closest confidant. Though Jewish, Kissinger seemed to tolerate Nixon's anti-Semitic views, even endorsing them on occasion. However, Kissinger's support for Nixon served his own quest for power; he could have used the Watergate debacle to take care of some personal scores.

✗ **General Alexander Haig, military aid to Henry Kissinger and later Nixon's chief of staff.** Haig has strongly denied that he was Deep Throat, particularly during his unsuccessful bid for the 1988 Republican presidential nomination. Uncharacteristically, Woodward confirmed that Haig was not Deep Throat. Denials aside, Haig remains, in the opinion of many, a leading contender because of his access to White House secrets.

✗ **Leonard Garment, special counsel to Richard Nixon.** Garment was known to be friendly with the press, and before joining the Nixon team he had been a liberal Democrat. Garment not only denies he was Deep Throat, but in a recent book, *In Search of Deep Throat*, he names his pick—John Sears.

✗ **John Sears, deputy counsel to President Nixon.** Leonard Garment says he favors Sears because he fits the partial description Woodward has given of Deep Throat as being a cigarette-smoking Scotch drinker who was fascinated by the rumors and scheming of the Nixon White House. Sears claims he didn't know Woodward until after Watergate and has threatened to sue Garment.

✗ **L. Patrick Gray, FBI Director.** Gray has been cited as a prime suspect because of his access to information about both the FBI and the White House. A 1992 CBS documentary said Gray was in Washington on all the dates Woodward gives for his clandestine

---

The Greek temple of Aphrodite, goddess of love, was discovered by archeologist Iris Love.

meetings with the informant. Gray lived just four blocks from Woodward in a building with an underground parking garage. He was an early morning jogger and could have easily marked Woodward's copy of the *New York Times* and seen the flower pot with the red flag on Woodward's balcony.

Gray reportedly became disillusioned with the Nixon White House as the Watergate scandal unfolded. In spite of being a Nixon appointee, Gray provided testimony to the Senate Judiciary Committee that was instrumental in pointing to White House involvement in the break-in.

✓ **Mark Felt, FBI Deputy Associate Director.** In July 1999, the *Hartford Courant* ran a story that quoted a 19-year-old named Chase Culeman-Beckman, who claimed that Carl Bernstein's son Jacob had told him at summer camp in 1988 that Felt was Deep Throat. Bernstein says he and Woodward never told their family members Deep Throat's identity.

Agents in the FBI also thought Felt was Deep Throat, according to former *Washington Post* investigative reporter Ronald Kessler in a recent book, *The Bureau: The Secret History of the FBI*. Felt clearly had reason to try to influence the course of the investigation. He had protested White House interference and may have resented not being appointed FBI director after the death of J. Edgar Hoover. But in a 1979 book, *The FBI Pyramid: Inside the FBI*, he denied that he had ever leaked information to Woodward.

STILL A MYSTERY

In spite of the long list of suspects, we may never know Deep Throat's identity. Many believe Deep Throat was a composite of several sources, or a fabrication. Bob Woodward insists that Deep Throat was real, and just one person. After Deep Throat dies, Woodward says, he will be released from his promise of secrecy and will reveal all. Will he? Perhaps…but one of the lessons of Watergate is that truth sometimes falls victim to other motives.

*   *   *

"The biggest conspiracy has always been the fact that there is no conspiracy. Nobody's out to get you. Nobody cares whether you live or die. There, you feel better now?"
—Dennis Miller

Eyelashes are typically the darkest hairs on the body.

FUNNY MONEY

*Years ago, Uncle John owned a toy store. One day a customer tried
to pay him with a photocopy of a $20 bill. Did Uncle John fall for
it? Well, let's just say he doesn't think these stories are funny.*

TRUST ME—IT'S REAL MONEY

In 2004, 35-year-old Alice Pike tried to pay for $1,671.55
worth of merchandise at a Covington, Georgia, Wal-Mart
with a $1 million bill. The clerk sensibly refused it ($1 million
bills don't exist). Unfazed, Pike offered to pay with a Wal-Mart gift
card worth $2.32...*plus* the $1 million bill. The clerk then pre-
tended to take it, and while Pike was waiting for her $998,331.17
change, Wal-Mart called the cops. When they arrested her on
forgery charges, they found two more $1 million bills on her.

TRUST ME—IT'S REAL MONEY. REALLY.

Police in Saitama, Japan, discovered more than 400 phony 1,000-
yen bills in vending machines, but they don't know who made
them—or why. Real 1,000-yen bills have three colored strips. On
the fake bills, one strip is a photocopy, but the other two are real,
lifted from real currency. In other words, the counterfeiter cut up
real 1,000-yen bills to make fake ones. Police can't figure out why
someone would make counterfeit money that cost more to produce
than it was worth.

TRUST ME—IT'S REALLY REAL MONEY. REALLY.

During World War II, the German government recruited prisoners
with experience in typography, printing, and forgery for a special
assignment: to make counterfeit British money. The Nazis planned
to flood the world market with it, hoping to devalue the pound
and cripple the British economy. They made £134 million ($377
million) in phony £5, £10, £20, and £50 notes and then dropped
them over London. But they didn't count on one thing: the hon-
esty of the Brits. Most people picked the cash up off the
street...and turned it over to the police. The Bank of England
quickly changed the design of its bills, and an economic crisis was
averted. (All's fair: At the same time, the United States and
England were counterfeiting German currency.)

WOODEN YOU KNOW

*Uncle John may never see…a thing as splendid as
a tree—except for this article full of tree facts.*

• In 2002 Luis H. Carrasco of Santiago, Chile, produced the world's only five-fruited tree after grafting different species onto a single tree. The fruits: apricots, cherries, nectarines, plums, and peaches.

• In memory of his wife Rachel, President Andrew Jackson planted a sapling on the White House lawn, grown from a seed from her favorite magnolia tree. Look on the back of an old $20 bill: It's the tree covering the left side of the White House.

• The slowest-growing tree in the world: a white cedar in the Canadian Great Lakes region. It grew to a height of four inches and weighed only 17 grams (0.6 oz.) after 155 years.

• Studies have shown that viewing scenery of trees can speed up the recovery time of hospital patients, reduce stress levels in the workplace, and increase employee productivity.

• More than a million acres of land worldwide (and 100,000 people) are used for growing Christmas trees.

• Native to Malaysia, the cauliflorous jackfruit yields the largest fruit grown on a tree—almost three feet long and 75 pounds (and it's edible).

• In a single day a tree can transpire 100 gallons of water through its leaves, creating a cooling process equivalent to five window air conditioners running 20 hours a day.

• The desert baobab tree can store up to 35,000 gallons of water in its trunk.

• Have you ever come across an old pecan tree that bends down to the ground and then turns upward? The Comanche were nomadic Plains Indians who marked their campsites by bending a pecan sapling and tying it to the ground. The last known specimen died in 2003, but there may be more, undiscovered.

• Because they constantly produce new wood to thwart decay, yew trees can live to be 4,000 years old. With such an amazing regenerative ability, scientists theorize that there is no reason for yew to die.

A large tree can have as many as 400,000 leaves.

THE CIA'S FIRST COUP, PART III

Here's the third and final installment of the story of the 1953 coup in Iran. (Part II is on page 303.)

IF AT FIRST YOU DON'T SUCCEED...

Where was CIA agent Kermit Roosevelt when all of this was happening? When the coup fell apart, he met with General Zahedi at his hiding place north of Tehran. Comparing notes, they realized that they still might have a chance to pull it off. They still had the shah's signed decrees firing Mossadegh and appointing Zahedi prime minister. If they could go public with the document and get the shah to broadcast an address to the country, they could paint Mossadegh as the usurper and possibly drive him from power.

Roosevelt returned to the CIA station in Tehran and arranged for Iranian newspapers to publish the details of the decree. CIA headquarters cabled Roosevelt and told him to get out of the country, but Roosevelt cabled back, telling them that he wanted to stay a little longer, because there was "a slight remaining chance of success."

Roosevelt staged a mob drama on the streets of Tehran over the next few days. While his contacts in the Iranian military went from barracks to barracks recruiting pro-shah officers to participate in a second coup attempt, other Iranian agents worked the slums of Tehran, hiring thugs to form the nucleus of a pro-Mossadegh mob that would take to the streets on Monday, August 17, and again on Tuesday. This mob was instructed to riot—Roosevelt wanted them to smash storefronts, overturn cars, topple statues of the shah and his father, and even attack innocent bystanders. They were to do all of this, Roosevelt instructed, while shouting slogans praising Mossadegh and Communism.

ACT 1

The pro-Mossadegh mob hit the streets on Monday. As they marched through Tehran, many sincere Mossadegh supporters joined the crowd to show their support, swelling the ranks until tens of thousands of people were on the march. After two days of

---

rioting, the American ambassador, who was in on the plot, paid a visit to Mossadegh to complain (falsely) that the protesters were targeting Americans—especially embassy staff—with violence, threats, and abuse. Mossadegh, who believed in freedom of assembly and had been inclined to let the demonstrations continue, fell for the ruse and ordered the police to start cracking down. He also issued a decree banning any further public demonstrations, and phoned his political allies and told them to keep their people home.

Meanwhile, the CIA's Iranian agents were out on the streets of Tehran passing out thousands of copies of the shah's decrees. The CIA also planted fake stories in Iranian newspapers claiming that Mossadegh was behind the first coup, and had attempted to kick the shah off the throne and seize it for himself. This, combined with two days of rioting by supposed Mossadegh supporters, cast doubt on Mossadegh's legitimacy and made him, in the eyes of many, a symbol of chaos.

ACT 2
On Wednesday, Roosevelt called out his second group of paid demonstrators. This time he instructed the crowd to support the shah and to behave peaceably. Instead of engaging in random violence, they were only supposed to vandalize the newspapers and offices that supported Mossadegh. The ban on public demonstrations was still in place, but because this crowd was seen as being the public's nonviolent response to two days of rioting by an angry mob, the police did not disperse it.

Just as the first mob had, this one attracted many thousands of sincere Iranians who either supported the shah or were just outraged by the anarchy of the previous two days. Mossadegh's supporters honored his request to stay home, so few were in the streets to support him. No one, probably not even the paid demonstrators, realized they were being manipulated by the CIA.

ACT 3
As these demonstrators were marching in Tehran, Roosevelt sent his pro-shah Army officers and troops into action. They seized the main squares and other key points in the city, including the radio

station, which began announcing that Mossadegh had already been deposed and arrested, even as troops were still marching on his house to do just that.

The battle at Mossadegh's house lasted for more than nine hours, ending only when his forces ran out of ammunition and Mossadegh himself escaped over the back wall of his garden. He surrendered the next evening and was taken into custody.

FINALE

• Mossadegh spent 10 weeks in a military prison and then was hauled before a military tribunal and tried for treason. He was found guilty and served three years in prison. He lived the rest of his life under house arrest, with only family and close friends allowed to visit him. He died from throat cancer in March 1967.

• Even though the goal of the coup was to restore Anglo-Iranian's concession, the company was so despised that after the shah regained the throne he could not risk it. Instead, an international consortium of foreign oil companies was set up to administer the concession together. Anglo-Iranian was reduced to a 40% stake, and the remaining 60% of the consortium's shares were split between five American oil companies, one French oil company, and Royal Dutch/Shell.

In a final slap at Mossadegh, the foreign-owned, foreign-controlled consortium took the name of the company that he had created when Anglo-Iranian's assets were nationalized in 1951: the National Iranian Oil Company.

So how Iranian was the new National Iranian Oil Company? Not very—from now on profits would be split with Iran on a 50/50 basis, but just like before, Iranians were not allowed on the board of directors and were not allowed to audit company books.

Mohammed Reza Shah returned to the throne determined never to let anyone threaten his power again. He abolished opposition parties and set up a one-party state, and reinforced his rule by beefing up the military and police. With the help of the CIA, he also established his own secret police force, SAVAK. As the years passed, his rule became more autocratic and corrupt, causing opposition to grow steadily in the 1960s and 1970s. In January 1979, he was swept from power by Islamic fundamentalists.

WHAT MIGHT HAVE BEEN

How would Iran be different today, had Mossadegh not been overthrown in 1953? Well, the country might have gradually evolved into a full-fledged democracy, perhaps even becoming a model of freedom for other nations in the Middle East. Then again, Iran was an unstable, oil-rich nation that bordered the USSR. It had an active, growing Communist party with strong ties to the Soviet Union, which had a history of setting up puppet governments in other countries around the world. Joseph Stalin died in March 1953 and was replaced by Nikita Khrushchev, the man who triggered the Cuban missile crisis with the United States in 1962. Would he have been content to leave a weak, unstable oil-rich neighbor alone?

By overthrowing Mossadegh, the United States may have prevented Iran from developing into a democracy...or it may only have set up a U.S.-sponsored dictatorship in place of a Soviet-sponsored dictatorship, which might have turned out to be even worse. We'll never know.

AFTERMATH

It may not have seemed like it at the time, but the United States was as profoundly affected by the 1953 coup as Iran:

The CIA

The CIA was only six years old in 1953, and the coup in Iran was its very first attempt to overthrow a foreign government from behind the scenes. The coup's astonishing success inspired the CIA to attempt similar coups in other countries, including Guatemala in 1954, the Congo in 1960, Cuba (the failed Bay of Pigs Invasion) in 1961, and Chile in 1973.

Foreign Policy

In the early 1950s the United States was seen in many parts of the world as opposing colonialism and supporting the nationalist ambitions of developing countries. (The United States had fought for its independence from England, after all.) But the CIA coups, along with the Vietnam War, gradually turned world opinion against the United States. America came to be seen as a country that would support oppressive dictatorships over democracy whenever dictatorships suited its interests.

The cornea is the only body part with no blood supply. It gets oxygen directly from the air.

Middle East Conflicts

• After 1953 the United States replaced Great Britain as the shah's most important sponsor. Result: Opponents of the shah's regime turned against the United States. The shah was deposed in January 1979, and when he traveled to the United States for cancer treatment the following October, Iranian students stormed the U.S. embassy in Tehran, seized the Americans inside, and held them hostage for 444 days. Whatever hope there was for an improvement in relations between America and revolutionary Iran evaporated when Iran's new leader, Ayatollah Ruholla Khomeini, refused to release the hostages until the shah returned to Iran.

• Iran's neighbor, Iraq, tried to capitalize on the chaos that followed the Iranian revolution by invading in 1980. The United States sided with Saddam Hussein, providing weapons, intelligence, and economic assistance.

• The war raged for eight years, devastating the economies of both countries, before it finally ended in a stalemate. Hussein borrowed more than $14 billion from Kuwait to help finance the war, and a dispute over repayment was one of the major pretexts for his invasion of Kuwait in 1990. The Iraqi invasion of Kuwait, in turn, led to the Gulf War between the United States and Iraq in 1991.

9/11

The Islamic fundamentalist state that was set up in Iran following the revolution of 1979 supported Islamic terrorist groups around the world. It also served as an inspiration to Muslim extremists all over the world, including Afghanistan, where Muslim fundamentalists known as the Taliban established a similar theocratic state in 1996.

The Taliban, in turn, hosted Saudi terrorist Osama bin Laden as he planned his attack on the United States that took place on September 11, 2001. "It is not far-fetched," historian Stephen Kinzer writes in *All the Shah's Men*, "to draw a line from Operation Ajax through the shah's repressive regime and the Islamic Revolution to the fireballs that engulfed the World Trade Center in New York."

* * *

"There is nothing new in the world except the history you do not know."
—**President Harry S Truman**

FAMOUS FOR
15 MINUTES

Here it is—our feature based on Andy Warhol's prophetic remark that "in the future, everyone will be famous for 15 minutes." Here's how a few people have used up their allotted quarter hour.

THE STARS: Tom Anderson, 24, a bartender and his fiancée, Sabrina Root, 33, a hair stylist
THE HEADLINE: *Here Comes the Bride...Inc.*
WHAT HAPPENED: Anderson and Root wanted a big wedding, but couldn't afford to pay for it. At the time Anderson was trying to start an animation company. "It occurred to me that a startup company and a startup couple both need launch money," he said. So Anderson devised a marketing plan and hit the bricks, asking 80 different companies to sponsor his wedding. In return, he offered to plug their businesses six times: 1) in the invitation, 2) in a newspaper ad, 3) at the buffet table, 4) at each dinner table, 5) in a speech after the toast, and 6) in the thank-you cards the couple would send to their guests. "I made them realize that for the few hundred dollars they were putting in, they were going to get a ton of exposure," Anderson said.

Of the 80 companies he approached, 24 said yes. In all, they chipped in $30,000 worth of goods and services, while Anderson and his fiancée only paid about $4,000 out of their own pockets.
AFTERMATH: The story was picked up by news wire services and even got them invited onto *The Oprah Winfrey Show*. The publicity inspired cash-strapped couples in Ohio, Florida, and other states to copy the idea, and at least one company has sprung up to advise engaged couples on corporate sponsorship. (*Note:* They don't donate their services—you have to pay for it.)

THE STAR: Ashley Revell, 32, a professional poker player
THE HEADLINE: *High-Stakes High Jinks: Batty Brit Bets It All*
WHAT HAPPENED: In early 2004, Revell decided to sell all of his possessions and bet all the money he made on a single spin of a Las Vegas roulette wheel. Over the next several weeks, Revell sold

Termite mounds can grow to up to 20 feet high.

everything—his car, furniture, jewelry, and clothes—and raised more than $135,000. Then he flew to Las Vegas, went up to the roulette wheel at the Plaza Hotel and Casino, bet it all on red...and won! He walked out of the casino $135,000 richer. (Had he lost, he would have owned nothing, not even the clothes on his back—he was wearing a rented tuxedo.)

AFTERMATH: Revell became a celebrity in England when British TV made his story into a documentary called *Double or Nothing*. About the only thing he didn't accomplish was winning his father's respect. "He's a naughty boy," Revell's dad told a London newspaper. "I tell my kids they shouldn't gamble. I've got four others, and now they're all going to want to go the same way."

THE STAR: Norman Hutchins, 53, of York, England

THE HEADLINE: *Masked Man Makes Hospital History*

WHAT HAPPENED: In January 2004, Hutchins walked into a hospital and explained to a staffer that he was going to a costume party dressed as a doctor. Could he borrow a surgical gown, a mask, and some rubber gloves? The staffer was cooperative at first, but when Hutchins asked her to accompany him into the restroom, she became suspicious and called police.

The staffer's suspicions were quickly confirmed. Hutchins was a fetishist with an obsession for surgical clothing. For 15 years, he'd been visiting various English and Welsh hospitals with invented excuses like costume parties, stage plays, animal experiments, and charity "fun runs," hoping to con hospital staff into giving him masks, gloves, and other attire.

AFTERMATH: Hutchins had managed to avoid the notice of the National Health Service...until they set up a new computer system and began compiling statistics nationwide. In the first five months alone, Hutchins racked up 47 different incidents at hospitals all over England. That's when he made British medical history: in June 2004, he became the first person ever to be banned from every public and private hospital, medical office, and dental office in the country. (He can still get treated for a genuine medical emergency, but if he fakes it, he faces five years in prison.)

THE STAR: Kimberly Mays, 9, from Florida

THE HEADLINE: *Girl, Switched at Birth, Wants to Stay Switched*

WHAT HAPPENED: In 1988 a 9-year-old girl named Arlena Twigg died from a heart defect. Tissue samples taken from Arlena revealed something astonishing: she wasn't related to her biological parents, Ernest and Regina Twigg. How was that possible? The Twiggs began looking for an answer, and their search led them to Kimberly Mays, who'd been born at the same hospital as Arlena, within a few days of Arlena. Genetic test results proved the unthinkable—Arlena and Kimberly had been switched at birth.

The story made headlines worldwide but probably would have died out quickly if the Mayses and the Twiggs could have come to an agreement on custody and visitation rights. Kimberly's father, Bob Mays, agreed to give the Twiggs visitation rights at first, but when, after five visits, Kimberly became depressed and her grades started slipping, he reneged. The Twiggs sued and the fight for Kimberly dragged on for five years. Finally a judge ruled that although they were her biological parents, the Twiggs had no parental rights whatsoever.

AFTERMATH: The long public tug of war between two sets of parents took its toll on Kimberly Mays. Six months after the court decision, she ran away from the Mayses and went to live with the Twiggs. Then she ran away from them. At 18 she got married and gave birth to a son. But she wasn't taking a chance that what happened to her might happen to him. "I had him right beside me in the hospital," she says. "All the time."

*   *   *

ENGLISH SIGNS AND LABELS SEEN IN JAPAN

"For Restrooms, go back to your behind."

—In a restaurant

"Danger! This toy is being made for the extreme priority the good looks. The little part which suffocates when the sharp part gets hurt is swallowed is contained generously. Only the person who can take responsibility by itself is to play."

—Warning label on a children's toy

"Soft Drinks: Cola, Ginger Ale, Milk, Flesh Juice"

—On a restaurant menu

"My Fannie"

—Toilet paper brand name

Q: What was the brand name of the first television set? A: The Philco Predicta.

AND THEN WHAT HAPPENED?

Our next installment in the history of (almost) everything that ever happened.

PART IV: FROM THE DARK AGES TO THE NEW WORLD

• **850 A.D.** This is the Islamic golden age (Europe will remain in the Dark Ages for centuries), marked by continuing advances in the arts and sciences. Persian mathematician al-Khwarizmi writes *Kitab Al-Jabr wa al-muqabalah,* from which we get the term *algebra.*

• **871** Muslims now dominate sea trade; Islam spreads to southeast Asia. Alfred the Great becomes the first king of England.

• **930** The *Althing,* the oldest functioning parliament in world, is established in Iceland.

• **1000** Mississippian culture flourishes in North America. Native chiefs run territorial governments. Maize, beans, and squash are cultivated. The largest city, Cahokia (near present-day St. Louis) has a population of 10,000. Viking Leif Eriksson lands in North America.

• **1066** The Norman Conquest: William of Normandy, a French duke, conquers the English and becomes king, creating England's first stable monarchy. Many historians call this the true beginning of English history.

• **1075** Turkish Muslims take Jerusalem.

• **1095** The Christian Crusades begin, a series of nine holy wars started in Europe and sanctioned by the pope to reclaim the Holy Land from Muslims. They will last until 1291.

• **1206** Temüjin unites the Mongol peoples and becomes the "Universal Ruler"—Genghis Khan. He begins making conquests with a very mobile—and very brutal—army. In less than 100 years, he and his descendants will expand their small empire into the largest the world has ever known, extending from the Sea of Japan, through China and India, all the way to eastern Europe.

Garden State? Newark, New Jersey, was the site of the first asphalt paving in 1870.

- **1215** English barons force King John to adopt the *Magna Carta* ("Great Charter"), a seminal document in the history of constitutional government. Its provisions limited the power of royalty and guaranteed an individual's basic civil liberties. It is considered a predecessor of the American Bill of Rights.

- **1250** The Shona people build hundreds of cities in southwest Africa. The most elaborate: Great Zimbabwe, an 1,800-acre stone complex. Roger Bacon makes the earliest gunpowder recipe in Europe.

- **1300** Mayan civilization collapses. Islam becomes the official religion of the Mongol Empire, further helping its spread through Asia. Spectacles are invented in Italy.

- **1325** Osman I rules the Turks. He is regarded as the father of the Ottoman Empire, which will thrive until World War I. In Mexico, the Aztec Empire begins with the founding of Tenochtitlán.

- **1347** The bubonic plague sweeps across Europe, killing 25 million people.

- **1400** Europe emerges from the Dark Ages with an unparalleled era of advances in art, literature, and science known as the Renaissance (generally regarded as beginning in Florence, Italy).

- **1450** Johannes Gutenberg becomes the first in the West to invent movable type and a printing press, making possible the mass production of books. Constantinople is taken by the Ottoman Turks, ending the Byzantine (eastern Roman) Empire.

- **1478** The bloody Spanish Inquisition is formed to rid the nation of "heretics" and enemies of the Catholic Church. Incan civilization covers the entire western coast of South America; the Aztec Empire covers most of Central America and Mexico.

- **1492** Christopher Columbus sails west from Spain searching for a new route to India and accidentally "discovers" the New World.

And then what happened? A whole lot of stuff—Galileo, baseball, Elvis, Shakespeare, coffee, Canada, the Pilgrims, Huckleberry Finn, blue jeans, the French Revolution, Gilligan's Island...but we ran out of room, so we'll save it for another Bathroom Reader. See ya!

LET'S WATCH *KUNG FU!*

Were you a fan of the TV series Kung Fu? *You aren't alone—it was one of the most popular shows of its day. Along with the films of Bruce Lee, it helped launch the martial arts craze of the 1970s.*

EAST SIDE STORY

In the late 1960s, a man named Ed Spielman was studying radio and television production at Brooklyn College in New York City. He was also a martial arts buff and a big fan of Japanese movies. One day a martial arts instructor he knew happened to tell him in passing that his wife, who was trained in the Chinese martial art of kung fu, could knock him to the ground using only one or two fingers. Intrigued, Spielman began reading up on kung fu.

Spielman earned money writing comedy with his friend Howard Friedlander, who was also fascinated by the Far East. Whenever Spielman read anything interesting about kung fu, he shared it with Friedlander.

Friedlander had a favorite tale about a man who travels through China and meets up with a warrior-monk from the Shaolin temple, where kung fu has been practiced for more than 6,000 years. One afternoon the two men were walking down Broadway toward Times Square when Friedlander stopped suddenly, turned to Spielman, and said, "Ed, why don't we write an *Eastern* Western? We can take the monk from the temple and place him in the West."

RAISING CAINE

The pair set to work writing a film screenplay, and in early 1970 they finished a story about a half-Caucasian, half-Chinese Shaolin monk named Kwai Chang Caine who flees to the American West after he accidentally kills the nephew of the emperor of China. When Caine gets to the United States, he learns that he has a half brother, Danny Caine, and for much of the rest of the screenplay Caine searches for his brother.

Meanwhile, the Warner Bros. studio was looking for ways to use its Old West film sets now that Westerns were declining in popularity. Spielman and Friedlander's script seemed to fit this need, so the studio bought it in late 1970 and made plans for a feature film…only to shelve the idea indefinitely in 1971. Reason: According to studio spokesmen, *Kung Fu* was too violent, not to mention too expensive to film. Besides, they said, the Eastern themes were too "esoteric" for American audiences.

A few months later, Harvey Frand, the Warner Bros. liaison between the studio's feature film and television departments, happened to read the *Kung Fu* script and was impressed. He pitched it to the ABC network as an original movie-of-the-week, and they bought the idea and turned it into a 90-minute film.

SPLIT PERSONALITY

Since Caine was half-Caucasian and half-Chinese, casting either a white actor or an Asian actor in the part would have worked. Two actors were considered: Bruce Lee, then best known for the role of Kato in the *Green Hornet* TV series, and David Carradine, son of screen legend John Carradine. Carradine was the calmer, more serene of the two actors, and the creators thought he would make a better Caine than the tense, energetic Lee. (Besides, studio executives worried that American audiences would not be interested in a series with an Asian male lead.) Carradine got the part.

When the TV film aired on February 22, 1972, 33% of the American viewing audience tuned in to see it. In those days people had only the big three networks to choose from, along with an independent channel or two. Still, getting one in three viewers to tune in to a brand-new show was impressive. *Kung Fu* had something for everyone: peaceniks liked the fact that Caine lived his life according to an Eastern philosophy of nonviolence, and action fans loved how the bad guys got a beating at least once in every show. ABC ordered four more episodes, and when these pulled in large audiences, the network ordered 15 more.

IT'S A FAD!

Kung Fu's timing couldn't have been better—Americans were beginning to take an interest in martial arts, thanks in large part to the guy who *didn't* get the part of Caine, Bruce Lee. By the time Lee got the news that he'd lost the part to Carradine, he was already in Hong Kong filming the first of the "chop-socky" martial arts films that would make him an international star. That caused

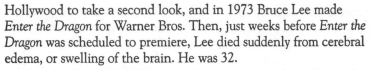

Hollywood to take a second look, and in 1973 Bruce Lee made *Enter the Dragon* for Warner Bros. Then, just weeks before *Enter the Dragon* was scheduled to premiere, Lee died suddenly from cerebral edema, or swelling of the brain. He was 32.

By then *Kung Fu* had been on the air for several months, and the combination of the TV show and Lee's movies—made all the more popular by his untimely death—helped launch the martial arts craze of the 1970s. People watched *Kung Fu* on TV, went to see chop-socky movies, and signed up for martial arts classes in greater numbers than ever before (or since). Elvis got a black belt. Kids wore *Kung Fu* T-shirts and read *Kung Fu* comic books and pulp novels while eating sandwiches out of *Kung Fu* lunchboxes. In 1974, when a singer named Carl Douglas spent 10 minutes recording what was supposed to be a B-side song called "Kung Fu Fighting," it went all the way to #1 on the *Billboard* pop chart. The song got it right—everybody *was* kung fu fighting.

KEEPING IT REAL

• The creators of *Kung Fu* were sticklers for authenticity, so they inserted real-life traditions from kung fu and other martial arts wherever they could. Walking across rice paper is a part of traditional ninja training in Japan, and snatching a pebble from the master's hand was inspired by a similar practice at the Shaolin monastery.

• Another scene taken from real life: the one where Caine, in his final act before leaving the temple, walks down a long corridor and lifts a red hot urn filled with coals with his wrists, branding a tiger and a dragon into his skin. Monks at the Shaolin temple ran a similar gauntlet: as they walked down a long corridor, they dodged acid dropped from the ceiling and spears thrust through holes in the walls and floors. If they made it to the end of the corridor, they branded themselves by lifting the urn with their arms or, if they needed to, with their stomach. "There's more to a disciple's leaving the temple than branding his arms," Carradine says. "We left the rest out because we doubted whether anyone would believe it."

KEEPING TRACK

Even when *Kung Fu* episodes are shown out of sequence, there are visual cues that viewers can use to place each episode in its proper chronological place in the series' three-year run:

• Carradine shaved his head at the start of the series and didn't cut his hair again until the final episodes. The longer Carradine's hair, the later the episode appears in the series.

• When Bruce Lee died in 1973, Carradine changed the color of the shirt he wore from brown to orange-yellow.

• The original martial arts advisor for the show was not a genuine Shaolin master, but he was eventually replaced with someone who was, which helped make the kung fu action sequences more authentic. Carradine marked the change by having Caine lose his signature fedora hat. "If you see me without a hat, it's genuine kung fu," he says.

BEHIND THE SCENES

• Spielman based the character of the blind, sympathetic Master Po on his grandfather, a Russian immigrant. "He was a moral and spiritual man. When he died," Spielman says. "I was only a teenager, too immature to thank him or tell him how much I loved him. The relationship between Master Po and young Caine was my way of doing that."

• Actor Keye Luke wore special opaque contact lenses to make him appear blind. He could see out of a tiny hole drilled into each lens, but other than that, he really was almost blind when he had them on, and he tended to leave them on all day—even when he wasn't filming a scene—to help him "get into character."

NOT AS THEY SEEMED

• One of the most famous scenes in the series is when Caine arrives as a young orphan boy at the Shaolin temple and is accepted as a student. Master Kan, who runs the temple, points to a pebble in his open palm and tells Caine, "As quickly as you can... snatch the pebble from my hand." Caine tries and fails, and Master Kan says to him, "When you can take the pebble from my hand, it will be time for you to leave." Filming the scene was tougher than you might think—actor Philip Ahn's reflexes were so slow that he couldn't stop Radames Pera from grabbing the pebble. Finally after about 15 takes, director Jerry Thorpe told Pera to signal with his left hand before grabbing with his right.

• In another important scene, young Caine is taught to tread lightly—symbolically and literally—by walking across fragile rice paper without breaking it. "When you can walk the rice paper without disturbing it," Master Kan explains, "then your steps will not be heard." But the prop department couldn't find any rice paper, so they used regular butcher paper instead, which is much stronger. Pera couldn't rip it no matter how hard he tried, even when the crew glued sandpaper to the bottom of his feet. They finally shot the scene by having Pera walk over paper that was already torn, but didn't show the paper until he'd already walked over it.

THE PRICE OF FAME

• Eleven-year-old Radames Pera, who played the young Caine, had his own problems. Child labor laws limited the number of hours he could be on the set each day, which meant that there was no time for makeup artists to apply a bald cap to his head—so they shaved him bald for much of the show's three-year run. He was a big TV star, but the bullies at his school picked on him anyway, slapping his bald head and calling him "eightball." Pera drew strength from the show's scripts. "As I was dealing with my personal struggles," he says, "young Caine was dealing with his. Asian philosophy helped us both."

• Like George Reeves (TV's Superman) before him, David Carradine had to worry about overly enthusiastic fans who really did believe he was an indestructible warrior monk. "People were throwing themselves at his car in the street," Harvey Frand says. It eventually got so bad that Carradine spent most of his free time on the set hiding in his dressing room.

SO LONG, GRASSHOPPER

Kung Fu might have continued for season after season save for one thing: David Carradine. Apparently worried that he would be typecast in the part, he was determined from the beginning not to play Caine for longer than three years. Just as he'd promised, he left the show. The last original episode aired on April 19, 1975.

Three attempts to revisit *Kung Fu* were made; two succeeded. *Kung Fu: The Movie* was a 1986 made-for-TV movie that starred Carradine as Caine and Bruce Lee's son Brandon as his son, Chung Wang. That did well enough to inspire a 1987 pilot for a show set in

the 1980s. Brandon Lee signed on to play Caine's great-grandson…
but Carradine thought the script was stupid—he called it "*Kung Fu
car crashes*"—and passed. The pilot aired in February 1986 but died
without Carradine's support. He did, however, agree to star in *Kung
Fu: The Legend Continues*, which ran from 1993 to 1997. In this
series, set in the 1990s, Carradine plays the original Caine's grandson (also a kung fu master named Kwai Chang Caine), and Chris
Potter plays Caine's son, Peter, a big-city police officer.

LASTING INFLUENCE

The original *Kung Fu* left an indelible mark on film and television. One huge fan was Quentin Tarantino, who lists the show as
one of his earliest inspirations. He even wrote the part of Bill in
his revenge flick *Kill Bill* with Carradine in mind (who got the role
after Warren Beatty dropped out). Carradine's Bill is sort of "an
evil Kwai Chang Caine, offering deep-sounding Chinese parables
with psychopathic twists, in between the soothing tunes of Caine's
trademark wooden flute," writes Chris Pepus, one of the many
critics who praised the film.

And *Kill Bill* is just the latest role in a long career for David
Carradine, who's appeared in more than 100 film and television
projects. Yet nearly every biography about Carradine echoes these
same words: "…best known for his role as Caine on the 1970s
series *Kung Fu*."

*   *   *

THE GREAT WIDE NORTH

It's a good thing Canada has free health care. Here are some less-
than-healthy (but still delicious) Canadian food favorites.

Poutine: French fries and a heap of cheese (or cheese curds)
immersed in brown gravy.

Trempette: Bread soaked in maple syrup and topped with heavy
cream.

Tire sur la neige: Heated maple syrup that congeals into taffy
when served on top of fresh snow.

Kraft Dinner sandwich: Macaroni and cheese on white bread,
topped with ketchup.

ANIMALS FAMOUS FOR 15 MINUTES

Here's our feature based on Andy Warthog's prophetic remark that "in the future, every animal will be famous for 15 minutes."

T HE HEADLINE: *O Brother, Boar Art Thou?*
THE STARS: Three male boars named Kalle, Oskar, and Willy; their mates Luise, Berta, and Sophie; and their 50 offspring

WHAT HAPPENED: In September 2003, a group called the German Hunting Protection League launched a Web site with 24-hour Web cams that let viewers watch the animals on a wildlife preserve in the Eifel Plateau in western Germany. The site didn't attract a whole lot of attention...until March 2004, when the league turned its cameras on the six adult boars and their babies. They happened to do this at about the same time that the German version of the reality TV show *Big Brother* launched the latest installment of the series.

Did Germans suddenly become more interested in nature? Or was it that after watching humans living together in a house crammed with cameras, boars seem a lot more fascinating? Whatever the reason, "Pig Brother," as the pig section of the site came to be known, was an instant hit. It attracted more than 1.5 million visitors in its first two weeks alone. Adding to the popularity: "We have microphones in the enclosure," says Anke Nuh, a spokesperson. "The mating calls are very impressive."

THE HEADLINE: *Cuddly Canine Captivates Calendar Consumers*
THE STAR: A tiny, fluffy, mixed-breed stray puppy
WHAT HAPPENED: One evening in 1996, a photojournalist named Lara Jo Regan got lost in Bakersfield, California, while on assignment for *Newsweek* magazine. She was driving around in circles when a tiny, dirty ball of fluff with big eyes and an oversized tongue suddenly appeared in her headlights. "I got out of my car and he just hobbled into my arms," she says. The abandoned puppy was "about the size of a Cornish game hen."

Regan took the tiny dog home and named him Mr. Winkle.

After nursing him back to health, she started taking pictures of the dog and quickly realized that he has a unique gift—he likes to pose. "He's like a pipe cleaner," Regan says. When she had enough pictures, she created a Web site and posted them. The site got so many hits that she decided to make a Mr. Winkle calendar…and the calendar sold so well that Regan landed a book deal with Random House.

AFTERMATH: So far Mr. Winkle has been the subject of five calendars and three books, and his fame continues to grow. He receives an average of 100 e-mails a day, many of them from fans who have seen him on *Today, The Rosie O'Donnell Show, Sex and the City,* and other TV shows. "I feel like I'm the keeper of a magical elf," Regan told the *San Francisco Chronicle.* "I'll take him to a party, and what was a staid affair is suddenly full of happiness and whimsy. It's almost as if he knows it's his mission to enchant people." (If Mr. Winkle's fame continues to grow, we'll have to rename this article "Famous for 25 minutes.")

THE HEADLINE: *Panicked Pair of Porkers Pinched by Pig Police*
THE STARS: Butch Cassidy and the Sundance Pig, two Tamworth pigs in central England
WHAT HAPPENED: In January 1998, a farmer named Arnaldo DiJulio brought his pigs to the local slaughterhouse to be butchered. The pigs must have known what was up because they escaped from the truck while they were being unloaded. Then, before anyone could catch them, they squeezed under a fence, ran across a field, and swam across the Avon River to safety.

Farmer DiJulio wanted the pigs returned to the slaughterhouse, but when Britain's tabloid newspapers picked up the story, animal lovers nationwide called for the renegade pigs—whom the press dubbed Butch and Sundance—to be spared. Were they? The hunt was on and soon more than 100 reporters from all over the world had descended upon the tiny town of Malmesbury to cover it. Butch (who turned out to be female) was the first caught—she was captured by animal lovers and whisked off to a shelter. Sundance was caught the next day. By then DiJulio had agreed to spare both pigs…by selling them to the highest bidder. The pigs were worth only $65 each when they escaped, but by the time the bidding was over, London's *Daily Mail* paid a rumored $24,500 for the pair.

AFTERMATH: Butch and Sundance are living out the rest of their days in an animal sanctuary in southeast England. In April 2004, they were the subject of a BBC-TV movie, *The Legend of the Tamworth Two*, billed as "the pigs that saved their own bacon."

THE HEADLINE: *Pet's Piano Playing No Trivial Pursuit*

THE STAR: Dinky Di, an Australian dingo

WHAT HAPPENED: Dingoes run wild in Australia and are considered pests because they prey on livestock. But when trappers caught some of the wild dogs near Jim Cotterill's roadhouse in the Northern Territory, Cotterill decided to take in one of the puppies and raise it as a pet.

One night, as Cotterill's daughter was practicing the piano in the bar, the puppy began to display an unusual talent. He started howling along to the music, and soon he was jumping on the keyboard as well. "When customers came in," Cotterill says, "someone would make a noise on the piano and he would literally sing to that piano playing."

AFTERMATH: Dinky Di became the most popular attraction at the roadhouse, bringing in tourists from all over the country. In 2003 someone entered him in a nationwide contest held by Trivial Pursuit to become the subject of a question for the 20th anniversary edition of the game—and Dinky Di won. "We wanted to find Australia's most trivial person," says game spokesperson Amanda Blackhall. "We just didn't think it would end up being an animal."

*   *   *

BATHROOM NEWS

The year 2000 was a toilet paper milestone—it marked the 15th anniversary of those jumbo roll toilet paper dispensers (JRTs) found in airports, restaurants, hospitals, and office buildings. Industry experts estimate that since 1985, JRTs have dispensed more than 293 billion feet of toilet paper, equal to the distance of 125 round-trips from the Earth to the moon. Weight: More than 494 million pounds—as much as 41,167 male African elephants. In honor of the occasion, Kimberly-Clark, the product's manufacturer, gave away 1,000 tape dispensers designed to look like jumbo roll toilet paper dispensers.

GIMLI GLIDER, PART III

Here's the final installment of our story on the world's
largest unintentional glider. (Part II starts on page 319.)

MEANWHILE, BACK IN COACH
So how were the passengers holding up while all this was
going on? Surprisingly well. One of the nice things about
this new Boeing 767 was that its engines were so quiet and the
cabin so well insulated for sound that few passengers were even
aware at first that both engines had stopped.

It wasn't until the flight attendants began preparing everyone
for an emergency landing that passengers realized the situation was
serious. People were instructed to remove their eyeglasses, dentures, and any sharp objects from their pockets and to fasten their
seatbelts low and tight around their hips. Then they were told to
assume the "crash position"—arms crossed, hands holding the top
of the seatback in front of them, head resting on their arms—and
prepare for a rough landing. In the galley, flight attendants were
tossing silverware, coffee pots, food trays, liquor bottles, and any
other loose items into the trash to keep them from becoming deadly projectiles.

Meanwhile, the air traffic controllers in Winnipeg had already
called ahead to the Gimli police and fire departments, and they
were racing to the old Air Force base as Flight 143 headed in for a
landing. People on the ground got their first hint that something
unusual was happening when a strangely silent jumbo jet suddenly
sailed into view, flying very low over buildings and the local golf
course. Terrified Gimlians scattered in all directions.

LOOK OUT BELOW

Had anyone other than Captain Pearson been flying the plane,
there's a good chance that Flight 143 would have already crashed.
But, on top of being one of Air Canada's best jet pilots, he was also
a licensed glider pilot with more than 10 years experience. It
turned out that he needed every minute of that experience as he
tried to wrestle the blind, crippled jumbo jet safely to the ground.

Pearson had a few mechanical backup instruments to help him,

You can't make snowballs at the South Pole...the snow is too dry and powdery.

including a magnetic compass, an artificial horizon (to help him keep the plane level) an altimeter (which gives the altitude), and an airspeed indicator. But since gliding a 767 to a landing had never been attempted before, what Pearson had to rely on more than any instrument…was his own judgment.

He knew that if he came in too fast, he'd send the plane hurtling off the end of the runway into whatever lay beyond. Coming in too slow was even worse—the 767 could stall and nosedive straight into the ground. He had to glide in at just the right speed. But what *was* the proper glide speed? He had no way of knowing…he was going to have to guess.

The normal landing speed for a 767 is between 115 and 153 knots (between 130 and 175 mph), depending upon the total weight of the aircraft including the passengers, cargo, and fuel. Pearson finally settled on 180 knots (about 205 mph). Coming in that fast was likely to blow out tires on the landing gear, but he decided he couldn't risk coming in any slower.

UH…ABOUT THE LANDING GEAR

As Pearson approached the Gimli landing strip, he suddenly realized he was coming in too high. He had to slow the plane down, which would cause it to lose altitude. Otherwise he risked overshooting the runway. To increase drag and slow the plane down, he told Quintal to lower the landing gear. Quintal pulled the lever to the down position and…nothing happened. The landing gear was powered by the hydraulic system, but the RAT (the pinwheel thingy) wasn't generating enough hydraulic pressure to lower them.

Luckily there's an emergency method: a switch that pulls the pins out of the landing gear doors. The landing gear then drops down and slams into the locked position. Quintal flipped the switch, and he and Pearson listened as the left and right landing gears noisily dropped and locked. But what about the nose gear? Suddenly another warning light came on in the cockpit—the nose gear had not locked into place, and there was no time to fix it.

SPIN CONTROL

Remember how the RAT propeller spins as the air rushes past it? Well, there's a catch—as the airplane comes in for a landing, the air speed drops, the propeller spins slower, and less hydraulic pressure is generated. That's why the landing gear didn't come down when it was supposed to, and it's also why the control yoke and rudder pedals were becoming increasingly stiff and unwieldy just when Captain Pearson needed them most.

More bad news: even with the landing gear down, Pearson was still coming in too fast. He wrestled the plane into a glider maneuver called a sideslip: he whipped the control yoke hard to the left, as if he were preparing to make a left turn, and practically stood on the right rudder pedal as if he were turning right. The effect of this maneuver was to greatly increase the drag, reducing airspeed. But it also caused the left wing to dip dangerously low to the ground. Witnesses say Pearson held this position until the wingtip was about 40 feet off the ground...*traveling at 180 knots.*

NO PLACE FOR A PICNIC

Could anything else go wrong? Yes. As you'll remember, Gimli Air Force Base had two parallel runways, 32 Left and 32 Right, one of which was still used by private aircraft. Captain Pearson didn't know which was which but he had to pick one, so he picked 32 Left. He held the 767 in the tilted position until the very last second, then leveled off the jet and prepared to land.

He had no power, no instruments, and hardly any brakes; the plane was coming in too fast; the controls were stiff, the nose gear was not locked into position; and some of the tires on the landing gear were certain to burst on impact. So what did Pearson see at the far end of the runway just moments before touching down? Race cars. Lots of race cars.

Winnipeg Air Traffic Control had told him that one of the runways was still used for aircraft, but what they didn't tell him (because they probably didn't know) was that the other runway— the one he was trying to land on—had been converted into the straightaway of an auto club racetrack. The Winnipeg Sports Car Club had held a race earlier in the day. The race was over, but the drivers, their families, and their cars—plus campers, tents, coolers, and barbecues—were all at the end of the runway. They were having a cookout.

Pearson didn't see the cars or the people until the very last minute, and because the 767 was coming in so silently, surprisingly few people saw the plane. Many who did see it coming in—tilted with its left wing nearly scraping the ground—were too stunned to move. But it didn't matter: there was no way everyone could have cleared the runway in time. Pearson was going to have to land the plane in a much shorter distance than he'd planned.

TOUCHDOWN!

Sure enough, when the 767 hit the runway, two tires on the right landing gear burst. But enough of them remained intact for Pearson to maintain control of the aircraft. He literally stood on the brake pedals, throwing his own weight into slowing down the plane.

Jet aircraft land on the rear wheels first; then, as the plane loses speed, the nose drops and the nose gear touches down. As Pearson had feared, when Flight 143's unlocked nose gear hit the runway, it buckled and collapsed, and the nose of the plane slammed onto the runway.

But that equipment failure may have been a blessing in disguise. The fuselage of a jumbo jet is engineered to be tough enough to land on its belly if necessary, and that's exactly what happened: the plane skidded and scraped down the runway, throwing up a cloud of sparks and smoke. But it also slowed the aircraft dramatically.

BRAKE DANCING

The plane was down, but Pearson still had to steer it to keep it centered on the runway. Normally you steer with the nose wheel, but since that was out of commission, he steered by shifting his weight from one brake pedal to the other, braking hard left when the plane veered to the right, and hard right when it veered to the left. Suddenly he noticed a metal guardrail off to one side. He headed for it. The 767 made a heck of a racket as it sheared one guardrail post after another, but the maneuver helped slow the plane even more.

The 767 finally came to a halt about halfway down the runway, 500 feet away from the auto club. The terrifying glide into Gimli lasted for what must have seemed an eternity, but only 29 minutes had passed since the first amber warning light came on in the cockpit. The time was 8:38 p.m. Had Flight 143 been scheduled for just an hour later, it would have been too dark to land.

A painting of a guide dog leading a blind man was found in Pompeii dating from 79 B.C.

TERRA FIRMA

The nose-down landing kicked up so many sparks that some insulation in the belly of the plane caught fire, but members of the race car club ran over with their fire extinguishers and put it out. Meanwhile, the flight attendants were working to evacuate the plane as quickly and safely as possible. Evacuating from the front of the plane was a snap—passengers just had a short jump onto the tarmac. The drop from the emergency exits at the rear was much longer, and a few people suffered minor injuries as they escaped the plane. Amazingly, they were the only people injured on Flight 143.

BLAME GAME

Air Canada's preliminary investigation into the disaster determined that the flight crew and the ground crew were ultimately responsible. Captain Pearson was demoted to first officer for six months, First Officer Quintal was suspended with pay for two weeks, and three members of the ground crew were suspended without pay for 10 days.

Critics immediately accused Air Canada of blaming its employees in order to protect its own reputation, and the ensuing public outcry prompted a much larger investigation, which lasted more than a year. *That* investigation blamed the accident on the airline's poor training and poor procedures, and questioned the wisdom of introducing a metric aircraft into an imperial air fleet.

The report not only exonerated Pearson and Quintal but also credited them with saving the passengers against very long odds. "The consequence would have been disastrous had it not been for the flying ability of Captain Pearson with valuable assistance from First Officer Quintal," the final report read.

THE REAL CULPRIT

But what had caused the fuel quantity processor to fail in the first place? Investigators took it apart to find out. The culprit: a single bad solder joint—a poor electrical connection that caused the system to send a weak signal to the fuel quantity processor instead of a strong one. It was actually worse than no connection at all.

The fuel quantity processor knew how to handle a *complete* loss of signal: it was programmed to switch to a backup signal if the first signal failed. But the processor didn't know how to respond to a *weak* signal, so rather than switch to the backup signal that was functioning properly, it shut down altogether and the fuel gauges went blank.

LESSON LEARNED

In the aftermath of Flight 143, Air Canada updated its procedures and improved its training. Most importantly, it assigned the task of calculating the fuel load to one individual who is qualified to do it even if the computers aren't working. The "Gimli Glider" experience has not been repeated, at least not at Air Canada. (In August 2001, an Air Transat Airbus A330 with a fuel leak ran out of fuel over the Atlantic Ocean. It glided some 60 miles to a safe landing at an airport in the Azores Islands.)

What happened to the 767? After the emergency landing, several mechanics were dispatched to Gimli to repair the jet enough so that it could be flown to Winnipeg for more extensive repair work. Believe it or not, their van ran out of gas on the way. The mechanics eventually made it to Gimli, and the plane made it back to Winnipeg. The damage was duly repaired, and the Gimli Glider was restored to the Air Canada fleet. It's been flying without incident ever since.

At last report the plane is still in service. Are you reading this on an Air Canada flight? A 767? Ask the flight attendant if you're riding on the Gimli Glider.

On second thought, maybe it's better to wait until you're back on the ground.

*　　*　　*

TECHNO-QUIZ

If you owned a model Mark IV FM, what would you have?

a. A new SUV.　　　　**c.** A top-of-the-line radio.
b. A DVD player.　　　**d.** A nuclear weapon.

Answer:

d. You'd have the atom bomb that was dropped on Nagasaki in 1945. The bomb was designated "Mark IV FM" on its blueprints.

When electric eels meet, they change frequencies so their electrical fields don't interfere.

HOW TO FIGHT A SPEEDING TICKET

Speeding tickets can cost a lot—in fines, legal fees, points on your license, increased insurance rates. Have you ever gotten a ticket you felt you didn't deserve but didn't know how to fight it? Here are some tips from the experts.

TIP #1: SHUT UP

Traffic officers will often ask you if you know why you were stopped. They aren't just curious—they're checking to see if you acknowledge guilt up front. If you do, it will make it that much harder for you to fight your ticket in court. Technically speaking, you *don't* know why the officer has pulled you over. And even if you were speeding, you may have been pulled over because a taillight is out. So if you're asked whether you know why you were stopped, just say no.

If you are charged with speeding and must speak, try to say something that will help your case, like, "Officer, I believe I was driving at a safe and reasonable speed." While you're at it, ask the officer to let you off with a warning. It never hurts to ask (and if they agree, you get to skip the rest of this article).

TIP #2: TAKE NOTES

Does your estimate of how fast you were going differ from the officer's estimate? If so, put some time and effort into researching your case and fighting your ticket. Experts say that if you can find a discrepancy in the officer's testimony, or identify a problem with the way the radar equipment was used, you may be in a good position to fight an unfair ticket. Make as many mental or—even better—written notes of the circumstances surrounding your traffic stop as possible. Here are some things to look for:

At the Scene

✔ Note the precise location where you were stopped, using street names and landmarks. You'll need this info if you decide to come back to the scene later to collect more information about your incident.

Forearmed is forewarned: Couples with forearms of the same length are more likely to stay together.

✔ Make a note of the weather—is it an unusually hot or cold day? Is it humid? Raining? Snowing? Windy? All of these factors can affect the accuracy of a radar gun.

✔ How heavy was the traffic when the officer clocked your speed? Were there any large vehicles (trucks, cars towing trailers, etc.) nearby? Make a note of it. Radar guns tend to detect the speed of the largest vehicle within their field of view.

The Radar Unit

✔ Where was the officer when you were clocked? The beam from a radar gun behaves like the light from a flashlight: the farther it travels, the more it spreads out and the more targets it's likely to hit. By the time the beam has traveled as little as 100 feet, it may be as wide as two lanes of traffic. Was a vehicle in the other lane traveling faster than your car? If so, your vehicle may not have been the one that was clocked.

✔ Ask the officer to let you see the radar unit that clocked your speed. Make a note of the make and model of the unit, and also the serial number if it is visible. If the officer refuses to let you see the unit, make a note of that too. It may come in handy later.

Returning to the Scene of the Crime

✔ As soon as possible after you get a speeding ticket, go back to the place where you were stopped. Bring a pencil and paper and a camera. Sketch a simple diagram of the surrounding area and make a note of any trees, curves in the road, or buildings that might have obstructed the officer's view.

✔ Note the speed limit in the area. Is it posted? In some states, if the speed limit isn't posted in the area where you were stopped, you may be able to get out of a ticket.

✔ Are there any signs that indicate the stretch of road is "radar enforced?" In some jurisdictions, the police are only allowed to use radar guns where such signs are posted—and if the signs aren't there, a judge can dismiss the charges against you.

✔ Power lines, microwave towers, bridges, overpasses, airports, hospitals, and even large neon signs can create electromagnetic interference affecting the accuracy of police radar units. If any such landmarks are nearby, be sure to photograph them and note them on your diagram.

TIP #3: CHECK THE EQUIPMENT

Now that you've made notes of the circumstances surrounding your traffic stop, you can check to see if any of them may have contributed to an inaccurate reading of your car's speed. If you suspect that the radar gun was malfunctioning or was used improperly, you can ask the court to instruct the police department to furnish you with documents that might help determine whether this is true. Some things to ask for:

✔ **Manuals.** Many training manuals include a few pages on the types of conditions that cause bad readings. Compare your notes with the instructions given in the manual. Did the officer use the radar gun in a way that the manufacturer warns is likely to generate a false reading? If you think poor weather on the day of the traffic stop was a factor, check to see if there's anything in the manual that warns against bad readings on days with similar weather.

✔ **Repair records.** Is the radar gun used to clock your speed in the repair shop all the time? Has it gone three years without being serviced even once? Repair records could indicate that the radar gun is faulty or badly maintained.

✔ **Calibration logs.** Radar guns are finicky instruments that must be calibrated with a tuning fork on a regular basis, sometimes at the start and end of every officer's shift. Ask to see the logs that certify the radar gun was properly calibrated and in good working order on the day it was used to clock your speed. If it wasn't recently calibrated, it may have been unreliable.

✔ **Vehicle information.** If the officer was in a moving vehicle when clocking your speed, ask for the vehicle's maintenance records, including information certifying that the speedometer has been calibrated recently and is working properly. If the police department declines to hand over what they have, or if their records are incomplete or poorly maintained, this, too, can serve as evidence in defending your case.

TIP #4: CHECK THE SPEED LAW

Let's assume that you *were* exceeding the posted speed limit. Is there anything else you can do to fight the ticket? According to experts, if you live in a state with a "presumed" speed law, the answer may be yes.

On a clear day, it is possible to see 50 miles from the top of the Empire State Building.

✔ Most states have "absolute" speed laws—if the sign says 55 mph and you are driving 56 mph, you're breaking the law. But some states have *presumed* speed laws: if the weather, traffic, and road conditions are favorable enough for you to safely exceed the speed limit, you may be okay.

✔ Look up the section of the vehicle code that you are accused of violating. It may include language that says you are breaking the law "unless the defendant establishes that the speed in excess of said limits did not constitute a violation at the time, place and under the road, weather, and traffic conditions then existing."

✔ Were you on a straight stretch of road? Was the road dry and the visibility clear? Was the traffic light? If so, you can argue that driving 52 mph on a 45-mph road was not breaking the law.

TIP #5: GO TO TRAFFIC SCHOOL

Nearly every state lets you wipe one traffic ticket off your driving record by going to traffic school. So should you go? The experts say *yes.* Here's why: If you fight a traffic ticket in court, there's no guarantee that you'll win, even if you know you are right. But if your ticket qualifies for traffic school, all it will cost you is a small fee and one Saturday afternoon spent in a classroom. Some states even offer online traffic school, so you can meet the requirements at home or anyplace else you have Internet access.

TIP #6: LOOK UP THE VEHICLE CODE

If you can't go to traffic school, experts say the next step is to read your ticket and do a little research to figure out what it means. Why bother? You may be able to find something in the language of the law that can help you argue your case.

Let's say you get ticketed for making an unsafe left turn at an intersection. The officer will write the applicable section of the vehicle code on the ticket. When you go to the library and look up that section in your state's vehicle code, it will list all of the conditions that must be met in order for your offense to be considered illegal. If any of the conditions are not met, you can go into traffic court and argue that your turn was *not* illegal.

For example: In some states the section of the code that covers unsafe left turns says the turn is considered unsafe if "a vehicle approaching from the opposite direction is within the intersection or so close as to constitute an immediate hazard."

But what if there was no vehicle approaching from the opposite direction? What if the driver of the vehicle slowed down and motioned for you to go ahead and turn? You can argue that the turn you made doesn't meet the definition of "unsafe" as described in the vehicle code. You can never predict what a judge will decide, but if you present your case well, you have a good chance that your ticket will be dismissed.

TIP #7: GO TO COURT

✔ Some ticket-fighting experts estimate that in as many as 20% of minor traffic court cases, the officer who wrote the ticket will fail to appear in court due to scheduling conflicts, illness, or for some other reason. In most cases, if the officer fails to appear, the judge will dismiss your ticket. (Warning: The more serious the offense, the more likely the officer will appear, and the less likely the judge will dismiss it even if he doesn't.)

✔ Would you want to go to traffic court on your day off? How about when you're on vacation? Police officers don't want to, either—and there's no law that says you can't call the police department and ask about an officer's days off and vacation time. If you can get the court to schedule your court date for a time when the officer is away from work, you increase the odds that they won't show up.

✔ Dress nicely. The judge is more likely to take you seriously.

✔ What if the officer does appear in court, and you lose the case? If you can't take care of the ticket by going to traffic school (for example, if you've already been), you can still ask the judge to assess a lower fine. They will often comply, so if nothing else, you've still got a good chance at saving some money on the ticket.

Good luck!

*　　*　　*

"This is my simple religion. There is no need for temples; no need for complicated philosophy. Our own brains, our own heart is our temple; the philosophy is kindness."

—Dalai Lama

The contents of King Louis XIV's chamber pot were noted daily and entered in a log book.

JACK JOHNSON vs. THE GREAT WHITE HOPE

Nobody gives much thought nowadays to the idea of African-American athletes competing against Caucasian athletes—it's an everyday occurrence. But back in the early 1900s, it was unthinkable.

THE GALVESTON GIANT

Jack Johnson was the first black heavyweight boxing champion of the world. He won the title in 1908. He never considered himself an ambassador of his race and never tailored his public behavior to suit the racist social notions of the day. Instead, Johnson played on white America's fears and prejudices, creating a public persona designed to provoke. He flaunted his wealth with fancy clothes and fast cars and, perhaps most distasteful to the bigoted newspaper sportswriters and editors of that era, he traveled and appeared regularly with white mistresses—two of whom he eventually married.

FIGHT CLUB

John Arthur Johnson was born in Galveston, Texas, in 1878. At the age of 13 he began participating in the notorious Battles Royale—contests between three to five fighters, usually black, with the last man standing taking the purse. By the time he turned 16, Johnson had become a full-time professional boxer.

Pugilism at the dawn of the 20th century was a rougher sport than it is today. Boxing gloves, which had been used to reduce injury during training for over 100 years, were only just replacing bare knuckles in sanctioned, professional bouts. There were no set limits for the number of rounds in a fight—bouts went on until one of the contestants could no longer continue. Professional boxers often fought once a week or more for relatively small purses and in unforgiving circumstances.

Black fighters weren't offered opportunities to fight for world titles—particularly not in the glamorous heavyweight division. The best black boxers traveled the country fighting white contenders in non-title contests, or fighting one another. Two of the best black heavyweights of Johnson's era, Sam Langford and Joe Jeanette, fought each other 15 times. Johnson fought Jeanette 10 times before winning the title but then never offered Jeanette a title match. They would only fight again in 1945 at the respective ages of 67 and 66 for a war bonds promotion in New York.

IN THIS CORNER...

It was in this harsh and undeniably racist atmosphere that Johnson, after nearly 100 fights and four years as "Black Heavyweight Champion of the World," got his World Heavyweight title shot against reigning champ Tommy Burns. On the eve of the fight, held in Australia, a Sydney newspaper wrote that "citizens who never prayed before are supplicating Providence to give the white man a strong right arm with which to belt the coon into oblivion."

Burns was paid a record $30,000 for the fight; Johnson, $5,000. Johnson beat Burns decisively; police had to stop the fight in the 14th round for Burns's safety. American author Jack London, writing in the *New York Herald*, observed that "the battle was between a colossus and a pygmy. Burns was a toy in Johnson's hands." London then called upon former champion Jim Jeffries, who'd retired undefeated to a Nevada farm, to avenge the white race. "Emerge from your alfalfa fields," he wrote, "and remove the golden smile from Johnson's face. Jeff, it's up to you. The White Man must be rescued."

The search for the Great White Hope was on.

DEFENDING THE TITLE

Boxing promoters quickly arranged for middleweight champ Stanley Ketchel to be the first of the Great White Hopes. For 11 rounds Johnson toyed with the smaller Ketchel, taunting him with insults and landing blow after blow. In the 12th round, the battered and bleeding Ketchel caught Johnson with a lucky shot that sent him to the canvas. The champion picked himself up and ended the fight with one last punch, knocking Ketchel's teeth out.

Several other white fighters followed, trying to dethrone Johnson. They all failed. Eventually, the undefeated Jim Jeffries was coaxed into taking up the challenge. White America was convinced that Jeffries was their last best hope for a white champ. The stage was set for one of the most socially explosive bouts in boxing history.

BEFORE THE FIGHT

James J. Jeffries was the only heavyweight champion ever to have retired undefeated. He'd been contentedly raising crops on his farm for six years when London and others convinced him to return to the ring. His fight with Johnson, scheduled for July 4, 1910, in Reno, Nevada, was one of the most anticipated sporting events of the age.

Promoter Tex Rickard sold a record 40,000 tickets to the contest. Eastern newspapers arranged to keep tabs on the fight via telegraph. Rickard spread rumors of celebrity referees, including H. G. Wells and Sir Arthur Conan Doyle, and hired former (white) champ James J. Corbett to make inflammatory publicity statements like, "Take it from me, the black boy has a yellow streak and Jeff will bring it out when he gets him into that ring."

The pre-fight hysteria over Jeffries's hope of "avenging his race" even affected the bookmakers—they made the aging, overweight Jeffries a 10 to 6 betting favorite, prompting Johnson to wire his brother Claude in Chicago to "bet your last copper on me." The fighters were to receive among the largest purses ever awarded in a prizefight at the time: $60,000 plus a $10,000 advance for Johnson, $40,400 to Jeffries, with an additional $50,000 apiece for the sale of film rights.

Leading up to the fight, Johnson continued to taunt his detractors. At his training camp two miles out of town (which was open to the press), he had two white women with him. The atmosphere surrounding the fight was summed up by playwright Howard Sackler in his 1967 play *The Great White Hope*:

> The fight was going to decide in the eyes of the world not just who was the better man, but who was the better race. The fear that underlay this was a nightmare fear, of this smiling black man, the strongest black man in the world, who made no bones about wanting and being able to have white women. That touched something very deep in the American consciousness.

AND THE WINNER...

The once-great Jeffries was humiliated in a 15-round knockout, Johnson making it clear that he was only toying with the ex-champ and that he could have ended the fight at any time. The news of Johnson's victory went out over the telegraph lines and within hours race riots broke out in every southern state, as well as Pennsylvania, Colorado, Missouri, Ohio, New York, Illinois, and the District of Columbia. Former president Theodore Roosevelt called for a ban on prizefighting, and Congress hastily passed laws prohibiting the interstate transportation of motion pictures, to prevent films of the fight being shown around the country. Before the dust settled, at least 14 black men had been lynched in the fallout over the fight.

THE WHITE SLAVE ACT

After the Jeffries debacle, Johnson continued to plow through his opponents and infuriate his enemies. Black journalists and social critics pressured him to tone down his antagonistic act and become a more acceptable black role model for the white press. But Johnson refused to yield.

Unable to find a match for him in the ring, white authorities arrested Johnson in 1912. The charge: Violation of the Mann Act, which prohibited the transport of women across state lines "for immoral purposes." Known as the "White Slave Act," the law had been created to stop interstate prostitution rings. The white woman Johnson was convicted of crossing state lines with was Lucille Cameron, his fiancée. The judge who convicted him was Kenesaw Mountain Landis, who, as Commissioner of baseball, would later work tirelessly to keep black players out of the major leagues.

Rather than face prison, Johnson fled to Europe, where he continued to box, fighting exhibition bouts all across the continent. After three years, he began to tire of the strain and agreed to defend his title against the new Great White Hope, the six-foot, seven-inch Jess Willard. Some writers believe the promoter convinced Johnson that a pardon could be arranged if he took the fight. Whether this is true remains uncertain. What is certain, however, is that no real pardon was ever offered.

ON THE ROPES

The fight was held close to home, but not quite on American shores—in Havana, Cuba, on April 5, 1915. It was a grueling bout, scheduled to last 45 rounds in 100-degree heat. But in the 26th round, Willard knocked out the 37-year-old Johnson.

In later years Johnson claimed to have thrown the fight. As

evidence, he pointed to films that show him lying on his back using his arms to shade his eyes from the sun as the referee counts him out. Was Johnson really knocked out, or was he faking? It didn't matter: he lost the fight, and white America felt redeemed.

FINAL ROUND

Johnson returned to the United States in 1920 and spent a year and a day in Leavenworth Prison, where he served as athletic director. On his release, he returned to the ring, where he earned decent money fighting exhibitions and non-title fights. He also continued his extravagant lifestyle, complete with white wives and fast cars. It was in such a fast car that Jack Johnson met his end in 1946. On his way to New York to watch the second black heavyweight champion, Joe Louis, defend his title against young Billy Conn (who also bore the Great White Hope burden), Johnson crashed his car in North Carolina and died at the age of 68. He is buried in a family plot in Chicago next to his two wives, in an unmarked grave to prevent vandalism.

RANDOM FACTS

• On April 18, 1922, Jack Johnson received U.S. Patent #1,413,121 for a type of wrench he invented.

• When Howard Sackler's play *The Great White Hope* opened in 1967, the actress playing Johnson's wife received hate mail and death threats over a scene depicting the interracial couple in bed. (James Earl Jones played Jack Johnson.)

• During World War I, a heavy artillery shell was referred to as a "Jack Johnson."

• "The possession of muscular strength and the courage to use it in contests with other men for physical supremacy," said Johnson, "does not necessarily imply a lack of appreciation for the finer and better things in life." Johnson *was* a man of refined tastes: he wrote two memoirs, played the cello, acted in plays and in vaudeville, and was romantically linked to exotic figures such as Mae West and German spy Mata Hari.

• Other celebrities arrested for violating the Mann Act: Charlie Chaplin in 1944 and Chuck Berry in 1962. Chaplin was acquitted. Berry served two years in prison. The act was repealed in 1986.

THE PINKERTON FILES

Before there was an FBI, Secret Service, or any other national law-enforcement organization, there was the Pinkerton Detective Agency. Founded by Allan Pinkerton in 1850, it existed for 145 years, sleuthing for government and big business, and chasing bank robbers, mobsters, and spies. Here are a few of Pinkerton's high-profile cases. (For more on Pinkerton, see page 265.)

SAVING PRESIDENT LINCOLN

Background: Weeks before Lincoln was to be sworn into office, a Pinkerton agent named Timothy Webster learned of a secessionist plot to assassinate the president-elect when he switched trains in Baltimore on the way to his inauguration.

What Happened: Pinkerton told Lincoln about the plot, and the future president agreed to change his travel plans. At the appointed hour, Lincoln, wearing a soft felt hat and an overcoat on his shoulders to disguise his features, slipped out of Harrisburg, Pennsylvania, hours ahead of schedule on a secret chartered train. When it left the station, Pinkerton had the telegraph lines cut so no one could warn the plotters that Lincoln was on his way.

Aftermath: Lincoln made it to Washington without incident, but his political enemies mocked him for sneaking into the capital. "I did not then, nor do I now, believe I would have been assassinated, had I gone through Baltimore as first contemplated," Lincoln later admitted. "But I thought it wise to run no risk, where no risk was necessary."

IN McCLELLAN'S SECRET SERVICE

Background: Following the start of the Civil War in April 1861, General George McClellan, who commanded the Army of the Potomac, asked Pinkerton to head his personal "secret service"—he wanted Pinkerton detectives to gather intelligence on Confederate forces. Pinkerton agreed; he and his men went to work, spying behind enemy lines and interrogating captured Confederate soldiers to find out what they knew.

What Happened: It was the single biggest failure of Pinkerton's career. He routinely overestimated enemy troop strength. In 1861, for example, he estimated that there were 150,000 Confederate troops near Manassas, Virginia, when there were only about 50,000. In April 1862, he estimated 120,000 troops near Yorktown, Virginia, when fewer than 17,000 troops were actually there. Two months later he calculated that General Robert E. Lee was leading a force of 180,000 men, when in fact they numbered only 50,000.

How did Pinkerton get the numbers so wrong? He was a great admirer of McClellan, who was obsessed with the idea that he was consistently outnumbered. Pinkerton willingly tailored his estimates to suit his boss. Even then McClellan wasn't above throwing out Pinkerton's numbers and making up his own higher ones.

Aftermath: At best, Pinkerton's failure helped the general lose his job—when McClellan botched the battle of Antietam in September 1862, Lincoln removed him from command. At worst, Pinkerton's inflated estimates may have caused the Civil War to drag on until 1865 when it might have been ended in 1862.

JESSE JAMES

Background: During the Civil War, Jesse and Frank James were members of a Confederate guerrilla group known as Quantrill's Raiders. They used hit-and-run tactics to terrorize Union troops and civilians along the Kansas-Missouri border, and when the war ended they used some of the same tactics against banks, trains, stagecoaches, and other targets.

What Happened: In March 1874, Pinkerton sent two of his top detectives, John W. Whicher and Louis Lull, to go undercover and try and get close to the James gang. Both men were found out and murdered; Pinkerton swore revenge against the Jameses.

He never got it. If anything, Pinkerton's vendetta against the James boys helped turn them into even bigger folk heroes than they had been before. In 1875 Pinkerton agents, acting on a tip, raided the Missouri farm of Frank and Jesse's mother, Zerelda. One of the agents threw an incendiary device into the house—Wild West buffs still argue over whether it was a bomb or just a flare— and it exploded, killing Zerelda's eight-year-old son, Archie. Public sympathy shifted to the James family, and Pinkerton detectives began to be seen as symbols of the ruthlessness of the giant railroads and the eastern money men who controlled them.

Holy Mackerel! A bluefin tuna can weigh over 1,000 pounds.

Aftermath: Pinkerton detectives were still chasing Jesse James when he was murdered in his own home by two members of his gang—brothers Robert and Charles Ford—while he turned his back to adjust a picture hanging on the wall. The Ford brothers hoped to collect the $10,000 reward on Jesse but instead only narrowly escaped being hanged for the crime. Fearing he was next, Frank James surrendered to the governor of Missouri, was tried for two different murders, and was acquitted both times.

THE MOLLY MAGUIRES

Background: The early 1870s were a time of labor unrest in the coalfields of Pennsylvania. Railroad cars were sabotaged, buildings were burned, and mine superintendents (as well as German and English miners) were beaten and killed. A secret society of Irish immigrant coal miners called the Molly Maguires was suspected of the violence, and in 1873 the Reading Railroad, which owned many of the mines, hired the Pinkerton agency to break up the group.

What Happened: In 1873 Pinkerton agent James McParland got a job in the coalfields posing as James McKenna, an Irish immigrant on the lam for a murder charge in Buffalo. Over the next two years he worked the mines while working his way up the ranks of the Molly Maguires, all the while sending written reports back to Pinkerton headquarters. By 1875 the Mollies knew they had an informer in their midst, and suspicion fell on McParland. He slipped out of town, having gathered enough evidence to shatter the Molly Maguires and send 10 of their leaders to the gallows.

Aftermath: The operation was a tactical success, but it further stigmatized the Pinkerton agency as the hired gun of big corporations, a reputation that would dog it for years to come.

JOINING THE MAFIA

Background: The American Mafia got its start in New Orleans in the 1870s. In 1890 members of that city's Provenzano crime family assassinated Chief of Police David Hennessey as he was preparing to testify in court against them. The police arrested 19 Provenzano mobsters and threw them in jail, but the case against them was weak and it looked like they were going to get away with murder.

What Happened: The Pinkertons joined the case. They arranged for detective Frank Dimaio to assume the identity of Anthony

Ruggiero, a real Mob counterfeiter doing time in Italy, then staged an arrest so that he was thrown in jail with the Provenzanos. Only six other men knew his true identity: three at the Pinkerton Agency, two at the U.S. Secret Service, and the district attorney. That made the assignment very dangerous: without the guards' protection, the mobsters were certain to kill Dimaio if they ever found out who he was. In his four months in jail, Dimaio contracted dysentery and malaria and lost 40 pounds, but he also gradually won the confidence of one of the Provenzano gang— Emmanuel Politz. Dimaio tricked Politz into admitting his role in the murder and then implicating the others.

Aftermath: Dimaio's evidence helped to build an ironclad case against the mobsters, but they still managed to intimidate witnesses and the jury, which returned a verdict of not guilty. The mobsters beat the rap, but not for long: the next morning an angry crowd stormed the jail and murdered them.

THE SCOTT-DUNLAP RING

Background: On January 25, 1876, a group of masked men stormed the home of John Whittelsey, chief cashier of the Northampton, Massachusetts, National Bank, and forced him to hand over the combinations to the bank's three safes. The robbers then went to the bank and made off with $1.2 million. It was the largest bank robbery in U.S. history and would remain so until 1950.

What Happened: While interviewing bank employees, Robert Pinkerton learned that William Edson, a representative from the vault company, had recently been to the bank. Edson was the one who had talked the bank into entrusting all three safe combinations to Whittelsey. Before that the bank had divided them among different employees, a much safer arrangement. Pinkerton put Edson under 24-hour surveillance. Another clue—that one of the robbers shrugged his shoulders continuously—led to the identification of the ringleaders, "Hustling" Bob Scott and his partner, Jim Dunlap. They were put under 24-hour surveillance, too, and when they were followed to a meeting with Edson, Pinkerton knew he was on the right trail. Detectives "interviewed" Edson several days in a row until he cracked and turned state's evidence against the gang.

Aftermath: Scott and Dunlap got 20 years; Edson went free.

BY THE TIME WE GOT TO WOODSTOCK, PART II

By August 15, 1969, the stage was set for one of the largest gatherings of the 20th century. No one knew how large it would be until the event unfolded. It was evident early on, though, that this was more than a mere rock festival. (Part I is on page 375.)

FRIDAY

Close to half a million hippies had converged on the site by evening, and estimates say that half a million more tried to get to Woodstock, but never made it past the 20-mile traffic jam leading into Bethel. Woodstock Ventures blamed the police for purposefully not maintaining the traffic flow in the hopes of ruining the event. In the end, thousands of people just abandoned their cars and walked to the farm. And when they got there, instead of going in through one of the two gates, the kids trampled the fence and walked right in. While Woodstock Ventures were overjoyed by the turnout, they were equally dismayed when they found out that very few of the concertgoers had paid. The largest concert of the century had suddenly become a free concert. And Rosenman, Lang, Kornfeld, and Roberts had no clue how they were going to pay for it.

When word got out on Friday afternoon that the bands could not make it through the gridlock, Woodstock Ventures rented a fleet of Army helicopters to ferry them in. But that would take time, and hundreds of thousands of kids were screaming for music. The only artist who had shown up—folkie Richie Havens—was ushered onto the stage at 5:00 p.m. His band hadn't arrived yet, so he played solo...for three hours. Every time he tried to stop, the promoters threw him back onstage. Next up was John Sebastian, who wasn't even scheduled to perform, but happened to be there. Lang was afraid that if the music stopped, the kids might riot. For that reason, the plan to stop playing every night at midnight was abandoned. If all went well, the music would go nonstop until Sunday evening.

Benjamin Franklin was a practicing nudist. (He got pretty good at it.)

SATURDAY

When the sun rose on Max Yasgur's field on Saturday morning, Woodstock was the third largest city in New York State. It was also one of the muddiest: five inches of rain had fallen in about three hours during the night. On the surface, the entire event looked like a mess. Greil Marcus, a reporter who covered the event for *Rolling Stone*, described the troubles:

> The sanitation facilities (600 portable toilets had been spotted across the farm) were breaking down and overflowing; the water from six wells and parked water tanks were proving to be an inadequate supply for the long lines that were forming, and the aboveground water pipes were being crashed by the humanity; the food concessions were sold out and it was impossible to ferry in any more through the traffic; the chief medical officer declared a "medical crisis" from drug use and subsequent freak-outs; police reported a shortage of ambulances, and those that were available had difficulty getting back to local hospitals through the metal syrup of the traffic jams.

Against All Odds

But even with all of the adversity, the music kept going through the afternoon and people banded together for survival. The Hog Farm, a group of communal hippies, was hired to manage the crowds, run interference, help people make it through bad drug trips, and keep the message of love flowing through the crowd. Their leader, known as Wavy Gravy, when asked how he intended to maintain law and order, replied, "With seltzer bottles and cream pies." Instead of the police force, they called themselves the "Please force." Woodstock Ventures would later maintain that the $16,000 they spent to get the Hog Farm to Woodstock was the best money they ever spent.

Even the locals, many of whom had tried to stop the event, pitched in when they heard how little food there was for so many people. Churches, the Boy Scouts, and even the local Air Force base went on food drives and donated provisions by the ton. Through it all, the music kept playing. And then at five in the afternoon on Saturday, it started raining again. Heavily.

No Pay, No Play

But the rain was the least of their problems. The three main acts for Saturday night—the Grateful Dead, Janis Joplin, and The

Who—informed Woodstock Ventures that they wouldn't play unless they were paid in advance, in cash. That added up to more than $30,000. Roberts didn't have that kind of money on him, so he pleaded with Charlie Prince, the owner of a local bank, to give him a cash advance. Roberts promised that he was good for it (he had a trust fund of more than $1 million). But Prince was still skeptical. Then Roberts told him that if the music stopped, they might have to deal with the largest riot in American history. Prince conceded, and the music went on.

SUNDAY

As the sun came up, The Who were just concluding the performance of their rock opera *Tommy*. Arriving by car (barely) the night before, they didn't realize how big the crowd was until dawn. As they were singing "Listening to you, I feel the music," the band saw almost half a million people looking back at them. Pete Townshend says it's one of the most amazing things he's ever experienced. (Less than an hour before, Townshend had another strange experience: yippie activist Abbie Hoffman ran onstage during The Who's set and started preaching politics to the crowd. Townshend, not recognizing Hoffman, bonked him on the head with his guitar.)

By noon on Sunday, torrential rain had given way to baking sun. All of the extra space at the festival, even the dressing rooms, had been converted to hospitals. Someone had spiked the water supply with LSD, so the Hog Farm was helping thousands of kids (and many band members) through bad trips. Local medics were treating people for heatstroke, cut feet from all of the broken glass, pneumonia from being drenched for two days, and even blindness—several tripped-out kids had been lying on their backs and staring at the sun.

The food situation was dire. Wavy Gravy tried to coordinate "breakfast in bed for 400,000," but supplies were woefully short. And by this time, the portable toilets were unusable. Three Days of Peace and Music had become a disaster area. The situation was so bad, in fact, that New York governor Nelson Rockefeller threatened to send in National Guard troops to break up the festival.

But luckily for everyone involved, calmer heads prevailed. And still, the music went on. Audiences were treated that day and throughout the night to sets by Crosby, Stills & Nash, Ten Years After, Johnny Winter, and Joe Cocker.

Woodstock's final act, headliner Jimi Hendrix, didn't even get to start his set until 9 a.m. on Monday morning. His instrumental version of "The Star-Spangled Banner" woke up the dozing crowd and gave them one last electrifying—but underappreciated—performance as they packed up their muddy belongings and left Yasgur's farm. The Woodstock Music and Arts Fair was over, but for the four men who formed Woodstock Ventures, that weekend would consume them for years to come.

AFTERMATH

The largest concert in history also left one of the biggest messes in history. It took several months and $100,000 to clean up all the garbage left behind—and it was years before Max Yasgur's land recuperated. The festival also left at least three people dead: one a 17-year-old boy who was asleep under a tractor trailer when it started up and pulled away, and two more people who died of drug overdoses. The final tally for those treated for medical problems was around 5,000. There were eight miscarriages and it was rumored that several babies were born. And with all of the free love, who knows how many babies were conceived at Woodstock.

By the festival's end, Woodstock Ventures was $1.3 million in debt. Promotional expenses had gone 70% over budget, and production expenses were 300% over budget. Throughout the 1970s, Woodstock Ventures was mired in lawsuits and faced criminal charges for illegal drug use, breach of contract, and even illegal burning from the plumes of smoke that rose over the field for weeks as all the trash was burned. Another lawsuit came from the town of White Lake for disturbing the peace (an ironic charge for an event whose goal was to promote peace), but that suit was dropped in 1978. So was it worth it? Yes, says Lang—the whole ordeal of organizing Woodstock was like "living a dream. My idea was just to get it done, whatever it took. We had a vision, and it all came true."

AFTER THE AFTERMATH

The saving grace for the concert promoters' monetary woes came from the movie *Woodstock*. Warner Bros. made a film of the event

---

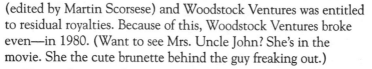
(edited by Martin Scorsese) and Woodstock Ventures was entitled to residual royalties. Because of this, Woodstock Ventures broke even—in 1980. (Want to see Mrs. Uncle John? She's in the movie. She the cute brunette behind the guy freaking out.)

Twenty-five years later, on August 12, 1994, around 300,000 people showed up in Saugerties, New York, to attend Woodstock '94, which was produced by Woodstock Ventures, still headed by Michael Lang, Joel Rosenman, and John Roberts.

CULTURAL LEGACY

Woodstock came at a time when the United States was at a cross-roads, but did it really change anything? On the day after the event, the *New York Times* ran an editorial that called Woodstock a "colossal mess." But just a day later, the paper changed its tune, calling it a "phenomenon of innocence. They came, it seems, to enjoy their lifestyle that is its own declaration of independence."

Elliot Tiber, the man who supplied the original permit for Woodstock Ventures to put on the festival, says in his essay, *How Woodstock Happened:* "True believers still call Woodstock the capstone of an era devoted to human advancement. Cynics say it was a fitting, ridiculous end to an era of naivete. Then there are those who say it was just a hell of a party."

Which of the three it actually was is still being debated, but one thing is for sure: as the summer of 1969 came to an end, the optimism that stemmed from seeing men land on the moon and 450,000 people gather peacefully in the rain was running out. On December 6 of that year, the Rolling Stones headlined the Altamont Festival in Livermore, California. The event was scarred by a near-riot and the stabbing death of an 18-year-old man at the hands of the Hells Angels. Altamont has since been called "the day the '60s died" and "the anti-Woodstock."

As the '70s rolled in, the nation would soon be rocked by the Watergate scandal and then an energy crisis, making that weekend in White Lake seem like a distant memory.

WHAT A LONG STRANGE TRIP

But Woodstock is by no means forgotten. It's one of the most enduring images of the 1960s. And it's likely there won't be a concert again of its magnitude. The original site now holds a monu-

---

The border between Italy and the Vatican City is marked by a painted white line.

ment to the event and an amphitheater that seats 16,000… comfortably. And as for the recording studio that sparked the whole idea in the first place, it was never built.

"I think you have proven something to the world—that half a million kids can get together and have three days of fun and music and have nothing BUT fun and music. God bless you all!"

—**Max Yasgur to the crowd at Woodstock**

*　　*　　*

LINEUP AT WOODSTOCK

Friday:
Richie Havens
John Sebastian
Country Joe McDonald (with his "Fixin-to-Die-Rag")
Swami Satchadinanda (the guru)
Bert Sommer
Sweetwater
Tim Hardin
Ravi Shankar (quit due to rain)
Melanie
Arlo Guthrie
Joan Baez

Saturday:
Quill (threw stuff at the audience)
Keef Hartly
Santana
Mountain
Canned Heat
The Incredible String Band
Grateful Dead
Creedence Clearwater Revival
Janis Joplin
Sly and the Family Stone
The Who
Jefferson Airplane

Sunday/Monday:
Joe Cocker (followed by a huge rainstorm)
Max Yasgur (with a speech)
Country Joe & the Fish
Ten Years After
The Band
Blood, Sweat & Tears
Johnny Winter
Crosby, Stills & Nash (joined for a few songs by Neil Young)
Paul Butterfield Blues Band
Sha-Na-Na
Jimi Hendrix

The tallest sunflower on record: 23 feet, 6 inches.

BIRTHSTONES

Birthstones are like horoscopes—even if you don't believe in them, it's fun to look them up and see what they mean.

R OCK STARS
Many gem scholars attribute the tradition of birthstones to the jeweled "breastplate of Aaron" described in the Bible (Exodus 28, 15-30). The breastplate was a ceremonial religious garment worn by Aaron, the brother of Moses; it was set with 12 gemstones representing the 12 tribes of Israel and perhaps, say folklorists, the 12 months of the year.

Around that same time, the Assyrians began assigning gemstones to each region of the zodiac according to a color system that they believed controlled its power. Each stone had its own distinct magical, protective, and curative qualities that corresponded with the attributes of the astrological sign. Over time the stones came to be associated more with calendar months than astrological signs.

The custom spread to other cultures—including Arabic, Jewish, Hindu, Polish and Russian, each of which modified the list of birthstones. Over the centuries, other changes and substitutions were made: sometimes accidentally by scribes, sometimes by royalty who didn't like their birthstones, and sometimes according to fashion and availability.

ROMANCING THE STONE

In 1912 the American National Association of Jewelers came up with the Traditional Birthstone List, a standardized list that combined contemporary trends with all the birthstone lists from the 15th to the 20th centuries. A few years later, it was revised and renamed the Modern Birthstone List. The association hoped the modern list would eliminate confusion among jewelers.

Did it work? Not entirely. The old lists didn't go away, so there are still variations in jeweler's lists. And those aren't the only lists, either. There's a Mystical Birthstone list that's based on ancient Tibetan culture, an Ayurvedic list originating from the 1,000-year-old system of Indian medicine, a zodiac list, and a planetary list, to name just a few. What's *your* birthstone? Look it up on the Modern Birthstone List and see for yourself:

Yell for 8 years, 7 months, and 6 days and you'll burn enough energy to heat 1 cup of coffee.

January Birthstone: Garnet (most commonly red, but it can be found in all colors except blue)

Background: The garnet got its name from the ancient Greeks because the stone looks like a *granatum*, or pomegranate seed. It was used in the 13th century to repel insects and evil spirits. Egyptians placed them in tombs as payment to the gods to guarantee the spirit's safe passage to the nether world. The garnet is considered the gem of faith and truth. Today, when you give someone a garnet, it is a token of your loyalty and devotion.

February Birthstone: Amethyst (all hues of purple)

Background: The amethyst was worn by the ancient Romans to ward off the temptations of Bacchus, the god of wine. The name itself is from the Greek term meaning "not drunk." It was also believed to bring its wearers peace of mind by controlling evil thoughts. If you want to keep negative energy away from you, wear amethyst. It is the most valued stone in the quartz family. The deeper its color, the more valuable it is.

March Birthstone: Aquamarine (light blue to blue-green to dark blue)

Background: Legend says that Neptune, god of the sea, presented it as a gift to his mermaids, which may explain why sailors used aquamarine as a talisman for safe travel. In the 14th century, Europeans wore it as an antidote for poison. It is said to increase intelligence, enhance youth, and relieve anxiety. Giving your bride an aquamarine necklace on your wedding day will ensure a healthy marriage.

April Birthstone: Diamond (all colors—from clear to pink, yellow, brown, red, green, blue, and even black)

Background: The diamond is the hardest natural mineral—four times harder than the next hardest, sapphire and ruby. Ancient cultures wore it to ward off cowardice, and to insure love and harmony in relationships. Jewelers say that "diamonds are forever" because they have the longest endurance of any other mineral substance. On average, they date back 3.4 billion years. World's largest diamond: the Cullinan Diamond from South Africa, at 3,106 carats.

May Birthstone: Emerald (deep green to yellow-green to blue-green)

Background: Emeralds were historically one of the most prized gems. Both King Solomon and Cleopatra owned emerald mines (the Egyptians believed emeralds could kill poisonous snakes, but that didn't help Cleopatra—she died from a snakebite). Bestowing upon its wearer wisdom, patience, everlasting love, faithfulness, and the ability to foretell the future, an emerald is regarded as an amulet for general good fortune. Large emeralds are rare; high-quality stones are valued at $3,000 to $4,000 per carat.

June Birthstone: Pearl (depending on the type of shellfish and water it comes from, it can be white, silver, pink, brown, or black)

Background: Pearls have been treasured throughout history by cultures around the world—Indian, Arabian, Chinese, Persian, and Egyptian, to name a few. They are believed to offer the power of love, money, and wisdom, to hasten the laws of karma, to cement relationships, and to keep children safe. Pearls are valued by their size, their color, and their "orient," the deep inner glow and iridescence found in natural pearls. The more "orient" a pearl has, the more valuable it is.

July Birthstone: Ruby (various shades of red—blue ones are called sapphires)

Background: Rubies were used in the 13th century as a prescription for liver ailments and were believed to preserve mental and physical health. They were given as offerings to Buddha in China and to Krishna in India. Ground to a powder, rubies were once thought to be a cure for indigestion. High quality rubies are rarer and more valuable than diamonds. Largest, most expensive ruby ever: a 15.97-carat stone that sold for $3.6 million in 1988.

August Birthstone: Peridot (mostly varying hues of yellow-green, but also yellow, brown, and orange)

Background: Hawaiians believed peridot to be the divine tears wept by Pele, goddess of the volcano. The Romans believed it would protect them from death in battle, but only when "pierced" (made into a bead) and "strung on the hair of an ass," then worn on the right arm. South American shamans still use it to ward off snakebites and mosquitoes. Wear it to clear your mind of envy.

The largest prime number known (so far) is 7,235,733 digits long.

September Birthstone: Sapphire (most commonly blue, but also found in yellow, clear, orange, pink, green, and purple)

Background: In Biblical times, sapphires were believed to transmit innocence and good health, and to protect against evil spirits. Later they were believed to heal mental illness. Ivan the Terrible wore them to give him strength and courage. New Age advice: Wear a sapphire to enhance spiritual enlightenment and inner peace, or to aid in telepathy, clairvoyance, and astral projection. The choicest sapphires are the rich blue ones that come from Kashmir.

October Birthstone: Opal (generally either opaque or translucent white, they show almost every color in a variety of combinations)

Background: In medieval times, blonde maidens wore opals to guarantee their hair would neither darken nor fade. The stones were also thought to grant wearers the power of invisibility, giving it the nickname *Patronus furum* ("patron of thieves"). Arabs believed the opal got its fiery color because it fell from the heavens in a lightning flash.

November Birthstone: Topaz (clear, yellow, orange, red, peach, blue, gold, and green, ranging from transparent to translucent)

Background: The topaz was named after the island in the Red Sea where the gem was first discovered, *Topazios* (meaning "to guess" —the island was hard to find because it was almost always covered in fog). During the Middle Ages, the stone was thought to heal mental and physical disorders and even to prevent death. Ancient Greeks believed that the topaz improved eyesight. It's rare to find a "precious topaz" (gold with pink hues) over three carats. If you do, it's worth about $500 per carat.

December Birthstone: Turquoise (blue to green and most combinations in between)

Background: In 13th-century Persia, turquoise was believed to protect riders from falling off their horses, so it was often set into bridles. American Indians—particularly Navajos and Apaches—believe turquoise to be sacred and use it in their jewelry, artwork, and ceremonies. The Aztecs reserved it strictly for the gods—no mortal was allowed to wear it. Turquoise attracts success, promotes healing, and relaxes the mind. Arizona turquoise generally has the highest value; "robin's egg blue" is the rarest.

How many hairs does the average human scalp contain? Between 120,000 and 150,000.

ANSWER PAGES

BASKETBALL 101
Answers for page 102

1. b, **2.** d, **3.** b, **4.** d, **5.** c, **6.** a straight line,
7. d, **8.** d **9.** c, **10.** a curved line

The test was so easy that nobody had to cheat, right? *Wrong.*
Coach Harrick let three athletes skip all the classes (and the final
exam) and then gave them A's anyway. Game over? No—the
NCAA got wind of Harrick's exam in 2004 and launched an
investigation. Outcome: Pending.

KNOW YOUR GLOBE
Answers for page 136

1. a) Louisiana. It has 64 parishes. (*Parish* comes from the administrative subdivisions of the Catholic Church.)

2. c) La Paz, Bolivia, at 12,000 feet above sea level.

3. b) Belgium. The Walloons, from southern Belgium (originally
called Walloonia), are descendents of the Celts. The Flemings,
from northern Belgium (originally called Flanders), are descendants of German Franks. Only 10% of the population is bilingual.

4. a) The Nile, which is more than 4,100 miles long.

5. d) Death Valley. It lies 282 feet below sea level.

6. b) *Uluru*, which means "Great Pebble," was formed more than
600 million years ago.

7. a) Steppes, most common in Russia, Asia, and central Europe,
are generally areas that were once lush and forested but became
barren from cultivation and overgrazing.

8. a) Mesa. An arroyo is a deep gully; an atoll is a coral island
and reef; and a piedmont is the area of land at the base of a
mountain.

9. d) Underwater earthquakes. A *tsunami* is a series of waves generated by oceanic disturbances—earthquakes, volcanic eruptions,

---

landslides, or impact from cosmic bodies such as meteorites.

10. d) Mandarin. More than one billion people speak it (500 million speak English; 450 million speak Hindi).

11. a) Greenland. It's about 840,000 square miles—a third the size of Australia. (Australia is a continent, which means it's technically too large to be considered an island.) Greenland is a territory of Denmark.

12. a) Botswana, located completely within South Africa, comprises 225,953 square miles and has a population of close to 1.5 million. It is one of 15 landlocked countries in Africa. The world's largest landlocked country is the Asian nation of Kazakhstan.

13. d) Igneous. Metamorphic rocks have undergone some type of change due to heat and pressure; sedimentary rocks are formed by the accumulation and squeezing together of layers of sediment (particles of rock or remains of plant and animal life). The term stratus has nothing to do with rocks—it's a low cloud formation with gray horizontal layers.

14. d) 180 degrees—it's an imaginary north-south line in the Pacific Ocean, the place where the date is one day earlier east of the line than west of the line. 0 degrees is the Prime Meridian, located in Greenwich, England, the place where longitude lines begin. (There is nothing significant about 45 and 90 degrees.)

15. a) Wyoming. It has a population of 450,000 (California's population is 30 million).

16. c) Sapporo. It's the name of a city in Hokkaido, the northernmost island (and the name of a Japanese beer). Kyushu is the fourth and southernmost island of Japan.

17. b) Seasons. The sun's rays hit the northern and southern hemispheres unequally—when direct rays hit one hemisphere (making it summer), diffused rays hit the other (making it winter). Fall and spring occur as the rays change hemispheres.

18. a) Pretoria. South Africa isn't the only country with more than one capital. Bolivia has two capitals: Sucre and La Paz.

19. a) Nauru. This Pacific island nation gained its independence from UN Trusteeship status in 1968. It's also the smallest independent nation in the world.

20. c) Esperanto. Despite being taught in universities around the world even into the 20th century, Esperanto has never been accepted as an international language.

OL' JAY'S BRAINTEASERS
Answers for page 166

1. The cup was filled with dry, ground coffee.

2. Sam's father was 50 when he married. His bride was 25; her father was 45. When Sam was born a year later, his father was 51 and his grandfather on his *mother's* side was 46.

3. A goose.

4. David ("D" is the Roman numeral for 500, "V" is the Roman numeral for 5, "a" is the first letter of the alphabet, and "I" is the first person.)

5. Boxing.

6. A relationship.

7. A mirror.

8. To cover cows.

9. He's a barber.

10. An egg.

11. A snake.

12. They're all abbreviations of U.S. states:
HI: Hawaii
MA: Massachusetts
PA: Pennsylvania
ME: Maine
ID: Idaho
IN: Indiana
OR: Oregon

13. They're the kings in a deck of cards.

14. The moon.

GRANDMA CELIA, CARD SHARK
Answers for page 357

SPLIT PERSONALITY. "Dave had 7 cards to start with," Grandma Celia explained. "Half of 7 is 3-1/2, so when Dave gave the oldest brother 'half the cards plus half a card,' he gave him 3-1/2 cards plus half a card, or 4 cards."

- "He had 3 cards left, and gave half of these cards plus half a card (1-1/2 plus 1/2) or 2 cards to the middle brother."
- "He had 1 card left, so when he gave the youngest brother half his remaining cards plus half a card (1/2 plus 1/2), he had 0 cards left."

BY THE NUMBERS. Grandma Celia always picks a 3. Whatever numbered card the other person picks (if they do the math right), the digits on their card, plus the 3 on her card, will form the answer—if they pick a 4, the answer will be 43; if they pick a nine, the answer will be 93, and so on.

TURNING 30. Grandma Celia knew that as long as she picked up the 9th card, the 16th card, and the 23rd card, she was guaranteed to win. She kept a running total of how many cards were picked up, and adjusted her picks accordingly. It didn't matter if she went first or second—when she went first, she only picked up 2 cards. That way no matter how many cards I picked up on my first turn, she could pick up as few or as many cards as she needed to pick up the 9th card. She did the same thing to get to the 16th, the 23rd, and the 30th cards. (Once I knew the secret, I was able to beat her once in a while.)

ELEVENSES. As long as Grandma Celia picked cards between 2 and 9 (or even aces if you count them as 1s), and the first card and the third card add up to the value of the middle card, the 3-digit number they form will always be divisible by 11.

THE ZOMBIE QUIZ
Answers for page 233

1. d) There really is a rum-soaked tropical drink called a zombie, but that's got nothing to do with real zombies.

2. c) You can also get infected if a zombie rubs up against an open cut or wound.

3. d) Zombies live off the liquid in the flesh they eat.

4. b) We know that zombies have some rudimentary form of intelligence, because they can tell humans from zombies, and they tend to congregate in places they frequented when they were alive.

5. c) Zombies are still dead, after all, and they're still decomposing, although at a much slower rate. Only a very young, very well-preserved corpse will last beyond five years.

6. b) A zombie's strength peaks early, then declines as it decomposes.

7. b) You must destroy the brain, or at the very least remove the brain from the rest of the body, so that even if the zombie is still "alive," it can't harm you.

8. c) Watch your step! Zombies have a mean bite.

9. d) A hand grenade sends shrapnel and ripped chunks of zombie meat flying in every direction, and anyone who gets hit by the zombie-soaked shrapnel will *become a zombie.* Using a hatchet puts you too close to the zombie for comfort, and if you use a flamethrower, the burning zombie will stumble around for a while before going down, creating a significant fire hazard. A rifle or shotgun lets you shoot the thing from a safe distance, with minimal risk of collateral damage.

10. d) But it wouldn't be a bad idea to teach your dog the "get away from that zombie" trick…just in case.

UNCLE JOHN'S PUZZLERS
Answers for page 301

1. UND, to form underground.

2. a. Michael Jordan
   b. Geraldo Rivera
   c. Madonna
   d. Bill Gates
   e. Tony Blair
   f. Keanu Reeves
   g. Uncle John

3. The answer is 3. The series shows the number of letters in the words o-n-e, t-w-o, t-h-r-e-e, etc.)

4. The answer is not 25. If you *divide* 30 by 1/2, you get 60. Add 10 and the answer is 70.

5. The answer is 36. Add up the value of all the letters in the names (1=a, 2=b. etc.)

Riveting fact: There are an estimated 2,500,000 rivets in the Eiffel Tower.

6. PAS

7. $18 \times 8 - 2 \div 2 = 71$

8. TYPEWRITER

9. Dwell, dwindle, dweeb, dwarf.

PALINDROMIA
Answers for page 420

1. Otto

2. kayak

3. Yo, Banana Boy

4. Ed, a general, a renegade

5. race car

6. a Toyota

7. Wow

8. If I had a hi-fi

9. DVD

10. Pull up, pull up

11. L.A. Ocelots Stole Coal

12. King Ognik

13. Eye

14. Was it a rat I saw

15. Ed is on no side

16. oozy rat in a sanitary zoo

17. Otto made Ed a motto

18. Now, sir, a war is won

19. step on no pets

20. gnu dung

21. lonely Tylenol

22. senile felines

23. bird rib

24. llama mall

25. laminated E.T. animal

26. DNA Land

27. stack cats

28. Aha

29. ewe

30. bar crab

31. Strapgod's Dog Parts

32. swap for I a pair of paws

33. borrow or rob

34. lion oil

35. Miss Sim

36. peep

37. Tangy Gnat

38. Dammit, I'm mad

39. top spot

40. tons o' snot

41. TNT

42. not a ton

43. go deliver a dare, vile dog

44. deified

45. live forever of evil

46. party booby-trap

47. poop

48. maps, DNA, and spam

49. He did, eh

50. name no one man

51. civic

52. Yreka Bakery

More *Bathroom Reader* titles

Uncle John's Bathroom Reader
For Kids Only! © 2002, $12.95

Uncle John's **Electrifying**
Bathroom Reader For Kids
Only © 2003, $12.95

Uncle John's **Top Secret!**
Bathroom Reader For Kids Only © 2004, $12.95

Uncle John's Bathroom Reader
Plunges Into The Presidency © 2004, $12.95

Uncle John's Bathroom Reader
Plunges Into History Again © 2004, $16.95

To Order

Contact:
Bathroom Readers' Press
PO Box 1117,
Ashland, OR 97520
Phone: 888-488-4642
Fax: 541-482-6159
orders@bathroomreader.com
www.bathroomreader.com

Shipping & Handling rates:
- 1 book: $3.50
- 2 – 3 books: $4.50
- 4 – 5 books: $5.50
- 5 – 9 books: $1.00/book

Priority Shipping also
available.
We accept checks and
credit card orders.
Order on-line, fax, mail,
email, or phone.

• Wholesale Distributors •
Publishers Group West (U.S.):
800-788-3123
Raincoast Books (Canada):
800-663-5714

THE LAST PAGE

FELLOW BATHROOM READERS:
The fight for good bathroom reading should never be taken loosely—we must do our duty and sit firmly for what we believe in, even while the rest of the world is taking pot shots at us.

We'll be brief: now that we've proven we're not simply a flush-in-the-pan, we invite you to take the plunge: Sit Down and Be Counted! Become a member of the Bathroom Readers' Institute. Log on to our Web site, www.bathroomreader.com, and place your first order at our online store, or, if you don't want to buy anything, send a self-addressed, stamped, business-sized envelope to: BRI, PO Box 1117, Ashland, Oregon 97520. You'll receive your free membership card, plus discounts when ordering directly through the BRI, and you'll earn a permanent spot on the BRI honor roll!

Well, we're out of space, and when you've gotta go, you've gotta go. Tanks for all your support. Hope to hear from you soon. Meanwhile, remember:

Keep on flushin'!